QUESTIONS &
ANSWERS

Law of Contract

D0265814

QUESTIONS & ANSWERS SERIES

Other titles in preparation

QUESTIONS &
ANSWERS

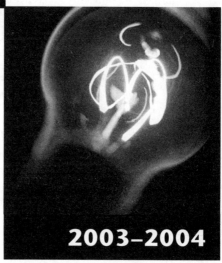

2003–2004

Law of Contract

FOURTH EDITION

Ian Brown

LLB, DPhil
Reader in Law, Faculty of Law,
University of the West of England, Bristol

Adrian Chandler

LLB, LLM, PhD
Associate Dean, Faculty of Law,
University of the West of England, Bristol

OXFORD
UNIVERSITY PRESS

OXFORD
UNIVERSITY PRESS

Great Clarendon Street, Oxford OX2 6DP

Oxford University Press is a department of the University of Oxford.
It furthers the University's objective of excellence in research, scholarship,
and education by publishing worldwide in

Oxford New York

Auckland Bangkok Buenos Aires Cape Town Chennai
Dar es Salaam Delhi Hong Kong Istanbul Karachi Kolkata
Kuala Lumpur Madrid Melbourne Mexico City Mumbai Nairobi
São Paulo Shanghai Taipei Tokyo Toronto

Oxford is a registered trade mark of Oxford University Press
in the UK and in certain other countries

Published in the United States
by Oxford University Press Inc., New York

First published by Blackstone Press 1996

© Ian Brown, Adrian Chandler, 2003

The moral rights of the authors have been asserted
Database right Oxford University Press (maker)

First published 1994
Second edition 1996
Reprinted 1998
Reprinted 1999
Third edition 2001
Fourth edition 2003

British Library Cataloguing in Publication Data
Data available

Library of Congress Cataloging in Publication Data
Data available

ISBN 0-19-926089-3

3 5 7 9 10 8 6 4 2

Typeset by RefineCatch Limited, Bungay, Suffolk
Printed in Great Britain by
Ashford Colour Press Ltd, Gosport, Hampshire

Contents

Preface

In this fourth edition, we have added succinct plans to each answer as an aid to students' learning and understanding skills. We hope that these plans will be valuable both before and after reading the full answers to the questions. We have also included several diagrams as an aid to logical progression through areas of the law which students often find exacting and tortuous.

There are several important new decisions that have been considered in this edition. The House of Lords evaluated the Unfair Terms in Consumer Contracts Regulations 1994 in *Director General of Fair Trading* v *First National Bank plc* [2001] UKHL 52, [2002] 1 AC 481 and, in so doing, reversed the decision of the Court of Appeal. In the area of undue influence, the House of Lords' decision in *Royal Bank of Scotland* v *Etridge (No. 2)* [2001] UKHL 44, [2001] 4 All ER 449 is of fundamental importance and, most recently, the Court of Appeal has held that the (always controversial) decision in *Solle* v *Butcher* [1950] 1 KB 671 was not good law (see *Great Peace Shipping Ltd* v *Tsavliris Salvage (International) Ltd* (2002) *The Times*, 17 October). This latter decision is most significant in establishing that the House of Lords' decision in *Bell* v *Lever Brothers Ltd* [1932] AC 161 is both dominant and definitive. Although the EU Directive on *Certain Aspects of the Sale of Consumer Goods and Associated Guarantees* (99/44/EC, 25 May 1999) should have been implemented by January 2002, there have been delays and the latest word from the Department of Trade and Industry is that Regulations based upon the Directive will probably become law sometime in the first half of 2003.

As always, our aim has been to devise answers that are comprehensive, critical and readable: we hope we have hit the target.

Ian Brown
Adrian Chandler
1 November 2002

The Q&A Series

Key features

The Q&A series provides full coverage of key subjects in a clear and logical way. This new edition contains the following features:

- **Question**
- **Commentary**
- **Bullet point list**
- **Suggested answer**
- **Further reading**
- **Diagrams**

Table of Cases

Table of Statutes

Offer and Acceptance

Introduction

It must be possible to ascertain the precise moment at which a binding contract is formed between the offeror (O) and the offeree (A), the process of offer and acceptance being concerned with the mechanics by which agreement is reached. Throughout a myriad of factual situations, English Law demands that the cogs of offer and acceptance enmesh harmoniously: O's definitively certain offer must be followed by A's similarly unequivocal acceptance. This nineteenth century paradigm of contract formation matched the relatively simple bargains of that era but its simplistic rigidity was increasingly subjected to criticism in the twentieth century. In *New Zealand Shipping Co. Ltd v AM Satterthwaite & Co. Ltd (The Eurymedon)* [1975] AC 154, Lord Wilberforce said:

> It is only the precise analysis . . . into the classical offer and acceptance . . . that seems to present difficulty . . . English Law, having committed itself to a rather technical and schematic doctrine of contract, in application takes a practical approach, often at the cost of forcing the facts to fit uneasily into the marked slots of offer, acceptance and consideration.

Many commercial contracts involve a protracted process of negotiation and bargaining (often through the medium of agents acting on behalf of O and A) which results in eventual *agreement* even though it may be difficult to ascertain O's precise offer and A's related acceptance. Indeed many relatively simple situations in which there has been held to be a binding contract cannot be equated satisfactorily with offer and acceptance (see *Brogden v Metropolitan Ry Co.* (1877) 2 App Cas 666; *Clarke v Earl of Dunraven and Mount-Earl, The Satanita* [1897] AC 59; *Blackpool & Fylde Aero Club Ltd v Blackpool Borough Council* [1990] 1 WLR 1195). Having such difficulties in mind, Lord Denning suggested that the sole test should be whether the parties have reached *agreement* rather than 'forcing the facts' into the template of offer and acceptance (see *Butler Machine Tool Co. Ltd v Ex-cell-O Corp. (England) Ltd* [1979] 1 WLR 401; *Gibson v Manchester City Council* [1978] 1 WLR 520). Such an approach was rejected by the House of Lords in *Gibson* and it is arguable that its adoption would substitute uncertainty and unpredictability for the prescriptive rigidity of offer and acceptance. It is, therefore, only a superficially attractive solution.

Structure

Most contract law exam papers contain an orthodox problem question on offer and acceptance, demanding an analysis of whether offers have been made, their possible termination and the validity of acceptances. The best approach would be to pose five questions.

First, has an offer been made? An offer is a specific and definite proposition manifesting the offeror's clear intention to be bound. Such statements must be contrasted with mere invitations to treat (ITT) which lack any contractual significance. For example, there is a strong presumption that an advert constitutes an ITT because: (a) the advert will often lack specific details (e.g. sale of a car where the mileage is omitted), (b) the advert is often couched in eulogistic terms (e.g. 'a chance to win the opportunity of a lifetime'), (c) the responsibility for making an offer may be firmly placed on the enquirer (e.g. '£1000 or nearest offer'); and (d) a reasonable person would not intend to expose himself to limitless actions for breach of contract where a limited supply of goods has become exhausted (e.g. one bicycle offered for sale, ten acceptances). Nevertheless, there are situations where an advertisement contains all the necessary ingredients of an offer. For example, in *Carlill* v *Carbolic Smoke Ball Co. Ltd* [1893] 1 QB 256 the advertisement was specific and definite ('£100 reward *will* be paid . . . to anyone contracting influenza') and demonstrated the requisite intent to be bound ('£1000 has been deposited with the Alliance Bank . . . showing our sincerity in this matter'). *Carlill* emphasises the vagaries of offer and acceptance in this area: it cannot be certain whether a statement constitutes an offer or an ITT. This will depend upon the circumstances and the specificity of the language employed, so never attempt to be too dogmatic in your answer (compare *Bigg* v *Boyd Gibbins Ltd* [1971] 1 WLR 913 with *Harvey* v *Facey* [1893] AC 552 and *Bowerman* v *Association of British Travel Agents Ltd* (1995) NLJ Rep 1815).

Secondly, if an offer has been made, has the offeree unequivocally accepted this offer? In particular: (a) does the purported acceptance contain any new terms? If so, it may constitute a counter-offer, requiring the other's acceptance before a contract is formed (see *Hyde* v *Wrench* (1840) 3 Beav 334); (b) does the acceptance display the requisite degree of intent? For example, there is a strong presumption in land law that accepting 'subject to contract' creates no contractual liability (but see *Alpenstow Ltd* v *Regalian Properties plc* [1985] 1 WLR 721 and *Branca* v *Cobarro* [1947] KB 854); (c) has the conduct of the offeree clearly established the fact of acceptance? Silence rarely constitutes acceptance but actions sometimes speak louder than words (see *Brogden* v *Metropolitan Ry Co.* (1866) 2 App Cas 666); and (d) has the acceptance been authorised and communicated by the offeree or his agent (see *Powell* v *Lee* (1908) 99 LT 284)? It will be seen that this is a far stricter rule than the communication of an offer's revocation through a third party.

Thirdly, has the acceptance been communicated effectively? In particular: (a) is the acceptance effective on receipt or must it be actually read and understood by the offeror? Traditionally, communication has implied more than mere receipt (see *Entores Ltd* v *Miles*

Far East Corp. [1955] 2 QB 327) but there is recent authority for suggesting that receipt may be sufficient in commercial dealings if it equates with the intentions of the parties or achieves a just solution having regard to the allocation of risks (see *The Brimnes* [1975] QB 929, *Brinkibon Ltd* v *Stahag Stahl et al* [1983] 2 AC 34). This might have far-reaching consequences for acceptances recorded on answering machines or faxes received outside office hours (see *Mondial Shipping & Chartering BV* v *Astarte Shipping Ltd* [1995] CLC 1011; (b) has the offeree used the correct mode of communication? If a particular mode is pre-scribed by the offeror and the offeree uses an alternative means the acceptance will not be valid unless the alternative mode is equally expeditious (compare *Eliason* v *Henshaw* (1819) 4 Wheat 225 with *Tinn* v *Hoffmann & Co.* (1873) 29 LT 271); (c) does the postal rule apply to the acceptance? The rule states that a postal acceptance is effective on posting but this will be subject to a test of reasonableness and the express reservations contained within the offer (see *Quenerduaine* v *Cole* (1883) 32 WR 185; *Holwell Securities Ltd* v *Hughes* [1974] 1 WLR 155). Note that where the postal rule applies there is a preponderance of persuasive authority favouring the view that any withdrawal of the acceptance is impossible after the acceptance has been posted (see *A to Z Bazaars (Pty) Ltd* v *Minister of Agriculture* (1974) 4 SA 392). Is any other view logical? (d) if dealing with more modern forms of technological communication, how has the common law approach to 'communication' been affected by the Electronic Commerce (EC Directive Regulations 2002, SI No. 2013, and the Consumer Protection (Distance Selling) Regulations 2000, SI No. 2334).

Fourthly, at the moment when the acceptance is *deemed* to have been effective, is the offer still open? In particular: (a) has the offer lapsed? Expiry of a specified acceptance period, death of the offeror, and rejection of the offer are just some of the circumstances where the offer may no longer be capable of acceptance (see *Ramsgate Victoria Hotel & Co.* v *Montefiore* (1866) LR 1 Exch 109, *Bradbury* v *Morgan* (1862) 1 H & C 249; (b) has the offer been revoked? Revocation is effective at any time before the date of effective acceptance, provided it is communicated to the offeree personally or through a reliable third party source (see *Byrne* v *Van Tienhoven* (1880) 5 CPD 344, *Dickinson* v *Dodds* (1876) 2 Ch D 463).

Finally, is there any precedent for suggesting a departure from the aforesaid rules of offer and acceptance? Two important issues may arise in this context. First, there is a growing number of cases where courts have been prepared to modify the traditional rules in the light of the parties' clear intention to enter into formal contractual arrangements (see *Blackpool & Fylde Aero Club Ltd* v *Blackpool Borough Council* [1990] 1 WLR 1195 and the Court of Appeal's decision in *Gibson* v *Manchester City Council* [1978] 1 WLR 520 reversed by the House of Lords [1979] 1 WLR 294). Similarly, where a transaction has been *executed*, it is easier for the courts to dispense with the formalities of offer and acceptance (see *G Percy Trentham Ltd* v *Archital Luxfer Ltd* [1993] 1 Lloyd's Rep 25). See also **Chapter 2** which deals with agreements that lack the required degree of certainty (e.g. *Hillas & Co. Ltd* v *Arcos Ltd* (1932) 147 LT 503). Secondly, if an *offer* of a unilateral contract has been made the offeror may be unable to revoke the offer even though the potential offeree has not yet accepted (see the extended commentary on Question 4). In particular, there is authority for the suggestion that once the offeree has embarked upon a course of performance leading ultimately to a completed act of acceptance the offeror cannot withdraw the offer (see *Carlill* v *Carbolic Smoke Ball Co. Ltd, Daulia Ltd* v *Four Millbank Nominees Ltd* [1978] Ch 231, *Errington* v *Errington and Woods* [1952] 1 KB 290 — cf *Luxor (Eastbourne) Ltd* v *Cooper* [1941] AC 108).

Conclusion

Dealing with the rules of offer and acceptance as a first topic in a Contract syllabus is criticisable in that it tends to inculcate an undesirable, mechanical approach to the subject. However, the good student will realise that the rules were largely formulated in the nineteenth century and that there is scope for their criticism if the rules are redundant or inapplicable in modern conditions. Moreover, always remember that the application of these rules to new factual situations will rarely result in definite decisions. This is an advantage as it ensures that students focus on the *analytical processes* by which tentative conclusions can be justified, rather than the conclusions themselves. It is vital therefore to keep an open mind when attempting an offer and acceptance question and to consider all the possible variations. For example, if a statement potentially represents either an offer or an ITT consider the justifications for *both* propositions — if there are plausible arguments on both sides, adopt a flow diagram approach, considering the impact of either argument's proving successful. This approach is demonstrated in the diagram below.

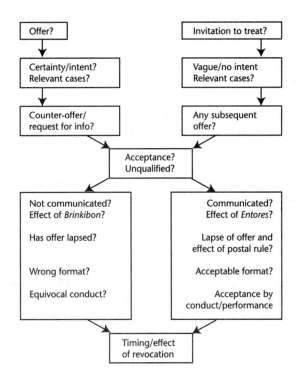

Q Question 1

Margaret, the sales director at TechMech, is approached by Philip, a local businessman, who outlines the size and nature of his business enterprise and asks Margaret to quote a price for the installation of TechMech's new accounts software system. Margaret, realising that her monthly sales quota has not yet been reached, replies: 'I am sure that for a business of your size we can guarantee a price of £3,000, covering all installation costs and appropriate staff training. But please get back to me quickly, I cannot hold that price for more than a week.'

Later that day, Philip receives an advertisement by email from CostPlus Ltd which states: 'We can offer "state-of-the-art" accountancy software for small businesses at a price guaranteed not to exceed £2,500.' He immediately telephones CostPlus and places an order. However, after discussing the matter further with a CostPlus representative, it becomes apparent that the actual costs of installation would exceed £4,000. Philip thereupon withdraws his order.

Next day, Philip telephones TechMech. He leaves a message on the answering machine accepting the offer of £3000 made by Margaret, at the same time asking whether the cost could also include on-site training for any new staff he takes on over the next six months. Subsequently, Philip has second thoughts and telephones TechMech to cancel his order. The secretary, now on duty, points out that she has passed all the answering service tapes over to Margaret who would be listening to them shortly, but that she would make a note of his wishes.

Advise Philip whether he has concluded a contract with TechMech and/or CostPlus and, if so, on what terms?

Commentary

This is a traditional offer and acceptance question incorporating a number of well-known principles such as the contractual effect of advertisements, the termination of an offer and the communication of acceptance and/or its withdrawal. Adopting a logical structure for your answer may be quite difficult so consider the possibility of using sub-headings, thereby avoiding unnecessary confusion for the examiner.

Although a technical, schematic approach is demanded, there is considerable scope for better students to demonstrate their analytical abilities. For example, the average student will apply the general rule of communication of acceptance in *Entores* v *Miles Far East Corp.* [1955] 2 QB 327 whereas the good student will explain the limitations possibly imposed upon this principle by the subsequent decisions in *The Brimnes* [1975] QB 929 and *Brinkibon Ltd* v *Stahag Stahl und Stahl* [1983] 2 AC 34.

- Does the CostPlus advertisement demonstrate sufficient intent and clarity to constitute an offer or is it merely an invitation to treat?

- If an offer, will CostPlus be in breach of contract in attempting to increase the price after Philip has placed an order?

- Is Margaret's response to Philip's enquiry an offer or an invitation to treat?

- Does Philip's attempted acceptance constitute a counter offer, a request for information or an acceptance subject to a preferred dispensation?

- If Philip's recorded message constitutes an unqualified acceptance, when was it actually communicated to TechMech?

- Did Philip revoke his 'acceptance' in time?

:Ó: Suggested answer

There are two possible contracts that Philip may have entered into: a contract negotiated personally with Margaret (of TechMech) and a contract with CostPlus. The question is whether Philip is contractually bound to purchase the relevant accounts software from either of the two firms. Naturally, if two contracts are found to have been concluded then Philip will automatically be in breach of contract regarding one of those agreements unless, of course, he is willing to pay twice!

CostPlus Advertisement

Clearly the original terms of the advertisement are extremely advantageous to Philip. The question is whether the advertisement constitutes an offer or an invitation to treat (ITT). Whereas an ITT merely represents a preliminary stage in negotiations, an offer constitutes a definite proposition by the offeror signifying his willingness to be bound by the terms stated therein as soon as it has been accepted by the offeree. The basic distinction between an offer and an ITT is that an ITT lacks the required objective intent and specificity to transform it into an offer. Traditionally, courts have preferred to view an advertisement as an opening gambit in future negotiations (i.e. an ITT) for two reasons. First, the wording of the advertisement is often too vague (cf *Grainger & Son* v *Gough* [1896] AC 325). Here the advertisement simply states a maximum price that presumably means that a lower price might be negotiated; moreover, no precise details are included about the software specifications, nor its inherent limitations or performance targets relevant to its intended business use. Secondly, sound business sense may dictate that a business 'supplier/seller' would prefer to choose its customers to avoid being inundated with acceptances that could not be fulfilled from existing stock (see *Partridge* v *Crittenden* [1968] 1 WLR 1204). Finally, there seems little difference between advertising goods in a shop-window, which courts have normally considered to be an ITT (see *Fisher* v *Bell* [1961] 1 QB 394) or advertising them via some other medium. The above reasoning points to the advertisement's being an ITT, reinforced by the subsequent conversation which demonstrates that CostPlus required further information before it could actually quote a definite price. Finally, if the advert was an offer, what *is* the price at which Philip is accepting — £2,500, or less? The fact that no definite answer can be given again suggests that the advert lacked the certainty required of an offer — drawing an analogy with the facts of *Harvey* v *Facey* [1893] AC 552 would reinforce this argument.

However, there are two points that might arguably alter the position here. First, in *Partridge* v *Crittenden* Parker LJ, in a strong *obiter dictum*, excluded manufacturers' catalogues from the presumption that an advert represented an ITT. Should this approach be extended to the supplier of specialist software who quotes a definite upper limit? Secondly, in *Carlill* v *Carbolic Smokeball Company Ltd* [1893] 1 QB 256 an advert was held to be an offer because the clarity of its wording, linked with an intention to be bound as evidenced by the deposit of money with the bank, demonstrated the required degree of intent and specificity. Similarly, does CostPlus's advert incorporate a statement of clear intent or is it a mere advertising puff? One might emphasise, for example, that the words 'price guaranteed not to exceed £2,500' demonstrates a clear contractual intent and that any further discussions will result in a lower price being agreed.

In the end, the argument that an ITT was made initially is probably stronger, in which case no contract will result (at any price). What is important here is that if the advertisement does constitute an offer, Philip has accepted its terms before Costplus increased its quote (i.e. offer) to £4,000. Specifically, the normal rule is that an offer can be accepted, subject to the need for communication, at any time before notice of its withdrawal has reached the offeree (see *Byrne* v *Van Tienhoven* (1880) 5 CPD 344). Thus, if a contract was formed when Philip placed his order, any post-contractual attempt by CostPlus to increase the quote would represent a breach of contract.

Discussions with TechMech

Does Margaret's statement of price represent an offer or an ITT? Adopting the analysis in the previous section, the required degree of intent and clarity of language must be isolated. Crucially, Margaret has used the words 'I am sure', suggesting a clear intent to be bound. One might compare this with *Gibson* v *Manchester City Council* [1979] 1 All ER 972 where the defendants' statement that they 'may be prepared to sell' was considered by the House of Lords to constitute an ITT — especially when linked with the later statement in the letter inviting the tenant to 'make a formal application'. In our facts, a specific price has been given, with a definite time limit. It is therefore more likely that the price constitutes an offer (Note: if it was definitely an ITT, the remainder of the question would have no purpose). One final point is that the offer can be withdrawn at any time before acceptance unless Philip has provided consideration for the offer to be kept open (e.g. payment).

Unqualified Acceptance?

Has Philip unequivocally accepted the terms of TechMech's offer? At first glance he appears to have added a new term; namely that the cost includes the training of new staff recruited over the next six months. If this represents a counter-offer then the placing of his order cannot constitute an acceptance — TechMech can choose to accept or reject this counter-offer (see generally *Hyde* v *Wrench*).

Could Philip argue that he was simply requesting information in order to clarify the position, i.e. is it clear that the quoted price applied only to the training of existing employees? This seems a weak argument as Philip's recorded message is not really phrased as a question of clarification, but rather as a favour. However, he may find greater support from *Society of Lloyd's* v *Twinn* (2000) *The Times*, 4 April where the Court of Appeal recognised that there was no reason why an offeree should not unconditionally accept an offer whilst, at the same time, making a separate offer collateral to the original offer. If the collateral offer was rejected then the unconditional acceptance of the original offer still created a binding agreement. On the facts, Philip's acceptance seems unconditional with his plea for indulgence regarding the training of subsequently recruited staff representing a collateral offer that TechMech is free to accept or reject.

Communication of Acceptance

Philip attempts to accept by telephone. The general rule is that acceptance must be communicated to the offeror or his agent in order to be effective. In this case Philip's acceptance has been recorded on an answering machine: is it effective when recorded or when it has been listened to? In *Entores* the Court of Appeal suggested that communication was equivalent to understanding, e.g. if the offeror does not hear the acceptance it is not effective. On this basis no contract has yet come into existence. But, as ever, there are arguable alternatives.

First, it is possible that the answering machine is a mechanical agent (see *Thornton* v *Shoe Lane Parking Ltd* [1971] 2 QB 163). If so, a contract has been formed and Philip has no chance of withdrawing from it.

Secondly, more recent decisions may have tempered the strictures of the *Entores* decision. In *The Brimnes*, the plaintiffs exercised their right to withdraw from the contract. The question was whether the plaintiffs' telex, incorporating the withdrawal, was effective when it was received during designated office hours or when it was read the following morning. The Court of Appeal concluded that the telex was effective on receipt as the plaintiffs had been told that it was the defendants' ordinary practice to read such telexes immediately. Whether one can apply this reasoning to communications of acceptance is, at present, a moot point. If it were applicable the following arguments might be advanced: (i) if the answering service implied that recorded messages would be listened to before the end of normal business hours of that day then acceptance would have been effectively communicated at some time during that day and a contract would come into existence, subject to the timing of Philip's attempted withdrawal; (ii) if the answering service suggested that messages would be listened to on the following day then it would seem that Philip's revocation would have already become effective, i.e. no contract would come into existence (see *Mondial; Shipping & BV* v *Astarte Shipping Ltd* [1995] CLC 1011.

A first class student *might* even elaborate on the suggestion, in *The Brimnes*, that a court could employ the indeterminate time between the receipt of a letter or telex, and its being read, to secure a just result; e.g., should TechMech be entitled to argue that a message is effective at the moment of its recording when the obvious consequence of using an answering service is to delay the actual time when communication takes place? Such flexibility was supported by the House of Lords in *Brinkibon Ltd* v *Stahag Stahl und Stahl* [1983] 2 AC 34: the time at which a telexed acceptance was effectively communicated would depend on the intentions of the parties, sound business practice and even a judgment as to where risks should lie. Is the receipt of a telexed acceptance similar to the telephone recording of an order? If so, can one assume that the intention of the parties was that Philip's order would only be communicated when his recorded message was heard, thereby allowing him the freedom to withdraw the order until that time? Conversely, does the use of an answering machine imply that a busy company does not wish to miss any opportunity to receive an order and that tapes will be listened to as quickly as possible, thereby suggesting that recording is tantamount to communication? Either argument is possible, again showing the inherent flexibility which the courts enjoy when applying the normal rules of offer and acceptance.

To summarise: if Philip's acceptance is effective only when his message has been listened to then his revocation is effective — an offeree can withdraw any acceptance provided the withdrawal is communicated prior to the acceptance (see *Byrne* v *Van Tienhoven*). If his acceptance is effective when recorded then a contract is immediately created, preventing him from attempting a revocation.

Q Question 2

Arnold has decided to try and sell his car by parking it outside his house with a notice on the windscreen stating: 'For sale. Pristine example — one owner. £4,750 or near offer. Please call at number 34 or telephone 713850, only.'

On Monday at 9.00 am, Bertram sees the car, but as he is late for work he is unable to stop. He telephones Arnold from work and makes an offer of £4,500 which Arnold says he will consider.

Charlie calls at Arnold's house on Monday at 11.00 am but Felicity, Arnold's daughter, is the only person there. He therefore leaves a note reading: 'Monday

11.05 am. Please keep car for me — here is a cheque for £4,750, Charlie.' Felicity leaves the note on Arnold's desk in his study.

On Monday afternoon, Arnold decides to accept Bertram's offer and posts a letter at 2.30 pm to Bertram's business address saying: 'I agree to sell on your terms. Because of the lower price can you pay in cash?'

At 4.30 pm on Monday, Arnold reads Charlie's acceptance and immediately telephones Bertram's business address, leaving a message on the recorded answering service: 'Ignore the letter you will receive — deal off. Arnold.' Bertram is away on business and only listens to the tape on Wednesday evening.

At 2.15 pm on Monday, Doris sees the notice and hurriedly posts a letter of acceptance and cheque for £4,750 in time for the 3.00 pm postal collection. Unfortunately, as Doris misaddresses her letter, it only arrives on Friday.

Advise all the parties as to their legal position.

Commentary

This question deals with a variety of technical offer and acceptance points. Amongst others, they include: Is Arnold or Bertram making a counter-offer? What is the importance of Arnold's telephoning Bertram's business office for the purposes of withdrawing his acceptance? When is Charlie's acceptance effectively communicated? Has Doris used the specified mode for communicating her acceptance?

One of the difficulties in answering the above question is that your answer will depend upon your interpretation of the first paragraph — is the windscreen notice an offer or an ITT? You can circumvent this difficulty by giving reasons for and against the advert as an offer and then employing appropriate sub-headings as a means of demonstrating a logical structure to the examiner. This will clarify the issues in your own mind and will also send a clear signal to the examiner that you do not expect answers in a Contract Law examination to be dogmatic, with only one possible solution.

- Is Arnold's advertisement sufficiently clear to constitute an offer, or even an offer of a unilateral contract, or would a court normally consider his efforts to be no more than an invitation to treat?

- Assuming Bertram's statement is an offer and/or a counter-offer, what is the effect of Arnold's saying that he will 'consider' it?

- Is Arnold's eventual acceptance unqualified and, if so, when was it communicated?

- If the original advert was an offer, has Charlie accepted that offer by calling at the house and leaving his note? Has the acceptance been communicated?

- Does the postal rule apply to Doris's purported acceptance?

:Q: **Suggested answer**

The first issue is whether the windscreen notice constitutes an offer or an ITT, for if it is the latter, Charlie and Doris never receive an acceptance to their offer. Does the notice demonstrate a clear willingness to be bound without any need or desire to prolong negotiations? An affirmative answer might suggest that the notice constitutes an offer. On the one hand the notice states a definite price, the car is subject to an external inspection and there is a prescribed method of communication. This latter point allows Arnold to vet each acceptance personally and, when a buyer has been found, place a notice of retraction on his car windscreen before any further acceptances are received (one might draw the analogy with *Shuey* v *US* (1875) 92 US 73).

Conversely, the price stated invites different bids ('or near offer'), it is unlikely that a buyer would come forward without an internal inspection of the car and test-drive, and an advertisement is normally considered to be a means of generating interest rather than a final stage before a contract is concluded. Is a notice on a windscreen any different from a price displayed in a shop window (e.g. *Fisher* v *Bell* [1961] 1 QB 394)? Moreover, the presumption generated by *Partridge* v *Crittenden* [1968] 1 WLR 1204 allows a private seller the discretion to choose their buyer.

Thus, as the contractual status of the notice is debatable, the answer below will assume that either proposition is valid.

Windscreen Notice is an ITT

(a) *Arnold* v *Bertram*   Bertram is clearly making an offer to Arnold to buy the car for £4,500. Arnold attempts to accept this offer by posting a letter in which he states that payment must be made in cash. What is the effect of this letter? First, by introducing a new condition that payment should be made in cash Arnold's response may be classified as a *qualified* acceptance, i.e. a counter-offer. If so, the counter-offer destroys Bertram's original offer (*Hyde* v *Wrench* (1840) 3 Beav 334). Bertram would have to accept this counter-offer before any contract came into existence (there is no evidence of this occurring). Moreover, Arnold's subsequent recorded telephone message would effectively revoke this counter-offer, at the very latest when Bertram listened to it on Wednesday morning.

But there is an alternative view. By specifying that payment should be made in cash, Arnold may simply be clarifying the position. How else would Bertram pay, especially as payment by cheque is considered to be equivalent to payment in cash (*D & C Builders Ltd* v *Rees* [1966] 2 QB 617)? This could be contrasted with the hypothetical position of Bertram's asking for a week to pay and then receiving Arnold's letter requesting immediate payment, in which case a clear counter-offer would have been made.

If Arnold's acceptance is considered to be unqualified, when is it effective? As the letter is posted, it may attract the postal rule, whereby acceptance is effective on posting (*Adams* v *Lindsell* (1818) 1 B & Ald 681). If so, modern authority would consider Arnold's subsequent retraction to be ineffective (e.g. *Wenkheim* v *Arndt* (1873) IJR 73 (NZ)). However, one must question the reasonableness of using the post in these circumstances. The advertisement was communicated *inter praesentes*, Bertram was required to visit Arnold's home or telephone him personally. An instantaneous communication is clearly contemplated by the parties, lest other people show an interest in the car whilst a letter is in transit. In these circumstances the rule may not apply on grounds of reasonableness or, put another way, because the offeror did not intend it to do so.

If the postal rule does not apply then the letter is only effective when it arrives — the final result depending upon whether the letter was delivered before Bertram listened to the recorded message on Wednesday morning, in which case a contract appears to have come into existence.

(Note: here again the better student might wish to (a) comment on the *obiter* statements in *The Brimnes* [1975] QB 929 which suggest that if the postal rule does not apply then a letter of acceptance is effective a reasonable time after it has been delivered during business hours at a business address (Arnold's letter might have arrived on Tuesday) and, (b) whether Arnold's retraction is effectively communicated when it was recorded or only when Bertram heard it — see extended analysis of this point in Question 1.)

(b)   *Arnold* v *Charlie*   As the windscreen notice is only an ITT Charlie has made an offer to Arnold to buy his car for £4,750. As there is no evidence that Arnold has communicated his acceptance, no contract can yet exist. Note that Arnold's mental acceptance of Charlie's offer is insufficient, unless Charlie dispensed with the need to communicate acceptance. (Note: arguably, if Arnold cashed Charlie's cheque then this might be effective communication provided Charlie's bank was acting as an agent for its customer when clearing the cheque.)

(c)   *Arnold* v *Doris*   Doris is in the same position as Charlie, assuming the windscreen notice is an ITT. There is no evidence that Arnold has accepted her offer.

Windscreen Notice is an Offer

(a)   *Arnold* v *Bertram*   Arnold's position is identical whether or not his notice constitutes an offer or an ITT. If Arnold has made an offer, then clearly Bertram's reply constitutes a counter-offer: he is offering a lower price. As with the above, the question is then whether Arnold has countered Bertram's response, in which case no contract yet exists, or is clarifying Bertram's offer, wherein the problem is resolved by whether Arnold's acceptance is communicated before or after his attempted retraction was communicated.

(b) *Arnold* v *Charlie* Charlie has accepted Arnold's offer without qualification. When is his acceptance effective? Is it when the letter arrives at Arnold's house (i.e. receipt) or when Arnold reads it (i.e. comprehension)?

Two arguments could be advanced in support of the receipt theory: (i) Felicity is Arnold's agent, thus communication takes place when Charlie delivers his acceptance into her hands. In fact, this is an unlikely result as it is doubtful whether a daughter would have the authority to act as an agent or, (ii) Charlie complied with the terms of the notice, visiting Arnold's house personally and has now left his acceptance. There is nothing to suggest that Arnold's notice required face to face communication. If either argument is successful then a contract is formed at 11.05 am on Monday.

Alternatively, Charlie's acceptance may only be effective when read by Arnold on Monday at 4.30 pm: until that time the acceptance has not been effectively communicated (see *Entores* v *Miles Far East Corp.* [1955] 2 QB 327). But by then Arnold may have entered a contract with Bertram earlier that afternoon (e.g. if the postal rule applies to his acceptance sent at 2.30 pm). If so, then either the circumstances in which the offer was made impliedly demand its immediate lapse after the sale of the car has been secured, or, if there is no implied lapse, Arnold is in breach of contract to Charlie by selling the car to Bertram. In the latter situation Charlie will have a remedy in damages based on the loss of bargain suffered.

(c) *Arnold* v *Doris* If the notice is an offer, Doris will argue that her posted acceptance has created a contract with Arnold. Two questions are worth posing: (i) does the postal rule apply to her letter of acceptance? and (ii) by using a different means of communication is her acceptance valid?

For the postal rule to apply, the acceptance must be properly addressed, the rules must not be excluded by the terms of the offer (e.g. *Holwell Securities Ltd* v *Hughes* [1974] 1 WLR 155), and the post must be a reasonable means of communication. In the present case Doris fails on all three counts. First, she has misaddressed her letter. Secondly, the terms of the offer stipulate a personal visit or a telephone call (see below). Thirdly, the situation demands immediate communication between the parties, thereby preventing unknown acceptances in the post creating unexpected liabilities. Thus, it is not reasonable for the postal rule to apply. But this does not exclude the possibility that her letter might be effective when it is delivered, creating the same difficulties for Arnold as he has with Bertram and Charlie; namely, is Arnold in breach of contract to Doris by selling the car to another party? To answer this we must consider whether Doris's acceptance is valid in the first place.

Clearly Doris has not used the prescribed means of communication. The general rule is that the offeree must adhere to the prescribed mode provided it is explicit and dogmatic, otherwise the acceptance is invalid (*Eliason* v *Henshaw* (1819) 4 Wheat 225). However, if there is not this degree of precision, the offeree may choose an equally expeditious means of communication (*Tinn* v *Hoffmann & Co.* (1873) 29 LT 271). In the present case, Arnold has used the word 'only' in his offer, thereby excluding use of the postal service, so Doris's acceptance is unlikely to be valid on receipt. Moreover, even if alternative forms of communication were not excluded by the terms of the offer, as the post is not as fast as the telephone, nor as immediate as a personal visit, Doris's attempted acceptance should still be invalid.

Q Question 3

On Wednesday Oftmark Ltd offers to sell 100 tonnes of steel to Aftercool Ltd at £500 per tonne. The offer to Aftercool states: 'Please telephone or email an acceptance by noon today. Delivery will take place next Monday.'

Aftercool Ltd faxes an acceptance at 10.00 am, the fax machine informing the clerical assistant that the message has been properly relayed to Oftmark. Unfortunately, the Oftmark fax machine has not been fitted with a new printing cartridge so the acceptance is not received. Moreover, as Aftercool Ltd believes that a firm contract exists, it enters into a binding contract with Torquecar Ltd to produce car body panels, using the anticipated delivery of steel on Monday.

Advise Aftercool Ltd whether there is a binding contract with Oftmark Ltd.

Would your advice differ in the following circumstances?

(a) Aftercool emailed a withdrawal of its acceptance before noon, but the email was accidentally deleted by an Oftmark employee.

(b) Aftercool telephoned an acceptance to Oftmark in the afternoon.

(c) Instead of a telephoned acceptance Oftmark's offer had specified: 'Please notify us of your acceptance by first class registered post sent before noon.' Aftercool sent a letter of acceptance before noon by unregistered post which was never received by Oftmark Ltd.

Commentary

This question is concerned with the problems of adapting the rules of offer and acceptance to new developments in communications technology. Communicating an acceptance by hand-delivered note or by post, or simply by using the telephone, has been overtaken in recent years by the ubiquitous telex and fax machines. Their advantages are clear: they combine speed and low operating costs with the benefits of a written record of any exchange of correspondence. Moreover, in these days of transnational negotiations and attendant time-zone difficulties, they provide commercial organisations with a means of immediate access to the offices of foreign clients. However, these forms of communication create their own difficulties. What happens if the recipient's telex machine is not permanently supervised? What if the equipment is improperly maintained? The House of Lords decision in *Brinkibon* v *Stahag Stahl und Stahl* [1983] 2 AC 34 provided some guidance on how courts should approach such difficulties, emphasising the importance of the parties' intentions and current business usage as well as requiring the court to make a judgment as to where the *risks* should lie.

To provide a complete answer to the above question, students must have a reasonable knowledge of the decisions in *Entores Ltd* v *Miles Far East Corp.* [1955] 2 QB 327, *The Brimnes* [1975] QB 929 and *Brinkibon* v *Stahag Stahl*. In particular, the *obiter* comments made in the judgments will address the problem of Oftmark's fault in not maintaining the fax machine properly and the reliance of Aftercool Ltd in entering into a contract with Torquecar Ltd.

- **What is the effect of Aftercool Ltd's employing a mode of acceptance different from that stipulated by Oftmark Ltd?**

- **As Aftercool Ltd has used an instantaneous means of communication, when is its acceptance effective? What flexibility does *Brinkibon* offer either party in these circumstances?**

- **(a) At what point was Aftercool Ltd's e-mailed acceptance effective: when it was capable of being accessed or only when it was actually read?**

- **(b) When did Oftmark Ltd's offer lapse, thereby negating any subsequent acceptance?**

- **(c) Did Oftmark Ltd impliedly exclude the postal rule?**

:Q: Suggested answer

It would appear that the requirements of an offer have been made out in that there is sufficient certainty (price and quantity) and intention (business context). The significant feature here is that the offeror has clearly prescribed a mode of acceptance. The general rule is that the offeree must adhere to the prescribed mode provided it is explicit and dogmatic, and if he does not, the acceptance is invalid (*Eliason* v *Henshaw* (1819) 4 Wheat 225). However, if this degree of precision is absent the offeree may choose an equally expeditious means of communication (*Tinn* v *Hoffmann & Co.* (1873) 29 LT 271). Into which category does this offer fall? On the one hand, the mode of acceptance is clearly specified but, on the other hand, use of the word 'please' suggests a degree of informality rather than a curt prescription. It is arguable that there is considerable room for manoeuvre here and, perhaps, the offeree is placed in a difficult position — does O want speed or a particular mode? If speed is of the essence then A has clearly complied with O's wishes by an immediate near-instantaneous communication which should have the added benefit of a permanent record (i.e. the printed fax). However, if the telephone or email mode is an absolute requirement then Aftercool's acceptance is invalid.

Assuming A has employed a valid mode of acceptance has a contract been formed? When does the acceptance take place? The general rule is that acceptance is only effective once it has been 'communicated' to O (*Entores* v *Miles Far East Corp.*); normally this means its understanding and/or receipt by O. In the instant case O does not receive any acceptance because of the malfunctioning fax machine. Does this mean that the acceptance is invalid?

Entores is a strong and sensible rule but it is not inflexible. The rule can be modified in various situations, e.g. if O is at fault with his defective communications equipment (turning off his 24-hour telex machine) then acceptance may be deemed to occur at the moment when it would have been received (see generally *Brinkibon* v *Stahag Stahl und Stahl* and *The Brimnes*). If this is the case then A may argue that, as O was at fault in failing to replace the printing cartridge on his fax machine, acceptance was deemed to be effective at 10.00 am (subject to the comments below). As fault and business usage are the determining factors, a different answer might be forthcoming if A clearly recognised that the fax had not been properly transmitted.

There is a further line of argument based on estoppel. In *Entores*, Lord Denning considered the possibility of O's telex machine running out of ink and, therefore, being incapable of receiving A's acceptance. His Lordship suggested that if an offeree reasonably believed that the acceptance had been received, and the offeror was at fault, then the latter would be estopped from saying that the acceptance was not received. This estoppel might be more easily established on the present facts as Aftercool Ltd relied to its *detriment* upon the assumed communication by entering into a binding agreement with Torquecar Ltd (cf *Argy Trading Development Co. Ltd* v *Lapid Developments Ltd* [1977] 1 WLR 444 where it was questioned whether a promissory estoppel could operate without a *pre-existing* contract).

Difference with (a)

There is as yet no case authority dealing with the use of email communication in the context of offer and acceptance. One must therefore extrapolate relevant principles from existing authority that might be appropriate to deal with the current situation. The basic principle stays the same: to be effective the revocation of an offer must be communicated prior to the time when any effective acceptance has become valid. In the context of faxes we have seen that communication normally occurs on receipt (*Entores*) but that this rigid rule is subject to flexible interpretation (*Brinkibon*). Treating the email like a fax would mean that Aftercool could argue that: (i) communication had taken place on receipt (relying on *Entores*); (ii) no estoppel could operate in Oftmark's favour as Aftercool's actions could not have induced any alteration of position; and (iii) even if communication of Aftercool's original acceptance had occurred, neither party should be allowed to take advantage of their own fault in order to create or prevent the formation of a contract (see *The Brimnes*).

However, one important difference between a fax and an email is that the latter often requires some positive action by the offeror before the acceptance can be read whilst the former is simply received in printed form. In particular, apart from switching on a PC, the offeror needs to access the email. In many ways, opening an email is very similar to opening an envelope in order to read its contents. Seen in this light, email communication is not instantaneous and may not be governed by the *Entores* principles. If so, consider *The Brimnes* where the Court of Appeal, *obiter*, suggested that a letter (that is not protected by the postal rule) delivered during normal business hours is assumed to have been read a reasonable time after its delivery. If the same can be said of emails then Aftercool could argue that the email was presumptively read a reasonable time after its 'delivery'. (Note: Article 11(2) of the E-commerce (EC Directive) Regulations 2002, S.I. No. 2013, in the context of internet contracting, appears to follow the logic of this approach by assuming that communication takes place once the recipients of emails 'are able to access them', although how this is applied to emails sent outside office hours remains a moot point.)

Difference with (b)

What is the effect of A's telephoning an acceptance after the noon deadline? An offer will lapse in accordance with its terms or, if this is unclear, a reasonable time after it has been made (see *Ramsgate Victoria Hotel Co.* v *Montefiore* (1866) LR 1 Exch 109). 'Reasonable' will depend on the circumstances, such as the implicit need for urgency displayed in *Quenerduaine* v *Cole* (1883) 32 WR 185 and the nature and perishability of the goods. On the present facts O has stipulated a reply before noon by telephone or email. It would seem, therefore, that the offer has impliedly lapsed by the time A attempted to accept the terms of the offer. (Note: the offeror would have expected to receive an acceptance before noon.) Another possible argument is that A, by not complying with the conditions of the offer, has made a counter-offer which was not accepted by O (*Wettern Electric Ltd* v *Welsh Development Agency* [1983] QB 796).

Difference with (c)

Two issues arise to be discussed. First, does the postal rule apply? The post is clearly contemplated as the expected medium for communicating acceptance. However, the postal rule can be excluded by express contrary intent, provided it is specified in the terms of the offer. For example, when completing a football pools coupon there is a clear statement that the coupon must be received by a certain time before any liability ensues. The present facts are similar to *Holwell Securities Ltd* v *Hughes* [1974] 1 WLR 155 where the offeree was requested to exercise his option by 'notice in writing'. These words were held to exclude the postal rule as the offeror was specifying the need to see the acceptance (i.e. have 'notice' of it) before any contract was formed. Equally,

O appears to be imposing a similar condition. If so, no contract would come into existence as the postal acceptance never reached O.

The alternative argument is that the court in *Holwell* was applying the provisions of s. 196 of the Law of Property Act 1925 in which, *inter alia*, the exercise of an option by post was deemed effective 'at the time at which the . . . letter would in the ordinary course be delivered'. Thus *Holwell* is limited to contracts affecting interests in land. Moreover, whereas 'notice in writing' implies delivery, notification by post might suggest that the act of posting is sufficient; in particular, only O can 'notice' an acceptance, but only A can notify it. If this argument were accepted the postal rule would be applied: the acceptance would be effective on posting irrespective of its subsequent loss.

Secondly, by using unregistered post has Aftercool sent a valid acceptance? Previous comments have suggested that this will depend upon the offer's prescription. If registered post is a pre-condition for acceptance, no contract will exist, whereas if any equally expeditious means of communication is acceptable, a contract should be formed as registered and unregistered delivery have the same time scale for delivery. However, there is a further argument. What is the purpose of stipulating registered post? It cannot help O as the acceptance is either delivered, in which case it is known, or it is not delivered, in which case it remains unknown. In *Yates Building Co. Ltd* v *RJ Pulleyn & Sons (York) Ltd* (1975) 119 Sol Jo 370, the court concluded that the instruction to use registered post was intended to protect the offeree. A took a risk by using ordinary post as he would lack proof of transmission if the letter was lost before its delivery.

In conclusion, if the postal rule applied then A's acceptance is effective on posting, provided there is sufficient evidence that the letter was actually posted. If the postal rule does not apply, no communication of acceptance has taken place so no contract can exist.

Q Question 4

Scrumptious Ltd, a manufacturer of chocolate and confectionery, places the following advertisement in a national newspaper in June:

> We have hidden 15 Scrumptious Badges in various parts of the UK. If you find one and send it to us we will give you £10,000 in cash! Simply buy 6 Scrumptious Candy Twirls and post us your wrappers and we will send you a free book of clues which will help in the fun Summer search for the badges! Good Luck!

On 15 July, Scrumptious Ltd places a prominent notice in all national newspapers stating that the prize has been withdrawn.

Discuss the legal position of the following entrants:

(a) Alan retrieves a discarded copy of the book of clues from a dustbin on 26 June and finds a badge on 16 July.

(b) Andrew buys 6 Candy Twirls and receives the book of clues. He locates a badge at the top of a flagpole. Before climbing the pole, Andrew is informed by a passer-by of Scrumptious Ltd's revocation. He nevertheless starts to climb the pole but before reaching the top he falls and breaks both legs. Consequently, he has to cancel his annual summer holiday and loses £3,000 in expected earnings whilst he is away from work.

Commentary

This problem concerns formation and performance of unilateral contracts about which there is much controversy and very few clear rules: students must be able to balance arguments and be aware that there are no definitive answers to such questions.

A bilateral contract entails an exchange of promises between O & A but the essence of a unilateral contract is that O's offer is accepted by A's *act of performance*. The contract is unilateral in the sense that only O is bound initially, for A may decide not to commence performance of the stipulated acceptance. These undertakings have been described as 'if' contracts by Goff LJ in *Daulia Ltd* v *Four Millbank Nominees Ltd* [1978] Ch 231, e.g. O offers A £100 if A will walk to York. Moreover it is clear that A need not communicate any acceptance — his performing the act of acceptance is sufficient without more. The paradigm unilateral contract is that in *Carlill* v *Carbolic Smoke Ball Co.* [1893] 1 QB 256 where the acceptance necessarily involved a course of conduct.

Two difficulties are immediately apparent. First, when is A's act of acceptance sufficiently clear and unequivocal to create a binding contract? A may want to establish the commencement of his act as an acceptance but O's retort will be that he has bargained for nothing short of a completed performance. Apply these two different perspectives to the *Carlill* case. When did Mrs Carlill accept the offer?

Secondly, may O legitimately revoke his offer once A has commenced performance? A conclusive answer to the first question would also resolve the revocation issue for the general rule is that revocation of an offer is permissible at any time prior to its acceptance. Strict adherence to this latter rule can often be inequitable in unilateral contracts if A has commenced performance and much of the analysis in this area seeks a measure of protection for A against O's power of revocation. A great deal may hinge on the facts and students must balance O's right to demand a completed act and correlative power to revoke before A's completion against the reliance and expectation interests of A which are generated by O's offer and may well be worthy of protection.

• **Is Scrumptious Ltd's advertisement an offer of a unilateral contract or an invitation to treat? Can you draw an analogy with *Carlill*?**

- If it is an offer, what act must Alan and/or Andrew perform in order to accept?
- At what point is it too late for Scrumptious Ltd to revoke its offer: once performance of the required act has commenced or at any time before completion?
- Can Alan accept the 'offer' when he did not purchase any Candy Twirls?
- When is notification of revocation by a third party effective? Does *Dickinson* v *Dodds* suggest that the third party must be reliable?
- What difficulties emerge when attempting to compensate the offeree for the offeror's revocation of his offer of a unilateral contract?

:Q: Suggested answer

This problem concerns the difficulties inherent in the formation and breach of unilateral contracts.

First, it must be asked whether the advertisement of Scrumptious Ltd (O) is an offer or an invitation to treat (ITT). An ITT is merely the precursor to an offer and hence incapable of acceptance whereas an offer is an unequivocal proposition made with an intention to be legally bound. The advertisement contains the necessary specificity and it is arguable that as it is made by a manufacturer the tendency is to construe it as an offer (see *Carlill* and *Partridge* v *Crittenden* [1968] 1 WLR 1204). It would be difficult for O to argue that the advertisement's jocular tone meant that it lacked the relevant intent because there is both an immediate benefit and detriment to O and A respectively in the purchase of the Candy Twirls and a continuing reliance by A in commencing a search. This would appear to be a unilateral offer which can be converted into a binding contract by A's act of acceptance. Secondly, it is necessary to consider when A's acceptance occurs. The presumption in unilateral contracts is that only the completion of A's act can amount to acceptance as, in the majority of cases, that is what O has bargained for, e.g. O's dog *returned* to him. In the instant problem O should not be under any liability to A if A cannot locate a badge: O had not promised to reimburse A for time and money spent in failed endeavours. In *Luxor (Eastbourne) Ltd* v *Cooper* [1941] AC 108 the agreement was that O would pay A £10,000 if he could find a purchaser for two cinemas at a minimum price of £185,000. A introduced a prospective purchaser who agreed, subject to contract, to pay that price but O sold the cinemas to a third party. The House of Lords held that A's acceptance would entail a completed sale to the purchaser he introduced and, accordingly, O could revoke his offer at any time before A's acceptance was complete. Moreover, the House was unable to imply a term that O would not revoke his offer as this was not necessary to give business efficacy to *both* parties' intentions. In *Errington* v *Errington and Woods* [1952] 1 KB 290 however, a father promised his son and daughter-in-law that, if they paid the mortgage instalments on his house, the house would belong to them when the mortgage was paid off. The Court of Appeal suggested that the father's promise could not be revoked once the couple had 'entered on performance of the act' but that it would cease to bind him if they left it 'incomplete and unperformed'. In *Luxor*, it is arguable that the huge potential reward (£10,000 on a sale price of £185,000) meant that A acknowledged both the risk of his not finding a purchaser and O's revoking before completion, whereas in *Errington* the couple who diligently paid their instalments did not consider that they were running any sort of business risk. *Ward* v *Byham* [1956] 1 WLR 496 (no permissible revocation) may also be justified using this latter argument. Furthermore, in *Errington*, A was conferring a *tangible benefit* on O with every payment made, thereby making the possible revocation more inequitable as time progressed. In short, the courts balance three principles in arriving at a decision: *reliance* of A, *benefit* conferred on O and the inherent *risk* which A may accept. Most unilateral contracts fall into the first two categories and the weight of authority is against revocation once performance has commenced (see also *United Dominions Trust (Commercial Ltd)* v *Eagle Aircraft Services Ltd* [1968] 1 All ER 104; *Daulia Ltd* v *Four Millbank Nominees Ltd*, above).

Alan

As Alan has not bought any Candy Twirls it is arguable that he does not comply with the terms of the offer and may not be a potential offeree. Moreover, the court might decide that the initial purchase amounted to an unequivocal beginning of performance thus preventing a subsequent revocation, Alan also failing to satisfy this requirement. Alternatively, Alan's searches may attract publicity which could be advantageous to Scrumptious and his subsequent reliance in seeking a badge is as great as any other competitor (draw the analogy with *Esso Petroleum Co. Ltd* v *Commissioners of Customs & Excise* [1976] 1 WLR 1). *If* revocation is possible, the question is met head-on with Alan. It was held in *Shuey* v *US* (1875) 92 US 73 that an offer of reward was revocable by giving the revocation 'the same notoriety' as the offer even if A had no actual knowledge of it. This is justifiable where O does not know his potential offerees (in *Shuey* the offer was made to the public) but Scrumptious may have a record of the purchasers of the wrappers thereby making such an attempted revocation unreasonable. In Alan's situation this would be inapplicable, arguably moving his case closer to *Luxor* in his acceptance of risk.

Andrew

Andrew's situation has the added difficulty that a third party communicates the revocation to him. *Dickinson* v *Dodds* (1876) 2 Ch D 463 established that a reasonable third party may communicate revocation to A even though he is not authorised by O to perform the task. *Dickinson* was arguably coloured by notions of lack of *consensus* between the parties and is criticisable today: how is A to ascertain the reasonableness of his informant? It is suggested that, on the facts, this mode of revocation would be unreasonable. Moreover, several points militate against the possible revocation in Andrew's case. First, Andrew has bought the Candy Twirls thereby conferring a benefit on Scrumptious Ltd and arguably commencing his performance. Secondly, Scrumptious Ltd may have a record of purchasers' addresses meaning that the attempted newspaper revocation might be unreasonable. Finally, Andrew places maximum, detrimental reliance on the offer.

In both Alan's and Andrew's case there is the problem of the measure of damages if O revokes before A's completion. If the parties do not have a *contract* until completion O cannot be in breach of contract and there would similarly be difficulties if O's offer was deemed to be irrevocable as in *Errington* — A still does not have a binding contract until completion. The courts might consider the revocation to be a breach of a collateral contract not to revoke, but, if not, damages might be assessed on a tortious basis. Similarly, it is arguable that in placing the badge at the top of the flagpole, Scrumptious is in breach of the duty of care which it may owe to Andrew in the tort of negligence.

In conclusion, perhaps a compromise of interests would be to allow O's power of revocation subject to an obligation to reimburse A to the extent of his justifiable reliance on the offer. Whilst not a perfect solution, in that it leaves open the question of how reliance is to be quantified (a detriment suffered by A, a benefit conferred upon O or some evaluation of both?), it would allow a court to *apportion* loss rather than take the all-or-nothing approach evidenced in *Errington* and *Luxor* respectively.

Certainty of Terms and Intention

Introduction

Contractual certainty

If businesspeople are often not overly-concerned with the niceties of offer and acceptance it follows that their contracts may not be all-embracing and complete in every respect. The parties may have reached an agreement in principle and then prefer to rely on experience from previous dealings, business practice and goodwill. The law's overall policy is to uphold bargains wherever possible and although businessmen tend to record their agreements in 'crude and summary fashion' the law should not be 'too astute or subtle in finding defects' (*Hillas & Co. Ltd* v *Arcos Ltd* (1932) 147 LT 503, 514, *per* Lord Wright). However, the parties must fix the boundaries of their own obligations and the law cannot paternalistically intervene to *create* a contract on their behalf. Consequently, in seeking to clarify and enforce agreements the law must tread a middle line, avoiding wanton destruction of agreements on one side and the imaginative creation of bargains on the other (compare *Hillas* (*supra*) with *Scammell (G) & Nephew Ltd* v *Ouston* [1941] AC 251). In pursuit of the general policy of upholding bargains, the law may (a) ignore a meaningless clause if it adds nothing to an otherwise complete agreement (see *Nicolene Ltd* v *Simmonds* [1953] 1 QB 543), (b) enforce an agreement where one party is under a duty to resolve the uncertainty (see *David T Boyd* v *Louis Louca* [1973] 1 Lloyd's Rep 209), (c) refer to previous dealings and trade practices (see *Hillas* (*supra*)) and, (d) resolve vagueness by reference to custom (see *Shamrock SS Co.* v *Storey & Co.* (1899) 81 LT 413).

Often the parties attempt to allow for fluctuating economic conditions by introducing a variable provision into their agreement, e.g. dates of payment and delivery to be fixed from time to time in the future. Such a provision may be regarded by the courts as 'an agreement to agree' and be so uncertain as to be incapable of enforcement (see *May & Butcher* v *R* [1934] 2 KB 17n; *Smith* v *Morgan* [1971] 1 WLR 803). As the courts are reluctant to strike-down provisions which are intended to have legal effect, they may uphold some agreements even if further terms are to be agreed by the parties (see *Foley* v *Classique Coaches Ltd* [1934] 2 KB 1; *British Bank for Foreign Trade* v *Novinex* [1949] 1 KB 623) and this is particularly so where there are criteria for resolving the uncertainty (see *Brown* v *Gould* [1972] Ch 53; *Sudbrook Trading Estate Ltd* v *Eggleton* [1982] 1 AC 493).

Letters of intent cause problems with certainty. Here the sender of the letter states that he intends to contract with the recipient and the latter may act in reliance on the letter in commencing performance. It is quite possible to establish a certain, binding contract in such cases (see *Trollope & Colls Ltd v Atomic Power Constructions Ltd* [1963] 1 WLR 333; *Wilson Smithett & Cape (Sugar) Ltd v Bangladesh Sugar and Food Industries Corporation* [1986] 1 Lloyd's Rep 378). Similarly, letters of comfort may be either binding contracts or informal and uncertain assurances resting entirely upon business goodwill (see *Kleinwort Benson Ltd v Malaysia Mining Corporation Berhad* [1989] 1 WLR 379).

The House of Lords has recently considered the status of a contract to negotiate and denied the existence of an enforceable, positive contract to negotiate in good faith as lacking sufficient certainty (see *Walford v Miles* [1992] 2 AC 128) although it is clear that a purely negative lock-out arrangement, for a specific period of time, is an enforceable contract (see *Pitt v PHH Asset Management Ltd* [1993] 4 All ER 961).

Contractual Intent

As well as the other elements required for the formation of a contract, there must be an intention to create legal relations, this being assessed objectively. In commercial contracts there is a presumption of intention and the onus is on the party who asserts that no legal effect is intended to rebut the presumption. The parties may expressly deny any intent but, in the absence of such an express denial, rebuttal is extremely difficult (see *Edwards v Skyways Ltd* [1964] 1 WLR 349; *Rose & Frank Co. v J R Crompton & Bros Ltd* [1923] 2 KB 261; *Jones v Vernons Pools Ltd* [1936] 2 All ER 626). The litigation in *Kleinwort Benson Ltd v Malaysia Mining Corporation Berhad* [1989] 1 WLR 379, is important. The first instance decision applied the presumption of intention ([1988] 1 WLR 799) but the Court of Appeal's reasoning appears to allow a circumvention of the presumption rather than its rebuttal.

A statement inducing a contract may be a 'mere puff' and the test is one of intention (see *Weeks v Tybald* (1605) Noy 11; *Carlill v Carbolic Smoke Ball Co. Ltd* [1893] 1 QB 256). Similarly, intention determines whether a statement is a term of the contract or a 'mere representation' (see *Heilbut, Symons & Co. v Buckleton* [1913] AC 30).

Many social and domestic agreements lack sufficient intent to make them legally binding (see *Balfour v Balfour* [1919] 2 KB 571) but a husband and wife, for example, can make a binding contract (see *Pearce v Merriman* [1904] 1 KB 80; *Merritt v Merritt* [1970] 1 WLR 1211). Similarly, other domestic arrangements can involve difficulties of intention (see *Jones v Padavatton* [1969] 1 WLR 328; *Simpkins v Pays* [1955] 1 WLR 975; *Parker v Clark* [1960] 1 WLR 286).

Q Question

It is a basic axiom of English law that, although the courts cannot make a contract for the parties, they will strive to uphold a bargain wherever possible.
Discuss.

Commentary

This question calls for an understanding of certainty of terms and, to a lesser extent, intention to create legal relations. Students must be able to make an accurate analysis of the lengths to which the courts will go in enforcing contracts. The decisions tend to make technical distinctions but students should be aware of the important substantive issues raised in *Kleinwort Benson Ltd* v *Malaysia Mining Corporation Berhad* [1989] 1 WLR 379 and *Walford* v *Miles* [1992] 2 AC 128.

* What is meant by the rule that a contract must have certainty of terms?

* To what extent will the courts strive to uphold a bargain and seek to clarify the terms of the contract?

* To what extent can the parties leave a term of the contract to be agreed upon in the future

* Do recent decisions adopt a more rigorous approach than formerly in demanding that intent and certainty must unite to forge an intelligible and enforceable undertaking?

;Q: Suggested answer

It is the parties who make their own contract and fix its boundaries whilst the courts enforce the bargain thus created. It follows that if the agreement is uncertain and imprecise the courts will be unable to enforce it and may decide that it also lacks the requisite intention to create legal relations. In *Scammell (G) & Nephew Ltd* v *Ouston* [1941] AC 251 there was an agreement to acquire goods 'on hire-purchase terms' but the House of Lords held that this could not be a binding contract as it was 'so vaguely expressed that it cannot, standing by itself, be given a definite meaning'. Similarly, in *Jacques* v *Lloyd D George & Partners* [1968] 1 WLR 625 there was an uncertain and unenforceable agreement where an estate agent was to be paid commission should he be 'instrumental in introducing a person willing to sign a document capable of becoming a binding contract'.

However, the courts will uphold bargains whenever possible and, as Lord Wright emphasised in *Hillas & Co. Ltd* v *Arcos Ltd* (1932) 147 LT 503, the courts should not be 'too astute or subtle in finding defects' even though commercial agreements may be crudely drafted by businessmen. In *Hillas*, the plaintiffs agreed to buy from the defendants a quantity of Russian softwood timber of a particular quality, the agreement containing an option for the plaintiffs to buy more timber at a later date but with no particulars of size or quality. When the plaintiffs sought to exercise the option, the defendants objected that the clause was vague and indeterminate and provided, at best, a basis for future negotiations. The House of Lords held that, having regard to previous dealings, there was sufficient intention to be bound and the agreement could be rendered certain by referring to the parties' previous dealings and the normal practice in the timber trade. *Hillas* is illustrative of the courts willingness to imply terms thereby making commercial sense of the agreement, but an alternative method of resolving uncertainty is to delete a meaningless, subsidiary provision, leaving the remainder of the contract complete and enforceable. In *Nicolene Ltd* v *Simmonds* [1953] 1 QB 543, the defendant agreed to sell a quantity of steel bars to the claimant on terms which were clear except for the statement that 'we are in agreement that the usual conditions of acceptance apply'. It was held that the words were meaningless but that they did not destroy the contract as they were severable, leaving the core of the obligation intact. The rationale of this decision was explained by Denning LJ in that, if the opposite conclusion had been reached, defaulters would be 'scanning their contracts to find some meaningless clause on which to ride free'. However, the *Nicolene* principle cannot function if the meaningless clause is intended to govern an undertaking central to the agreement, for then its uncertainty may vitiate the whole agreement.

The courts look favourably on agreements which, although leaving some issue to be resolved in the future, provide the machinery or criteria for its resolution. Thus, an agreement will not fail simply because it provides for the resolution of outstanding issues by arbitration, and, in *Brown* v *Gould* [1972] Ch 53, an option to renew a lease 'at a rent to be fixed having regard to the market value of the premises' was binding in that it provided a criterion, albeit somewhat elusive, for resolving the vagueness. Moreover, this notion was extended in *Sudbrook Trading Estate Ltd* v *Eggleton* [1983] 1 AC 444. A lease gave the tenant an option to purchase the premises 'at such price as may be agreed upon by two valuers' who were to be appointed by each party. The landlord refused to appoint a valuer but the House of Lords held that the option did not fail for uncertainty. The substance of the undertaking was an agreement to sell at a reasonable price to be determined by valuers and the extra stipulation that each party should nominate a valuer was 'subsidiary and inessential'. Furthermore, provided that the machinery is 'subsidiary' the court may institute its own procedures for resolving the uncertainty should the original machinery break down, e.g. ascertain the price with the help of expert evidence (see *Re Malpas* [1985] Ch 42).

The courts will thus not be deterred from clarifying uncertainty where there is a determinate intention of the parties to form a binding contract but the vagueness in question may relate to a fundamental obligation which the parties have deliberately left open-ended. This may occur where both parties are reluctant to enter into a finalised contract for a lengthy period of time, preferring to leave questions such as the price and manner of payment for later consideration and agreement. Are such agreements enforceable? In *May & Butcher* v *R* [1934] 2 KB 17n, an agreement for the sale of tentage provided that the price, dates of payment and manner of delivery should be agreed 'from time to time'. On these facts, the House of Lords held that the agreement was incomplete as it amounted to nothing more than an agreement to agree in the future. If the agreement had been silent on these issues, the House thought that s. 8(2) of the Sale of Goods Act 1893 might have applied meaning that a reasonable price should be paid, but the parties had shown that this was not their intention by providing for a further agreement. *May & Butcher* has been distinguished in several cases and it is very difficult to make generalisations in this area but it seems that the courts look for substantial agreement between the parties and, if this is present, it accords with commercial practice that some points may be left for future resolution without vitiating the agreement. It is nevertheless very difficult to ascertain the nature and extent of the issues which may be left for future agreement. In *Foley* v *Classique Coaches Ltd* [1934] 2 KB 1, the plaintiff owned a petrol station and adjoining land which he agreed to sell to the defendants on condition that they should agree to buy all the petrol for their coach business from him. The agreement regarding the petrol was executed and provided that it was to be supplied 'at a price to be agreed by the parties in writing and from time to time'. The land was conveyed and the petrol agreement was acted on for three years but the defendants then repudiated it arguing that it was incomplete in relation to the price of the petrol. The Court of Appeal held that the agreement was enforceable and that, consequently, the defendants must pay a reasonable price for the petrol. The most influential factors in the decision appeared to be that the contract had been acted upon for several years and that the petrol agreement formed part of a linked bargain with the sale of the land, the defendants paying a price for the land which no doubt reflected the fact that they would buy their petrol from the plaintiffs.

Two recent and important decisions cast doubt upon the notion that the courts will strive to uphold the parties' bargain. *Kleinwort Benson Ltd* v *Malaysia Mining Corporation Berhad* [1989] 1 WLR 379 concerned a letter of comfort which the defendant issued to the plaintiff in respect of a loan of £10 million to one of the defendant's subsidiary companies. Comfort letters possess varying degrees of formality but here the letter was negotiated between the parties and contained the statement by the defendant that it was its 'policy to ensure that the business of [the subsidiary] is at all times in a position to meet its liabilities to you under the above arrangements'. The defendant argued that neither party intended this statement to be contractually binding. At first instance, it was held that the plaintiff should succeed as: (a) the presumption of intention to create legal relations which applies to commercial contracts had not been rebutted by the defendant; (b) the wording was unambiguous and 'crystal clear'; and (c) the undertaking was of crucial importance and the plaintiff had acted in reliance on it in advancing the loan. The Court of Appeal reversed the decision and held that the wording of the undertaking did not amount to a contractual promise and thus the question of rebutting the presumption of intention to create legal relations never arose. Moreover, the court considered that the statement was only one of present intention in that the defendant's 'policy' could change in the future. The Court of Appeal's reasoning appears to ignore the presumption of intention and, if that presumption has not been rendered redundant by the decision, it is very difficult to ascertain in which circumstances it will apply. The second decision, *Walford* v *Miles* [1992] 2 AC 128, concerned the enforceability of a contract to negotiate. The plaintiff and defendant were negotiating the sale of the defendant's business and an agreement was reached by which the plaintiff would provide the defendant with a letter of comfort from the plaintiff's bankers confirming that a loan would be granted to the plaintiff. In return, the defendant agreed to terminate any negotiations with third parties and not to consider any alternative offers. The comfort letter was provided but the defendant withdrew from the negotiations and sold the business to a third party. The House of Lords held that the plaintiff's action must fail. The House considered that it was possible to have a contract *not* to negotiate with third parties provided that the duration of this 'lock-out' was specified expressly but that the parties could never be 'locked-in' by such an arrangement to negotiate positively as this would amount to an uncertain and unenforceable contract to negotiate.

Kleinwort and *Walford* are paradigmatic of *laissez-faire* principles of self-reliance and judicial non-interventionism. It is suggested that the decisions ignore English law's basic tenet that agreements should be validated wherever possible and, in so doing, will encourage bad faith in commercial transactions.

Consideration

Introduction

If offer, acceptance and certainty of terms relate to the *machinery* of agreement, consideration and intention are the tests for ascertaining the validity of its *substance*. Whilst enforcement of all promises is theoretically possible, it is very unrealistic and so there must be limits on enforceability. Various methods of control can impose restrictions. First, rules regarding the *form* the contract must take, e.g. deeds or writing, can draw unequivocal boundaries and prescribe detailed formalities (e.g. the requirements of the Consumer Credit Act 1974). A requirement of form deters sharp practice and fraud whilst encouraging the desirable elements of a seriously intended, voluntary agreement. An over-emphasis on form is the hallmark of the early stages of a legal system which, as it develops, begins to recognise the intent/substance of the agreement behind the formalities. Moreover, it would clearly be impossible to demand writing for every contract and so a more general test of enforceability is required. This could have several possible bases. First, the test might be dependent upon the intention of the parties, serious agreements thus being enforceable. Secondly, B's *reliance* on A's promise might simultaneously establish a nexus and a good reason to enforce the agreement (see American Restatement (Second) of Contracts, section 90). Thirdly, the agreement might involve an *exchange* thereby becoming a bargain. A would thus not be bound unless he received *consideration* from B in the form of a return promise or actual performance of the undertaking. The proponents of reliance theory suggest that if B has relied to his *detriment* on A's promise he has a stronger claim to redress than if he merely gives a return promise without any actual performance. Whilst this appears to be theoretically logical, it lacks practical merit as a universal ground of liability. How, exactly, can reliance be ascertained? If A promises to give £100,000 to B hospital and two weeks later the hospital buys new equipment, has it relied on A's promise? What if the alleged reliance is *negative* in nature? Must reliance involve B in economic loss? Because of such difficulties, the test of reliance has found no overall favour in English law but there are clearly elements of justifiable reliance which the courts recognise (see Estoppel, *infra*). English law thus has elements of form, reliance and exchange but it is the exchange model which has been adopted as the dominant test of enforceability and referred to as the doctrine of consideration. One notable exception to the doctrine of consideration is that an agreement under seal need not be supported by consideration.

The exchange or bargain envisaged by the doctrine of consideration would classify the hospital example above as an unenforceable gift unless it were by deed. The reciprocity demanded by consideration thus characterises it as a commercial notion and with its paradigm of profit-making contracts in a free-market economy, it became a corner-stone of *laissez-faire* ideals. Consideration is said to be *executory* when it is present in an exchange of promises and *executed* when it is a promise in return for an act. The essence of a bargain struck between the parties is maintained in two distinct rules. First, consideration must move from the promisee, meaning that a party must provide consideration if he is to sue on a promise (see *Tweddle* v *Atkinson* (1861) 1 B & S 393), although the Law Commission in its 1996 Report on Privity of Contract (Law Com. No. 242, 1996, Cm 3329) interpreted the decision in *Tweddle* as simply demonstrating that consideration must be provided by the main contracting parties in order to support the exchange of promises, in which case the third party was not also required to furnish additional consideration (see now Contracts (Rights of Third Parties) Act 1999). Secondly, consideration cannot be past, meaning those situations where a promise follows a completed act, as it would be regarded as independent and therefore gratuitous and unenforceable, e.g. without any request, B rescues A from a car accident and A later promises to reward B (see *Eastwood* v *Kenyon* (1840) 11 A & E 438; *Roscorla* v *Thomas* (1842) 3 QB 234; *Re McArdle* [1951] Ch 669). It is often said that an exception to this rule occurs where A, without a prior, *express* promise to pay, requests that B perform services for him and subsequently promises to reward B (see *Lampleigh* v *Brathwait* (1615) Hob 105). The better view is, however, that the subsequent promise merely *quantifies* the amount owing to B, as payment is implicit in A's original request (see *Re Casey's Patents* [1892] 1 Ch 104). Certainly if the rule were otherwise many business arrangements would be unenforceable when an account is sent only on completion of services rendered.

Freedom of contract demands that the parties make their own bargain and fix the economic values of their exchange, the parties thereby running the risk of concomitant loss or gain. It follows that the law does not seek to value that exchange or ensure that it is fair provided that there is something promised or exchanged which amounts to consideration. Most confusingly, this is expressed in the rule that consideration need not be *adequate*. That is, the exchange can be unequal in value, but must be *sufficient* i.e., an insufficient consideration is *not* deemed to be a valid consideration.

Adequacy of Consideration

The rule that the parties fix their own bargain which the courts then enforce finds its clearest illustration in those bargains where the consideration is a mere token but is nevertheless regarded as adequate (see *Bainbridge* v *Firmstone* (1838) 8 A & E 743; *Haigh* v *Brooks* (1839) 10 A & E 309; *Thomas* v *Thomas* (1842) 2 QB 851; *De La Bere* v *Pearson* [1908] 1 KB 280; *Chappell & Co. Ltd* v *Nestlé Co. Ltd* [1960] AC 87; *Midland Bank & Trust Co. Ltd* v *Green* [1981] AC 513). This rule allows gratuitous promises to become binding by the addition of a nominal consideration (a 'peppercorn bargain') but whilst this amounts to a tangible consideration, it is arguable that it is really evidence of serious intent.

Sufficiency of Consideration

Under this heading are those cases where B does or promises to do something which he is already legally obliged to do, e.g. B owes A £1,000 and promises to pay him £750 in final settlement of the debt. Could £750 be consideration for A's promise to accept it? The orthodox view is that as B is under an existing obligation to perform the completed act (i.e. pay £1,000) payment of £750 cannot be either a *legal* detriment to him or a legal benefit to A. On the other hand, there may clearly be a *factual* benefit and detriment — B's payment of £750 may be more onerous to him than the risk of being sued by A and the partial settlement may be more beneficial to A than either waiting indefinitely or running the risk of suing for the £1,000. Accordingly, Lord Denning advocated that a promise to perform or actual performance of an existing duty should amount to good consideration provided that there is nothing in the transaction contrary to the public interest (see *Ward* v *Byham* [1956] 1 WLR 496; *Williams* v *Williams* [1957] 1 WLR 148). In the absence of effective rules concerning duress, the function served by consideration in this area was to protect A against the duress of B by invalidating *all* performances of existing contractual obligations as insufficient consideration, but an important recent decision establishes that such an agreement will be enforceable *provided* that there is no duress and the arrangement results in a factual benefit (or obviates a disbenefit) for A (see *Williams* v *Roffey Bros & Nicholls (Contractors) Ltd* [1991] 1 QB 1). The decision may lead to a radical change in this area of the law of contract. *Williams* was, however, distinguished in *Re Selectmove Ltd* [1995] 1 WLR 474. At present, *unless* B does something beyond his existing duty or obligation owed to A, his promise to perform or actual performance of his existing obligations is insufficient consideration in the following situations:

(a) Performance of a public duty: see *Collins* v *Godefroy* (1831) 1 B & Ad 950; *England* v *Davidson* (1840) 11 A & E 856). For cases where B's performance has entailed something extra, see *Glasbrook Brothers Ltd* v *Glamorgan County Council* [1925] AC 270; *Ward* v *Byham* [1956] 1 WLR 496; *Harris* v *Sheffield United FC Ltd* [1988] QB 77.

(b) Performance of a contractual duty: see *Stilk* v *Myrick* (1809) 2 Camp 317. For an additional performance by B see *Hartley* v *Ponsonby* (1857) 7 E & B 872, and now see *Williams* v *Roffey* [1991] 1 QB 1.

(c) Part payment of debts: see *Pinnel's Case* (1602) 5 Co Rep 117a; *Foakes* v *Beer* (1884) 9 App Cas 605; *D & C Builders Ltd* v *Rees* [1966] 2 QB 617. *Pinnel's* rule was recently reaffirmed in *Re Selectmove Ltd* which did not extend the *Williams* v *Roffey* reasoning to cases of part-payment of debts. Numerous exceptions have been established to this rule which has often been criticised as arbitrary and divorced from commercial reality (see *Couldery* v *Bartrum* (1881) 19 Ch D 394).

Thus the following variations regarding the debt, or disputes regarding the bare obligation of B, will be sufficient consideration for A's promise: (a) A's claim is disputed in good faith (see *Re Warren* (1884) 53 LJ Ch 1016) or is unliquidated (see *Ibberson* v *Neck* (1886) 2 TLR 427); (b) at A's request, payment of less at an earlier date (see *Pinnel's Case, supra*) or place (see *Vanbergen* v *St. Edmund's Properties Ltd* [1933] 2 KB 233); (c) at A's request, payment of less plus the delivery of a chattel or a chattel alone (see *Pinnel's Case*); and, (d) payment of less by a third party (see *Welby* v *Drake* (1825) 1 C & P 557 — debtor's father paid half in full satisfaction of claim) and composition agreements with creditors, i.e., all creditors agree to accept less (see *Good* v *Cheesman* (1831) 2 B & Ad 328).

One situation within the sufficiency rules is anomalous: a promise to perform or actual performance of a contractual duty owed to a third party, i.e., A and B are contractually bound and C promises A an extra amount if A will simply perform his contract with B. In the two-party scenario of *Stilk* v *Myrick* this is not good consideration but it is arguable that consideration is present here in that by accepting C's promise A gives up any right to vary his contract with B. However, it is now beyond doubt that there is good consideration in the three-party scenario and A may successfully sue C on his promise (see *Shadwell* v *Shadwell* (1860) 9 CB (NS) 159; *Scotson* v *Pegg* (1861) 6 H & N 295; *New Zealand Shipping Co. Ltd* v *AM Satterthwaite & Co. Ltd (The Eurymedon)* [1975] AC 154; *Pao On* v *Lau Yiu Long* [1980] AC 614 — it is arguable that these decisions are logical and that now *Williams* v *Roffey* accords with them).

Promissory Estoppel

Estoppel introduces the notion of reliance to the rules of consideration but only in a limited sense. The principle of estoppel is that, if one party has induced another to act in a certain way, he may subsequently be prevented from denying that fact and is thus said to be estopped. A variation of a contract normally requires consideration, but in those situations where a variation benefits one party only, equity's perspective focuses upon the conduct of the party granting the forbearance and its effect on the other party. It may therefore be inequitable for A to revoke a serious promise made to B, particularly where B has acted upon it to his detriment (see *Hughes* v *Metropolitan Ry* (1877) 2 App Cas 439; *Central London Property Trust Ltd* v *High Trees House Ltd* [1947] KB 130).

In identifying promissory estoppel within an exam question, the following questions will need to be answered in the affirmative:

(a) Do the parties have an existing contractual relationship or, possibly, any relationship which gives rise to rights and duties (see *Durham Fancy Goods Ltd* v *Michael Jackson (Fancy Goods) Ltd* [1968] 2 QB 839)?

(b) Has there been a clear and unequivocal promise by words or conduct that existing rights will not be enforced (see *Scandinavian Trading Tanker Co. AB* v *Flora Petrolera Ecuatoriana (The Scaptrade)* [1983] QB 529)?

(c) Is it inequitable for the promisor to revoke his promise (see *D & C Builders Ltd* v *Rees* [1966] 2 QB 617; *Société Italo-Belge pour le Commerce et l'Industrie* v *Palm & Vegetable Oils (Malaysia) Sdn Bhd (The Post Chaser)* [1981] 2 Lloyd's Rep 695; *Re Selectmove Ltd* [1995] 1 WLR 474)?

(d) Has the promisee relied upon the promise? Although some earlier cases considered *detriment* of the promisee incurred by his reliance to be important (see *Ajayi* v *RT Briscoe (Nigeria) Ltd* [1964] 1 WLR 1326) it now appears that reliance and inequity are dominant (see *Alan (WJ) & Co. Ltd* v *El Nasr Export & Import Co.* [1972] 2 QB 189; *The Post Chaser*).

(e) Is the promisee using the doctrine as a shield rather than a sword? Promissory estoppel is defensive in nature in that the promisee's reliance on a gratuitous prom-ise excuses his non-performance of an existing obligation rather than creating new causes of action (see *Combe* v *Combe* [1951] 2 KB 215). If the rule were otherwise the requirement of consideration would be abolished (see *Brikom Investments Ltd* v *Carr* [1979] QB 467).

If an estoppel has been established what are its effects? Normally it will suspend rights which can be revived by giving reasonable notice (see *Tool Metal Manufacturing Co. Ltd* v *Tungsten Electric Co. Ltd* [1955] 1 WLR 761) but it can extinguish rights if it is impossible for the promisee to resume his position (see *Birmingham & District Land Co.* v *L & NW Ry* (1888) 40 Ch D 268) or if it is *very* inequitable to insist that he should so resume it (see *Nippon Yusen Kaisha* v *Pacifica Navegacion SA (The Ion)* [1980] 2 Lloyd's Rep 245).

A diagram may be helpful to demonstrate the potential enforceability of promises to modify existing contracts (see p. 34).

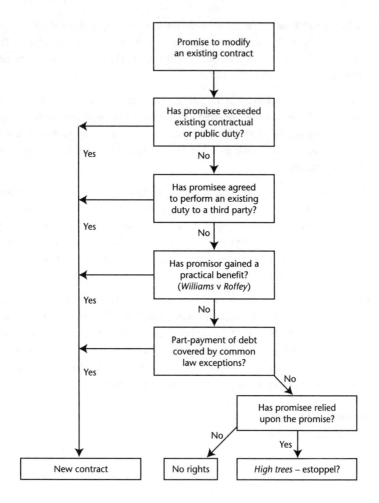

Q Question 1

Fiste is the leader of a newly-formed political party called 'Stronghold'. He organises an open-air rally in Hyde Park to publicise the party.

Perkup contracts with Fiste to provide catering facilities at the rally at a cost of £4,000.

Wilful agrees to fly an aircraft over the rally trailing a banner showing the party's emblem of the 'all-seeing eye'. Wilful declines payment for these services saying that his commitment to the party will be reward enough.

Grippe, a prominent supporter of the party, writes to Fiste saying that he 'hopes the rally will be the first step towards putting some backbone into the country' and that, accordingly, he will provide £10,000 'to help with expenses'.

Fiste is determined that the rally should be successful and, at the last minute, he agrees to pay Perkup 'a bonus of £1,000 to ensure that things run smoothly'. Similarly, fearing trouble from the 'Urban Vigilante Party', Fiste asks for an increased police presence for which service he agrees to pay £2,500.

The rally is a success but Fiste refuses to pay the £1,000 bonus to Perkup and the £2,500 to the police. Wilful finds that his costs were more than anticipated and Fiste promises to 'reimburse him fully in due course'. Grippe informs Fiste that he cannot pay the £10,000 as his business is not prospering. Consequently, Fiste refuses to reimburse Wilful.

Discuss the legal position of all the parties involved.

Commentary

This is a wide-ranging analytical problem concerning consideration. The problems posed are precise and the better student should be able to construct a concomitantly precise answer. As there is little overlap between the characters in the problem and most of the issues are not interlocked, an answer might profitably separate the various scenarios for individual attention.

- Is Perkup performing only his existing contractual duty in promising to ensure smooth performance of the contract and does he, therefore, furnish no consideration for Fiste's promise to pay him a bonus of £1,000?

- Do the police provide consideration for the promised payment of £2,500 from Fiste or, in supervising the rally, do they perform only their existing public duty?

- Is Fiste's promise to reimburse Wilful's costs an example of past consideration because the promise is made after Wilful has performed his services or, alternatively, are the conditions of *Lampleigh* v *Brathwait* and *Re Casey's Patents* satisfied, meaning that Wilful will be successful in his claim?

- Does the arrangement between Grippe and Fiste amount to nothing more than a vague, gratuitous promise from Grippe with no consideration being furnished by Fiste? Does the undertaking possess sufficient certainty of terms and intent to create legal relations?

۬ Ϙ֟ Suggested answer

This question concerns sufficiency of consideration, past consideration and gratuitous promises. It is proposed to divide the question into its composite parts.

Fiste (F) v Perkup (P)

This agreement involves an analysis of sufficiency of consideration. F and P clearly have an initial contract with consideration and intent but the issue is whether P can claim the 'bonus' of £1,000 from F. The general rule of consideration is that the courts will not investigate the adequacy of consideration and the relative values exchanged provided that there is *some* consideration supporting the bargain, that is 'something of value in the eye of the law'. It is arguable, therefore, that if a party does, or promises to do something which he is already bound to do, he provides no consideration for a promise made to him. As he is already bound to perform the act in question, he suffers no legal detriment nor does he confer a legal benefit on the other party who is entitled to performance. In *Stilk* v *Myrick* (1809) 2 Camp 317, several sailors deserted during a voyage, the captain promising to share their wages amongst the remaining crew if they would get the ship home safely. It was held that the claim brought by one of the sailors for the extra amount must fail as no consideration had been provided in performing the existing contractual duty to work the ship home. An alternative ground for the decision is that it provides a deterrent to extortion and duress: if the sailor's claim had been successful such illegitimate pressure might be encouraged. In fact, this *is* the stated decision in the alternative report of *Stilk* by Espinasse (see (1809) 6 Esp 129). If the promisee does, or promises to do, *more* than his basic contractual duty he is said to provide consideration. Thus, in *Hartley* v *Ponsonby* (1857) 7 E & B 872 the crew became so depleted by desertion (36 reduced to 19) that it became dangerous to continue the voyage thereby freeing the sailors and enabling them to enter into a new contract with increased remuneration. On this basis, it is arguable that P does no more than his contractual duty as he should ensure that 'things run smoothly' and cannot therefore claim the extra £1,000.

Nevertheless, if there is no duress and both parties obtain what they desire from the bargain why should it be unenforceable? It is not difficult to envisage that the promisee may incur a *factual* detriment and the promisor a factual benefit meaning that enforcement of the bargain would sensibly acknowledge commercial reality. This has always been the view of Lord Denning in the analogous cases of performance of an existing *public duty* (see *Ward* v *Byham* [1956] 1 WLR 496; *Williams* v *Williams* [1957] 1 WLR 148). Moreover, performance of an existing contractual duty owed to a third party is sufficient consideration to support an independent contract (see *New Zealand Shipping Co. Ltd* v *AM Satterthwaite & Co. Ltd (The Eurymedon)* [1975] AC 154; *Pao On* v *Lau Yiu Long* [1980] AC 614). If, therefore, a third party had offered P the bonus of £1,000 for performing his contract with F, the bonus could be successfully claimed. In this light, it is extremely difficult to justify the two party rule of *Stilk*. A recent decision, *Williams* v *Roffey Bros & Nicholls (Contractors) Ltd* [1991] 1 QB 1, alters the law in this area. The defendants were building contractors who had a contract to refurbish a block of flats, the carpentry being sub-contracted to the plaintiff who was in financial difficulties and falling behind with the work. Delays might have resulted in the defendants paying liquidated damages under the refurbishment contract and, accordingly, they offered the plaintiff an extra amount to complete the work on time. The Court of Appeal held that the plaintiff should succeed, emphasising that the defendants obtained a factual, real benefit and there was no duress tainting the bargain. In the problem, it seems that *Williams* v *Roffey* should apply to P and F thereby enabling P to claim his £1,000 bonus.

Fiste v Police

This problem also concerns sufficiency of consideration but here it is performance of a *public duty* which is at issue. The rule is the same as performance of a contractual duty and the promisee's bare performance of a public duty is insufficient consideration to support a promise to pay for its execution. In *Collins* v *Godefroy* (1831) 1 B & Ad 950, the plaintiff was subpoenaed to give evidence on the defendant's behalf and alleged a promise of the defendant to pay him six guineas for his trouble. The court held that as the plaintiff was under a public duty imposed by law to attend, he gave no consideration to the defendant. Just as the rationale of *Stilk* is explainable as the need to deter duress, public policy underlies this area: to allow a public official to be paid extra by members of the public for doing his job encourages both extortion and bribery and corruption. On the other hand, the act in question might not be contrary to public policy. In *England* v *Davidson* (1840) 11 A & E 856, a policeman successfully claimed a private reward for giving information which could lead to a criminal's arrest and conviction. The court held that the officer had done more than his public duty and that his acts were not contrary to public policy. In 1840, with an embryonic police force, such offers of reward encouraged people to seek out information and thus promote the *desirable* end of law enforcement. Accordingly, subject to the question of public policy, a person who performs more than his public duty may recover the promised payment. In *Ward* v *Byham* [1956] 1 WLR 496, a mother whose statutory duty was to support her child did more by keeping the child 'well and happy' and thus could claim the promised £1 per week from its father. Similarly, in *Glasbrook Brothers Ltd* v *Glamorgan County Council* [1925] AC 270, the police provided extra protection for a coal mine during a strike and could claim the payment under the contract and in *Harris* v *Sheffield United FC Ltd* [1988] QB 77, a claim for payment was upheld for policing a football match. The position is now governed by statute, s. 15(1) of the Police Act 1964 allowing payment for 'special police services' rendered at the 'request' of the other party. It appears beyond doubt that F must pay the £2,500 to the police.

Fiste v Wilful (W)

This problem concerns past consideration. The doctrine of consideration demands that a bargain be struck between the parties and, therefore, a single transaction with contemporaneous consideration is required. If the act constituting the consideration has been performed before any promise to pay for it is given, the consideration is said to be 'past' and unenforceable. Consequently, in *Roscorla* v *Thomas* (1842) 3 QB 234, a promise that a horse was sound given *after* the horse had been sold was held to be past consideration. Similarly, in *Eastwood* v *Kenyon* (1840) 11 A & E 438, a promise to repay the guardian of a girl who had earlier paid for her maintenance was held to be unenforceable. However, an act performed before the promise was made can be good consideration if the conditions specified in *Lampleigh* v *Brathwait* (1615) Hob 105 and *Re Casey's Patents* [1892] 1 Ch 104 are satisfied. First, the promisor must request the act. Secondly, it must be assumed and understood that it would be remunerated and, finally, the payment must have been legally enforceable had it been promised in advance. If these three conditions are established, the subsequent promise is regarded as *fixing expressly* the amount to be paid, the fact of payment being implicit in the original request. In the problem, much would depend upon whether F 'requested' W's flight and whether it was understood that payment would be forthcoming. This latter condition would seem impossible to satisfy however, as W has said that he does not want payment and this is not a business arrangement as in *Re Casey's Patents* and *Pao On* v *Lau Yiu Long* [1980] AC 614. It would seem that W has no valid claim against F.

Fiste v Grippe (G)

G's promise to pay £10,000 appears to be gratuitous in that F offers nothing in return and any reliance F may have made on the faith of the promise is, without more, insufficient to found a contract in English law. On the facts, this could not be construed as a promise to pay £10,000 in return for the organisation of a political rally, particularly as F does not even reply to G. Moreover, G's 'promise' is very vague and might not possess the requisite certainty and intent to be binding (see *Kleinwort Benson Ltd* v *Malaysia Mining Corporation Bhd* [1989] 1 WLR 379) thereby emphasising one merit of consideration, certainty and intent in that these notions guard against the enforcement of rash promises. Reliance theories would lead to the same conclusion: F could show neither the fact nor extent of his reliance upon G's promise. Similarly, the principles of promissory estoppel cannot help F as that doctrine cannot be used as a ground of action (*Combe* v *Combe* [1951] 2 KB 215). F appears unable to claim the £10,000 from G and it is suggested that this is a perfectly reasonable outcome.

Q Question 2

Cheatham & Steele wish to expand the productivity and efficiency of their manufacturing processes. They borrow £100,000 from Grabbit and Runne, merchant bankers. The agreed period of the loan is five years, £20,000 to be repaid each year together with interest at 40% on the capital outstanding.

After repayment of £20,000 with interest, Cheatham & Steele suffer a lengthy industrial dispute which makes it impossible for them to pay the next £20,000 due. The difficulties of Cheatham & Steele are so acute that there is a possibility that the company may become insolvent. Cheatham & Steele draw the attention of

Grabbit & Runne to this and the consequential risk to their unsecured loan. With this in mind, Grabbit & Runne agree to the postponement for a year of payment of the £20,000 due and the waiver of all interest payable.

However, four months later, Grabbit & Runne also experience severe financial problems and request Cheatham & Steele to pay the outstanding instalment and interest owing without further delay. Cheatham & Steele refuse to do this and suggest that only £10,000 of the loan could be paid but that this would cause them severe hardship in the circumstances.

Advise Grabbit & Runne.

Commentary

This problem relates to promissory or equitable estoppel. Students commonly find estoppel perplexing. This may be because having just mastered an arcane but somewhat mechanistic world of offer and acceptance, they have to contend with metaphysical notions of reliance and inequity. In fact, estoppel is the simplest of notions in the abstract but more difficult to apply in reality. When has B relied on A's promise? Why is it inequitable for A to revoke his promise? It is this balance of interests which students must make in order to understand estoppel and answer a question on this topic satisfactorily. A mechanical reiteration of the requirements of estoppel with little or no application to the problem will result in a poor mark.

Throughout the law, there is no substitute for reading the primary materials but this is particularly true here. Many of the leading decisions contain judgments by Lord Denning which should be read for their chronological symmetry and clarity of exposition.

- Cheatham & Steele (C&S) provide no consideration for the variation of the contract of loan which is agreed with the lenders, Grabbit & Runne (G&R). May G&R therefore demand the repayment of the loan in accordance with the contract terms or, alternatively, might they be estopped from doing so?

- What is meant by the principle of promissory estoppel and what are the requirements of this doctrine?

- Have C&S relied on the promise of G&R regarding the variation of the contract's terms?

- Is it inequitable for G&R to revoke that promise?

- Is the effect of the estoppel to suspend the rights under the original contract which can thus be revived if G&R give reasonable notice to C&S or, alternatively, might those rights be extinguished?

☼ Suggested answer

Cheatham & Steele (C&S) clearly have a contract with Grabbit & Runne (G&R) which is varied so as to confer a benefit on C&S only. Thus C&S provide no consideration to G&R for the postponement of the loan instalment and, although there might be some factual benefit to G&R in that their unsecured loan is still subsisting, there is no legal benefit as they have a pre-existing contractual right to full and prompt payment. With payment of debts the rule is unequivocal that a creditor is not bound by a promise to accept a partial payment in full settlement and may claim the remainder from his debtor (see *Pinnel's Case* (1602) 5 Co Rep 117a; *Foakes* v *Beer* (1884) 9 App Cas 605). The rule has been much criticised as being divorced from commercial reality (see *Couldery* v *Bartrum* (1881) 19 Ch D 394) but, although numerous exceptions surround it, its core remains intact and was recently reaffirmed in *Re Selectmove Ltd* [1995] 1 WLR 474. The reason for preserving *Pinnel's Case* is frequently said to be that it protects a creditor from the economic duress of his debtor (e.g. *D & C Builders Ltd* v *Rees* [1966] 2 QB 617) but the relatively recent development of independent principles of economic duress render this justification redundant. Often a partial settlement of a debt or a suspension of instalments due is a commercially sensible arrangement which should be enforceable in the absence of duress. However, the unbending rigour of *Pinnel's Case* is mitigated by principles of promissory estoppel.

The basic notion of estoppel, which permeates many areas of the law, is that A makes certain representations or promises to B upon which B relies or acts in some way. Should A wish to change his mind and deny any efficacy to the representations, he may be prevented or estopped from doing so. In *Central London Property Trust Ltd* v *High Trees House Ltd* [1947] KB 130, Denning J introduced the notion of promissory estoppel to the law of contract by way of the equitable principles in *Hughes* v *Metropolitan Ry* (1877) 2 App Cas 439. In *High Trees*, the plaintiffs leased a block of flats to the defendants in 1937 at a ground rent of £2,500 per annum but in 1940 agreed to reduce this rent by half because few of the flats were let in the wartime conditions. At the start of 1945 most of the flats were let again but the defendants were still paying the reduced rent. Accordingly, the plaintiffs demanded the full rent, testing their claim by suing for the last two quarters of 1945. It was held that the claim should succeed as the agreement of 1940 was only intended as a temporary arrangement for wartime conditions and it had ceased to operate early in 1945. Most importantly, Denning J also said that, although the defendants had provided no consideration for the plaintiffs' promise to reduce the rent, the plaintiffs could not have recovered the full rent for the period covered by the 1940 agreement. The plaintiffs would thus be estopped from denying the force of the 1940 agreement where the promise was 'intended to be binding, intended to be acted on and in fact acted on' (*per* Denning J).

From such fragile beginnings promissory estoppel has flourished and the requirements for its operation are now firmly established. First, the parties must have a legal relationship which gives rise to rights and duties between them. C&S and G&R have a contractual relationship which is the paradigm of this requirement. Secondly, there must be a promise or representation that the promisor will not insist on his strict legal rights. This promise must be clear and unequivocal but it can be implied or made by conduct (e.g. *Hughes* v *Metropolitan Ry*) and need not be express. In the problem, this requirement is satisfied in an unambiguous, express promise. Thirdly, unlike proprietary estoppel, the *High Trees* principle does not ground a cause of action but is defensive in nature only. In *Combe* v *Combe* [1951] 2 KB 215, it was established that promissory estoppel may be used 'as a shield but not a sword' (*per* Birkett LJ) but in the problem C&S are only defending themselves and may thus plead the equitable principle. Fourthly, as this is an equitable notion the pivotal and inter-connected requirements are that the promisee must have relied or acted upon the representation in some way and that it must be inequitable for the promisor to revoke his promise. In the common law doctrine of estoppel by representation, the promisee must show a *detrimental* reliance on the promise by, for example, incurring expenditure on the faith of the promisor's representation i.e. he must be worse off, this factor thereby grounding the estoppel. Whilst detriment has been an ingredient in many of the cases on promissory estoppel and should strengthen the promisee's claim, there has always been a difference of opinion as to whether it is a *necessary* ingredient. It would appear that there was no detriment in *High Trees*: the promisee was not worse off as a result of the promise and it is arguable that an emphasis on detriment is over-restrictive in seemingly moving estoppel closer to orthodox theories of consideration. Lord Denning consistently argued both judicially (see *WJ Alan & Co. Ltd* v *El Nasr Export & Import Co.* [1972] 2 QB 189; *Brikom Investments Ltd* v *Carr* [1979] QB 467) and extra-judicially (see (1952) 15 MLR 1) that repudiation of the promise is, in itself, inequitable. More recently, in *The Post Chaser*, The [1981] 2 Lloyd's Rep 595, Robert Goff J emphasised that the fundamental principle was established by Lord Cairns LC in *Hughes* v *Metropolitan Ry* that a promisor will not be allowed to enforce his rights 'where it would be inequitable having regard to the dealings which have thus taken place between the parties' and that a promisee could *benefit* from the promise and it might still be inequitable to revoke. In the problem, C&S clearly benefit immediately from the postponed payment but suffer hardship when it is revoked, meaning that such revocation might be inequitable. Detrimental reliance may therefore be relevant in deciding upon the inequity of the revocation and this is the emphasis which must be placed upon it instead of insisting that it be present as a separate requirement. In *The Post Chaser* it was not inequitable to revoke the promise two days after it had been made because, as a question of fact, the promisee had not suffered prejudicially in so short a period of time.

G&R can point to their own dire financial position as a valid reason to retract the promise and the court thus has to balance G&R's alleged ability to withdraw against C&S's plea of estoppel. Should the promisee exact the promise by duress it would not be inequitable for the promisor to resile. The promisee's conduct must therefore be blameless if he is to be afforded equitable protection for 'he who comes to equity must come with clean hands'. In *D & C Builders Ltd* v *Rees* [1966] 2 QB 617, the plaintiffs agreed to accept £300 from the defendant in settlement of £482 principally because of their desperate financial position, there being evidence that the defendant knew of this and took advantage of it in securing the plaintiffs' promise. Accordingly, it was not inequitable for the plaintiffs to withdraw the promise. There is no clear evidence of duress in the problem but C&S do 'draw the attention of G&R' to their financial position and the possible risk to G&R's loan. However, there is insufficient information in the problem to resolve this issue.

The final question raised by the problem is the effect of the *High Trees* doctrine on the obligations owed by the parties. It is usually said that promissory estoppel suspends rights rather than extinguishing them and that, accordingly, the promisor may revive his normal rights provided that he gives reasonable notice to the promisee of his intention to do so — as in *Tool Metal Manufacturing Co. Ltd* v *Tungsten Electric Co. Ltd* [1955] 1 WLR 761. The suspensive nature of the doctrine can be seen in the *High Trees* case itself but it may have an extinctive effect if it is impossible for the promisee to return to the previous position and perform the original obligation, as in *Birmingham & District Land Co.* v *L & NW Ry* (1888) 40 Ch D 268. It is arguable that impossibility can never apply to debts as they involve simply a payment of money. However, there is authority that the doctrine may be extinctive even though such performance is not impossible if it is, nevertheless, very inequitable to revoke. In *Olgivie* v *Hope-Davies* [1976] 1 All ER 683, a vendor of land indicated on 15 August that he would not insist on the completion date of 30 August and it was held that the original date could not be reinstated 'because the time was far too short'. The question of notice is thus entwined with the estoppel's effect but even if it is suspensive it is not entirely clear what this effect might be in a continuing obligation such as a payment of rent or a debt in instalments. If there is an agreed reduction in the debt coupled with a postponement can the promisor claim, on the expiry of the notice, the full amount for the future only or is he entitled to future payments and the balance of those which fell due during the period of postponement? Much depends on the intentions of the parties and it would appear that in the problem there is only an agreed postponement of time with an intended revival of full rights on its expiry but it is arguable that the right to interest on one year's payment might be extinguished.

In conclusion, the court must balance the equities of the parties, i.e., deferment of payment against insistence on an immediate reinstatement of existing contractual rights. It is suggested that this balance can be achieved by requiring the promisor to give reasonable notice before his rights can revive. This conclusion would also reconcile the rule in *Foakes* v *Beer* with the doctrine of estoppel in that the creditor's rights are not extinguished but merely suspended.

Q Question 3

Consideration is often a mere fiction devised to make a promise enforceable and, as such, serves little purpose. It would be advantageous to abolish consideration and leave the more satisfactory requirement of intention to create legal relations as the test of an agreement's enforceability.

Discuss.

Commentary

In order to answer such an essay question well, it is imperative that students *think* about the quotation and *discuss* it. This appears to state the obvious but all too often students take such a question as a *carte blanche* to reiterate all they know about consideration. Examiners are very familiar with a regurgitation of case law followed by the trite conclusion 'thus it can be seen that it would/would not be advantageous to abolish consideration'. The 'would/would not' are often used interchangeably with no difference in the essay's content. Moreover, students proliferate examination myths (e.g. the essay title must be agreed/disagreed with) when, in fact, the examiner looks for an answer which shows that its author can *think*, *criticise* and reach *sensible conclusions*.

- What rules *could* a legal system adopt as tests for the enforceability of agreements?

- What is meant by the doctrine of consideration in English law and what is the test of enforceability demanded by this doctrine?

- Are there any illogicalities in the principles of consideration and any rules which should be amended or abrogated?

- Would it be more logical to substitute intention to create legal relations as the sole test for an agreement's enforceability?

- What difficulties might be encountered if intent was the sole test of enforceability?

- Are there signs that the common law is beginning to place greater emphasis on intent in contract formation?

☼ Suggested answer

Offer, acceptance and certainty are the requirements which prescribe the skeletal structure of a contract's formation while consideration and intent relate to its body and substance. Any legal system may adopt one of a variety of options as a requirement for the enforceability of contracts. First, in order to be enforceable, all contracts might require a degree of form such as writing or a deed. Such a rule undeniably provides the requisite degree of certainty, deters fraud and embodies as a necessity that the parties intend legal relations but it would be virtually impossible to insist upon form for *all* contracts in the twenty-first century. Form is demanded in exceptional cases, most importantly that contracts for the sale of land must be in writing and strict formalities are demanded in some situations where one party might seek to abuse the other's inexperience and lack of bargaining power, e.g. hire-purchase and consumer credit. At the other extreme, it is theoretically possible to make *all* agreements enforceable but this notion is as untenable and impractical as the opposite rule which might stipulate a form for all contracts. Other options might look to the seriousness of intent alone or evidence of reliance on the promise or a combination of both. If A makes a serious promise to B upon which it can reasonably be assumed that B will rely, possibly to his detriment, there are clearly good grounds both morally and legally to enforce A's promise. In principle, many European countries adopt the stance that all lawful and serious agreements are contracts. On the other hand, English law uses consideration as its test for a contract's enforcement and, in so doing, is said to look for a bargain or exchange between the parties. The difference of approach between the English and European systems is traceable to historical development: the remedy of *assumpsit* in English law was based upon commercial needs and the element of bargain whereas continental law developed in the middle ages and was much influenced by canon law and notions of good faith. However, in addition to consideration English law demands intention to create legal relations as a separate requirement for a contract's enforcement (see *Balfour* v *Balfour* [1919] 2 KB 571). The role played by consideration must be ascertained therefore and it should be asked whether intention might perform it better.

The dominant theory of consideration, at least in the nineteenth and twentieth centuries, was that of a bargained-for exchange between the parties: A must show that he has bought B's promise. But the overall influence of *laissez-faire* and freedom of contract meant that, although some consideration was necessary (i.e. sufficiency of consideration), it need not be adequate. Bargains might thus be grossly unequal, this being a pre-requisite of the free-market economy where capitalism was to flourish. In *Thomas* v *Thomas* (1842) 2 QB 851 for example, rent of £1 per annum was regarded as adequate consideration and it was emphasised in *Chappell & Co. Ltd* v *Nestlé Co. Ltd* [1960] AC 87 that a contracting party may stipulate for whatever consideration he desires, even if it is valueless. It is evident that consideration does not ensure fairness of bargains and it is even questionable whether such nominal bargains should be classified as bargains in the true sense of the word. The doctrine of consideration thus distinguishes onerous from gratuitous promises by stipulating for a token exchange. Furthermore, Professor Atiyah has argued (*Essays on Contract, Consideration: A Restatement*) that consideration was originally the *reason* for the enforcement of a promise, i.e. those considerations which were relevant in assessing this issue. It is a small step to see the token element in bargains as merely evidence that both parties take the agreement seriously, in other words, as evidence of intention to create legal relations. One advantage in the token agreement is that it provides concrete evidence of intention and it was, therefore, particularly apt for administering the less sophisticated contracts of earlier centuries. Viewed thus, consideration is simply one test of enforceability and serves the same function as intent. But does it perform the function as efficiently as intent? What would happen to the established problems within consideration if intent were the sole yardstick for enforcement?

Many of the difficulties of consideration spring from the fact that is has been elevated as a 'doctrine' with concomitant mystification and rigidity. The underlying purposes behind many of the orthodox rules of consideration are clear and yet they have become obscured by language such as 'sufficiency' and 'adequacy' which admit the uninitiated into the twisting doctrinal corridors. In relation to adequacy of consideration, it is arguable that in supporting the notion of unequal consideration the law may cloak the duress in some so-called bargains. Adequacy of consideration assumes there is a valid consideration where A sells his Rolls Royce car to B for a token amount, but it is perhaps more reasonable to infer the opposite and consider that some duress or blackmail might lie at the root of such an arrangement. In sufficiency of consideration, the cases which establish that performance of an existing contractual duty are insufficient consideration (e.g. *Stilk* v *Myrick* (1809) 2 Camp 317; *Hartley* v *Ponsonby* (1857) 7 E & B 872) are really concerned with protecting the creditor from the economic duress of his debtor. The rule is carried to a logical conclusion in *Foakes* v *Beer* (1884) 9 App Cas 605, that part payment of a debt cannot amount to consideration which would discharge the debtor, thereby leaving the creditor free to claim the amount owing. Similarly, the cases on performance of a public duty such as *Collins* v *Godefroy* (1831) 1 B & Ad 950 seek to curb possible extortion and corruption in public life. Consideration thus achieves a purpose but at a cost. The price paid is that, at its worst, the rigidity of consideration means that the desirable contract worthy of enforcement cannot be distinguished from the undesirable and unworthy. Thus *all* part-payments of debts are invalidated, even those where a freely-negotiated, sensible business arrangement is sought by both parties. It is almost unbelievable that the serious discharge of a debt by simple payment of a lesser amount cannot be accommodated within consideration. The decision in *Re Selectmove Ltd* [1995] 1 WLR 474, indicates that the House of Lords' decision in *Foakes* v *Beer* must be reconsidered by the House itself or abrogated by legislation. At its best, consideration spawns innumerable technical exceptions to its rigid code, the rule that part-payment of money plus the addition of a chattel will discharge the debt, for example. If intention to create legal relations became the sole test, the courts would be free to examine and enforce legitimate bargains and invalidate those that are illegitimate as having been exacted through improper threats or pressure. It was clearly necessary to keep the rules of consideration in the absence of any coherent rules regarding economic duress but the necessity has disappeared with the common law's evolution of that doctrine and its awareness that duress must be distinguished from commercial hard-bargaining.

Concern is often expressed that gifts would become enforceable as serious promises if intention were the sole test of a contract's enforceability. This seems to be an illusory concern. Intent would simply become the test for the formation of *contracts* and the parties would still not intend that most social and domestic gifts should be contracts. However, the courts would have the ability to examine factors other than consideration in deciding whether promises should be enforceable. Much would depend on the nature of the promise and the promisee's response to it; the presence of writing or other formalities, for example, might be paramount. The promisee's direct reliance on the promise would also clearly assume significance in some situations.

Similarly, it is sometimes said that the rules of intention would have to be devised by the courts in order to cope with new problems but, again, this criticism is unfounded because intention is an existing and established requirement for the formation of a contract. Atiyah (above) argues that it is 'nonsensical' to talk of the abolition of consideration as the courts would 'have to begin all over again the task of deciding what promises are to be enforceable' but he concedes that there is 'something to be said' for beginning again whilst questioning whether intention would work any better as a formula. But why should intention not be elevated as the dominant requirement with the essence of consideration preserved but thus relegated and subservient to intent? The courts would not have to 'begin again' but would be required merely to adjust the concept of a bargain within the more logical rules of intention. It is arguable that such an approach would simply modernise consideration whilst preserving its vitality. If the parties genuinely intended a token bargain it would not cease to be enforceable, yet a freely-negotiated part-payment of a debt, for example, would become validated with the evidence of intention manifested in the mutual benefits received.

The recent decision in *Williams* v *Roffey Bros & Nicholls (Contractors) Ltd* [1991] 1 QB 1 seems to point the way ahead. The defendants were building contractors who had a contract to refurbish a block of flats, the carpentry being sub-contracted to the plaintiffs who were in financial difficulties and falling behind with the work. Delays might have resulted in the defendants paying liquidated damages under the refurbishment contract and, accordingly, they offered the plaintiffs an extra amount to complete the work on time. The Court of Appeal held that the plaintiffs should succeed, emphasising that, although the plaintiffs were only performing their existing contractual duty, the defendants obtained a factual, real benefit and there was no duress tainting the bargain. *Stilk* v *Myrick* was thus subjugated to the rules of intent and the freely-negotiated variation was enforced by the court but *Williams* preserves the essence of consideration in emphasising the question of benefit received. Perhaps the most significant fact is that the court could almost certainly have found consideration in the revised methods of payment which were introduced by the parties, as the plaintiffs were paid on the completion of each flat. The decision might thus have accorded with established doctrine but the Court of Appeal deliberately chose the more radical route of its actual decision.

Williams v *Roffey* has the potential to revolutionise the rules of consideration or, alternatively, remain limited to variations of existing contracts where a realistic benefit is obtained. Although the court in *Re Selectmove Ltd* was constrained by the House of Lords' decision in *Foakes* v *Beer*, Peter Gibson LJ saw 'the force of the argument' in extending *Williams* to part-payment of debts. Some critics have already argued that it is undesirable to substitute the vagaries of intent and duress for the certainty of consideration. This timid approach would presumably wish to see the opposite conclusion reached on the facts of *Williams* but it is artificial and outmoded to justify such an outcome in the context of the modern law. Similarly, it is difficult to see why there is such apprehension regarding intent in this context when, for example, criminal law is almost totally reliant on the concept. Furthermore, promissory estoppel functions well with the notions of intent, reliance and inequity. It is to be hoped that intent becomes the dominant principle in the formation of contract, with the essence of consideration preserved in a re-adjusted perspective of a freely-negotiated bargain.

Q Question 4

On 5 May, Sponge borrowed £20,000 from Maxwell and agreed to repay the loan plus interest of 12% on 1 August. Advise Maxwell of the legal position in the following separate situations:

(a) On 5 July, Maxwell accepted £17,500 from Sponge 'in full and final settlement' of the debt. On 1 August, Maxwell decided to claim the full amount of the debt from Sponge.

Would your advice differ if payment of £17,500 was made on 1 August?

(b) On 1 August, Maxwell accepted Sponge's collection of antique Derby porcelain in lieu of the debt. Maxwell considered that the porcelain was worth £25,000 but has now discovered its true value to be closer to £15,000. Accordingly, Maxwell has decided to commence proceedings for £5,000 plus interest on the debt.

Would your advice differ if Sponge knew that the porcelain was worth only £15,000 but did not disclose that fact to Maxwell?

(c) Sponge's father wrote to Maxwell enclosing a cheque for £18,000. Maxwell cashed the cheque but has decided to sue Sponge for the remainder of the debt.

Commentary

Students often make errors of technique in answering such a question which is split into separate parts. First, answers often give too much weight to one part at the expense of the others. If the question does not specify how marks are awarded, treat each part equally. Secondly, this does not mean that relevant material should be repeated *ad nauseam* in each part. It is both permissible and sensible to make cross-references in the answers and so part (a) may be longer than parts (b) and (c) as it will contain general information relevant to (b) and (c), the answers to these two parts consequently referring the examiner to material in part (a).

(a)
- Explain the rule in *Pinnel's Case* which establishes that the part-payment of a debt, without more, can never discharge the entire debt.

- Explain the rule that payment of a lesser sum, in *early* settlement of the debt, discharges the entire debt.

- Although there is no doubt regarding the efficacy of *Pinnel's Case*, can the reasoning underpinning the case be exposed as flawed and illogical?

(b)
- Explain the rule that an agreement to accept goods in full settlement of the debt amounts to an effective discharge of the entire debt.

- Explain the rule, inherent in the doctrine of consideration, that *either* party's knowledge regarding the value of the goods would not affect the validity of the settlement. Consequently, Sponge's failure to disclose the true value of the goods would, in the absence of any misrepresentation, fraud, duress or fiduciary relationship, be irrelevant.

(c)
- Explain the rule that part-payment of a debt by a third party amounts to a discharge of the entire debt. What justifications are advanced for this rule?

- Has Maxwell accepted unequivocally the part-payment in full and final settlement? What does acceptance entail in this context?

☀️ Suggested answer

(a) This problem concerns consideration and the question of whether a part-payment of a debt may discharge the whole of the debt. At common law, the position is that a creditor is not bound by either a promise to accept a smaller sum or its actual payment by the debtor. Such a promise or payment amounts to nothing more than a promise to perform or performance of *part* of an existing duty owed to the creditor, the debtor consequently providing no consideration. The position is thus very similar to *Stilk* v *Myrick* (1809) 2 Camp 317 except that in part payment of debts the debtor seeks the *discharge* of an existing obligation rather than extra payment for its *performance*. It follows that a debt may only be released by an agreement for valuable consideration or by an agreement under seal. The general rule that part-payment is no satisfaction was established in *Pinnel's Case* (1602) 5 Co Rep 117a and finally approved in *Foakes* v *Beer* (1884) 9 App Cas 605. Beer had obtained a judgment against Foakes for £2,090. 19s but a written agreement was made whereby Beer undertook not to take 'any proceedings whatsoever' on the judgment in consideration of an immediate payment of £500 with the remainder to be paid in specified instalments until the entire sum was satisfied. When the £2,090.19s had been paid, Beer claimed £360 interest on the judgment debt and the House of Lords held that she must succeed. Just as the captain of the ship was protected against duress in *Stilk*, *Pinnel's* rule protects the creditor from the duress of his debtor (see *D & C Builders Ltd* v *Rees* [1966] 2 QB 617). It is suggested that there is now little utility in the rule. First, it may well be that the duress is exercised by the creditor and, where the agreement is procured illegitimately, the developing law of duress is better able to cope with this problem than the rigid rule of consideration which invalidates *all* part payments. Secondly, it is evident that many partial settlements are reasonable and sought positively by the creditor. Lord Blackburn emphasised in *Foakes* that it is often more beneficial for the creditor to receive a part payment than to insist on his strict legal rights.

Although *Pinnel's Case* has been subjected to sustained criticism it has never been overruled and the decision was recently reaffirmed in *Re Selectmove Ltd* [1995] 1 WLR 474. It is, however, subject to numerous limitations which are testimony to its inutility. Relevant to this problem are those situations where there is some variation in the debtor's performance at the request of the creditor. In fact, it was established in *Pinnel's Case* that payment of a lesser sum at an earlier date is good consideration for there is clearly both a benefit to the creditor and detriment to the debtor in early settlement. It seems beyond doubt that the payment of £17,500 thus discharges Sponge. Moreover, it is possible that promissory estoppel might apply on these facts, although there is not enough detail given to decide the issue.

The advice would differ if payment of a lesser sum were made on 1 August, as here there would be no variation of the obligation which could amount to consideration and *Pinnel's Case* would be applicable, meaning that Maxwell could claim the remainder of the debt. It is clearly arguable that such an agreement to accept less without any variation should be a binding contract provided that it is made without duress. This was the point made by Lord Blackburn in *Foakes* and was at the heart of the criticisms of *Pinnel's Case* made by Sir George Jessel MR in *Couldery* v *Bartrum* (1881) 19 Ch D 394. It is impossible to justify the rule that a peppercorn may settle a debt of any amount when an agreement to accept 99p in the pound is insufficient consideration. Moreover, the decision in *Williams* v *Roffey* is that performance of an existing contractual duty may, without more, be sufficient consideration to support a promise to pay extra if the contract is duly performed by the promisee. There is a difference, however, between complete performance in *Williams* and partial perform-ance in the settlement of debts and it is clear from *Re Selectmove Ltd* that the *Williams* reasoning cannot be extended to part-payment of debts. In principle, the *Williams* variation is no different from the variation of paying a lesser sum and it is to be hoped that *Pinnel's Case* may soon be abrogated.

(b)   The variation in this problem involves a substitution of goods for money. If goods are requested by the creditor and accepted freely it is clear from *Pinnel's Case* itself that 'a horse, hawk or robe' is good consideration for a promise to forgo the balance of the debt on the basis that this may be 'more beneficial' than money. The notion of adequacy of consideration thus applies here and the courts do not seek to quantify the relative values of the bargained-for exchange. It seems clear therefore that Sponge and Maxwell have a binding contract and the debt is discharged. Again, these rules entail an inversion of logic. In the absence of duress, the creditor's agree-ment to accept a lesser sum must be subjectively beneficial and objectively valuable when compared with 'canary-birds or tomtits, or rubbish of that kind' (*Couldery* v *Bartrum, per* Sir George Jessel MR).

If Sponge knew the true value of the porcelain but did nothing more than not disclose that fact to Maxwell, the advice would not differ. Freedom of contract means that there is no duty of disclosure in this situation just as it could not be suggested that Maxwell should inform Sponge if he thought the porcelain was worth £25,000. This is the essence of a bargain where speculative profit and loss are inherent. Sponge does not actively mislead Maxwell, the parties are dealing at arm's length and are not, for example, in a fiduciary relationship where disclosure would be necessary. More-over, on the facts there could be no operative mistake and there is no duress.

(c)   This final situation involves a third party's intervention in the part-payment of a debt. In *Welby* v *Drake* (1825) 1 C & P 557, a creditor sued a son after having accepted half the amount of the debt from his father in full settlement. It was held that he must fail for 'by suing the son he commits a fraud on the father, whom he induced to advance money on the faith of such advance being a discharge of his son from further liability'. The same result was reached in *Hirachand Punamchand* v *Temple* [1911] 2 KB 330 but a variety of doubtful reasons was given for the decision. First, Fletcher Moulton and Vaughan Williams LJJ considered that the agreement to accept less meant that the debt became 'extinct'. Secondly, Fletcher Moulton and Farwell LJJ thought that there was an agreement between the father and the creditor, made with good consideration, to the effect that the latter would not sue the son. Fletcher Moulton LJ considered that the consideration could be 'in meal or in malt' and the amount given need bear no relation to the debt. It would thus be an abuse of the process of the court to allow the creditor to sue. Finally, following *Cook* v *Lister* (1863) 13 CB (NS) 543, Vaughan Williams LJ thought it would be 'a fraud upon the stranger who pays part of a debt' to allow an action for the debt. All these justifications are somewhat dubious, particularly the 'fraud' idea which is most often cited as the rationale of these decisions. The difficulty is that the creditor is barred from suing his debtor even though no consideration moved from the debtor and no promise was ever made to him, meaning that the debtor and creditor had no contract. Although the reasoning in the cases appears doubtful, it is arguable that Sponge will be discharged by the father's payment, provided that there is clear evidence that Maxwell has accepted the payment in full and final settlement. On the facts, is the cashing of the cheque a sufficient act of acceptance? Perhaps Maxwell feared the possibility that Sponge's father might countermand payment and therefore acted quickly by cashing the cheque. Is this an act of unequivocal acceptance? The recent decision in *Ferguson* v *Davies* [1997] 1 All ER 315 suggests that more evidence is required before the simple act of cashing can be deemed an acceptance of the part-payment.

Minors' Contracts

Introduction

In the law of contract, a minor or infant is a person under 18 years of age, the age of majority having been reduced from 21 by the Family Law Reform Act 1969. The general rule is that a minor's contracts are voidable at his option but are binding on the other party. Voidable contracts are sub-divided into two categories. First, those contracts which bind the minor unless repudiated during minority or within a reasonable time of attaining majority. Secondly, contracts which are *not* binding upon the minor unless he ratifies them after attaining majority but which do bind the other party. The contracts within this second category are, perhaps, better described as unenforceable contracts. The only contracts which are fully binding on minors are contracts for necessaries which include contracts of apprenticeship and education. The Infants Relief Act 1874 complicated the law but that Act only remains applicable for contracts made before June 1987. The Minors' Contracts Act 1987 applies to contracts entered into after that date.

Binding Contracts: Necessaries

Section 3 of the Sale of Goods Act 1979 provides that 'where necessaries are sold and delivered to a minor . . . he must pay a reasonable price for them'. Section 3(3) defines necessaries as 'goods suitable to the condition in life of the minor . . . and to his actual requirements at the time of the sale and delivery'.

Necessities are within this category but 'necessaries' has a wider connotation and it is a relative term which is interpreted having regard to the minor's age and the antiquated and ethereal notion of his 'position in society' (see *Peters* v *Fleming* (1840) 6 M & W 42). For items which have been held to be necessaries see, e.g. *Elkington & Co. Ltd* v *Amery* [1936] 2 All ER 86; *Clyde Cycle Co.* v *Hargreaves* (1898) 78 LT 296; *Fawcett* v *Smethurst* (1914) 84 LJ KB 473. For non-necessaries see, e.g. *Ryder* v *Wombwell* (1869) LR 4 Ex 32; *Nash* v *Inman* [1908] 2 KB 1; *Stocks* v *Wilson* [1913] 2 KB 235. Services supplied can also be necessaries (see *Helps* v *Clayton* (1864) 17 CB (NS) 553; *Chapple* v *Cooper* (1844) 13 M & W 252). A considerable latitude is given to the minor because:

(a) The burden of proving that goods are necessaries is on the supplier and the goods must be to the minor's actual requirements at the time of sale and delivery (see *Nash* v *Inman*).

(b)   A contract for necessaries will be void if it contains harsh or onerous terms (see *Fawcett* v *Smethurst; Flower* v *London & North Western Ry Co.* [1894] 2 QB 65).

(c)   A minor's trading contracts are not contracts for necessaries and he is not liable either for goods or services supplied to him to enable him to carry on his trade (see *Re Jones, Re, ex p Jones* (1881) 18 Ch D 109; *Mercantile Union Guarantee Corp. Ltd* v *Ball* [1937] 2 KB 498) or where, as a tradesman, he fails to deliver goods (see *Cowern* v *Nield* [1912] 2 KB 419).

(d)   A loan advanced to a minor to enable him to buy necessaries is irrecoverable (see *Darby* v *Boucher* (1694) 1 Salk 279) but if the loan is actually spent on necessaries, the lender can recover the amount so spent under the equitable doctrine of subrogation. Any security given in respect of the loan is unenforceable even if the loan was required to pay for necessaries (see *Martin* v *Gale* (1876) 4 Ch D 428) and accounts stated with minors are unenforceable even if some of the goods listed are necessaries.

(e)   It is very debatable whether a minor is liable on an executory contract for necessary goods as the Sale of Goods Act 1979, s. 3, specifies that goods must be 'sold and delivered'. One view is that he is liable normally on a contract for necessaries but the better view is that he is liable *quasi ex contractu* by virtue of the delivery of the goods, this being strengthened by the fact that he need only pay a reasonable price under s. 3 (see *Nash* v *Inman*; cf *Roberts* v *Gray* [1913] 1 KB 520).

Binding Contracts: Employment, Apprenticeship, Education and Analogous Contracts

Contracts of service, education and apprenticeship are regarded as advantageous to minors and hence binding, but the undertaking must be to their overall advantage (see *Clements* v *London and North Western Ry Co.* [1894] 2 QB 482; *De Francesco* v *Barnum* (1890) 45 Ch D 430; *Sir WC Leng & Co. Ltd* v *Andrews* [1909] 1 Ch 763). This category of beneficial contracts has been extended to analogous situations, e.g, a contract between a minor and a publisher for the publication of the minor's autobiography (see *Roberts* v *Gray* (supra); *Doyle* v *White City Stadium Ltd* [1935] 1 KB 110; *Chaplin* v *Leslie Frewin (Publishers) Ltd* [1966] Ch 71; *Denmark Productions Ltd* v *Boscobel Productions Ltd* (1967) 111 SJ 715). However, it is not possible to postulate a general rule that any contract beneficial to a minor is binding upon him.

Voidable Contracts: Contracts Binding on a Minor unless Repudiated

This category is limited to contracts where the minor acquires an interest in property of a permanent nature with continuing obligations. The contract is voidable at his option before or within a reasonable time of attaining majority, but until repudiation, he is bound by the contract and its obligations (see *North Western Ry* v *McMichael* (1850) 5 Exch 114). There is no general rule that *all* contracts conferring an interest in property of a permanent nature come within this category and contracts of hire or hire-purchase, for example, are not encompassed in this group. This classification is limited to four types of contract: (a) contracts to lease or purchase land; (b) purchase of shares; (c) partnerships; (d) marriage settlements. If the minor repudiates, he is free of obligations which have not yet accrued at the time of repudiation but there are conflicting *dicta* on the question of whether accrued obligations are extinguished by repudiation (see *McMichael's* case; *Cork & Brandon Ry Co.* v *Cazenove* (1847) 10 QB 935). He cannot recover any money paid under a voidable contract unless there has been a total failure of consideration (see *Steinberg* v *Scala (Leeds) Ltd* [1923] 2 Ch 452; *Corpe* v *Overton* (1833) 10 Bing 252).

Voidable Contracts: Contracts Unenforceable against a Minor unless Ratified

The general rule in minors' contracts is that the minor may enforce the contract but it is not enforceable against him unless he ratifies it on reaching majority. This is the legal position in all contracts apart from necessaries, beneficial contracts of service and contracts for the minor to acquire an interest in property. The ratification may be express or implied and will bind the minor even though there is no consideration for the new promise. The 1874 Act had prevented the enforcement of a ratification but that Act is now repealed by the 1987 Act and the common law rule of an enforceable ratification is thus reinstated. Similarly, s. 5 of the Betting and Loans (Infants) Act 1892 which invalidated contracts to repay loans advanced during minority is repealed by the 1987 Act.

Once a contract in this category has been executed, the infant cannot recover back money paid or property transferred under it on the basis that it was unenforceable against him — he only has this right if the remedy would be available to an adult, e.g., a total failure of consideration. Moreover, property in goods passes to the infant by delivery: this was the position under the 1874 Act when the contract was 'absolutely void' and almost certainly it should be the same where the contract is simply unenforceable against the minor (see *Stocks* v *Wilson* [1913] 2 KB 235). Section 3 of the 1987 Act appears to assume that property may pass by referring to 'property acquired' by the minor. Similarly, it appears that property may pass from a minor to the other party in an unenforceable contract (see *Chaplin* v *Leslie Frewin (Publishers) Ltd* (above)). Finally, where the other party knows that he is contracting with a minor, he may prudently seek a guarantee from an adult. The position is now governed by s. 2 of the 1987 Act which provides that such a guarantee shall be enforceable against the guarantor/adult even where the obligation is unenforceable against the minor or where he repudiates the contract.

Liability of Minors in Tort

The general principle here is that a minor is not liable for a tort directly connected with a contract which is unenforceable against him, for, otherwise, the protection available to the minor would be illusory (see *Jennings* v *Rundall* (1799) 8 Term Rep 335; *Leslie Ltd* v *Sheill* [1914] 3 KB 607; *Fawcett* v *Smethurst* (1915) 84 LJ KB 473). However, the minor can be liable if the tort arises independently of the contract or is outside its ambit (see *Burnard* v *Haggis* (1863) 14 CB (NS) 45; *Ballett* v *Mingay* [1943] KB 281).

Liability of Minors to make Restitution

A minor may use fraud to obtain non-necessary goods, for example, and thus not be liable in either tort or contract, but where there has been fraud, equity may compel him to restore the goods. The overall principle is that 'restitution stops where repayment begins' and thus restitution could not apply to a loan obtained by fraud as this would amount to a direct enforcement of the debt (see *Leslie Ltd* v *Sheill supra*) However, in *Stocks* v *Wilson* (*supra*) it was held that a minor could be compelled to account for the proceeds of sale of the goods in question. This decision, although criticised in *Leslie*, is often justified by commentators on the basis of the equitable doctrine of tracing.

The Minors' Contracts Act 1987, s. 3, provides an effective means by which restitution can be ordered and, unlike the equitable remedy, it is not limited to cases of fraud. Under s. 3, where a contract is unenforceable against a minor or where he repudiates it, the court may, if it is just and equitable to do so, order the minor to transfer to the other party 'any property acquired . . . under the contract, or any property representing it'. There are difficulties here. First, it is not clear whether 'property' is meant to cover money but it appears from the Law Commission report which led to the Act (Law Com No 134, 1984) that, where the minor sells the goods which were the subject of an unenforceable contract, the proceeds of sale should be recoverable. Secondly, the phrase 'any property representing it' allows the court to restore property acquired by the minor's exchanging the contract goods for other goods, for example. The Law Commission did not intend that s. 3 should allow the court to order payment of a price or reasonable value where the contract goods have been consumed, or the proceeds of sale dissipated, for example, as this goes beyond the scope of restitution and amounts to enforcement of the contract. Thirdly, it is unclear to what extent the court may order statutory tracing, e.g., if the goods are sold and the proceeds paid into a bank account which contains other monies. Finally, the court has a discretion to award restitution and it may take into account whether unfair advantage was taken of the minor or whether a tracing order would, in effect, enforce the contract. Most particularly, it will want to strike a balance between protection of the minor and the other party's interests in seeking restitution.

Q Question 1

Crammer is a student aged 17 who lives on the campus of Passmore College. He buys a new 1,200 cc motorbike from Ace Machines Ltd, paying a deposit of £500, and purchases a £1,750 word processor on credit terms from Computo Ltd. One of the purposes of buying these goods was to attract his girlfriend, Ivy, back to him and to further this possibility, he moves out of the hall of residence at the college and takes a lease of a luxury flat from Rory at £2,000 per month. Crammer owed £400 in rent to the hall at the date he left.

As his examinations are pending, Crammer borrows £300 from Buster and orders several textbooks from Swotters Ltd. Being under great strain, Crammer begins to develop obsessive religious tendencies and he therefore abandons his studies and joins 'The Heavenbent', a strict religious sect which promotes self-denial. Consequently, on his way home from a meeting of the sect, he pushes the motorbike over a cliff. He then repudiates the lease of the flat, refusing to pay Rory the £2,000 rent owed, and cancels the order for the books from Swotters Ltd. Crammer is unable to repay the loan to Buster and refuses to pay £400 to the hall of residence. Moreover, Crammer has not paid any instalments on the word processor. 'The Heavenbent' have informed Crammer that if he does not pay £3,000 for the 'spiritual guidance' given, they will commence proceedings for these 'fees'.

Discuss the legal position of all the parties.

Commentary

Students should be careful to separate the various transactions in this problem and follow each through to its conclusion for, otherwise, a jumbled and confused answer will result. Material should not be repeated in the answer but, instead, appropriate cross-references should be made. The use of headings in the answer is desirable for each relationship/problem.

- Is the purchase of the motorbike a contract for 'necessaries' meaning that Crammer must pay a 'reasonable price' for it?

- Is Crammer liable in tort for pushing the motorbike over the cliff?

- Is the contract for the purchase of the word processor one for necessaries?

- Can the seller of the word processor successfully order its return under the Minors' Contracts Act 1987, s. 3?

- Is Crammer liable on the executory contract for the textbooks which are, indisputably, necessaries?

- May Buster recover the money lent to Crammer?

- Is Crammer liable for the rent owed to the hall of residence

- Is Crammer liable for the rent owed under the lease of the luxury flat?

- Is the contract with the 'The Heavenbent' a beneficial contract of education or training which is binding on Crammer?

 Suggested answer

As he is under 18 years of age, Crammer is a minor who does not have full contractual capacity. The policy of the law is to protect minors against both their own inexperience and unscrupulous adults who might take unfair advantage of the position. Sometimes these roles appear to be reversed and, accordingly, the law must strike a balance between protecting the minor and not unduly prejudicing the other contracting party.

Ace Machines Ltd/1,200 cc Motorbike

The only contract which is fully binding on a minor is a contract for necessaries, this category encompassing contracts for the sale of goods, the supply of services and beneficial contracts of employment and education. Section 3 of the Sale of Goods Act 1979 provides that where necessaries are 'sold and delivered' a minor must pay 'a reasonable price' for them. Section 3(3) defines necessaries as goods 'suitable to the condition in life of the minor and to his actual requirements at the time of sale and delivery'. The term 'necessaries' is clearly a relative one and in deciding whether goods fall within this classification the court (and the other contracting party) must make a decision based upon the minor's age, requirements and 'position in society' (*Chapple* v *Cooper* (1844) 13 M & W 252, 258 *per* Alderson B.) It is arguable that a means of transport could be a necessary for Crammer (C) but it is unlikely that such a powerful, expensive motorbike would be deemed necessary. However, in *Fawcett* v *Smethurst* (1914) 84 LJ KB 473, the hire of a car to fetch luggage from a station six miles away was held to be a necessary and so was a racing bicycle for a youth earning 21 shillings a week in 1898 (*Clyde Cycle Co.* v *Hargreaves* (1898) 78 LT 296). Alternatively, a hunter for an impecunious cavalry officer was held not to be a necessary in *Re Mead* [1916] 2 IR 285. It is suggested that the motorbike would not be a necessary, meaning that the contract would not be enforceable against C. However, C might be liable in tort for pushing the motorbike over the cliff. The general rule is that a minor is not liable for a tort directly connected with the contract for this would amount to indirect enforcement of the contract but he can be liable for torts not so connected. In *Jennings* v *Rundall* (1799) 8 Term Rep 335, a minor who hired a horse for riding was not liable when he injured it through excessive riding but in *Burnard* v *Haggis* (1863) 14 CB (NS) 45, a minor was liable when he hired a mare for riding but lent her to a friend who killed her by taking her jumping. It seems that C would be liable in tort to Ace Machines Ltd. Although the contract does not bind C, he cannot recover the deposit of £500 (*Chaplin* v *Leslie Frewin (Publishers) Ltd* [1966] Ch 71) but it would be considered in any award of damages.

Computo Ltd/Word Processor

As with the motorbike, such an expensive word processor is unlikely to be a necessary and the contract would be unenforceable against C. However, C appears to be in possession of the word processor and it seems indisputable that the court would order its return to Computo Ltd. There is no evidence that C has been fraudulent in inducing Computo Ltd to contract with him and so the equitable doctrine of restitution could not apply, but the most effective remedy is provided by s. 3 of the Minors' Contracts Act 1987. This provides that, where the contract is unenforceable against the minor (or he repudiates it), the court may, 'if it is just and equitable to do so', order the minor to transfer to the other party 'any property acquired . . . under the contract'. It is clearly just to order the return of the goods and, as C is in possession, there is no obstacle to a simple restitution of the property.

Swotters Ltd/Textbooks

Almost certainly, textbooks for a student would be necessaries if not necessities, but C has cancelled the order and the question is therefore whether a minor is liable on an executory contract for necessary goods. The position is unclear but the better view is that a minor is liable in quasi contract because he has been *supplied*, not simply because he has made a promise to pay. This is supported by *Nash* v *Inman* [1908] 2 KB 1 and s. 3 of the Sale of Goods Act 1979 which refers to goods 'sold and delivered'. Moreover, the minor need only pay 'a reasonable price' for the goods which, as emphasised in *Pontypridd Union* v *Drew* [1927] 1 KB 214, is not suggestive of full, consensual liability. Alternatively, a minor was liable on an executory contract for education and training in *Roberts* v *Gray* [1913] 1 KB 520. On balance, it would seem that, perhaps unjustly, this contract could not be enforced against C.

Loan from Buster

A contract of loan is unenforceable against a minor unless he ratifies it on attaining majority, and a loan taken to pay for necessaries was irrecoverable at common law (*Darby* v *Boucher* (1694) 1 Salk 279) on the basis that 'it may be borrowed for necessaries but laid out and spent at a tavern' (*Earle* v *Peale* (1711) 1 Salk 386). However, if the loan is actually spent on necessaries, the lender can recover the amount so spent under the equitable doctrine of subrogation (*Marlow* v *Pitfield* (1719) 1 P Wms 558) whereby the lender is given the same rights as the seller of the goods. Unfortunately for Buster, C cancels the order for the textbooks/necessaries and there is no evidence that the loan has been spent on other necessaries. If C had bought goods with the loan, Buster could have sought restitution of those goods under the Minors' Contracts Act 1987, s. 3, as 'property representing' the loan but there is no evidence of such a purchase. Consequently, Buster cannot recover the loan.

Hall of Residence

This is almost certainly a valid contract for necessaries in the sense that basic food and clothing would be so classified as necessities and the hall is suitable to the minor's 'condition in life'. Alternatively, the contract might be valid as being analogous to beneficial contracts of service and education — in *Pickering* v *Gunning* (1629) Palm 528, for example, a minor was liable for board, lodging and schooling. It would appear that C has been supplied with accommodation rather than being liable for rent in advance. If the contract is one for necessaries and he has been supplied he will be liable for the £400. However, it seems that executory contracts for necessary services are enforceable against a minor, at least if they are classified as beneficial contracts of education (*Roberts* v *Gray*, above — minor who had contracted to tour with a professional billiards player liable in damages for failing to proceed). Nevertheless, contracts for necessaries must contain no harsh or onerous terms (*Fawcett* v *Smethurst*, above) and, similarly, contracts of service and education must be to the minor's overall advantage, so that a provision for rent in advance would probably not satisfy these requirements.

Lease of the Luxury Flat from Rory

A lease of property is voidable at the minor's option either before reaching majority or within a reasonable time thereafter, but until he does avoid it he is subject to the liabilities of the contract. Accordingly, it is clear that C is liable for rent (*Davies* v *Benyon-Harris* (1931) 47 TLR 424) and since the decision in *North Western Ry Co.* v *McMichael* (1850) 5 Exch 114 it would appear that the minor is bound even if the contract is not beneficial. Thus, there could be no argument that, this being a 'luxury flat', C was not bound. C may repudiate the lease but it is essential to ascertain the effects of repudiation in relation to C's liabilities. It is beyond doubt that repudiation ends all liability for *future* obligations but there are conflicting *dicta* as to whether it extinguishes liabilities accrued before repudiation. *McMichael's* case favours the retrospective extinction of liabilities but in *Blake* v *Concannon* (1870) IR 4 CL 323, an Irish decision, a minor who repudiated a lease was nevertheless liable for rent which had accrued while he was in possession. It is suggested that *Blake* represents the better view and it accords with the principle that, in this class of voidable contract, the minor cannot recover any money paid to the other party unless there has been a total failure of consideration (*Steinberg* v *Scala (Leeds) Ltd* [1923] 2 Ch 452). It seems that it is accrued rent which Rory wishes to claim in the problem and it is suggested that C is liable to pay it.

The Heavenbent

This may be a valid contract within the category of beneficial contracts of employment, education and training but the contract must be to the minor's overall advantage (*De Francesco* v *Barnum* (1890) 45 Ch D 430). The rationale of these contracts is that they equip the minor for his future trade or profession and it is unlikely that the court would find the contract binding in the absence of clear evidence to this effect. Accordingly, it is suggested that this contract would be unenforceable against C unless he ratified it on reaching majority.

Q Question 2

Sprint, aged 17, is a trainee racing driver apprenticed to Flash. Sprint borrows £10,000 from Basil and with the money enters into the following transactions: (a) being an obsessive hi-fi enthusiast, he buys new equipment from Watts Ltd to the value of £4,000, and (b) he purchases shares to the value of £6,000 in Surefire Ltd.

In order to supplement his income, Sprint starts a business specialising in the 'race-tuning' of cars. He orders parts to the value of £5,000 from Wrenchit & Co. in order to start the business.

Sprint wishes to accept an offer from Dream Team & Co. to drive racing cars for them but has discovered that the terms of the agreement with Flash provide that he is to be apprenticed for a further four years at the same salary.

Angered by this turn of events, Sprint refuses to repay the loan to Basil. He then refuses to pay for the hi-fi and sells it for £2,000 to Ben. With the £2,000 he books a holiday in the Seychelles. He then repudiates the contract with Surefire Ltd and seeks the return of the £2,000 paid and refuses to continue working for Flash. Just before leaving for holiday, Wrenchit & Co. inform Sprint that they are to commence proceedings for the cost of the parts supplied to Sprint.

Discuss the legal position of all the parties.

Commentary

As with the previous question, it is vital to answer this problem in a definite order thereby avoiding repetition and preserving the answer's internal consistency. Thus, although the loan from Basil is chronologically the first problem, it is not advisable to answer it first. This is because its recovery may depend on later facts in the problem which have not yet been discussed in the answer. In other words, aim at symmetrical progression in the answer.

- Is the contract for the (expensive) hi-fi equipment one for 'necessaries' under which Sprint must pay a 'reasonable price'?

- Can the seller of the hi-fi successfully claim the amount obtained by Sprint when he sold the hi-fi to Ben?

- Has property in the hi-fi passed to Sprint and from Sprint to Ben?

- May Sprint repudiate the contract for the purchase of the shares and recover the £2,000 purchase price?

- May Basil recover the money lent to Sprint?

- Is Sprint bound by the contract of apprenticeship with Flash?

- Is Sprint liable for the parts supplied by Wrenchit & Co for use in Sprint's business?

 **Suggested answer**

For the purposes of the law of contract, Sprint is a minor as he is not yet 18 years of age. Accordingly, he has a limited contractual capacity, the overall policy of the law being to protect the minor against both his own inexperience and those who wish to take advantage of it.

Hi-Fi from Watts Ltd

The problem here is to decide whether this is a contract for necessaries which would be valid and binding upon Sprint (S). Section 3 of the Sale of Goods Act 1979 provides that where necessaries are 'sold and delivered' a minor must pay 'a reasonable price' for them. Section 3(3) defines necessaries as goods 'suitable to the condition in life of the minor and to his actual requirements at the time of sale and delivery'. Necessities such as clothing and food are clearly within this definition but beyond this the test is relative and based upon the minor's age, needs and position in society. It is a difficult test for the court to apply but it is arguably almost impossible for a retailer to make such a decision with regard to a total stranger and yet the burden of establishing that goods are necessaries is always on the supplier. It is very unlikely that such expensive hi-fi equipment could be a necessary for Sprint, as it is arguably a 'mere luxury' as opposed to a 'luxurious article of utility' (*Chapple* v *Cooper* (1844) 13 M & W 252). In *Ryder* v *Wombwell* (1868) LR 3 Ex 90, it was held that jewelled solitaire cuff links for the son of a deceased baronet were not necessaries and likewise a collection of snuff boxes and curios in *Stocks* v *Wilson* [1913] 2 KB 235. Moreover, S is an 'obsessive enthusiast' of hi-fi and this is 'new' equipment which might indicate that he is already well-supplied with hi-fi. If so, this is fatal to the seller's claim to establish the goods as necessaries for, by s. 3(3) of the Sale of Goods Act 1979, the goods must be suitable 'to the infant's "actual requirements at the time of the sale and delivery" '. In *Nash* v *Inman* [1908] 2 KB 1, a tailor who supplied an undergraduate with 11 fancy waistcoats could not establish them as necessaries as it was shown that the minor was sufficiently supplied with suitable clothing. This is the position even if the minor's sufficiency of supply is unknown to the seller. It is suggested that the purchase of the hi-fi is therefore unenforceable against S.

Are any other remedies available to Watts Ltd? The Minors' Contracts Act 1987, s. 3, provides that the court may, 'if it is just and equitable to do so', order the minor to transfer to the other party 'any property acquired . . . under the contract, or any property representing it'. As S has sold the hi-fi, the proceeds of sale become 'property representing' the hi-fi. In *Stocks* v *Wilson* (above), the minor sold goods in this way and was held liable to account for the proceeds of sale and, although the decision was criticised in *Leslie (R) Ltd* v *Sheill* [1914] 3 KB 607, it was clearly the intention of the Law Commission report which led to the 1987 Act (Law Com No 134, 1984) that proceeds of sale should be recoverable under s. 3. However, *restitution* is the rationale of this area and there should be no indirect enforcement of the contract in the guise of restitution — this being the criticism of *Stocks* that was made in *Leslie*. The Law Commission recognised that where property has been sold and the proceeds of sale dissipated the minor should not have to *account* for the proceeds or compensate the other party. This is almost certainly the position with S as he has used the money to pay for a holiday. However, it should be emphasised that the court has a wide discretion under s. 3 and the Law Commission proposals did not rule out tracing orders, for example. But when the property has been dissipated the remedy of tracing similarly evaporates.

It is also clear from *Stocks v Wilson* that property in non-necessary goods can pass from the seller to the minor 'by the delivery'. As this was the position in *Stocks* when the contract was 'absolutely void' under the Infants Relief Act 1874, it must surely be the position now when the contract is only unenforceable against the minor. This also means that S can transfer a valid title in the hi-fi to Ben. Moreover, the fact that property passes to S means that he cannot be liable to Watts Ltd in conversion and neither can the third party, Ben.

Purchase of Shares in Surefire Ltd

This is clearly a contract which is voidable at the minor's option during minority or within a reasonable time of reaching majority but which is valid and binding in the absence of such repudiation. This category is limited to those specific situations where the minor acquires an interest in property of a permanent nature with continuing obligations. Thus, S can repudiate but it is clear that if the shares have been allotted he cannot recover what he has paid for them. In *Steinberg* v *Scala (Leeds) Ltd* [1923] 2 Ch 452, a minor was allotted shares in a company and paid the amounts due on allotment and on the first call but she attended no meetings and was paid no dividends. After 18 months she repudiated the allotment, but it was held that she could not recover the amounts paid as she had received 'the very consideration for which she had bargained'. A minor may only recover back in this way if there has been a total failure of consideration, as in *Corpe* v *Overton* (1833) 10 Bing 252.

Loan from Basil

The contract of loan is unenforceable against S unless he ratifies it on attaining majority and, as S has not used the loan to purchase necessary goods, Basil cannot invoke the equitable doctrine of subrogation in order to be given the rights of the seller of the goods. However, might Basil utilise s. 3 of the 1987 Act arguing that the hi-fi bought with the loan becomes 'property representing' the loan? Unfortunately, as the hi-fi has been sold, Basil is met with the same obstacle as Watts Ltd in that the property has been dissipated. Furthermore, if Basil were to be allowed the proceeds of sale this would amount to *actual* enforcement of the contract to repay the loan and, as such, might be disallowed. It is interesting to speculate what would have happened if the hi-fi had *not* been sold, for then both Basil and Watts Ltd would have had a claim to it under s. 3 and it is unclear how this conflict could be resolved.

However, S has used part of the loan to purchase shares in Surefire Ltd, this being a voidable contract. It appears from *Nottingham Permanent Benefit Building Society* v *Thurstan* [1908] AC 6 that the lender is entitled to stand in the shoes of the other party to the voidable contract and may recover the loan from the minor by this method. In other words, this is a parallel remedy to the lender's subrogation to the rights of the seller of necessary goods.

Apprenticeship with Flash

A contract of apprenticeship is valid and binding on a minor provided that the contract as a whole is beneficial to him at the date it is entered into. In *De Francesco* v *Barnum* (1889) 45 Ch D 430, a girl of 14 bound herself by an apprenticeship deed for seven years to be taught stage dancing, the terms of the contract placing her entirely at the will of the claimant. It was held that the contract was unreasonable and invalid. The question of fairness may often be tested by comparing the contract with other undertakings in the same trade to see if restrictions are justified (*Leslie* v *Fitzpatrick* (1877) 3 QBD 229), but the four-year period in S's case with no increase in salary seems, prima facie, to be unreasonable.

Parts Supplied by Wrenchit & Co.

It is indisputable that trading contracts are not contracts for necessaries and the law accords great protection to a minor in this context. Thus a minor who 'trades' (there being no clear definition of 'trade') is not liable for goods supplied to him for use in his trade (*Mercantile Union* v *Ball* [1937] 2 KB 498) nor can he be liable for failing to deliver goods which he has sold as a tradesman (*Cowern* v *Nield* [1912] 2 KB 419). It is somewhat perplexing that a minor may be bound by contracts of employment, education and training yet cannot be liable on business/trading contracts. However, it is clear that Wrenchit & Co. have no remedy against S.

Terms of the Contract

Introduction

The terms of the contract are its heart and lifeblood in that they define both the content and scope of the parties' mutual rights and obligations. In a contract for the sale of goods, for example, the price of the goods, the date of delivery, mode of payment and the requisite standard of quality which must be met are all likely to be contractual terms. A breach of contract is defined as breach of a term. There are two distinct levels of enquiry here. First, there must be an *ascertainment of the terms* of the contract and, secondly, a *classification and determination of the relative importance of the terms* thus established as part of the contract.

There are four principal difficulties in ascertaining the terms of the contract. First, the parties' negotiations may be extensive. Which, if any, of the promises and statements made during several months of negotiation are to be treated as part of the concluded contract? Secondly, the *general* rule is that there is no particular form demanded for contracts which can run the gamut from a deed (specialty) or writing to a purely oral contract (parol contract). If the contract is embodied in a deed or wholly in writing, might other evidence be adduced to establish oral statements as terms or is the writing a final manifestation of intent? Thirdly, apart from the express terms upon which the parties have agreed, there may be *implied* terms derived from a variety of sources, which dictate the content of the contract. In a contract for the sale of goods, for example, the minimum standards of quality are prescribed by ss. 13 and 14 of the Sale of Goods Act 1979. Fourthly, the contract may contain exclusion clauses by virtue of which one party seeks to exclude or restrict a liability which he would otherwise owe to the other. To what extent should special rules govern the incorporation of such onerous clauses in the contract or prohibit their use completely? Exclusion clauses are considered separately in **Chapter 6**.

It is important to realise that, as the law has developed, three stages are evident in the processes employed for determining the terms of the contract. First, a rigid adherence to freedom of contract and the *implementation* of the parties' intentions. Secondly, a degree of cloaked judicial interventionism based upon *ascertainment* of the parties' intentions and, thirdly, open judicial and legislative interventionism *imposing* a just solution upon the parties. The three stages necessarily merge and overlap.

Ascertainment of the Express Terms of the Contract

The first task is to distinguish the terms of the contract from mere representations. A truthful, mere representation is legally valueless but if it is factual and untrue it is a misrepresentation for which there are now potent remedies (see **Chapter 7** on misrepresentation). Differentiating a term from a mere representation involves ascertaining the *intention* of the maker of the statement (*Heilbut, Symons Co.* v *Buckleton* [1913] AC 30). Did he warrant its accuracy and truth or is it merely a legitimate 'puff' praising and enhancing the contract's subject matter? The test of intention gives the courts considerable latitude in answering this question, many of the earlier decisions reflecting a *laissez-faire* attitude (e.g. *Heilbut*) whilst modern cases have increasingly used an objective test in ascertaining the effect of the statement on the other party and whether his reliance on it is justified (see *Oscar Chess Ltd* v *Williams* [1957] 1 WLR 370; *Bentley (Dick) Productions Ltd* v *Harold Smith (Motors) Ltd* [1965] 1 WLR 623; *Esso Petroleum Co. Ltd* v *Mardon* [1976] QB 801). Although the cases are necessarily ambivalent, some delineation of the test of intention is possible.

Where an agreement was embodied in a deed or reduced to writing the *parol evidence rule* might mean that parol (or other extrinsic) evidence could not be admitted to add to, vary or contradict the writing. The rule sought to implement the finality of the parties' intentions as expressed in their all-embracing written contract but it is now surrounded by so many exceptions relating to form and substance that it has become subsumed within the overall test of intention. A written contract is therefore only one pointer, albeit an important one, to the parties' intent. In 1976, the Law Commission considered that the parol evidence rule might be abolished (WP No 70) but the final report in 1986 decided that no reform was needed as the rule was not as troublesome and extensive as traditionally expounded (Law Com No 154, Cmnd 9700). Many of the exceptions are understandable, however, when it is realised that their *raison d'être* was the need to avoid this technical and arbitrary rule, e.g., parol evidence was allowed to prove the *invalidity* of a contract as this did not purport to *alter* its *content*.

In seeking to implement the parties' intentions and decide whether a statement is a term or a mere representation, the courts will consider (a) the lapse of time between the making of the statement and the contract's conclusion: if the interval is short the statement is more likely to be a term (see *Schawel* v *Reade* [1913] 2 IR 64; *Routledge* v *McKay* [1954] 1 WLR 615); (b) whether the maker of the statement had specialist knowledge or was in a better position than the other party to verify the statement's accuracy (see *Harling* v *Eddy* [1951] 2 KB 739; *Oscar Chess Ltd* v *Williams Ltd supra*; *Bentley (Dick) Productions Ltd* v *Harold Smith (Motors) Ltd*); (c) the importance of the truth of the statement as a pivotal factor in finalising the contract (see *Bannerman* v *White* (1861) 10 CB (NS) 844, *Esso Petroleum Co. Ltd* v *Mardon supra*); and, (d) whether the statement was omitted in a later, formal contract in writing (see *Gilchester Properties Ltd* v *Gomm* [1948] 1 All ER 493; *Birch* v *Paramount Estates* (1956) 16 EG 396).

The notion of the collateral contract developed rapidly in the twentieth century as a significant means by which the difficulties of fixing a statement with contractual force may be circumvented. The courts may be prepared to find both a primary and secondary collateral contract, the consideration for which is, classically, entry into the primary contract, e.g., 'If you take a lease of this property, I will confirm that the drains are sound'. Nevertheless, in *Strongman (1945) Ltd* v *Sincock* [1955] 2 QB 525, the ambit of the collateral contract was widened in that such a contract was established where the primary contract was *unenforceable* for illegality. A collateral contract is particularly useful where (a) the parol evidence rule might otherwise bar a statement's inclusion in the final contract (see *Mann* v *Nunn* (1874) 30 LT 526) — note that the collateral contract may *contradict* the writing, see *City and Westminster Properties (1934) Ltd* v *Mudd* [1959] Ch 129; (b) an exclusion clause in the written contract attempts to invalidate the collateral promise (see *Andrews* v *Hopkinson* [1957] 1 QB 229; *Evans (J) Son (Portsmouth) Ltd* v *Andrea Merzario Ltd* [1976] 1 WLR 1078); (c) the statement would not qualify as a misrepresentation (see *Andrews*, above: 'It's a good little bus, I would stake my life on it'); (d) the primary contract is made between the claimant and a third party but the defendant has made a collateral promise (see *Andrews*, above; *Shanklin Pier Ltd* v *Detel Products Ltd* [1951] 2 KB 854).

Ascertainment of the Implied Terms of the Contract

A court may be required to imply a term into a contract if the parties have specified only the rudimentary obligations or if a disagreement ensues from which it is apparent that the parties have not provided for the contingency at issue. There are two broad categories of implied term. First, those implied terms where the courts attempt to implement the unexpressed intention of the parties. Here there is no question of imposing a solution or attempting to make the contract more reasonable. Instead the implication must be necessary and not inconsistent with the express terms of the contract. A term may be implied in this first category if (a) it is *necessary* to give *business efficacy* to the contract (see *The Moorcock* (1889) 14 PD 64); (b) it is so obvious that *both* parties must have intended it to be part of the contract, i.e., the 'officious bystander' test (see *Shirlaw* v *Southern Foundries (1926) Ltd* [1939] 2 KB 206); and (c) there is a custom of a trade or locality which is certain, notorious, reasonable and lawful (see *Hutton* v *Warren* (1836) 1 M & W 466; *Les Affréteurs Réunis Société Anonyme* v *Walford* [1919] AC 801). The second broad category is based more upon the notion that in certain relationships and contracts the law seeks to impose a model or standardised set of terms as a form of regulation — this approach resembling more closely an implication of reasonable, rather than necessary, terms (see *Liverpool City Council* v *Irwin* [1977] AC 239; *Shell UK Ltd* v *Lostock Garage Ltd* [1976] 1 WLR 1187 and the views expressed therein regarding such implied terms). It is apparent that the central issue throughout implied terms is the extent to which *interventionism* in contracts is appropriate when freedom of contract is still the philosophical notion underpinning the law of contract.

Legislation increasingly dictates that certain terms be implied in contracts thereby seeking to maintain minimum standards of performance. Even statutory intervention can be linked with the parties' intentions and classical theories of contract if the legislation codifies the common law. Such a tenuous connection is becoming increasingly unrealistic, particularly in those situations where such implied obligations cannot be excluded (e.g., the Sale of Goods Act 1979, ss. 13 and 14 and the Unfair Contract Terms Act 1977, ss. 6 and 12 which restrict the exclusion of the implied terms contained in ss. 13 and 14). It is clear, therefore, that legislation may impose a paradigm contract by way of implied terms.

Classification and Determination of the Relative Importance of Terms

Classically, terms of the contract have been divided into either *conditions* or *warranties* which are, respectively, the contract's major and minor stipulations. Breach of condition entitles the innocent party either to treat himself as discharged from further performance or affirm the contract and claim damages whichever course is chosen, whereas a breach of warranty only gives rise to a claim for damages. Again, the nature of these stipulations and the consequences of their breach are said to be based upon the intention of the parties as manifested in their agreement (see *Bentsen* v *Taylor, Sons & Co.* [1893] 2 QB 274; *Schuler (L) AG* v *Wickman Machine Tool Sales Ltd* [1974] AC 235). Alternatively, a statute may provide that a particular implied term is either a condition or a warranty (e.g., the Sale of Goods Act 1979, ss. 12–15).

It follows that if the parties have expressly agreed upon their obligations, a breach of a term entails that the appropriate remedies be available without considering the seriousness of the breach or its consequences. A trifling breach of condition may thus allow repudiation of the entire contract (see *Arcos Ltd* v *EA Ronaasen & Son* [1933] AC 470) although in non-consumer contracts for the sale of goods, the Sale of Goods Act 1979, s. 15A now provides that the buyer cannot reject the goods for a 'slight' breach of the conditions implied in ss. 13–15 of the 1979 Act. In *Hongkong Fir Shipping Co. Ltd* v *Kawasaki Kisen Kaisha Ltd* [1962] 2 QB 26, the Court of Appeal recognised that there are many contractual undertakings of a complex character which can be the subject of a major or minor breach e.g. the condition that a ship be seaworthy could be breached by the ship's hull being defective at one extreme, or, at the other, by the first-aid box being inadequately stocked. The court considered that such undertakings should not be categorised *beforehand* as either conditions or warranties but, rather, the *consequences of the breach* should dictate the appropriate remedy. The *Hongkong* decision firmly established the innominate or intermediate term which is only 'classified' by the courts at the date of breach and not by a retrospective investigation of the parties' intentions (see also *Cehave NV* v *Bremer Handelsgesellschaft mbH, The Hansa Nord* [1976] QB 44; *Reardon Smith Line Ltd* v *Yngvar Hansen-Tangen* [1976] 1 WLR 989). The innominate term is clearly interventionist in approach even if its rationale is the supposed ascertainment of the parties' intentions. Although the innominate term is capable of universal application, there is still scope for the orthodox classification of conditions and warranties in mercantile contracts where certainty is at a premium. There may be cogency, therefore, in treating stipulations as to the time of performance (see *The Mihalis Angelos* [1971] 1 QB 164; *Bunge Corporation* v *Tradax Export SA* [1981] 1 WLR 711) and, for example, the precise description of unascertained future goods (e.g. a sale of commodities) as conditions entitling the innocent party to repudiate in the event of a breach (see also *Barber* v *NWS Bank plc* (1995) *The Times*, 27 November).

Finally, the above classifications relate to *promissory conditions* but there may also be *contingent conditions* which either suspend or cancel contractual liability. A *condition precedent* generally means that the contract will not become binding unless a condition is fulfilled (see *Aberfoyle Plantations Ltd* v *Cheng* [1960] AC 115) and a *condition subsequent* involves a contract which is binding immediately but which may cease to bind the parties or allow one party the option to cancel on the operation of the condition (see *Head* v *Tattersall* (1871) LR Ex 7).

Q Question 1

It is illogical and unjust that the law sanctions a prior determination of contractual obligations as either conditions or warranties and allows a claimant the concomitant remedy for breach of such terms without considering the consequences of that breach.

Discuss.

Commentary

This essay title requires a *critical* examination of conditions and warranties, the consequences of their breach and the development of the innominate term. In particular, students must be able to make both a close analysis of the leading cases and display a critical awareness of the problems which have shaped the new developments in the law. In conclusion, an appraisal should be undertaken of the relative merits of orthodox conditions and warranties as compared with the innominate term.

- Explain what is meant by the classification of contract terms as either conditions or warranties.

- How, and when, is the differentiation made between conditions and warranties? Do the consequences of the breach of contract play any part in this evaluation?

- Explain what is meant by an 'innominate term'. Has the development of this term brought greater flexibility to this area of the law of contract?

- Are there any instances where a prior classification of contract terms as either conditions or warranties may still have significance?

⌀ Suggested answer

The promissory obligations of a contract are its terms, classified as either conditions or warranties. Conditions are the important and fundamental obligations whereas warranties are less important, subsidiary promises. In the nineteenth century 'warranty' was often used by the judges to encompass all contract terms and the strict, two-fold demarcation is relatively recent, having been expedited by a definition of these phrases in the Sale of Goods Act 1893 (see now the Sale of Goods Act 1979, ss. 11(3) and 61). Most importantly, a breach of condition allows the innocent party to repudiate or affirm the contract and claim damages in either case whereas a breach of warranty allows only a claim in damages. The overriding notion of freedom of contract means that the court must assess the parties' intentions in order to decide whether a particular statement or clause in a written contract is a condition or a warranty. Alternatively, statute may dictate that certain implied terms are conditions as in the Sale of Goods Act 1979, ss. 12–15. The distinction is a crucial one as the right to repudiate is of such importance: an unscrupulous party must not be allowed to use a breach of condition as a sham, enabling him to evade his contractual obligations with the concomitant opportunity of entering into a more profitable contract with a third party. It is vital to establish how the differentiation is made between the two types of term and whether the courts will always pay paramount attention to the parties' intentions.

The orthodox theory is that conditions and warranties are determinable as such at the date of the contract. This approach has two peculiarities. First, it is based upon the assumption that there is some essential substance which defines these obligations in the abstract and, secondly, it takes no account of the seriousness of the breach and its consequences. It is arguable that the only reason which justifies one party's repudiation is a breach by the other party which goes to the root of the contract meaning that further performance is futile. Nevertheless, many undertakings have become definitive conditions by virtue of commercial usage, the operation of the doctrine of precedent and statutory implied terms which are expressly declared to be conditions. In *Arcos Ltd* v *EA Ronaasen & Son* [1933] AC 470, the contract was to sell wooden staves of half-an-inch thick for making cement barrels. Only a small percentage conformed with the specification but the remainder were nearly all less than nine-sixteenths of an inch thick. Although this made no difference to the manufacture of cement barrels (i.e., the goods were merchantable and fit for their purpose) it was held that the buyer was entitled to reject the entire consignment for breach of the implied condition of description in s. 13 of the Sale of Goods Act 1893. There was evidence that the motive for the buyer's rejection was that the market price of timber had fallen. A similar conclusion was reached regarding a breach of condition occasioning no loss in *Re Moore & Co. and Landauer & Co.* [1921] 2 KB 519, where Scrutton LJ pointed out that the breach *might* have had drastic consequences. With respect, such a hypothesis did nothing to justify the repudiation where there was no loss on the facts. This tunnel-vision has little to commend it and developments in recent years are infinitely preferable.

First, where the contract labels its terms as conditions or warranties the court must attempt to implement the parties' intentions, but it is clear that the form of the contract should not be allowed to dictate its substance or injustice would surely follow. *Schuler (L) AG v Wickman Machine Tool Sales Ltd* [1974] AC 235 concerned a 'condition' in a four-and-a-half-year distributorship agreement that the distributor, Wickman, should visit six named customers once a week to solicit orders. This entailed an approximate total of 1,400 visits during the subsistence of the contract. Clause 11 of the contract provided that either party might determine it if the other committed 'a material breach' of its obligations. The House of Lords refused to accept the contention that a single failure to make a visit should allow Schuler to repudiate the entire contract. Lord Reid said that the House was trying to discover intention as disclosed by the contract as a whole and whilst the use of 'condition' was a strong indication of intention, it was not conclusive. He considered that 'the fact that a particular construction leads to a very unreasonable result must be a relevant consideration. The more unreasonable the result the more unlikely it is that the parties can have intended it'.

Secondly, the development of the innominate or intermediate term introduces a more logical flexibility to this area of law. In *Hongkong Fir Shipping Co. Ltd v Kawasaki Kisen Kaisha Ltd* [1962] 2 QB 26, the Court of Appeal emphasised that the orthodox division of conditions and warranties could be rigid and inflexible in operation, meaning that a negligible breach of condition might allow repudiation whilst only damages would be available for a catastrophic breach of warranty. The condition that a ship should be seaworthy could thus be breached across a spectrum of possibilities from inconsequential inconveniences at one extreme to calamities involving substantial loss at the other. Diplock LJ held that such undertakings could not be categorised as conditions or warranties but that the legal consequences of the breach should 'depend upon the nature of the event to which the breach gives rise and . . . not . . . from a prior classification'.

The *Hongkong* reasoning has been endorsed in subsequent decisions. In *Cehave NV v Bremer Handelsgesellschaft mbH, The Hansa Nord* [1976] QB 44, the contract was for the sale of citrus pulp pellets for use in animal food. The contract price was £100,000, an express term being that the goods should be shipped 'in good condition'. The buyer sought to reject the goods for a relatively minor breach. In fact, the market in such goods had fallen dramatically at the delivery date and the buyer eventually bought the same goods from a third party for £30,000 *and* used the pellets for cattle food. The buyer argued that rejection was permissible under both the statutory implied condition of merchantability and the express condition relating to quality. The court held that the Sale of Goods Act did not exhaustively define all obligations as either conditions or warranties and that the express provision was an innominate term, breach of which, on the facts, did not permit rejection of the goods. The court assumed that merchantability was an immutable statutory condition but that, on the facts, the sellers were not in breach of that condition. The notion of the innominate term was similarly approved by the House of Lords in *Reardon Smith Line Ltd* v *Yngvar Hansen-Tangen* [1976] 1 WLR 989 with Lord Wilberforce casting doubt upon the decisions in *Arcos* and *Re Moore*, considering them 'excessively technical' and probably applicable only to their facts.

Although the innominate term is an attractively logical proposition, there may nevertheless be instances where the necessity for commercial certainty and predictability demand that the parties should be able to allocate the risks of the contract at the time of its formation. This is particularly so if there is no disparity of bargaining strength between them. Provisions relating to *time* are often crucial as are the precise descriptions of unascertained, future goods, such as a sale of commodities. In *The Mihalis Angelos* [1971] 1 QB 164, for example, a stipulation as to when a ship should be 'expected ready to load' under a charterparty was held to be a condition and, likewise, a notice of readiness to load in *Bunge Corporation* v *Tradax Export SA* [1981] 1 WLR 711.

Thirdly, the Sale of Goods Act 1979, s. 15A now provides that where the buyer 'does not deal as consumer' and the breach of any of the implied conditions in ss. 13–15 is 'so slight that it would be unreasonable for him to reject [the goods]', the breach 'is not to be treated as a breach of condition but may be treated as a breach of warranty'. The principal target of s. 15A is thus the decision in *Arcos Ltd* v *EA Ronaasen & Son*, referred to earlier (see also the SGA, s. 30(2A)). However, s. 15A(2) allows the parties to exclude expressly the operation of s. 15A.

In conclusion, there is still room to implement the definitive intentions of the parties expressed as conditions and warranties. Lord Wilberforce dissented vigorously in *Schuler* and would not assume 'contrary to the evidence, that both parties to this contract adopted a standard of easygoing tolerance rather than one of aggressive, insistent punctuality and efficiency'. Such tensions will always be present where freedom of contract meets policy-interventionism but combining innominate terms with the orthodox classification of conditions and warranties allows the courts to tread a middle-path between rigid, and sometimes unjust rules on one side, and indeterminate flexibility on the other.

Q Question 2

In contracts for the sale of goods, the development of the statutory implied terms relating to the description, quality and fitness for purpose of the goods sold has reflected changing social needs and recognised the vulnerable position of the consumer buyer. However, the latest EU Directive concerning consumer guarantees carries consumer protection to new heights.

Discuss.

Commentary

The essay title calls for knowledge of the development of the statutory implied terms in sales of goods from the Sale of Goods Act 1893 to the present Act of 1979. As the question mentions 'changing social needs' it invites a discussion of the way the implied terms have been adapted throughout a period of 100 years to cope with disparity in bargaining power. A knowledge of the extent to which the implied terms may be excluded is also clearly very important to the answer. The question seeks a broad, critical awareness of the problems in this area, rather than intimate detail concerning the *substance* of the implied terms. An appraisal of the recent European Directive (99/44/EC, 25 May 1999) on *Certain Aspects of the Sale of Consumer Goods and Associated Guarantees*, is also required.

- Explain the purpose and scope of the implied terms relating to description, quality and fitness for purpose in the (original) Sale of Goods Act 1893.

- Originally, these implied terms could be freely excluded or varied: was this just and realistic in 1893?

- What were the changing commercial conditions which rendered this policy of unrestricted exclusion unjust and unrealistic?

- How does current legislation ensure that consumers are protected from the exclusion of the implied terms whilst business buyers and sellers are at liberty to apportion risks under their contract?

- What are the key provisions of the EU Directive on *Certain Aspects of the Sale of Consumer Goods and Associated Guarantees*?

☼ Suggested answer

The Sale of Goods Act 1893 was a radical piece of legislation in that it attempted to codify the common law concerning the sale of goods. During the nineteenth century the courts had developed the notion of *caveat emptor* (let the buyer take care) but, significantly, the 1893 Act introduced statutory implied terms relating to the description, quality and fitness for purpose of the goods sold. These implied terms had a logical scheme reflecting the Act's purpose in prescribing broad statutory standards for *commercial* sales of goods. The object of the Act was thus to draw a distinction between specific goods and those bought by description. In relation to specific goods the rules did not favour the buyer as, normally, he could inspect the goods and make his own judgment as to their quality. *Caveat emptor* therefore applied to specific goods, there being no implied term as to their quality. However, the buyer could make his specific purpose known to the seller and, if he did so, there was an implied condition that the goods should be reasonably fit for that purpose. In relation to sales by description however, there was an implied condition that the goods should reach a standard of merchantable quality. In fact, litigants were unsure of the meaning of both 'merchantable' (the word was not defined in the Act) and 'sale by description' and the particular purpose provisions seemed more accessible — they were consequently invoked more often with the result that the courts gave this provision an extended interpretation. Moreover, as the first hurdle in a complaint regarding merchantability was to prove that the sale was 'by description', description was similarly broadened in meaning by the courts. The courts therefore ensured protection for both commercial buyers and the increasingly common phenomenon in the twentieth century of the private 'consumer' buyer.

Reflecting *laissez-faire* philosophy, s. 55 of the 1893 Act allowed the implied conditions to be freely 'negatived or varied by express agreement or by the course of dealing between the parties, or by usage'. Based upon the premise of rough equality of bargaining power between commercial buyers and sellers, this provision was undoubtedly reasonable and allowed the parties freedom to allocate risks under their contract. However, *laissez-faire* ideals could not foresee the changed nature of commerce which developed in the twentieth century. Large retailers selling to private consumers began to deploy written standard-form contracts with ample exclusion clauses negating or restricting the Sale of Goods Act implied terms. The contract of adhesion combined with inequality of bargaining power meant that the aspect of freedom of contract which began to dominate was freedom to exploit the weaker party. It was with the Supply of Goods (Implied Terms) Act 1973 that radical provisions were introduced restricting the seller's ability to exclude the implied terms. In relation to consumer buyers, attempts at excluding the implied terms relating to quality and fitness were rendered void, but those implied terms could be excluded between two businesses provided the exclusion clause could pass a 'reasonableness' test.

By 1973 the function of the implied terms had thus changed in recognition of social needs. For the consumer, the implied terms provided a strict code of standards which could not be excluded, a development which could not possibly have been envisaged by the 1893 Act. Yet there were still thought to be weaknesses in the buyer's protection: the 1973 Act meant that an exclusion of the implied terms was void but it did not *prevent* the attempted exclusion of the implied terms. Unscrupulous sellers thus continued to display exclusion clauses and deploy them in contracts until the practice was rendered a criminal offence by the Consumer Transactions (Restrictions on Statements) Order 1976 made under The Fair Trading Act 1973. The basic scheme of the Supply of Goods (Implied Terms) Act 1973 was re-enacted in the Unfair Contract Terms Act 1977, ss. 6 and 12, the latter section providing a comprehensive definition of 'dealing as consumer'.

An insidious practice appears to be growing which may deprive buyers of the protection of the implied terms without infringing the statutory controls. The seller may attempt to define or 'shrink the core' of his obligations by, for example, warning that the buyer should examine the goods and rely on his own judgement. The extent of the seller's obligations may thus be *shaped* rather than excluded or restricted. In *Harlingdon and Leinster Enterprises Ltd* v *Christopher Hull Fine Art Ltd* [1991] 1 QB 564, the seller had two paintings by Gabriele Münter for sale which were examined by the buyer. The seller told the buyer that he did not like the paintings and had never heard before of the artist. A price of £6,000 was agreed and an invoice supplied with the artist's name and lifespan. Although the picture was subsequently revealed to be a forgery, the Court of Appeal held that this was not a sale by description within s. 13 of the Sale of Goods Act 1979, as the buyer had not *relied upon* any description. Stuart-Smith LJ dissented and particularly warned against the practice of allowing vague statements as to the limited expertise and knowledge of the seller to nullify the protection of the statutory implied condition within s. 13.

The implied terms of the Sale of Goods Act 1979 have proved to be infinitely adaptable and have performed an excellent function in protecting the consumer buyer by implying a paradigm set of contract terms which cannot be excluded whilst allowing business buyers and sellers the requisite degree of freedom to contract on equal terms. It is arguable that *Harlingdon* falls into this latter category, but vigilance is needed to ensure that the practice endorsed by the decision does not start to erode the protection which the law sees fit to afford consumer buyers of goods.

Substantial amendments to the Sale of Goods Act 1979 (SGA) will be needed as a consequence of the new EU Directive (99/44/EC, 25 May 1999) on *Certain Aspects of the Sale of Consumer Goods and Associated Guarantees*. Although the Directive should have been implemented in Great Britain by 1 January 2002, it has been delayed and will not become law until 2003. The new Directive applies only where *businesses* deal with *consumers* and, most significantly, the new provisions will add considerably to the range of remedies available to consumers. Article 1 delineates the scope of the Directive and defines the relevant parties. 'Consumer' is defined in art. 1(2)(a) as 'any natural person who, in the contracts covered by this Directive, is acting for purposes which are not related to his trade, business or profession'. 'Seller' means 'any natural or legal person who, under a contract, sells consumer goods in the course of his trade, business or profession' (art. 1(2)(c)). 'Consumer goods' are also defined very widely in art. 1(2)(b) as 'any tangible movable item' with the exception of water and gas (where 'they are not put up for sale in a limited volume or set quantity'), electricity and 'goods sold by way of execution or otherwise by authority of law'. It is thus clear that 'consumer goods' are not restricted to those which are normally supplied to consumers; on the contrary, the definition encompasses goods which are normally supplied only to businesses, e.g., cement mixers.

Undoubtedly, the new provisions are aimed primarily at sales of new, consumer goods made directly between a business seller and a consumer buyer. However, whilst the definition of a 'seller' demands that he must sell the goods, the 'consumer' who seeks a remedy need not *buy* the goods from that seller. Article 2(1) provides that 'the seller must *deliver* goods to the consumer which are in conformity with the contract of sale' and so it is plain that the seller could sell consumer goods to a buyer who is either a consumer or a non-consumer, with a condition that the goods be delivered to a consumer donee who will then have the rights and remedies against the seller which are prescribed under the Directive. This will constitute a revolutionary reform for English law as the implied conditions in the SGA 1979 currently apply only where the seller and buyer have a direct contract of sale.

Article 2 is the central core of the Directive as it provides that the 'seller must deliver goods to the consumer which are in conformity with the contract of sale'. Article 2(2) delineates the requirements of the notion of 'conformity' (e.g., goods must 'comply with the description given by the seller') and here many of the Directive's demands will already be realized by the implied conditions in the SGA 1979, ss. 13–15. In one respect, however, art. 2(2)(d) is revolutionary. In assessing the quality which the consumer can 'reasonably expect', account must be taken of 'any public statements on the specific characteristics of the goods made about them by the seller, the producer or his representative, particularly in advertising or on labelling'. The Directive uses the phrase 'public statements' and this is aimed, principally, at advertisements. The new provisions will enable consumers to rely on advertising produced by a *manufacturer* of the goods when seeking to render the *seller* liable where those goods are not in conformity with the contract of sale. It is suggested that the extra liability imposed on a seller by art. 2(2)(d) does not seem unreasonable in the light of modern advertising and marketing practices by which consumers are attracted directly to brand-name goods because of the manufacturer's claims.

The Directive clarifies the position regarding time-limits and consumer claims for redress in that art. 5(1) provides that the seller shall be liable 'where the lack of conformity becomes apparent within two years as from delivery of the goods'. This provision is not intended to impose a two-year durability requirement for consumer goods, as art. 3(1) provides that the non-conformity of the goods must exist at the date of *delivery*. Under English law, a buyer has six years in which to pursue a claim for goods which can be shown to have been defective at the time of delivery but, in some Member States, the consumer can lose his right to complain of defective goods very soon after delivery. Indeed, this conclusion might currently be reached in English law if the consumer is deemed to have accepted the goods under the SGA 1979, s. 35. Accordingly, art. 5(1) will improve consumer rights in those countries where the lack of conformity was present at the date of delivery but a defect materializes subsequently in the two-year period. It should also be emphasized that art. 5(1) does not impose a limitation period in the sense that the consumer must commence proceedings within the two-year period. Provided that the defects were present at the date of delivery and became apparent within the two-year period, the consumer may commence proceedings at any time within the limitation period prescribed by national law. Should a Member State have a period of limitation which is less than two years, art. 5(1) will, of course, effectively extend that period to two years.

As regards time-limits, art. 5(3) introduces an important new right for consumers in providing that 'unless proved otherwise, any lack of conformity which becomes apparent within six months of delivery of the goods shall be presumed to have existed at the time of delivery unless this presumption is incompatible with the nature of the goods or the nature of the lack of conformity'. This rebuttable presumption has caused concern amongst many retailers who fear that it will lead to an increase in fraudulent claims being made, but this assertion overlooks the fact that the presumption is not applicable where it is 'incompatible with the nature of the goods or the nature of the lack of conformity'. This indicates that the presumption will apply only where the nature of the goods means that it would be unusual for defects to appear in six months and the stress on the nature of the lack of conformity means that sellers can establish, where apt, that the goods have been mistreated or maintained inadequately by the consumer.

Finally, art. 6(1) provides that 'a guarantee shall be legally binding on the offerer under the conditions laid down in the guarantee statement and the associated advertising'. This provision relates to the standard, commercial guarantees offered by sellers or manufacturers of goods. The legal status of manufacturers' guarantees has always been in doubt because, where the buyer has no direct contract with the manufacturer, the difficulties of consideration and intent to create legal relations are formidable hurdles placed in the path of enforceability. In view of these difficulties, art. 6(1) is welcome in providing that guarantees shall become legally binding.

Q Question 3

Steven advertises in an antiques journal that he has an aeroplane for sale. The advertisement appears on 1 March and reads:

> A rare opportunity to acquire a collector's item. A bi-plane which belonged to the early flying ace, Sir George Ditcher, has come on the market for the first time. Sir George was an early member of the Royal Flying Corps and was the person upon whom Wiggles, the fictional flying hero, was based. £85,000, or nearest offer.

Boris, the owner of a museum dedicated to items connected with the First World War, contacts Steven on 15 March to discuss the sale. Steven shows Boris a large collection of letters written by Sir George Ditcher which describe an aeroplane of the same type as the one offered for sale as 'my little buzz-bomb'. He also points out numerous letters written to Sir George Ditcher by the author of the Wiggles books. On 10 April, Boris agrees to buy the aeroplane for £85,000 and a brief written contract is entered into which makes no mention of Sir George Ditcher or Wiggles.

Boris displays the bi-plane at his museum describing it as 'previously owned by Sir George Ditcher, the real-life Wiggles'. It has now been established that, although he did fly it, the aeroplane never belonged to Sir George Ditcher and that there were ten other people who had as strong a claim as Sir George Ditcher to be the basis of the Wiggles character.

Advise Boris.

Commentary

This question focuses upon the terms of the contract and their breach. Three broad questions should be answered. First, where is the contract to be found? Secondly, what are its terms? Thirdly, what remedies exist if the seller is in breach of a term of the contract? It is important to keep this chronological progression if a logical and readable answer is sought. There is a large amount of material to include in this question and not all points can be given equal weight — for example, reference should be made to misrepresentation but not in any depth. A good student will show the examiner an overall knowledge of the area and be able to put the law in perspective when delineating the options available to the disgruntled buyer.

- Explain briefly the advantages of establishing a statement as a term of the contract. Might misrepresentation provide an attractive remedy for Boris?

- As there is an advertisement describing the aeroplane, the parties have personal negotiations and a written contract is entered into, where are the terms of this contract of sale to be found? What are the tests for deciding if a statement is a term of the contract?

- Once the terms of the contract have been located, it must be decided whether they are conditions, warranties or innominate terms. How is this achieved?

- As this is a contract for the sale of goods, might the implied terms of the Sale of Goods Act 1979 provide the most desirable remedy for Boris or should he seek to establish breach of an express term of the contract?

:Q: Suggested answer

This question concerns terms of the contract and remedies for breach of a term. Not all statements are contractual in nature as some may be mere representations or commendatory 'puffs' which, if true, lack any legal value. It is obvious that a seller of goods must be able to praise them *within a certain latitude* without legal consequence but if his statements are untrue statements of fact which induce the buyer to enter into the contract, an action may lie in misrepresentation. If the parties have a contract, it is natural to think of contractual remedies first and misrepresentation second and that was certainly the position prior to the Misrepresentation Act 1967. However, s. 2(1) of that Act introduced potent remedies for negligent misrepresentation and placed the burden of discharging negligence on the representor. This is therefore an attractive remedy but there are still advantages in proving a term. If the contract is in writing the term may be easier to prove than a misrepresentation. Secondly, it is not an essential requirement that a term must *induce* the buyer and, thirdly, although the statement constituting the term is usually one of fact, there is no requirement that it *must* be. Where is the contract to be found between Steven and Boris and what are its terms?

It was established in *Heilbut, Symons & Co.* v *Buckleton* [1913] AC 30 that *intention* is the overall guide as to whether a statement is a term of the contract. This test emphasises the intent of the *maker of the statement* in asking if he warranted its truth and accuracy rather than merely expressing an opinion, and it is criticisable in that it does not sufficiently accentuate the effect of the statement on the other party and his justifiable *reliance* upon it. More recent cases have tended to emphasise these factors and in *Evans (J) & Son (Portsmouth) Ltd* v *Andrea Merzario Ltd* [1976] 1 WLR 1078, Lord Denning, referring to *Heilbut*, said that 'much of what was said in that case is entirely out of date'. Sub-divisions of the single test of intention can be attempted in this context however.

First, a lengthy interval between the making of the relevant statement and the conclusion of the contract may indicate that the statement does not have contractual force. In *Routledge* v *McKay* [1954] 1 WLR 615 an interval of one week between statement and contract was sufficient to deny any contractual intent to the statement. There it was the sale of a motorcycle but much depends on the facts, and if the contract and its subject matter are complicated, longer time must be allowed in order to verify statements. The interval of some five weeks between advertisement and contract is thus not necessarily fatal to Boris's claim.

Secondly, the courts are influenced in their decision by any special knowledge that the maker of the statement may possess. It is presumed that an owner of goods knows their condition and consequent weight attaches to his statements (see *Harling* v *Eddy* [1951] 2 KB 739 — owner of a heifer who 'absolutely guaranteed' her sound condition) but it is possible that Boris, as an expert on the First World War, knows more than Steven and should have verified the statements in the five weeks before contract. This reasoning was influential in the decision in *Oscar Chess Ltd* v *Williams* [1957] 1 WLR 370, where it was held that the statement of a car's age made by its owner was not a term of the contract as the claimant car dealer had specialist knowledge and could/should have verified the statement. This test may therefore militate against Boris.

Thirdly, it is important to assess the overall importance of the statement in the light of the contract and its effect on the other party. Is the statement both crucial and pivotal in the contract's formation? In *Schawel* v *Reade* [1913] 2 IR 64 and *Bannerman* v

White (1861) 10 CB (NS) 844 this test meant that the statements were terms. In *Schawel*, the buyer stopped his examination of a horse when he was told that it was sound, and in *Bannerman*, a buyer of hops asked whether they had been treated with sulphur adding that he would not bother to ask the price if they had been so treated. Similarly, in *Esso Petroleum Co. Ltd* v *Mardon* [1978] QB 801 the defendant's doubts as to the claimant's forecasted 'throughput' of petrol were quelled by the latter, and the statement was thus held to be a term. It is arguable that the provenance of the aeroplane is the dominant factor in this contract as evidenced by the fact that it is displayed with its history at Boris's museum.

Finally, the presence of a written contract might indicate that the parties' intentions are crystallised therein. The parol evidence rule is surrounded by countless exceptions and it is quite possible to have a contract which is partly written and partly oral *if the parties so intend* (*Couchman* v *Hill* [1947] KB 554 — oral assurance dominated the written sale catalogue). Alternatively, the court might construe the statements regarding the aeroplane's history as a collateral contract, thereby avoiding the parol evidence rule. In *Andrews* v *Hopkinson* [1957] 1 QB 229, for example, the claimant had a primary contract with a finance company to take a car on hire-purchase and a collateral contract with the defendant car dealer that it was 'a good little bus'. It is suggested that Boris may succeed in establishing a term but subject to the *caveat* that he is a specialist/expert buyer who cannot be bothered to provide for his requirements in a written contract. As some prominent recent decisions show a distinct tendency to revert to nineteenth century principles of *laissez-faire* (e.g. *Photo Production Ltd* v *Securicor Transport Ltd* [1980] AC 827) a court might thus castigate Boris's laxity.

If the statements are terms of the contract it must be decided whether they are conditions, warranties or innominate terms. A condition is a major stipulation which allows the innocent party either to repudiate or affirm the contract and claim damages in both cases whereas a warranty sounds only in damages. Again, the distinction between these two types of term depends upon the parties' intentions at the date of contract. As the statements are not in the written contract they cannot be *labelled* as either conditions or warranties and the contract is not one of an established commercial type where precedent may classify certain undertakings as conditions (e.g. insurance or carriage of goods by sea). It is likely that the court would consider the statements regarding the aeroplane to be innominate terms which means that, instead of a prior classification of contract terms, the effects of the breach will provide the necessary yardstick for the court's decision. In *Reardon Smith Line Ltd* v *Yngvar Hansen-Tangen* [1976] 1 WLR 989, for example, it was held that a different numbering of a ship (showing the yard where it was built) from the one specified in the contract was insufficient to allow rejection of the vessel when it was up to specification in every other respect. It is arguable that the statements regarding the aeroplane cause a serious breach which goes to the root of the obligation thereby allowing Boris to repudiate the contract. On the facts of the problem, damages alone could not compensate Boris for this breach.

It is imperative that Boris attempts to establish an express term of the contract as it would appear that the implied terms of the Sale of Goods Act 1979 will be of little avail. The implied conditions in s. 14 relating to satisfactory quality and fitness for purpose probably do not extend beyond physically defective goods; for example, in *Harlingdon and Leinster Enterprises Ltd* v *Christopher Hull Fine Art Ltd* [1991] 1 QB 564, a forged painting was held not to be physically defective. Moreover, s. 13 relating to the description of the goods would seem to be equally ineffective on the facts of the problem. The reason for this is that, apart from commercial sales of future, unascertained goods where description is crucial, the courts have restricted s. 13 to descriptive words which *identify the subject-matter* of the contract. This involves a metaphysical distinction between the subject-matter of the contract and its attributes but, as defective food was still held to be food in *Ashington Piggeries Ltd* v *Christopher Hill Ltd* [1972] AC 441, it is very arguable that Boris has nevertheless bought an aeroplane, there being compliance with the essence of the bargain within s. 13.

Exclusion Clauses

Introduction

An exclusion clause is a term of the contract which attempts to exclude or restrict one party's liability which he would otherwise owe to the other. In the nineteenth century, at the high-water mark of freedom of contract, such clauses were regarded as unexceptional, their use being viewed as a legitimate exercise of bargaining power. It was principally in the twentieth century that there was a growth in the disparity of bargaining strengths between the parties, with the consequence that the economically superior party was sometimes able to impose his will on the weaker party. This situation escalated as limited liability companies amalgamated and deployed standard form contracts with ample exclusion clauses offered on a take it or leave it basis. These contracts consequently became known as contracts of adhesion. The courts were hampered by the theory of freedom of contract and consequently unable to prohibit exclusion clauses, but within this theory they developed strict rules relating to the incorporation of such clauses as terms of the contract as well as interpreting them *contra proferentem*. Statute, however, is not thus confined by theory and may take the bold step, for example, of both rendering void certain exclusion clauses and stipulating that any attempt to use them should be a criminal offence.

Common Law Restrictions upon Exclusion Clauses

Signature

A party who signs a document containing an exclusion clause is normally bound by its terms irrespective of the degree of notice given and whether he has read it (see *Parker* v *South Eastern Ry* (1877) 2 CPD 416; *L'Estrange* v *F Graucob Ltd* [1934] 2 KB 394). Should the signature have been exacted by fraud or misrepresentation, however, it will not bind the signatory (see *Curtis* v *Chemical Cleaning and Dyeing Co.* [1951] 1 KB 805).

Adequate Notice

Most commonly, the document containing the conditions is handed to one party and, in this case, he must receive adequate *notice* of the terms although he need not have *read* the document in order to be bound by its terms (see *Parker*, above). Indeed, it is irrelevant if the party receiving the document is illiterate or blind (see *Thompson* v *L M & S Ry* [1930] 1 KB

41). Whether adequate notice has been given is a question of fact but cases of inadequate notice include terms obscured by a printed date stamp (see *Richardson, Spence & Co. v Rowntree* [1894] AC 217) and conditions printed on the reverse of a document with no notice of them on its face (see *Henderson v Steven* (1875) LR 2 HL (Sc) 470). If the particular clause relied upon is unusually wide or onerous, it may require unusually explicit notice (see *Thornton v Shoe Lane Parking Ltd* [1971] 2 QB 163; *Interfoto Picture Library Ltd v Stiletto Visual Programmes Ltd* [1989] QB 433).

Pre-Contractual Notice

The exclusion clause must be drawn to the attention of the other party before or at the time the contract is entered into, the courts preserving the maximum discretion as to the moment of the contract's completion (see *Olley v Marlborough Court Ltd* [1949] 1 KB 532; *Thornton*, above).

Contractual Document

The document containing the exclusion clauses must be one which a reasonable man would expect to contain contract terms and, again, the courts preserve a wide discretion in deciding this question in cases, for example, involving tickets and receipts (see *Chapelton v Barry UDC* [1940] 1 KB 532; *Burnett v Westminster Bank* [1966] 1 QB 742; *McCutcheon v MacBrayne (David) Ltd* [1964] 1 WLR 125; *Thornton*, above).

Course of Dealing

The court may infer notice of the exclusion clause from a consistent course of dealing between the parties, e.g., the relevant document containing the exclusion clause sent consistently to the other party, post-contractually, over a period of ten years (see *Spurling (J) Ltd v Bradshaw* [1956] 1 WLR 461; *Hollier v Rambler Motors (AMC) Ltd* [1972] 2 QB 71; *Kendall (Henry) & Sons v Lillico (William) & Sons Ltd* [1969] 2 AC 31). Such an incorporation of terms may be easier where both parties are businesses of equal bargaining power (see *British Crane Hire Corp. Ltd v Ipswich Plant Hire Ltd* [1975] QB 303).

Common Law Rules of Construction and Interpretation

Exclusion clauses must be clear and unequivocal or they will be inoperative, the common law's interpretation being *contra proferentem* (see *Baldry v Marshall* [1925] 1 KB 260; *Andrews Bros Ltd v Singer & Co. Ltd* [1934] 1 KB 17; *Webster v Higgin* [1948] 2 All ER 127; *Houghton v Trafalgar Insurance Co. Ltd* [1954] 1 QB 247). The courts have particularly strict rules of construction where there is an attempted exclusion of liability in negligence and will construe any doubt regarding the ambit of the clause against the *proferens* (see the guidance given in *Alderslade v Hendon Laundry Ltd* [1945] 1 KB 189; *Canada Steamship Lines Ltd v The King* [1952] AC 192; *White v John Warwick & Co. Ltd* [1953] 1 WLR 1285; *Lamport & Holt Lines Ltd v Coubro & Scrutton (M & I) Ltd* [1982] 2 Lloyd's Rep 42).

These rules of interpretation have undoubtedly become less significant since the advent of the Unfair Contract Terms Act 1977 and the courts have warned against a strained and hostile construction of clauses (see *Ailsa Craig Fishing Co. Ltd* v *Malvern Fishing Co. Ltd* [1983] 1 WLR 964; *George Mitchell (Chesterhall) Ltd* v *Finney Lock Seeds Ltd* [1983] 2 AC 803).

Exclusion Clauses and Fundamental Breach of Contract

There is a clear authority for the notion that certain obligations in contracts are fundamental to the entire undertaking such that their non-performance amounts to a failure to perform the *contract itself* (see *Chanter* v *Hopkins* (1838) 4 M & W 399). The common law considered that such a fundamental breach could not be excluded or restricted in any circumstances as this would amount to giving with one hand and taking with the other. This non-applicability of exclusion clauses to fundamental breaches thus became elevated as a *rule of law* (see *Pinnock Bros* v *Lewis and Peat* [1923] 1 KB 690; *Karsales (Harrow) Ltd* v *Wallis* [1956] 1 WLR 936). The rule of law approach was rejected in *UGS Finance Ltd* v *National Mortgage Bank of Greece* [1964] 1 Lloyd's Rep 446, on the basis that it conflicted with freedom of contract and the intention of the parties; rather, the question of whether a clause could exclude liability for a fundamental breach was held to be a question of construction. The *UGS* case was unanimously approved by the House of Lords in *Suisse Atlantique Société d'Armement Maritime SA* v *NV Rotterdamshe Kolen Centrale* [1967] 1 AC 361 and the rule of construction put beyond doubt by *Photo Production Ltd* v *Securicor Transport Ltd* [1980] AC 827. After this decision, it seems that there is not even a presumption that the parties do not intend an exclusion clause to apply to a fundamental breach.

The Unfair Contract Terms Act 1977

The Unfair Contract Terms Act 1977 has three broad areas of control but does not interfere with the common law concerning the *integration* of an exclusion clause in the contract. First, exclusion of liability for negligence, secondly, general control of exclusion clauses which seek to exclude or restrict one party's liability for breach of contract, and thirdly, control over certain specific contract terms which exclude or restrict liability for breach of certain terms implied by statute in the sale of goods, hire purchase and supply of goods. If the Act applies to the clause in question, control may take one of two forms: the clause may be rendered absolutely void and ineffective or it may be effective only to the extent that it satisfies the test of reasonableness.

Liability for Negligence

Section 2 restricts the ability of one party to exclude his business liability (see ss. 1(3) and 14) for negligence (see s. 1(1)). He cannot by reference to any contract term or a notice, exclude or restrict his liability for death or personal injury resulting from negligence (s. 2(1)). In the case of other loss or damage, he cannot exclude or restrict his liability *except* in so far as the term satisfies the test of reasonableness (s. 2(2)).

Liability in Contract

Section 3 applies generally to contract liability but one of the contracting parties must 'deal as consumer' *or* on the other's 'written standard terms of business'. The section then specifies that one party cannot, by reference to any contract term, exclude or restrict his own liability for breach of contract or render any performance substantially different from that expected of him, or render no performance at all, *except* in so far as the term satisfies the test of reasonableness.

The Sale of Goods and Hire-Purchase

Section 6 provides that the statutory implied obligations as to quality, fitness for purpose, etc., in sale and hire-purchase contracts cannot be excluded or restricted by reference to any contract term as against someone 'dealing as consumer', but for non-consumers the exclusion is possible *if* the clause passes the reasonableness test. Furthermore, the section stipulates that the statutory implied undertaking as to title *cannot* be excluded in either the consumer or non-consumer category. See s. 7 for the corresponding provisions in other miscellaneous contracts. See s. 12 for the definition of 'deals as consumer' and *R & B Customs Brokers Co. Ltd* v *United Dominions Trust Ltd* [1988] 1 WLR 321.

Other Major Provisions

Section 4 — a person 'dealing as consumer' cannot be made, by the use of a contract term, to indemnify another for liability arising from the other's negligence or breach of contract unless the term is reasonable (see *Thompson* v *Lohan (Plant Hire) Ltd* [1987] 1 WLR 649).

Section 5 — renders absolutely ineffective provisions in manufacturers' guarantees excluding or restricting liability for loss or damage resulting from the manufacturer's negligence when the goods have proved 'defective' in 'consumer use'.

Section 9 — affirms the common law's approach to fundamental breach.

Section 10 — an anti-avoidance provision which prevents the rights preserved under one contract from being removed by a secondary contract (see *Tudor Grange Holdings Ltd* v *Citibank NA* [1991] 3 WLR 750).

Section 13 — gives a wide definition of an exclusion clause and may be useful for invalidating provisions which seek to *define* liability rather than *exclude* it (see *Smith* v *Eric Bush* [1990] AC 831; *Harlingdon & Leinster Enterprises Ltd* v *Christopher Hull Fine Art Ltd* [1991] 1 QB 564).

Reasonableness under the 1977 Act

This test emphasises that exclusion clauses may be *negotiated* between the parties and thus represent their allocation of risks (see *Photo Production*, above) rather than being *imposed* as in contracts of adhesion. Section 11 provides that, for a contract term, the moment that reasonableness is to be assessed is the time that *the contract is made* but for a notice excluding liability in tort and not having contractual effect, the relevant time is when the *liability arose* and whether it is then reasonable *to rely* on the notice. The test in contract is, therefore, very strict (see *Stewart Gill Ltd* v *Horatio Myer & Co. Ltd* [1992] 1 QB 600). Section 11(4) specifies that if liability is restricted to a specific sum of money, regard is to be had to the resources of the person inserting the clause and whether he could have taken out insurance.

In relation to the substance of the reasonableness test and its assessment, sch. 2 of the Act specifies important factors to which the court must have regard. Although these are not exhaustive and are only expressly applicable for the purposes of ss. 6 and 7, *they are most important and show the balancing exercise which the court must perform.* Reported cases on the reasonableness test are still scarce and some concern the earlier test of reasonable reliance in s. 55 of the Sale of Goods Act 1893. Decisions to consider are: *George Mitchell (Chesterhall) Ltd* v *Finney Lock Seeds Ltd* [1983] 2 AC 803 (old test); *Walker* v *Boyle* [1982] 1 WLR 495; *Stag Line Ltd* v *Tyne Shiprepair Group Ltd* [1984] 2 Lloyd's Rep 211; *Phillips Products Ltd* v *Hyland* [1987] 1 WLR 659; *Stewart Gill, supra; St Alban's City and District Council* v *International Computers Ltd* [1996] 4 All ER 481.

Unfair Terms in Consumer Contracts Regulations 1999

The original Unfair Terms in Consumer Contracts Regulations 1994 (SI 1994, No. 3159) came into force on 1 July 1995 in order to implement an EC Council Directive (93/13/EEC) *Unfair Terms in Consumer Contracts,* but the 1999 Regulations (SI 1999, No. 2083), which came into force on 1 October 1999, revoke and replace the original Regulations and reflect more closely the wording of the Directive.

The wording of the Unfair Terms in Consumer Contracts Regulations 1999 (UTCCR) has been clarified and the powers of enforcement granted by them have been extended considerably. In terms of substance, there is one significant change from the position under the 1994 Regulations. Previously, the UTCCR 1994 applied only to the business supply of goods and services to consumers under the terms of a standard-form contract, and there was doubt as to whether interests in land were covered. However, the amended definition of a 'supplier' in the 1999 Regulations omits any reference to goods and services. It is thus clear that standard-form business contracts for the supply to consumers of goods, services and interests in land, are within the 1999 Regulations.

The purpose of the Directive was to harmonize the laws of Member States of the EC and ensure that contracts with consumers did not contain unfair terms but, regrettably, no attempt was made to dovetail the UTCCR with the Unfair Contract Terms Act 1977 (UCTA 1977). The result is a complex, overlapping set of rules which is most undesirable in the sphere of consumer protection where remedies should be accessible and understandable. A contract term can thus be subject to both the UTCCR and the UCTA 1977, and this means that a term might satisfy the requirements of the Act and yet fail the requirements imposed by UTCCR 1999, and vice versa. The overall effect of the UTCCR 1999 is that an 'unfair term' in a contract concluded between a consumer and a seller or supplier 'shall not be binding on the consumer' (reg. 8(1)).

It is important to stress that, ultimately, it is the Directive which is paramount and thus, in interpreting the UTCCR 1999, the court must have regard to the purpose and wording of both the Directive and its recitals (see *Marleasing SA* v *La Comercial Internacional de Alimentacion SA,* Case C-106/89 [1990] ECR I-4135; *Lister* v *Forth Dry Dock and Engineering Co. Ltd* [1990] 1 AC 546).

Scope of the Regulations

The UTCCR reg. 4(1), broadly defines the scope of the regulations:

> ... these Regulations apply in relation to unfair terms in contracts concluded between a seller or supplier and a consumer.

Sellers, Suppliers and Consumers

'Seller' and 'supplier' are defined in reg. 3(1) as 'any natural or legal person who, in contracts covered by these Regulations, is acting for purposes relating to his trade, business or profession, whether publicly owned or privately owned'. The 1994 Regulations previously defined a 'seller' as 'a person who sells goods' and a 'supplier' as 'a person who supplies goods or services'. Most significantly, the new definition omits any reference to selling goods and supplying services. It is thus plain that, whilst the selling of goods and the supply of services is still the most significant target at which the UTCCR 1999 are aimed, the Regulations now cover the creation or transfer of interests in land, e.g., terms contained in tenancy agreements. There is no definition of either 'goods' or 'services' within the UTCCR 1999.

There is, likewise, no definition of a 'trade, business or profession' in the UTCCR 1999, and no further delineation of when the seller or supplier will be regarded as 'acting for purposes relating to' his trade, business or profession. It remains to be seen how this latter phrase will be defined but its counterpart in the UCTA 1977, s. 12 ('makes the contract in the course of a business') has been interpreted by the common law as requiring a *regularity* of business dealings (see *R & B Customs Brokers Co. Ltd* v *United Dominions Trust Ltd* [1988] 1 WLR 321).

'Consumer' is defined in reg. 3(1) as 'any natural person who, in contracts covered by these Regulations, is acting for purposes which are outside his trade, business or profession'.

Unfair Terms within the UTCCR 1999

When is a Contract Term Unfair?

An 'unfair term' is defined in reg. 5(1) as:

> A contractual term which has not been individually negotiated shall be regarded as unfair if, contrary to the requirement of good faith, it causes a significant imbalance in the parties' rights and obligations arising under the contract, to the detriment of the consumer.

There are thus four crucial elements in the operation of the UTCCR unfairness test:

(i)   the contract term must not have been 'individually negotiated' (see reg. 5(2)–(4));

(ii)   an absence of good faith;

(iii) a significant imbalance in the parties' rights and obligations under the contract;

(iv) detriment to the consumer.

Assessing Unfairness

Regulation 6(1) provides that:

> Without prejudice to regulation 12, the unfairness of a contractual term shall be assessed, taking into account the nature of the goods or services for which the contract was concluded and by referring, at the time of conclusion of the contract, to all the circumstances attending the conclusion of the contract and to all the other terms of the contract or of another contract on which it is dependent.

It is under reg. 6(1) that the court must assess the factors leading to the contract's conclusion and, having regard to the goods or services themselves, weigh in the balance the contract terms which seek to favour the seller/supplier against those which are advantageous to the consumer. In this way, the court might conclude that there is a significant imbalance in the parties' rights and obligations to the detriment of the consumer. The House of Lords has recently considered the question of unfairness under the UTCCR 1994 in *Director General of Fair Trading* v *First National Bank plc* [2001] UKHL 52; [2002] 1 AC 481.

Schedule 2: the Indicative List of Unfair Terms

An important feature of the UTCCR 1999 is that reg. 5(5) refers to sch. 2 as providing 'an indicative and non-exhaustive list of the terms which may be regarded as unfair'. Schedule 2 contains a copious list of 17 potentially unfair terms. It must be stressed that these are merely *examples* of terms which *might* be unfair and it is not practical to list and analyze all the examples provided in sch. 2. The Office of Fair Trading produces regular bulletins on unfair contract terms, with abundant examples of such terms and the amendments ordered by the Director General of Fair Trading under his powers of enforcement. These bulletins are an indispensable aid to understanding the practical operation of the UTCCR 1999.

Terms Concerning Adequacy of the Price or Defining the Subject Matter of the Contract

One crucial limitation on the scope of the test of unfairness in the UTCCR 1999 is contained in reg. 6(2), which stipulates that:

> In so far as it is in plain, intelligible language, the assessment of fairness of a term shall not relate—
>
> (a)   to the definition of the main subject matter of the contract, or
>
> (b)   to the adequacy of the price or remuneration, as against the goods or services supplied in exchange.

Paragraph (a) means that the parties are at liberty to define clearly the subject matter of their contract. An example of such a core term, referred to by the Office of Fair Trading (*Unfair Contract Terms*, Bulletin No. 6, April 1999, para 1.24 and Case Report 56, p. 49) is that retail 'gift vouchers' may, plainly and intelligibly, state the date upon which they expire and thus become invalid.

Paragraph (b) means that adequacy of consideration will not be challenged *per se*, and thus the price charged for the goods or services remains within the central core of freedom of contract — an undertaking cannot be impugned simply because the consumer has, voluntarily and openly, made a bad bargain.

Assessing Good Faith

The UTCCR 1994 contained, in sch. 2, a list of four factors to be taken into account in making an assessment of good faith: (a) the strength of the parties' bargaining positions; (b) whether the consumer had an inducement to agree to the term; (c) whether the goods or services were sold/supplied to the special order of the consumer; and (d) the extent to which the seller/supplier had dealt fairly and equitably with the consumer. These factors have been deleted from the body of the 1999 Regulations because they are contained in recital 16 to the Directive and the 1999 Regulations sought to reflect more accurately the wording of the main text of the Directive. Accordingly, these four factors remain crucial, as reference must be made to the recitals in interpreting the Regulations, and, of course, reg. 5(1) stipulates that the absence of 'the requirement of good faith' is crucial in assessing the unfairness of a contract term. On the question of good faith, see *Director General of Fair Trading* v *First National Bank plc* (above).

Prevention of the Continued Use of Unfair Terms

Regulations 10–15 relate to the machinery for challenging unfair terms and the prevention of their continued use. Under reg. 10(1), it is the duty of the Director General of Fair Trading to consider complaints made to him regarding unfair terms and, under reg. 12(1), he may apply for an injunction against the person using such a term. In deciding whether or not to apply for an injunction, the Director may have regard to any undertakings given to him by the person as to the continued use of the term in question (reg. 10(3)).

Regulation 11 extends the power to seek an injunction to other regulatory bodies which are specified in sch. 1, e.g., the Data Protection Registrar and the Directors General of Electricity, Gas and Water, provided such bodies have notified the Director General of their intention to apply for an injunction at least 14 days before the application is made, unless the Director consents to the application being made within a shorter period (reg. 12(2)(a) and (b)). Most importantly for consumers, this power to seek injunctions extends to every weights and measures authority in Great Britain and the Consumers' Association.

Intelligibility in Written Contracts

Regulation 7 provides that 'a seller or supplier shall ensure that any written term of a contract is expressed in plain, intelligible language' and that, 'if there is doubt about the meaning of a written term, the interpretation which is most favourable to the consumer shall prevail'. Although the common law might achieve this result by a combination of the rules on reasonable notice and interpretation *contra proferentem*, the express articulation of principle in reg. 7 is most welcome.

Q Question 1

Harvey buys a country mansion in Gloucestershire and decides to have the gardens landscaped. He contacts Capability Ltd after seeing the company's advertisement in the local newspaper stating: 'Paths, fencing and garden maintenance our speciality — also quotations given for larger jobs.' Before concluding any contract, Harvey discovers that there is a local builder, Scrapitt, who offers to do the work at '5% less than whatever price Capability quotes'. Harvey has little confidence in Scrapitt and he therefore decides to enter into a contract with Capability Ltd.

A price of £10,000 is agreed and Harvey is given a document headed 'Memorandum of Terms'. This document sets out the job specification, price and date of completion. The reverse has the following clauses added by rubber stamp:

Clause 1: The company accepts no responsibility for personal injury to the customer during performance of the contract.

Clause 2: Liability for any damage to the customer's home is limited to the sum of £500, and no liability can be accepted for loss of, or damage to, the customer's goods.

Reckless, employed by Capability Ltd, drives a dumper truck through the wall of Harvey's house. As Harvey returns home that night, he collides with the dumper truck which Reckless has left in the middle of the driveway. The car is completely ruined and Harvey is injured.

Advise Harvey.

Commentary

There are three areas for evaluation in this problem. First, the question of the common law and exclusion clauses: have these clauses been incorporated as terms of the contract? Secondly, the relevant sections of the Unfair Contract Terms Act 1977 must be considered and, finally, a brief mention must be made of third party liability and exclusion clauses in relation to Reckless, the employee of Capability Ltd.

• Have the exclusion clauses been incorporated as terms of the contract? What are the tests, at common law, for the effective incorporation of exclusion clauses in a contract?

• Explain which provisions of the Unfair Contract Terms Act 1977 and the Unfair

Terms in Consumer Contracts Regulations 1999 apply to these exclusion clauses.

• Explain the legal position of Reckless who is not party to the contract between Harvey and Capability Ltd. Does the Contracts (Rights of Third Parties) Act 1999 apply to Reckless?

ֺ☀ Suggested answer

This question concerns exclusion clauses and the extent to which Harvey (H) is bound by the attempted exclusion and restriction of Capability Ltd's (C) liability. Like any other term of the contract, an exclusion clause must be an integral part of the undertaking if it is to be effective but, as an exclusion clause attempts to remove a liability that would otherwise exist, there are particularly stringent rules regarding the incorporation of such terms in contracts. If H had signed the contract there would be a strong presumption that he was bound by its terms (*L'Estrange* v *F Graucob Ltd* [1934] 2 KB 394) but in the absence of a signature, H must be given adequate *notice* of the terms. It was emphasised in *Parker* v *South Eastern Ry* (1877) 2 CPD 416 that it is notice of the terms which is important, not their actual reading or understanding, and it follows that if the notice is illegible or obscured by a date stamp as in *Richardson, Spence & Co.* v *Rowntree* [1894] AC 217, it will be ineffective. The clauses in the problem appear to be quite legible but they are on the reverse of the document and there is no notice such as 'See over for conditions' on its face. This may well be fatal to C, for in *Henderson* v *Steven* (1875) LR 2 HL (Sc) 470 the court held that the absence of a notice on the front of a ticket referring to clauses on its rear rendered the clauses invalid. Most recently, in *Interfoto Picture Library Ltd* v *Stiletto Visual Programmes Ltd* [1989] QB 433, the court emphasised that if the clause is particularly stringent or onerous particular care must be taken to draw its attention to the other party. Furthermore, the notice that is given must be contemporaneous with the contract's formation (see *Olley* v *Marlborough Court Ltd* [1949] 1 KB 532; *Thornton* v *Shoe Lane Parking Ltd* [1971] 2 QB 163). The exclusion clauses in the problem are certainly not presented to H post-contractually as they are given to him *before* the price is agreed and this requirement would therefore appear to be satisfied.

Even if the conditions regarding notice are complied with, there are other demands made by the common law. The document containing the clauses must be a contractual document, i.e. one which a reasonable man would expect to contain the conditions of the contract. In *Chapelton* v *Barry UDC* [1940] 1 KB 532, a receipt which was given for the hire of a deck chair was not such a contractual document and neither was the front cover of a cheque book in *Burnett* v *Westminster Bank* [1966] 1 QB 742. The courts preserve great flexibility when deciding this question (see *McCutcheon* v *MacBrayne (David) Ltd* [1964] 1 WLR 125) and it may be that the 'Memorandum of Terms' in the problem will not suffice. There might be a full, written contract elsewhere which would mean that the court could strike-down this 'Memorandum'.

Before leaving the common law, it must be emphasised that, should the clauses be successfully integrated in the contract, any ambiguity will nevertheless be construed against C, that is *contra proferentem*. Particularly exacting standards are demanded of clauses which are alleged to exclude all liability for negligence and the law will preserve this head of liability wherever possible (see *Alderslade* v *Hendon Laundry Ltd* [1945] 1 KB 189; *White* v *John Warwick & Co. Ltd* [1953] 1 WLR 1285). The question is one of construction of the contract, but if the defendant disclaims liability for 'any loss' the court may consider that he is attempting to exclude all *types* of loss without being sufficiently specific as to their *cause* (see *Price* v *Union Lighterage Co.* [1904] 1 KB 412). The clauses in the problem certainly make no *express* reference to negligence and, as such, they will clearly be construed against C following the tests laid down by Lord Morton in *Canada Steamship Lines Ltd* v *The King* [1952] AC 192. However, the common law's powers to circumvent clauses by deft interpretation are now of less significance in the light of the Unfair Contract Terms Act 1977.

Section 2(1) of the 1977 Act invalidates any attempt by a contract term or notice to exclude or restrict liability for death or bodily injury resulting from negligence. It seems indisputable that it was negligent to leave the dumper truck in the driveway and clause 1 of the contract would be ineffective as regards H's claim for his injuries.

Section 2(2) further provides that in the case of 'other loss or damage' a person cannot exclude or restrict his liability for negligence except in so far as the term or notice satisfies the test of reasonableness. This is clearly applicable to C, as is s. 3, which subjects an attempted exclusion of liability for breach of contract to the reasonableness test where one party 'deals as consumer or on the other's written standard terms of business'. Apart from the difficult question of whether C's terms are 'written standard terms' (which the Act does not define and in relation to which there is no judicial guidance), it must be decided whether clause 2 can pass the reasonableness test. Section 11(1) provides that the time for determining whether the clause is reasonable is the time at which the contract is made. This is a very strict test and the seriousness of the loss or damage caused cannot be considered except to the extent to which it was, or ought reasonably to have been, in the contemplation of the parties at the time of contract. Following the interpretation given to s. 11 in *Stewart Gill Ltd* v *Horatio Myer & Co. Ltd* [1992] 1 QB 600, it seems most unlikely that C could justify the insertion of the exclusion clause in the contract. *Stewart Gill* also decides that the *whole* clause must be reasonable, not merely the part relied upon by the defendant: clause 2 may therefore fail in its entirety and this conclusion is fortified in that deliberate breaches of contract are within the literal wording of the clause. Section 11(4) provides that if the defendant limits liability to a specific sum of money, regard shall be had, in assessing reasonableness, to the resources which he could expect to be available to him for meeting the liability and how far it was open to him to cover himself by insurance. This provision was designed to alleviate undue hardship to small businesses but it is arguable that C could and should have insured against the risk in question and this would certainly be the case if C could insure without any material increase to H in the contract price.

It is also vital to consider the guidelines for assessing reasonableness in sch. 2 of the Act. Particularly relevant to this problem is the question of whether the customer was given any inducement to agree to the clause or had the opportunity of doing business elsewhere without having to accept the clause. As C charges more than one of its competitors (Scrapitt would give a 5% discount on C's prices) it is legitimate to ask whether Scrappit would use any exclusion clauses and, if so, whether they are more or less onerous than C's. C's exclusion clause might, therefore, be condemned using such a comparative assessment.

The decision in *Phillips Products Ltd* v *Hyland* [1987] 1 WLR 659 is particularly applicable to the problem. There the plaintiff hired an excavator from the second defendants on the latter's standard terms which provided that the driver should be regarded as employed by the plaintiff, the plaintiff thereby remaining liable for any loss arising from the machine's use. The driver negligently damaged the plaintiff's factory whilst carrying out work at the plaintiff's request. It was held that several factors meant that the clause failed to pass the reasonableness test. First, the plaintiff did not regularly hire machinery of this sort whereas the defendants were in the business of equipment hire. Secondly, the clause was not the product of any *negotiation* between the parties: rather it was simply one of the defendant's 43 standard conditions. Thirdly, the hire period was very short and the plaintiff had no opportunity to arrange insurance cover. Finally, the plaintiff played no part in the selection of the driver and had no control over the way in which he performed his job. On balance, it is suggested that C's clause would not be regarded as a reasonable one.

The Unfair Terms in Consumer Contracts Regulations 1999 (SI 1999, No. 2083) also apply to these facts. C is undoubtedly a business 'supplier', defined in reg. 3(1) as 'any natural or legal person who, in contracts covered by these Regulations, is acting for purposes relating to his trade, business or profession, whether publicly owned or privately owned', and H is a 'consumer' who is 'acting for purposes which are outside his trade, business or profession' (reg. 3(1)). The Regulations apply only to contract *terms* (reg. 4(1)) but, on the facts which are given, the 'memorandum of terms' would appear to contain contractual obligations. Moreover, the clauses added by rubber stamp have certainly not been 'individually negotiated' (reg. 5(1)) but, instead, have been 'drafted in advance' (reg. 5(2)). The contract between H and C would thus appear to be a 'pre-formulated standard contract' (reg. 5(3)) within the scope of the Regulations but, in any event, the remainder of the contract can be viewed as such a standard contract even if a 'specific term' has been individually negotiated, provided that an 'overall assessment of it indicates that it is a pre-formulated standard contract' (reg. 5(3)).

Having established that the 1999 Regulations apply to the contract between H and C, it must be asked whether any of the contract terms are unfair and thus not binding (reg. 8(1)) on H as being 'contrary to the requirement of good faith' and causing a 'significant imbalance in the parties' rights and obligations arising under the contract, to the detriment of the consumer'. Recital 16 of the Directive on *Unfair Terms in Consumer Contracts* (93/13/EEC) refers to several factors in the assessment of good faith. Applying these factors to the problem, there is no obvious disparity in the bargaining strengths of H and C and H has been given no inducement to agree to the term. Moreover, the services supplied by C are to H's 'special order'. However, it is arguable that *a unilateral imposition* of such terms means that C has not 'dealt fairly and equitably' with H and has failed to consider H's 'legitimate interests'. In addition, H may not have had a 'real opportunity of becoming acquainted' with the contract terms before the contract was concluded (sch. 2, para. (i)). In conclusion, these terms may be 'so weighted in favour of the supplier as to tilt the parties' rights and obligations under the contract significantly in his favour' (*Director General of Fair Trading* v *First National Bank plc* [2002] 1 AC 481, per Lord Bingham of Cornhill at 494).

When clauses 1 and 2 in the contract between H and C are examined more closely, there are further grounds for rendering them invalid. Schedule 2 of the Regulations provides an indicative, non-exhaustive list of terms which may be regarded as unfair, and a term excluding liability for death or bodily injury caused by negligence of the supplier heads the list of 17 examples. However, the Unfair Contract Terms Act 1977 (UCTA), s. 2(1), renders such an attempted exclusion of liability totally ineffective and the Act is thus more advantageous to H. Clause 2 would also seem to be unfair under the Regulations for 'inappropriately excluding or limiting the legal rights of the consumer vis-à-vis the supplier . . . in the event of total or partial non-performance or inadequate performance by the supplier of any of the contractual obligations' (sch. 2, para. (b)). However, the test of reasonableness under the UCTA may, once again, prove to be more advantageous to H as, under the UCTA, the burden is on C to prove that the exclusion clauses satisfy that test whereas, under the Regulations, the burden of proving that the terms are unfair is placed on H.

Finally, although C may attempt to claim protection under the exclusion clauses in the contract with H to the extent discussed above, Reckless (R), his employee, remains an unprotected third party. As such a third party, R remains liable for his negligence as in *Adler* v *Dickson* [1955] 1 QB 158. C would then be vicariously liable for R's negligent acts which have clearly been committed in the course of his employment. It follows from this circuitous procedure that C will ultimately carry the loss. One of the principal aims of the Contracts (Rights of Third Parties) Act 1999 is that, where a company agrees with its customer that its employees should be protected by an exclusion clause, the employees will be able to benefit from the agreement and seek shelter under the clause. Section 1 of the 1999 Act provides that:

... a person who is not a party to a contract (a 'third party') may in his own right enforce a term of the contract if—

(a) the contract expressly provides that he may, or

(b) subject to subsection (2), the term purports to confer a benefit on him.

Section 1(3) adds that 'the third party must be expressly identified in the contract by name, as a member of a class or as answering a particular description'. Finally, s. 1(6) stresses that 'where a term of a contract excludes or limits liability in relation to any matter, references in this Act to the third party enforcing the term shall be construed as references to his availing himself of the exclusion or limitation'. This is a most desirable reform as it means that the parties can now apportion risks accurately and correctly by means of insurance.

On the facts of the problem, there is no agreement between C and H that R should be able to benefit from the exclusion clauses and, indeed, there is no *mention* of R in the contract either personally or as an employee. The 1999 Act is, therefore, not applicable to these facts. Furthermore, it would be impossible to argue that C is acting as R's agent for the purpose of bringing R into direct contractual relations with H (see *New Zealand Shipping Co. Ltd v A M Satterthwaite & Co. Ltd (The Eurymedon)* [1975] AC 154).

Q Question 2

Patrick, a director of Dartsma Ltd, which manufactures computers, decided that the company should purchase a prestigious car which could be used principally for entertaining the company's customers but which would also be suitable for private use by Patrick and the other directors. Accordingly, the company bought a second-hand 'Lynx' car from Dependable Motors Ltd (DM). Patrick managed to negotiate a 15% 'trade discount' on the price of the car. The lengthy contract for the sale of the car, which Patrick signed, contained the following clause on page 10: 'DM Ltd will refund the price of any defective goods provided that such defects are communicated to the company in writing no later than 3 days after the contract of sale is concluded but the Company shall not otherwise be liable for any loss or damage caused by defects in the goods.'

Before leaving DM, Patrick noticed that the car's windscreen-wiper blades needed replacing. He therefore purchased two new blades from the parts department of DM Ltd, fitting them himself. The sales invoice contained the same exclusion clause as that in the contract for the sale of the car and was also signed by Patrick. After using the car for two weeks, Patrick had a minor accident whilst driving the car in wet weather and the car was damaged. He discovered that the rubber wiper blades had perished and had consequently failed to clear the windscreen of rain. In the third week of using the car, its gearbox seized-up and was ruined. DM Ltd had failed to refill the gearbox with oil during the pre-delivery service of the car.

Advise Patrick.

Commentary

This question involves a consideration of the extent to which the implied terms of the Sale of Goods Act 1979 relating to description, quality and fitness for purpose of the goods can be excluded in consumer and business sales. Sections 6 and 12 of the Unfair Contract Terms Act 1977 must be considered together with the courts' interpretation of those sections. It is also crucial to consider the Unfair Terms in Consumer Contracts Regulations 1999.

- Is Dependable Motors Ltd, the seller of the car, in breach of the implied terms of the Sale of Goods Act 1979 relating to satisfactory quality and fitness for purpose?

- Have the exclusion clauses been incorporated as terms of the contract?

- Is Patrick classifiable as a business buyer ('dealing otherwise than as consumer') or a consumer buyer ('dealing as consumer') within ss. 6 and 12 of the Unfair Contract Terms Act 1977 (UCTA)? What is the relevance of these distinctions in relation to exclusion clauses? How is a consumer buyer distinguished from a business buyer?

- Are any of the provisions of the Unfair Terms in Consumer Contracts Regulations 1999 applicable to Patrick? Does UCTA provide better remedies in this context than those available in the 1999 Regulations?

:ʘ: Suggested answer

This problem involves a consideration of whether the exclusion clauses in issue protect DM from breach of the implied terms of the Sale of Goods Act 1979 (SGA 1979), ss. 13–15, which cover the description, quality and fitness for purpose of the goods sold. First, it is almost certainly the case that DM are in breach of s. 14 of the SGA. Both the car and the wiper blades were sold 'in the course of a business' by DM (see *Stevenson* v *Rogers*, below) and the goods are both unsatisfactory and unfit for their purpose. Secondly, there can scarcely be any dispute regarding the integration of these exclusion clauses as terms in the contracts of sale as they are advanced by DM at the moment of the formation of both contracts (see *Olley* v *Marlborough Court Ltd* [1949] 1 KB 532) and both documents are probably contractual in nature (see *Chapelton* v *Barry UDC* [1940] 1 KB 532). There might only be some doubt in this respect regarding the 'sales invoice' for the wiper blades but the problem does not provide enough information to decide the issue. More importantly, both documents are signed by Patrick (P) and, in the absence of any misrepresentation or duress, the exclusion clauses will almost certainly be integrated as terms of the contract (see *L'Estrange* v *F Graucob Ltd* [1934] 2 KB 394). It is arguable, therefore, that at common law these exemption clauses would bind P.

However, the Unfair Contract Terms Act 1977 (UCTA 1977) ss. 6 and 12 restrict dramatically the extent to which ss. 13–15 of the SGA 1979 may be excluded. Section 6 provides that 'as against a person dealing as consumer' liability for breach of obligations arising from the SGA ss. 13–15 'cannot be excluded or restricted by reference to any contract term', but as against a person 'dealing otherwise than as consumer' liability can be excluded but 'only in so far as the term satisfies the requirement of reasonableness'. Section 12 defines a consumer sale stipulating three requirements. First, that one party does not make the contract 'in the course of a business' nor 'holds himself out as doing so'. Secondly, that the other party *does* make the contract in the course of a business and, thirdly, that the goods 'are of a type ordinarily supplied for private use or consumption'. It is clearly vital to decide into which category the sale in the problem falls.

No wider stipulation could be postulated than that in the UCTA 1977, s. 12, of making the contract in the course of a business, but there are two possible interpretations of the phrase. First, a business or person may contract in this way by, for example, purchasing goods for the business even though the business does not deal in the type of goods which have been purchased and the sale is thus not a normal and regular part of the business activity which is carried on, e.g., a solicitor who buys an electric fire for use in the office. It is plain that the definition is wide enough to encompass this example and it was arguably the intent of the legislature to cast the net very widely. Moreover, in *Stevenson* v *Rogers* [1999] QB 1028, the Court of Appeal held recently that the phrase 'sells goods in the course of a business' in the SGA 1979, s. 14(2), must be given a literal interpretation. In *Stevenson*, the defendant had an established business as a fisherman and he sold a fishing vessel which he used in the course of his business, replacing that vessel with a new one. The defendant's business was thus not that of buying and selling ships or boats. At first instance, it was held that there was an insufficient regularity of dealing to render the sale of the fishing vessel 'in the course of a business' within s. 14(2) and that, accordingly, the implied condition of merchantability in that section did not apply to the sale. The Court of Appeal reversed that decision and ruled that, having regard to the legislative history of the SGA 1979, the wording in s. 14(2) of the Act had been deliberately changed to widen the protection conferred upon a buyer of goods from a business seller. Consequently, it was held that s. 14(2) must be construed at face value and the sale of the fishing vessel was in the course of a business: the wording of the section did not demand any element of regularity of dealing and so there was no reason 'to reintroduce some implied qualification, difficult to define, in order to narrow what appears to be the wide scope and apparent purpose of the words' (p. 623, per Potter LJ). The second possible interpretation of the UCTA, s. 12 is that, to be in the *course* of a business, the goods in question must be bought for some definite business purpose with a degree of regularity. In contrast with the example, above, of the solicitor who buys an electric fire for his office, the regularity argument would mean that only a trader whose business is to purchase electric fires for resale would be making the contracts in the course of a business.

The courts are clearly adopting this second interpretation for s. 12. In *Rasbora Ltd* v *JCL Marine Ltd* [1977] 1 Lloyd's Rep 645, a private buyer of a boat substituted the plaintiff company as buyer for the purposes of avoiding payment of VAT. On her maiden voyage, the boat caught fire and sank. Lawson J held that this was a consumer sale (under SGA 1893, s. 55(7)) and, more importantly, that even if the company had been the *original buyer* the sale would still have been a consumer sale on the basis that the boat was to be used by the company's majority shareholder and not chartered to third parties. Similarly, in *Peter Symmons & Co.* v *Cook* (1981) 131 NLJ 758, the plaintiff firm of surveyors bought a second-hand Rolls Royce from the defendants which developed serious defects after 2,000 miles. It was held that the firm was acting as a consumer and that to buy in the course of a business 'the buying of cars must form at the very least an integral part of the buyer's business or a necessary incidental thereto'. It was emphasised that only in those circumstances could the buyer be said to be on an equal footing with his seller in terms of bargaining strength. This approach has been confirmed by the Court of Appeal in *R & B Customs Brokers Co. Ltd* v *United Dominions Trust Ltd* [1988] 1 WLR 321 where a director of the plaintiff company decided that the company should buy a new car and trade in its existing car in part-exchange, his intention being that the car would be used both for company and personal use. The car proved to be defective but, again, because the company was only an irregular purchaser of cars, it was held that it was acting as a consumer and the exclusion clauses were ineffective. Moreover, the court dismissed the argument that there was any holding-out that the contract was made in the course of a business under s. 12. These decisions are criticisable in that they evaluate the *purpose* for which the goods are bought and the *regularity of dealing*, neither of these factors being present in the objective statutory definition.

Although at first glance it appears unnecessary to have these conflicting interpretations, a moment's thought reveals the justice underlying them. If the regularity requirement is held to apply to business sellers, the buyer has no protection under the implied conditions in the SGA 1973, s. 14, where the seller sells goods which are not his stock-in-trade, as in *Stevenson* v *Rogers*. Equally, if the regularity stipulation did *not* apply on the facts of *R & B Customs Brokers*, and the buyer was thus characterised as acting in the course of a business, the exclusion clauses would not be declared void but would be subject to the reasonableness test only. In short, protection is secured for the buyers in both *Stevenson* v *Rogers* and *R & B Customs Brokers*.

In view of these decisions, it would seem that both the sale of the car and the wiper blades would fall within the consumer classification and *Rasbora* indicates that the 15% discount obtained by P would not alter this conclusion. The exclusion clauses would thus be ineffective. There is an additional problem with the wiper blades, however. Section 12 provides that the goods must be 'ordinarily supplied for private use or consumption'. There is no authority on this point but there are clearly goods which were once regarded as trade items, building materials, for example, which have become part of the 'do-it-yourself' consumer market. Wiper blades for cars are often bought and fitted by a car's owner rather than a mechanic and it seems likely that the court would regard these as consumer goods within s. 12. Finally, the damage to the car resulting from the defective wiper blades would almost certainly be a recoverable consequential loss, being reasonably in the contemplation of the parties at the time the contract was made. In sales of goods, the courts have treated such claims in the buyer's favour (see *Parsons (Livestock) Ltd* v *Uttley, Ingham & Co. Ltd* [1978] QB 791).

Should the purchases in the problem be regarded as made in the course of a business, the exclusion clauses would be subject to the reasonableness test, but it is most unlikely that they would pass that test. Having regard to the guidelines concerning reasonableness in sch. 2 of the UCTA 1977, the parties have roughly equal bargaining power and P has been given a 15% discount both of which favour DM. However, it is likely that P could have bought the same model of car elsewhere without such a restrictive clause but with as generous a discount. Similarly, perhaps P ought not reasonably to have known of the existence of the term in this lengthy document at page 10 and it seems that the time limit of three days for notifying defects could not be justified at the date the contract was entered into, this being the time that an evaluation is made under the UCTA 1977, s. 11. It is quite unreasonable to expect defects to manifest themselves and then be notified within three days (see *R W Green Ltd* v *Cade Bros Farms* [1978] 1 Lloyd's Rep 602). Furthermore, in *Rees Hough Ltd* v *Redland Reinforced Plastics Ltd* (1984) 1 Const L J 67, a clause in a contract between two businesses was held to be unreasonable because it provided that the sellers of piping excluded all liability unless notified of complaints within three months.

It is clear that the Unfair Terms in Consumer Contracts Regulations 1999 (UTCCR) *cannot* apply to the sale of the car as, although DM are clearly business sellers of goods within reg. 3(1), it is the *company* (Dartsma Ltd) which has bought the car and the definition of a 'consumer' in reg. 3(1) applies only to a 'natural person'. Provided that the 'sales invoice' given to P contains contract terms, the 1999 Regulations will apply to the sale of the wiper blades. P buys them in his capacity as a 'natural person' and, almost certainly, he is 'acting for purposes which are outside his trade, business or profession' (reg. 3(1)). Moreover, it is indisputable that the terms in the invoice have not been 'individually negotiated' (reg. 5(1)) but, instead, have been 'drafted in advance' (reg. 5(2)). This contract would thus appear to be a 'pre-formulated standard contract' (reg. 5(3)) within the scope of the Regulations. It is very likely that the terms are unfair and thus not binding upon P (reg. 8(1)) as being 'contrary to the require-ment of good faith' and causing a 'significant imbalance in the parties' rights and obligations arising under the contract, to the detriment of the consumer' (reg. 5(1)). In particular, the terms in the problem have been imposed unilaterally, meaning that DM has not 'dealt fairly and equitably' with P and has failed to consider his 'legitim-ate interests' (Directive 93/13/EEC, Recital 16). Similarly, P does not appear to have had a 'real opportunity of becoming acquainted' (UTCCR 1999, sch. 2, para (i)) with the terms before the contract was concluded. Moreover, the time limit of three days for notifying defects plainly has the effect of 'excluding or hindering the consumer's right to take legal action or exercise any other legal remedy' (sch. 2, para. (q)). There is little doubt that these terms are unfair as being 'so weighted in favour of the supplier as to tilt the parties' rights and obligations under the contract significantly in his favour' (*Director General of Fair Trading* v *First National Bank plc* [2002] 1 AC 481, 494 per Lord Bingham of Cornhill). However, as mentioned earlier, this is almost certainly a consumer sale of goods within the UCTA 1977, ss. 6 and 12 and, consequently, there is a total ban on excluding the implied conditions relating to description, satisfactory quality, and fitness for purpose of the goods within the SGA 1979, ss. 13 and 14. The provisions of the UCTA 1977 are thus obviously much more advantageous to P than his having to prove the unfairness of the contract terms under the 1999 Regulations.

Q Question 3

Exclusion clauses are offensive only where they are embodied in standard form contracts and there is a gross disparity of bargaining power between the parties. Discuss.

Commentary

In answering this essay title, the growth of inequality of bargaining power and abuse of exclusion clauses must be explained. Secondly, it should be asked whether the courts could, or would, be prepared to disallow exclusion clauses where one party had no realistic choice but to agree to the exclusion of liability. Finally, the controls imposed by the Unfair Contract Terms Act 1977 and the Unfair Terms in Consumer Contracts Regulations 1999 should be evaluated in the light of the essay title.

- Explain the predominant philosophy of *laissez-faire* during the nineteenth century and the effect of freedom of contract on the law's approach to exclusion clauses.

- Explain the development of multi-national corporations, inequality of bargaining power and contracts of adhesion.

- What was the common law's attitude to exclusion clauses and inequality of bargaining power during the early twentieth century? Did the perspective of the courts change during the latter part of the twentieth century?

- How do the provisions of the Unfair Contract Terms Act 1977 and the Unfair Terms in Consumer Contracts Regulations 1999 cope with the difficulties generated by standard form contracts and inequality of bargaining strengths?

☼ Suggested answer

During the nineteenth century, the predominant influence of *laissez-faire* meant that exclusion clauses were unexceptional terms of the contract agreed between parties with roughly equal bargaining strengths. In this context, it was the purpose and duty of the law to enforce the intentions of the parties as expressed in their sanctified agreement. In the middle of the nineteenth century, the quickening of the Industrial Revolution introduced radical social and economic changes which *laissez-faire* ideology could not foresee. Most particularly, commercial enterprises of ever-increasing size began to predominate at the close of the nineteenth century and the limited liability company was legally recognised by the decision in *Salomon v Salomon & Co. Ltd* [1897] AC 22. Companies began to amalgamate (eventually developing to have monopolistic and oligopolistic control of markets) and mass produced, standardised goods generated their counterpart in standard-form contracts with standardised exclusion clauses. These developments had massive implications for an individualistic theory of freedom of contract: individualism was destroyed as the benefits of standard-form contracts became evident. Large commercial companies with overriding bargaining strengths quickly realised that terms could be dictated to the weaker party whose only choice was to adhere to the exclusions of liability specified or seek the, often fictitious alternative, of doing business elsewhere. In a monopolistic situation there is simply no choice but to contract on the other party's terms. The contract of adhesion was thus born.

Where there is equality of bargaining power between the parties their prior knowledge of risks will be catered for in the standard-form contract which is then used throughout their particular trade or business. Here the standard-form has been *negotiated freely* and any exclusion of liability will amount to an allocation of risks between the parties which can be counter-balanced by appropriate insurance cover. In this situation, standard-form contracts are not objectionable and may possess many advantages in that they save expense, effort and time and engender security, as a ruling on one standardised contract will provide a stable precedent and guide for future eventualities. Potential hazards are thus minimised and the standard-form may not need re-evaluation for several years. Moreover, deployment of standard-forms may mean that production and distribution costs of businesses are reduced with a concomitant benefit to society as a whole.

Although inequality of bargaining power became manifest in the twentieth century, the courts continued to support notions of freedom of contract. The constant advocacy of freedom of contract meant that exclusion clauses could flourish: freedom to contract on any terms necessarily encompassed the freedom to oppress, thus enabling companies virtually to legislate in their own interests. *Thompson* v *L M & S Ry* [1930] 1 KB 41 was an outstanding decision. The plaintiff, who could not read, asked her niece to buy a railway excursion ticket for her. The ticket had a notice on its face reading 'see back', the back containing a statement that the ticket was issued subject to the company's conditions set forth in the company's timetables, a copy of which might be purchased for 6d. The conditions contained a clause on page 552 excluding the company's liability for 'any injury . . . however caused'. The plaintiff was injured but the Court of Appeal held that the company had taken reasonable steps to bring the conditions to the attention of the plaintiff and so she was bound by them. Moreover, the court held that the plaintiff's illiteracy was irrelevant.

After the Second World War, the judiciary and, most prominently, Lord Denning, began to acknowledge the 'consumer' interest and the stage was set for the rejection of exclusion clauses in deference to the ideals of social welfare. Even so, the common law was constrained by the abstract notion of freedom of contract and consequently unable to deny absolutely the legality and efficacy of exclusion clauses. In *L'Estrange* v *F Graucob Ltd* [1934] 2 KB 394, for example, the plaintiff was bound by her signature on a standard-form contract containing sweeping exemption clauses which she had not read, thinking the document was an order-form. Maugham LJ said: 'I regret the decision to which I have come, but I am bound by legal rules and cannot decide the case on other considerations.' The courts nevertheless developed an impressive array of techniques for the avoidance of such clauses whilst paying lip-service to freedom of contract. *Thornton* v *Shoe Lane Parking Ltd* [1971] 2 QB 163 is illustrative of the changed attitude of the courts, its facts being very similar to *Thompson*. The plaintiff parked his car in a multi-storey car park and received from a machine a standard-form ticket which carried a clause to the effect that it was issued subject to the conditions displayed on the premises. The plaintiff was injured in an accident in the car park, caused in part by the negligence of the defendants, who relied on conditions in the notices exempting them from liability. The Court of Appeal held that insufficient steps had been taken to draw the plaintiff 's attention to the conditions and consequently he was not bound by them. Megaw LJ pointed out how unrealistic it would be for customers to leave their cars and search for notices displaying the conditions thereby blocking all the entrances to the car park. But his Lordship emphasised that 'unless the defendants genuinely intended the potential customers to do just that, it would be fiction, if not farce, to treat those customers as persons who have been given a fair opportunity, before the contract is made, of discovering the conditions by which they are to be bound'.

A further method by which exemption clauses might be avoided in standard-form contracts was the courts' insistence that they be interpreted *contra proferentem*, meaning that any ambiguity would be construed against the party seeking the protection of the clause. In *Houghton* v *Trafalgar Insurance* [1954] 1 QB 247, a five-seater car was involved in an accident whilst carrying six passengers, the plaintiff's insurance policy exempting the defendants from liability for damage caused 'whilst the car is carrying any *load* in excess of that for which it was constructed'. It was held that the defendants were liable as the clause could not be extended to those situations where the car was carrying too many *passengers*.

The notion that an exclusion clause could not protect one party from the consequences of a fundamental breach of contract developed into a powerful weapon protecting the weaker party against exclusion clauses. In *Karsales (Harrow) Ltd* v *Wallis* [1956] 1 WLR 936, the principle was elevated to a rule of law that, no matter how clear the clause, it would not suffice to exclude liability for such a breach. This formulation virtually abandoned any pretence of compliance with freedom of contract and the parties' intentions and was finally rejected by the House of Lords, albeit on inappropriate facts, in *Photo Production Ltd* v *Securicor Transport Ltd* [1980] AC 827. The House insisted that whether an exclusion clause could excuse the consequences of a fundamental breach depended upon the proper construction of the contract and, on the facts, the exclusion clause was effective to protect the defendants. At first glance this seems to be a retrogressive step, exposing the weaker party to possible abuse, but this should not be so. The *Karsales* rule was so indiscriminate that it invalidated both the contracts which were the product of inequality of bargaining power and unworthy of enforcement along with those which resulted from carefully planned negotiation between equals. The court is now able to winnow the grain from the chaff, as the *Photo Production* reasoning is embodied in the Unfair Contract Terms Act 1977, s. 9.

The general scheme of the 1977 Act similarly allows for exclusion clauses to be invalidated where there is inequality of bargaining power and an involuntary agreement, but upheld where the clause is the product of equal bargaining strengths and able to pass the 'reasonableness' test. There is particular concern shown for consumers in that the implied terms of the Sale of Goods Act 1979, which relate to the quality and fitness of the goods, cannot be excluded where one party is 'dealing as consumer' (s. 6). In a non-consumer sale, however, the parties are able to exclude these implied terms but only in so far as the exclusion clause satisfies the reasonableness test. Section 3, which imposes general controls on the exclusion of liability for breach of contract similarly employs the reasonableness test at its heart. There should thus be ample scope under the 1977 Act for the exercise of discretion in differentiating the reasonable from the unreasonable clause without resorting to strained construction or dogmatic rules of the *Karsales* type. Crude inequality of bargaining power combined with swingeing exclusion clauses can be easily controlled by the 1977 Act but more problematical is the extent to which the courts should intervene in *commercial contracts* where inequality of bargaining power is infinitely variable and various shades of reasonableness are possible. It remains to be seen how this delicate balancing exercise will be performed, although after the decision in *Stewart Gill Ltd* v *Horatio Myer & Co. Ltd* [1992] 1 QB 600, there is little evidence that the law intends to pursue the non-interventionist policy advocated in *Photo Production*.

The Unfair Terms in Consumer Contracts Regulations 1999 certainly acknowledge that exclusion clauses are offensive when embodied in standard form contracts and there is gross disparity of bargaining power between the parties—indeed the major function of the Regulations is to render such clauses ineffective. The Regulations apply to standard form contracts used by businesses which contract with consumers for the sale of goods or the supply of goods or services and render ineffective any terms in the contract which are held to be unfair—in so doing, they control a wide range of contract terms and are not limited to simple exclusion or limitation clauses. Regulation 5(1) provides that 'a contractual term which has not been individually negotiated shall be regarded as unfair if, contrary to the requirement of good faith, it causes a significant imbalance in the parties' rights and obligations arising under the contract, to the detriment of the consumer'. Although English law is now familiar with the idea of 'reasonableness' under the Unfair Contract Terms Act 1977, the 1999 Regulations inject into commercial law the radical concept of dealing in 'good faith'. This notion is an accepted one in the civil law but it was expressly rejected by the House of Lords in *Walford* v *Miles* [1992] 2 AC 128 as having no realistic place in the adversarial context of buying and selling a business. This is, patently, an unacceptable approach to adopt in relation to the new Regulations and the recent decision of the House of Lords in *Director General of Fair Trading* v *First National Bank plc* [2002] 1 AC 481, acknowledges that good faith has both a procedural and a substantive element. The procedural aspect will control abuse in contract formation where, for example, misrepresentation or duress is employed to secure apparent acceptance of an unfair term. The real challenge to English law lies in the development of substantive notions of good faith and a delineation of when there is 'a significant imbalance in the parties' rights and obligations arising under the contract, to the detriment of the consumer'. In the *First National Bank* case, Lord Bingham of Cornhill considered that 'good faith' related to 'good standards of commercial morality and practice' (p. 494) and Lord Steyn thought that it demanded 'open and fair dealing' (p. 500). Equally important, although somewhat more prosaic, the 1999 Regulations have an important preventive effect (e.g., reg. 7(1), which provides that written terms must be expressed in 'plain, intelligible language'), and their breadth of operation will ensure that businesses which deal with consumers re-evaluate their standard form contracts in the light of the new controls.

Q Question 4

Both the radical concepts employed in the Unfair Terms in Consumer Contracts Regulations 1999 and the scope of the Regulations mean that the law's approach to exclusion clauses in consumer contracts must change dramatically.
  Discuss.

Commentary

Obviously this question demands an overall knowledge of the Unfair Terms in Consumer Contracts Regulations 1999 (UTCCR) and the scope of their operation but, in particular, it calls for a critical analysis of the notion of unfairness and the concept of good faith and transparency of dealing in commercial contracts. Where relevant, there is scope to compare the UTCCR with the Unfair Contract Terms Act 1977 (UCTA).

* What is the scope of the Unfair Terms in Consumer Contracts Regulations 1999?

* What are the central concepts employed in the 1999 Regulations? Explain the notions of good faith and fairness which are utilised by the Regulations.

* How has the House of Lords interpreted the Regulations in the recent decision in *Director General of Fair Trading* v *First National Bank plc* [2001] UKHL 52; [2002] 1 AC 481?

:Q: Suggested answer

The Unfair Terms in Consumer Contracts Regulations 1999 (SI 1999, No. 2083) (UTCCR) implement an EC Council Directive (93/13/EEC) on *Unfair Terms in Consumer Contracts*. The UTCCR 1999 revoke and replace the original Regulations (SI 1994, No. 3159) and reflect more closely the wording of the Directive. The Regulations have been clarified and the powers of enforcement granted by them have been extended considerably. The overall effect of the UTCCR 1999 is that an 'unfair term' in a consumer contract 'shall not be binding on the consumer' (reg. 8(1)).

The range of standard form consumer contracts (the contract term must not have been 'individually negotiated' (reg. 5(1)) to which the UTCCR apply is immense. Regulation 4(1) provides that '. . . these Regulations apply in relation to unfair terms in contracts concluded between a seller or supplier and a consumer'. The 1994 Regulations applied only to the business supply of goods and services to consumers under the terms of a standard form contract, and there was doubt as to whether interests in land were covered. However, the amended definition of a 'seller or supplier' in reg. 3(1) omits any reference to goods and services, stating that a 'seller or supplier' is 'any natural or legal person who, in contracts covered by these Regulations, is acting for purposes relating to his trade, business or profession, whether publicly owned or privately owned'. It is thus clear that standard form business contracts for the supply to consumers of goods, services and interests in *land*, are within the 1999 Regulations. Moreover, certain contracts were expressly exempted from the operation of the 1994 Regulations, namely 'any contract relating to employment . . ., succession rights . . ., rights under family law . . . and the incorporation and organisation of companies or partnerships' (UTCCR 1994, sch. 1). This list of excluded contracts has been deleted from the 1999 Regulations. It must be assumed that the rationale underpinning the deletion is that, in the recitals to the Directive (93/13/EEC, Recital 10), this group of contracts is said to be excluded from the ambit of the Directive itself and the 1999 Regulations have sought better to embody the wording of the Directive. It must be asked, therefore, whether these contracts are within or without the 1999 Regulations. The purposive construction which must be adopted when interpreting the Directive dictates that full consideration must be given to the recitals and, consequently, it seems that this group of contracts will continue to be excluded from the operation of the UTCCR 1999. Alternatively, but more improbably, it is arguable there is now nothing to prevent the 1999 Regulations from applying to this cluster of contracts. Employers might be perturbed to think that contracts of employment are within the 1999 Regulations and will argue that it is difficult, if not impossible, to envisage situations where the employer would be regarded as either a 'seller' or a 'supplier' and the employee cast as a 'consumer.' However, employers regularly supply goods such as tools, equipment and materials to employees in the course of their employment and, an employer's provision of training contracts for his employees might easily be regarded as a supply of services. If onerous, unfair conditions were to be attached to these undertakings for the supply of goods or services to employees, it is difficult to see, at least in principle, why the UTCCR 1999 should not render them unenforceable. Moreover, there is recent authority that the UCTA, s. 3, can apply to contracts of employment (see *Brigden* v *American Express Bank Ltd* [2000] IRLR 94).

The 'consumer' is defined in reg. 3(1) as 'any natural person who, in contracts covered by these Regulations, is acting for purposes which are outside his trade, business or profession'. Although this definition applies only to 'natural' persons and does not include limited companies (cf the UCTA and *R & B Customs Brokers Co. Ltd* v *United Dominions Trust Ltd* [1988] 1 WLR 321, where limited companies can be regarded as consumers), there is no restriction on the type of goods or services to be supplied (cf the UCTA, s. 12(1)(c), where consumer *goods* must be 'of a type ordinarily supplied for private use or consumption').

The principles utilized in the UTCCR 1999 are both broad and radical. Three pivotal elements feature in the definition of an 'unfair term' in reg. 5(1), namely: (i) an absence of good faith; (ii) a significant imbalance in the parties' rights and obligations under the contract; and (iii) detriment to the consumer. These factors are, potentially, much broader than the notion of 'reasonableness' in the UCTA, and it is plain that

English law must begin to develop the precept of good faith and fair dealing in consumer contracts. Good faith encompasses both a *substantive* test of fairness and the more accessible, *procedural* test of fairness in contract formation (e.g., misrepresentation, duress, and the notion that contract terms must be legible and understandable). The Office of Fair Trading (*Unfair Contract Terms*, Bulletin No. 2, September 1996, para. 2.22) has accentuated that, in assessing good faith, it takes account of the availability and use of explanatory pre-contractual brochures and whether, having signed a contract, consumers are given a reasonable 'cooling-off' period in which they may cancel the contract without penalty.

The House of Lords has recently considered the question of unfairness under the UTCCR 1994 in *Director General of Fair Trading* v *First National Bank plc* [2002] 1 AC 481. The agreement under scrutiny was a standard form loan agreement regulated by the Consumer Credit Act 1974 (CCA). Clause 8 provided that, should the borrower default on his repayments, interest continued to be payable at the contract rate on the outstanding principal plus accrued interest unpaid, until any judgment obtained by the bank was discharged. Interest thus continued to be payable before and after judgment until that judgment was discharged by payment. The Director General's contention was that cl. 8 would operate unfairly where (a) judgment was obtained against the borrower; (b) an order was made to pay the debt by instalments, e.g., a time-order under the CCA, s. 129; but (c) no order was made under the CCA, s. 136 to amend the agreement, with the result that interest would continue to accrue notwithstanding the due payment of the instalments ordered. The Court of Appeal had held ([2000] QB 672) that the clause had not been drawn to the borrower's attention at or before the conclusion of the contract and he would not be given notice of it at any later time prior to the making of an order nor in the order itself. The Court thus considered that cl. 8 was unfair in that it created 'unfair surprise'. That decision was reversed by the House of Lords. The House held that a 'significant imbalance' occurred where a term was so weighted in favour of the supplier as to tilt the parties' contractual rights and obligations in his favour and that 'good faith' connoted fair and open dealing. Accordingly, terms had to be expressed fully and clearly and suppliers could not take advantage of the consumer's weaker bargaining position. In assessing the fairness of cl. 8, the House held that the borrower's obligation to repay the principal in full together with interest was unambiguously and clearly expressed in the contract and contained nothing unbalanced or detrimental to the consumer. It was also pertinent to note that the CCA had not prohibited the use of a term such as that in cl. 8 and neither was there any scheme in the CCA under which notice of the protective provisions in ss. 129 and 136 had to be drawn to the borrower's attention at the date of contract. This meant that the borrower's difficulties stemmed from the lack of procedural safeguards which would bring the relief available to his attention. Lord Bingham of Cornhill had no doubt that this situation was 'unacceptable' (p. 496) but it did not indicate that the term was unfair *per se*.

As well as injecting into the mainstream of English law the radical concepts discussed above, there are certain other aspects of the UTCCR 1999 which add to their utility. First, sch. 2 contains an 'indicative and non-exhaustive list of the terms which may be regarded as unfair' (reg. 5(5)), the list comprising 17 potentially unfair terms. Secondly, under reg. 10(1), it is the duty of the Director General of Fair Trading to consider complaints made to him regarding unfair terms and, under reg. 12(1), he may apply for an injunction against the person using such a term. Regulation 11 extends the power to seek an injunction to other regulatory bodies which are specified in sch. 1, e.g., the Directors General of Electricity, Gas and Water. Further, the power to seek injunctions extends to every weights and measures authority in Great Britain and to the Consumers' Association.

It is indisputable that the scope of the Regulations and the broad notions of fairness, good faith and openness which underpin their operation, mean that businesses using standard form contracts can no longer take advantage of their superior bargaining strengths to abuse consumers and treat them unfairly.

Misrepresentation

Introduction

During the course of pre-contractual negotiations a number of statements may be made with a view to inducing the other party to enter into the contract. For example, the seller of a car may describe it as 'a good little runner' or 'accident-free' or as having 'very low mileage'. **Chapter 5** explained the circumstances in which such representations might constitute terms of the contract, depending upon the objectively defined intentions of the parties, their respective states of knowledge and so forth. If a breach of contract resulted (i.e. the statements proved false) the representee could claim damages and/or repudiation. However, the representee possesses an alternative course of action which is to sue in misrepresentation. Students are well advised to treat these two areas as forming one unit, for whereas damages in contract accentuate loss of bargain, damages for misrepresentation are based on reliance losses. The resulting difference requires close scrutiny when evaluating which course of action offers the greater benefits to a claimant in terms of damages for losses suffered. In particular, recent case law has drawn attention to the advantages of suing under s. 2(1) of the Misrepresentation Act 1967, where applicable, as opposed to pursuing a breach of contract action.

For most purposes the definition of a misrepresentation is as follows: a false statement of fact, made pre-contractually, which is intended to induce the representee to enter into a contract and which has that effect. If an actionable misrepresentation is found to exist a court will then need to consider the available remedies. On this basis, one would be well-advised to adopt the following structure for answering any problem question on misrepresentation.

Is it a Statement of Existing Fact?

As a *general* rule, statements of fact do not include vague or commendatory puffs, opinions, beliefs, statements as to the future, and statements of law. Thus the description of land as being 'fertile and improvable' was held not to give rise to any liability (see *Dimmock* v *Hallett* (1866) 2 Ch App 21). Note that all cases involving the description of property for sale should now be read in the light of the Property Misdescriptions Act 1993 which imposes strict limits on the use of estate agents' flowery jargon.

Even statements which are more precise may not be characterised as statements of *fact*, e.g., the unambiguous opinion of a declared amateur (see *Bisset v Wilkinson* [1927] AC 177). However, a statement of opinion or belief will generally, by implication, contain a representation that the person making it actually holds the belief or opinion. The test, often used, is whether the opinion or belief is held on reasonable grounds (see *Smith v Land & House Property Corporation* (1884) 28 Ch D 7). As a general rule of thumb one might say that the greater the expertise of the representor the more likely that a court will interpret his opinion as being a statement of fact (see *Reese River Silver Mining Co. v Smith* [1869] LR HL 64).

Thus, the types of question one should *initially* be considering are:

(a)   is the statement too vague?

(b)   is it stated as an opinion or as a fact?

(c)   how knowledgeable is the representor?

(d)   is the representor misrepresenting the state of his mind?

Statements as to the Future

A promise as to the future which is subsequently broken is not an actionable misrepresentation as there is no statement of *existing fact*. But there is a limit. For example, obtaining a loan by 'representing' that it *will* be used for one purpose but then using it for a different purpose creates no problems. However, liability would arise if, when the representation was made, the representor had no intention of using the money for the stated purpose (see generally *British Airways Board v Taylor* [1976] 1 All ER 65 and *Edgington v Fitzmaurice* (1885) 24 Ch D 459: 'The state of a man's mind is as much a fact as the state of his digestion' *per* Bowen LJ).

Statements of Law

It was normally assumed that a representation of law could not found an action merely because it was wrong — unless it had been fraudulent in which case the state of the representor's mind had been misrepresented. However, first, a court must distinguish between questions of *law* and *fact*; for example, a statement as to the effect of a private document (e.g. a will) might constitute a fact insofar as it related to the contents of the document rather than its meaning. Secondly, in *Vraj Pankhania v Hackney LBC* (2002) *unreported*, the High Court has stated that the distinction between law and fact is illogical and should be ignored.

Silence

In general, *caveat emptor* prevails so there is no duty of disclosure in pre-contractual dealings (see *Keates v Cadogan* (1851) 10 CB 591). However, silence or non-disclosure can lead to an active or implied misrepresentation so always consider the following questions:

(a) Does the defendant's conduct amount to an active concealment of a defect? For example, in *Gordon v Selico Ltd* (1986) 278 EG 53 it was held that painting over dry rot, immediately prior to sale of the property, was a fraudulent misrepresentation (see also *Walters v Morgan* (1861) 3 DF & J 718 which considered the overlap between oral statements and physical behaviour).

(b) Does the statement constitute a half-truth? Silence can distort a positive representation by conveying the wrong impression (see *Atlantic Estates plc v Ezekiel* [1991] 35 EG 118; *Gran Gelato Ltd v Richcliff* [1992] Ch 560; and *Spice Girls Ltd v Aprilia World Service BV* [2000] EMLR 478).

(c) Has there been a change in circumstances? A subsequent change in circumstances prior to the contract which falsifies an existing representation should be disclosed (see *With v O'Flanagan* [1936] Ch 575).

(d) Does the defendant's conduct incorporate an implicit guarantee of a factual character? If goods are bought there is an implied representation that they will be paid for, if goods are sold there is an implied representation that, to the seller's knowledge, they exist (see generally *Edinburgh United Breweries v Molleson* [1894] AC 96).

(e) Is there a fiduciary relationship between the parties? If so, a duty of disclosure will be implied (see *Tate v Williamson* (1866) 2 Ch App 55).

Is there Evidence of Inducement and Reliance?

There is no requirement that a misrepresentation must relate to a fundamental matter, merely that it constitutes a *material factor*, i.e. it must be something that would affect the judgment of a reasonable man in deciding whether, and on what terms, to enter a contract (see *Edgington v Fitzmaurice, supra*).

However, the representee must have actually allowed the representation to influence his mind. The following questions might be pertinent in this context:

(a) Was the representee ignorant of the misrepresentation? An uncommunicated misrepresentation is not actionable (see *Horsfall v Thomas* (1862) 1 H & C 90).

(b) Was the misrepresentation ignored by the representee? Note that the misrepresentation need not be the sole reason for entering the contract (see *Attwood v Small* (1838) 6 Cl & F 232; *Gran Gelato Ltd v Richcliff*, above).

(c) Was the representee aware of the true facts? Remember, even if there is an opportunity to verify the statements this will not prevent the defendant's liability arising provided that representees do not avail themselves of such opportunities (see *Redgrave v Hurd* (1881) 20 Ch D 1).

What Type of Misrepresentation has been Made?

Fraudulent Misrepresentation

A fraudulent statement is one that is made (a) knowingly, or (b) without belief in its truth, or (c) recklessly, careless whether it be true or false (see *Derry* v *Peek* (1889) 14 App Cas 337). The litmus test is clearly whether there has been an absence of honest belief, honesty in this context denoting a subjective appreciation of events, i.e. *did* rather than *could* the representor honestly hold that view (see *Akerheilm* v *Rolf De Mare* [1959] AC 789).

Negligence at Common Law

Since 1963, it has been possible to argue that a contract-inducing negligent statement may give rise to an action for damages in the tort of negligent misstatement (see *Hedley Byrne & Co.* v *Heller & Partners* [1964] AC 465). Success depends upon proof of a *special relationship* existing between the parties (see *Esso Petroleum Co. Ltd* v *Mardon* [1976] QB 801).

Section 2(1) of the Misrepresentation Act 1967

Unlike negligence at common law, s. 2(1) does not require representees to establish a duty of care. Moreover, it places the burden on representors to prove that they had 'reasonable grounds to believe and did believe up to the time the contract was made that the facts represented were true'. This burden may be difficult to discharge as shown in *Howard Marine & Dredging Co. Ltd* v *Ogden & Sons Ltd* [1978] QB 574, although where the representor is a private individual a court might adopt a more lenient approach (see *Cooper* v *Tamms* [1988] 1 EGLR 257).

Innocent Misrepresentation

This is a statement without any provable fault. Following s. 2(1) we must assume that proof of 'reasonable grounds' is sufficient to demonstrate innocence.

What Remedies are Available?

Fraud

The representee will be entitled to damages in the tort of deceit *and* rescission (subject to exceptions discussed later). The purpose of damages is to restore the victim to the position he occupied before the representation had been made. In fraud, the test is one of 'direct consequence' rather than foreseeability, with damages normally being broken down into two categories: diminution in value and consequential losses. More recently, in *Smith New Court Securities Ltd* v *Scrimgeour Vickers (Asset Management) Ltd* [1996] 4 All ER 769, the House of Lords stated that in cases of fraud the misrepresentor will be liable for all the damage *directly flowing* from the transaction. Although the damages need not be foreseeable, the damage must have been caused by the transaction (see *Doyle* v *Olby (Ironmongers) Ltd* [1969] 2 QB 158). Moreover, in a property transaction the misrepresentee is entitled to recover the full price minus any benefits resulting from the transaction. Normally such benefits will include the current market value at the date of the transaction, although this might be inapplicable if the continuing effect of the misrepresentation induces the claimant to retain the property, or the circumstances of the fraud are such that he is locked into the property. Finally, the misrepresentee can also recover consequential losses but must have taken reasonable steps to mitigate any losses on discovery of the fraud (see also *Standard Chartered Bank* v *Pakistan National Shipping Corp.* [1999] 1 Lloyd's Rep 747). In the words of Lord Steyn: 'the plaintiff is entitled to recover as damages a sum representing the financial loss flowing directly from his alteration of position under the inducement of the fraudulent representations of the defendants' (see *Smith New Court Securities*).

The above statement demonstrates the wide-ranging nature of damages for fraud. For example, they may include lost opportunity costs representing the loss that the misrepresentee has incurred in relying upon the fraud, and thereby not entering a different and more lucrative transaction with the misrepresentor or someone else (see *East* v *Maurer* [1991] 2 QB 297; *Clef Aquitaine SARL* v *Laporte Materials (Barrow) Ltd* [2000] 3 All ER 493).

Negligence at Common Law

The normal remedies are rescission (discussed below) and damages in the tort of negligence (incorporating a test of reasonable foreseeability).

Section 2(1) of the Misrepresentation Act 1967

This section imposes liability in a rather convoluted manner:

> if the person making the representation would be liable in damages . . . had the misrepresentation been made fraudulently, that person shall be so liable notwithstanding that the misrepresentation was not made fraudulently, unless he proves he had reasonable grounds to believe and did believe up to the time the contract was made that the facts represented were true.

Recent case law has shown that the successful claimant will be entitled to the same remedies as those available in fraud unless the representor discharges the burden of proof (see *Naughton* v *O'Callaghan* [1990] 3 All ER 191; *Royscot Trust Ltd* v *Rogerson* [1991] 2 QB 297; *Cemp* v *Dentsply R&D Corp. (No 2)* [1991] 34 EG 62). In particular, damages will be based on 'direct consequence' (tort of deceit) rather than reasonable foreseeability (tort of negligence). However, in contrast with fraud, there is a possibility that damages under s. 2(1) can be reduced by the court if there is evidence that the claimant has been contributorily negligent (see *Gran Gelato* v *Richcliff* [1992] 1 All ER 865).

Innocent Misrepresentation

At present this area is shrouded in mystery. It would seem that a court may follow one of two lines of authority: award rescission or damages at its discretion under s. 2(2) (consider *Watts* v *Spence* [1976] Ch 165 and *William Sindall plc* v *Cambridgeshire County Council* [1994] 1 WLR 1016), or award rescission with an indemnity (see *Whittington* v *Seale-Hayne* (1900) 82 LT 49 for the limited nature of an indemnity).

Rescission

Although rescission is available for all types of misrepresentation the remedy will be barred by: (a) lapse of time; (b) affirmation; (c) the impossibility of returning the parties to their original position; and (d) third parties having acquired rights to the subject matter prior to the claimant's avoidance of the contract.

Moreover, under s. 2(2) of the 1967 Act a court can award damages in lieu of rescission, for a non-fraudulent misrepresentation (note: it is still a moot point whether this power extends to purely innocent misrepresentations). This discretion will be exercised in accordance with the principles of equity, having regard to the nature of the misrepresentation, the loss that would be caused if the contract were upheld, as well as the loss that rescission would cause to the other party. Initially it appeared that the discretion to award damages in lieu of rescission under s. 2(2) applied even if the right to rescission had been lost (see *Thomas Witter Ltd* v *TBP Industries* [1996] 2 All ER 573), however this now seems unlikely in the light of *Government of Zanzibar* v *British Aerospace Ltd* [2000] 1 WLR 2333 and *Floods of Queensferry Ltd* v *Shand Construction Ltd* [2000] BLR 81.

Has Liability for Misrepresentation been Excluded?

Under s. 3 of the Misrepresentation Act 1967 (as amended by the Unfair Contract Terms Act 1977 (UCTA), s. 8) such an exclusion clause must satisfy the test of reasonableness contained in UCTA 1977, s. 11 (see *Walker* v *Boyle* [1982] 1 WLR 495; *Howard Marine & Dredging Co. Ltd* v *Ogden & Sons Ltd* [1978] QB 574; *Smith* v *Eric S Bush* [1990] AC 831 and the comments in **Chapter 6**).

Is there a Breach of Contract?

As mentioned earlier, this will depend upon considerations outlined in **Chapter 5**. If the statement is a term of the contract then the available remedies will depend upon whether the term is classified as a condition, a warranty or an innominate term. In answering a problem question on misrepresentation a student may be expected to consider the remedies available for breach of contract as compared with those available in misrepresentation. See diagram for a more detailed comparison.

Table 1 **Breach of Contract Section 2(1) Misrepresentation Act 1967**

Offer/Intent	Fact (not Puff/Opinion)
Acceptance of offer	Inducement/reliance
Burden on claimant to establish breach	Burden on defendant to establish 'reasonable grounds'
Repudiation? Is the term a condition, warranty or an innominate term?	Rescission – subject to bars (e.g. lapse of time) and/or section 2(2) of the 1967 act

(cont'd)

Damages	Damages
Robinson v Harman – protecting the expectation interest	Protecting the reliance interest – but see East v Maurer
Remoteness and reasonable contemplation – Hadley v Baxendale	Remoteness and reasonable consequence test – Royscot v Rogerson
Contributory negligence? Strict liability v duty to take reasonable care	Contributory negligence? Redgrave v Hurd, Gran Gelato v Richcliff
Limits on recovery of non-pecuniary losses	Fraud, and therefore s. 2(1), includes anxiety/distress

Q Question 1

Welton Bogg, a well-known singer, decides to use Bikton Concert Hall (BCH) as the first venue in his 'Round UK Music Tour'. During negotiations the BCH Manager, Jim, informs Welton that '. . . the hall will hold 3,000 people . . . [and] . . . the acoustics are suitable for the performance of your musical repertoire'.

Welton signs the contract of hire which contains the following clause: 'The management reserves the right to restrict the capacity of this Theatre on grounds of public safety and does not accept liability for any statements made by BCH staff concerning the quality of the facilities provided'.

Welton's concert is sold out. However, only 2,500 are admitted on the instructions of the local police, and the acoustics are so bad that a large percentage of the audience demands its money back.

The adverse media publicity affects ticket sales for the remainder of Welton's UK tour.

Advise the parties.

Commentary

Adopting the structure used in the introduction to this chapter you must consider the following questions: Do any of the pre-contractual statements made by Jim constitute statements of fact? If so, did any of these statements induce Welton to enter into the contract? What type of misrepresentation was made? What remedies are available? Do any of the statements constitute contractual terms? If so, what remedies are available for breach of contract? What is the effect of the exclusion clause?

- During the preliminary negotiations, did BCH's manager make any statements of fact, or were all his comments mere puffs/opinions?

- Was BCH's silence on any issue, such as audience capacity, capable of being construed as a 'statement of fact'?

- Were any of these 'statements of fact' sufficiently material to have induced Welton to enter into the contract?

- What type of misrepresentation, if any, was BCH guilty of making?

- Is rescission barred for any reason, such as lapse of time etc?

- What types of damages can Welton claim, especially under s. 2(1) of the Misrepresentation Act 1967?

- Would the exclusion clause be regarded as 'reasonable' under s. 8 of the Unfair Contract Terms Act 1977?

⚬ Suggested answer

Welton will need advice on his possible remedies in misrepresentation and for breach of contract. Furthermore, in considering which remedy to pursue, recourse will need to be made to recent decisions which have enhanced the ability to recover damages in misrepresentation.

Misrepresentation can be defined as a false statement of fact, made pre-contractually by one party (representor), with a view to inducing the other party (representee) to enter into the contract. The statement must have been intended to be acted upon and must actually induce the other party to enter the contract.

Did Jim make any false statements of fact? The first statement concerned the capacity of the hall. There is no suggestion that the statement is phrased as an opinion, moreover, even if it were, one would argue that Jim is an expert and that the figure is presumably based upon facts known to him. For example, in *Smith v Land & House Property Corporation* (1884) 28 Ch D 7, the vendor described the sitting tenant as 'desirable and a first class investment'. This constituted a misrepresentation as the only facts known to the vendor were in direct conflict with this summation.

There is, however, a further difficulty. Technically, the capacity of the hall *is* 3,000. Did Jim realise that this figure would be limited by the local police? Perhaps this was a common occurrence when such concerts were held. If so, Jim's silence regarding the safety feature effectively distorts his original statement, thereby conveying the wrong impression to Welton. In common parlance, the statement constitutes a half-truth and, therefore, a statement of fact (e.g. *Nottinghamshire Patent & Brick Tile Co.* v *Butler* (1889) 16 QBD 778).

The second part of Jim's statement is that the 'acoustics are suitable' for the intended performance. The word 'suitable' clearly causes problems as it is a relatively vague and ambiguous term. For example, in *Scott* v *Hanson* (1829) 1 Russ & M 128, the description of land as being 'uncommonly rich water meadow' was held only to constitute a misrepresentation with reference to non-meadow land, rather than meadow that was of poor quality. Perhaps, as in the above paragraph, Welton will need to show that Jim had no facts upon which to base his statement (e.g. *Smith* v *Land & House Property*) in which case he is misrepresenting the state of his mind. As Bowen LJ put it in *Edgington* v *Fitzmaurice* (1885) 29 Ch D 459, 483: 'The state of a man's mind is as much a fact as the state of his digestion.' Moreover, there is some precedent for suggesting that an actionable misrepresentation may lie where an opinion is stated and the representor is the only person to be in a position to know the true facts (*Brown* v *Raphael* [1958] Ch 636).

Assuming that the whole statement constitutes a false statement of fact the next question is whether it was made with an intention of inducing Welton to enter into the contract and, if so, whether Welton relied upon it in this way. In general terms, inducement involves the application of an objective test: would a reasonable man have considered the statement to be a *material* factor? Undoubtedly the answer is yes. The capacity of the hall will influence the hire charge. The standard of acoustics will determine suitability for its intended use.

Has Welton relied upon the statement in entering into the contract? The facts suggest that Welton had already decided to hire the concert hall before negotiations began. But an alternative argument is certainly apparent. Presumably if Jim had proposed a much greater hire charge or the capacity of the hall was embarrassingly low or the acoustics were only considered suitable for the performance of classical opera, then Welton would have withdrawn. In this way, Welton can demonstrate some form of potential reliance. Equally, the possibility of verifying Jim's statements by, for example, reading reviews in the musical press of previous concerts would not jeopardise Welton's case. As the House of Lords stated in *Redgrave* v *Hurd* (1881) 20 Ch D 1, constructive knowledge is insufficient to prove non-reliance.

The remedies for misrepresentation will be determined by the lack of care exercised by the misrepresentor. Traditionally, fraud has attracted the best remedies for the representee but it is difficult to establish. The burden of proof is a heavy one to discharge (e.g. *Derry* v *Peek* (1889) 14 App Cas 337). Moreover, in the light of recent case law concerning the Misrepresentation Act 1967, s. 2(1), it is unlikely that Welton would be advised to pursue a claim in fraud unless he had firm evidence that Jim was intentionally lying.

Alternatively, if a special relationship exists between the parties Welton might consider suing in the tort of negligent misstatement (e.g. *Esso Petroleum Co. Ltd* v *Mardon* [1976] QB 801). Here, Welton must affirmatively establish negligence on the part of Jim in making those pre-contractual statements. However, as we shall see, in view of s. 2(1) of the 1967 Act, it is pointless to pursue this line of argument.

Section 2(1) of the Misrepresentation Act 1967 reverses the burden of proof, requiring Jim to prove that he had 'reasonable grounds' for his belief. This may be difficult to establish, especially in the light of *Howard Marine & Dredging Co. Ltd* v *A Ogden & Sons (Excavations) Ltd* [1978] QB 574, where the Court of Appeal stated that a party had an 'absolute obligation' not to state facts which he had no reasonable grounds for believing were true. As honest belief is insufficient, it would seem difficult for Jim to argue that he was not expected to know of the theatre's capacity when negotiating the hire charge. Perhaps his only escape route would be if the capacity of the hall had never previously been restricted by police measures and the acoustics had always been found to be suitable at previous concerts of a similar nature. This seems unlikely. In the light of these comments, one could safely ignore the possibility of innocent misrepresentation which, in general terms, refers to false statements made without provable fault.

All misrepresentations attract the remedy of rescission although, here, as the concert has been performed, the right will be lost on grounds that *restitutio in integrum* is impossible. It remains a moot point whether damages can be awarded in lieu of rescission under s. 2(2) of the 1967 Act where rescission is barred (see the conflicting decisions in *Thomas Witter Ltd* v *TBP Industries* [1996] 2 All ER 573 and *Government of Zanzibar* v *British Aerospace Ltd* [2000] 1 WLR 2333, *Floods of Queensferry Ltd* v *Shand Construction Ltd* [2000] BLR 81).

Regarding the remedy of damages, Welton would be best advised to pursue his claim under s. 2(1) of the 1967 Act. Recent case law has emphatically stated that damages will be assessed in the tort of deceit, with all its concomitant advantages (e.g. *Royscot Trust Ltd* v *Rogerson* [1991] 2 QB 297). Welton will be entitled to reclaim all those damages which *directly* flow from his reliance upon the misrepresentation, such as the losses sustained in returning money to dissatisfied customers. This might also include any subsequent losses incurred on the remainder of the tour resulting from the adverse media publicity as well as any personal distress and anxiety suffered by Welton (see generally *Doyle* v *Olby (Ironmongers) Ltd* [1969] 2 QB 158; *Archer* v *Brown* [1985] QB 401). Finally, damages may encompass lost opportunity costs such as the profit that Welton would have made if he had booked a different concert hall in the vicinity (see *East* v *Maurer* [1991] 2 QB 297), or the additional profits which he would have made if the transaction with BCH had been more favourable but for any proven fraud (see *Clef Aquitaine SARL* v *Laporte Materials (Barrow) Ltd* [2000] 3 All ER 493).

However, Welton's claim is subject to the enforceability of the exclusion clause inserted into the contract. Assuming the clause has been properly incorporated under existing common law principles (e.g. adequate notice as demonstrated in *Parker* v *South Eastern Ry* (1877) 2 CPD 416) one needs to consider the effect of the Unfair Contract Terms Act 1977, s. 8, which subjects such clauses to a test of reasonableness. Adopting the guidelines in sch. 2 of the Act, the answer might depend upon what opportunity Welton was given of checking on the capacity, whether he received any inducement for agreeing to the clause, and the respective strength of the parties' bargaining positions. Note that with regard to the last point the House of Lords, in *Photo Production Ltd* v *Securicor Transport Ltd* [1980] AC 827, suggested that a very hard line would be taken where equality of bargaining power exists; i.e. freedom of contract prevails and Welton might therefore have to accept the effect of the clause. Welton's only escape route would be the Court of Appeal's decision in *Stewart Gill Ltd* v *Horatio Myer & Co. Ltd* [1992] 1 QB 600, which emphasised that all parts of a clause must be reasonable, irrespective of what reliance is being placed upon each part by either party. If a sub-clause is found to be unreasonable then the whole clause fails. On the present facts, although it *might* be reasonable to restrict admission for reasons of public safety, the whole clause might still fail owing to the breadth of the latter part, especially as it seems to absolve BCH from fraudulent statements.

Finally, Welton should consider the alternative possibility of claiming damages for breach of contract. The test for determining whether a pre-contractual statement has become part of the contract is one of objective intent (e.g. *Heilbut, Symons & Co.* v *Buckleton* [1913] AC 30). The courts have developed a variety of guidelines as aids to identifying the requisite degree of contractual intent. For example, Welton could argue that Jim possessed specialist knowledge (e.g. *Oscar Chess Ltd* v *Williams* [1957] 1 WLR 370), that he (Welton) attached considerable importance to the statement (e.g. *Bannerman* v *White* (1861) 10 CB (NS) 844), and that he was not encouraged by Jim to verify the statement. Jim would point out that the statement was not incorporated into the written contract (e.g. *Birch* v *Paramount Estates (Liverpool) Ltd* (1956) 16 EG 396), that Welton's previous experience of arranging musical venues should be taken into account as it created an equality of expertise between the parties (see generally *Bentley (Dick) Productions Ltd* v *Harold Smith (Motors) Ltd* [1965] 1 WLR 623) and, finally, that there was no evidence of a collateral contract as Welton did not place any specific emphasis on Jim's statement during the negotiations (unlike in *City and Westminster Properties (1934) Ltd* v *Mudd* [1959] Ch 129). The decision could go either way but it does seem that the statement lies at the heart of the hire contract and therefore would be intended to have some legal effect, especially with regard to the hall's capacity which is couched in a clear and definite manner.

If the statement constitutes a term of the contract, Welton's primary remedy would be damages. These would depend on whether, at the time of making the contract, they were in the reasonable contemplation of the parties as liable to result from the specified breach (see *Hadley* v *Baxendale* (1854) 9 Exch 341). For example, should the parties have foreseen the effect of the reduced hall capacity and/or below par acoustics, and their consequential impact on future tour receipts? (Note: it is unlikely that an examiner would expect an extended analysis of damages for breach of contract in a problem question so clearly based on the potential existence of an actionable misrepresentation.)

Q Question 2

On 11 January, Reckless, the purchasing manager of Addit Ltd was visited by Sharp, a sales representative of Calculo Ltd. Sharp showed Reckless the 'Perfecto Printing Machine' and during negotiations for its purchase Sharp said: 'If you buy this machine you will see that it is beyond belief — its multi-functions and speed leave all its competitors standing. Further, we guarantee it absolutely for two years from the date of delivery.' Reckless is very impressed with the machine when he briefly tests it. Being impressed and having in mind the alterations being done to his offices which would, when completed, easily accommodate the machine, Reckless agrees to buy one 'Perfecto'.

On 17 January, a brief written contract is entered into which makes no mention of a guarantee, nor are there any written specifications covering the machine's functions, capabilities or size.

The 'Perfecto' is delivered on 3 March and it develops a minor fault on 10 March which Calculo Ltd repairs free of charge. The machine is the same size as the demonstration model but it proves to be very large and cumbersome in the altered offices. The machine breaks down again on 1 April and is again repaired by Calculo Ltd, a service for which they charge the cost of labour. The machine is much slower in operation than the previous machine which it replaced, and when it fails again on 29 April, Reckless wants to return it and obtain a full refund of the purchase price. Calculo Ltd refuses to take back the machine or replace it.

Advise Reckless.

Commentary

This problem relates to terms of the contract and misrepresentation. First, the question of whether Reckless has a remedy for breach of contract should be considered. The better student will also consider whether a collateral contract might be established. Secondly, misrepresentation as a possible remedy must be evaluated. This question is both wide-ranging and technical and requires detailed knowledge if it is to be answered successfully.

- Are any of Sharp's statements capable of being terms of the contract? Is there scope for any collateral contract to exist in the circumstances?

- How would the terms that have been broken be classified?

- Does the parol evidence rule apply here?

- Did Sharp make any statements of fact, or were his statements mere puffs/ opinions?

- Was Reckless induced by Sharp, or by his own investigation, to enter into the contract?

- What type of misrepresentation has occurred, if any?

- What are the general remedies available to Reckless, e.g. rescission and/or damages? What if Reckless was considered to have contributed to his own loss?

:Q: Suggested answer

There are three grounds of action which Reckless (R) may try to pursue in this problem: breach of contract, breach of a collateral contract and misrepresentation. If R can establish that the statements made by Sharp (S) are terms of the contract he may repudiate the contract and claim damages for breach of condition or obtain damages for breach of warranty. It is more likely that the courts would consider the statements to be innominate terms thereby relating the remedy to the gravity of the breach. But can R show that the statements are terms of the contract as opposed to mere representations? It was emphasised in *Heilbut, Symons & Co.* v *Buckleton* [1913] AC 30 that determination of which statements constitute terms involves ascertaining the objective intention of the parties. The parol evidence rule, that extrinsic evidence may not be adduced to add to, vary or contradict writing, therefore embodies the strong presumption that if the parties have committed their agreement to an all-embracing written contract, it must represent their finalised intent. In the problem, the material facts are omitted from the written contract and an obvious obstacle is placed in R's path. Nevertheless, if the parties intend to contract on terms partly-written and partly-oral, the law will give effect to such intent (see *Allen* v *Pink* (1838) 4 M & W 140). As the problem refers to 'a brief written contract' this is in R's favour.

More detailed questions might disclose the parties' intentions. First, is there a substantial lapse of time between the oral statement and the writing? If the period is short, the courts may consider the oral statement to be a term but much may depend on the nature of the goods sold, for example, so no hard-and-fast rule can be established (see *Routledge* v *McKay* [1954] 1 WLR 615 in which the period was seven days). Secondly, has S any expert knowledge? If so, more weight attaches to his statements (see *Harling* v *Eddy* [1951] 2 KB 739) and as S is the sales representative of Calculo Ltd, it may be assumed that he has such knowledge and expertise. Thirdly, does R rely on this statement emanating from an expert. Some cases such as *Schawel* v *Reade* [1913] 2 IR 81, where the statement in question was a term, are justified on the basis that the statement was of crucial importance to the other party and thus the dominating factor in its formation. It is disputable whether this statement had such an influential effect on R as he tests the machine and is impressed by its performance. Finally, there is no suggestion that S has indicated that R should verify the statement thereby nullifying it as a term as in *Ecay* v *Godfrey* (1974) 80 Ll LR 286, or that verification is normal in R's business (see *Leaf* v *International Galleries* [1950] 2 KB 86). On balance, therefore, it is possible that R could establish this statement as a term of the contract.

R may try to establish a collateral contract which has the advantage of circumvent-ing some of the difficulties discussed above. Most particularly, the notion is an excep-tion to the parol evidence rule in that a separate contract is shown to exist, the consideration for which is entry into the main contract. Here the oral statement could amount to such a contract and add to the written undertaking which is silent on the material points as in *Mann* v *Nunn* (1874) 30 LT 526. The collateral contract has the singular advantage that apparently vacuous statements, such as S's promise that the machine is 'beyond belief ', may constitute its terms. In *Andrews* v *Hopkinson* [1957] 1 QB 229, the defendant's promise that the car in question was 'a good little bus' and that he 'would stake his life on it' was a collateral contract which was actionable when the car swerved into a lorry as a result of its defective steering mechanism.

R's last remedy may lie in misrepresentation. A misrepresentation is a false state-ment of fact made by the representor which is intended to induce and, in fact, does induce the representee to enter into the contract. The first sentence of S's claim seems to be too vague and ambiguous to amount to a statement of fact (see *Scott* v *Hanson* (1829) 1 Russ & M 128; *Dimmock* v *Hallett* (1866) 2 Ch App 21). However, should S assert that his statements are only opinions, as in *Bisset* v *Wilkinson* [1927] AC 177, he might be met with the argument that, as an expert, he is impliedly saying that he knows facts which justify his opinion (see *Smith* v *Land and House Property Corporation* (1884) 28 Ch D 7). Also, *Brown* v *Raphael* [1958] Ch 636 establishes that an opinion may be actionable as a misrepresentation where the representor is in a far stronger position to ascertain the facts than the representee. This is clearly relevant in R's case. In any event, the second sentence of S's claim would appear to be an unequivocal, false statement of fact in that Calculo Ltd refuses to replace the machine or take it back. As the statements emanate from S, who is an authoritative source, the fact of R's reliance upon them and his consequent inducement to enter into the contract would seem to follow as an objective fact. But are there any factors which might nullify such reliance and inducement? It is unlikely that R's testing the machine would mean that he relies upon his own judgment, as was successfully pleaded in *Attwood* v *Small* (1838) 6 Cl & F 232, for R's testing is brief and the machine does not exhibit the characteristics of the one that is delivered. Moreover, it is clear from *Redgrave* v *Hurd* (1881) 20 Ch D 1, that R's opportunity to discover any defects is irrelevant: construct-ive knowledge is insufficient. Finally, although R may have been partially induced to buy the machine because of the structural alterations to his offices, S cannot escape liability by pointing to other such contributory causes which induce R to enter into the contract. *Edgington* v *Fitzmaurice* (1885) 29 Ch D 459 emphasised that it is suf-ficient if the misrepresentation complained of is simply one of several competing inducements. It appears that R can thus establish an actionable misrepresentation.

It is most unlikely that R could establish a fraudulent misrepresentation as S would have to possess a 'wicked mind' (*Le Lievre* v *Gould* (1893) 1 QB 491; *Derry* v *Peek* (1889) 14 App Cas 337). Moreover, in view of the liability imposed by s. 2(1) of the Misrepresentation Act 1967, both an action in deceit and one for damages at common law under the principles of *Hedley Byrne & Co. Ltd* v *Heller and Partners Ltd* [1964] AC 465, are needlessly burdensome for a representee. In effect, s. 2(1) imposes liability for negligent misrepresentations and reverses the normal burden of proof; once the representee proves that there has been a misrepresentation, the burden shifts to the representor to show that he had 'reasonable ground to believe and did believe up to the time the contract was made that the facts represented were true'. It is clear from *Howard Marine and Dredging Co. Ltd* v *A Ogden & Sons (Excavations) Ltd* [1978] QB 574 that it is extremely difficult to discharge this burden: honest belief is insufficient in that the representor must positively establish reasonable grounds for his belief. The question here is thus whether S *ought* to know the comparative advantages of the machine and whether his statements could be verified objectively, e.g., reports from customers regarding the machine's superior capabilities.

As R wishes to return the machine and have his purchase price refunded, he would be seeking rescission of the contract. The purpose of rescission is to restore the *status quo ante* and whilst it may literally be possible on the facts, it is unlikely to be available as R may find his claim barred. He has probably affirmed the contract by both allowing the repairs to the machine (particularly by paying Calculo's labour charges) and continuing with its use, as in *Long* v *Lloyd* [1958] 1 WLR 753. Moreover, as the breakdowns and repairs occur over a two month period, there may be a sufficient lapse of time thereby adding to the presumption of R's affirmation (*Clough* v *L & NW Ry* (1871) LR 7 Ex 26).

Regarding the remedy of damages, R would be best advised to pursue his claim under s. 2(1) of the 1967 Act, as damages will be assessed in the tort of deceit, with all its concomitant advantages (see *Smith New Court Securities Ltd* v *Scrimgeour Vickers (Asset Management) Ltd* [1996] 4 All ER 769 and its explanation of the direct consequence test). R will be entitled to reclaim all those damages which *directly* flow from his reliance upon the misrepresentation such as the losses sustained in possessing a malfunctioning printing machine, the possible need to hire a substitute machine if the repairs were to take too long and the superior performance of R's original machine. This latter point would emphasise the reliance aspect of R's losses, but note that any failure to act reasonably once the misrepresentation has been discovered might leave R open to a charge of contributory negligence and a consequential reduction in any award of damages (see *Gran Gelato* v *Richcliff* [1992] 1 All ER 865). Finally, in the light of *East* v *Maurer* [1991] 2 QB 297, damages may encompass lost opportunity costs, i.e. the benefits that R would have obtained if he had purchased an alternative machine from a different source for the same price which *did* meet the standards originally claimed by S.

Q Question 3

Recent case law suggests that litigants are generally better advised to pursue a claim in misrepresentation rather than for breach of contract.
  Discuss.

Commentary

Although a general comparison of the remedies available for misrepresentation and for breach of contract is called for, the question clearly focuses upon the recent spate of Court of Appeal decisions in which damages under s. 2(1) of the Misrepresentation Act 1967 have been equated with those available for an action in deceit. Your answer should therefore include a comparison of the following points: (a) the availability of rescission and repudiation; and (b) the basis upon which damages are awarded in misrepresentation and for breach of contract.

- What is the difference between repudiation and rescission?

- How are contract terms classified? Why is this important?

- What is the basis for awarding damages for breach of contract?

- What is the basis of awarding damages for misrepresentation?

- What are the advantages of suing under s. 2(1) of the Misrepresentation Act 1967?

- What is the relevance of contributory negligence, fraud and direct consequences damages, and loss of opportunity damages?

☼ Suggested answer

The general remedies for breach of contract are repudiation and/or damages, whereas in misrepresentation the remedies are rescission and/or damages. The best means of comparing these remedies is to consider separately (a) the availability of repudiation and rescission, and (b) the basis for awarding damages in each area. One interesting feature will be that, whereas contract remedies will depend primarily upon whether the term which the defendant has broken is a condition or a warranty, in misrepresentation it is the culpability of the defendant which will determine the claimant's remedies.

Rescission v Repudiation

A victim of a breach of contract does not possess an automatic right to repudiate the contract. The right of repudiation generally arises only in two circumstances. First, where it is established that the term which has been broken constitutes either a condition or, following the decision in *Hongkong Fir Shipping Co. Ltd* v *Kawasaki Kisen Kaisha Ltd* [1962] 2 QB 26, that it is an innominate term breach of which has deprived the victim of a substantial part of the intended benefit under the contract. The second possibility is that the contract-breaker has intimated by words or conduct his refusal to perform outstanding contractual obligations as they fall due (see generally *Woodar Investment Development Ltd* v *Wimpey Construction (UK) Ltd* [1980] 1 WLR 277). If neither of the above situations applies the victim of a breach will be left with a remedy in damages.

The law on misrepresentation does not consider the relative importance of pre-contractual statements. Provided a false statement of fact has been made, the representee, in principle, will have the right to claim rescission and thereby avoid the contract. The representee need only establish that the statement induced him to enter the contract, i.e. that it was a material factor (see *Edgington* v *Fitzmaurice* (1885) 29 Ch D 459). This right is available for all types of misrepresentation — innocent, negligent and fraudulent. However, the right to rescission can be lost on the following grounds:

(a) by affirmation of the contract (see *Long* v *Lloyd* [1958] 1 WLR 753;

(b) by lapse of time (see *Leaf* v *International Galleries* [1950] 2 KB 86);

(c) where third parties have acquired rights in the subject-matter prior to avoidance of the contract (see *White* v *Garden* (1851) 10 CB 919); and

(d) where the parties cannot be restored substantially to their original positions (see *Clarke* v *Dickson* (1858) EB & E 148).

(Note: a good student might make three further points at this juncture.)

First, before the passing of the Misrepresentation Act 1967 a representee lost the right to rescind if the representation became part of the contract. In such cases the representee would seek repudiation, provided the term broken was a condition or the representor had shown a clear intention to repudiate the contract. However, s. 1(a) of the 1967 Act provides that the right of rescission remains, notwithstanding that the representation has become a term of the contract. This clearly provides litigants with a powerful weapon when comparing the remedies available in misrepresentation with those for breach of contract. Secondly, under s. 2(2) of the 1967 Act the court is given a discretion when dealing with non-fraudulent misrepresentations to declare the contract as subsisting and award damages in lieu of rescission, taking account of the equitable considerations affecting *both* parties. Thirdly, a misrepresentation renders a contract voidable *ab initio* (provided the representee elects to rescind) so the parties are restored to the positions they occupied before the contract was entered into (see *Abram SS Co.* v *Westville Shipping Co. Ltd* [1923] AC 773). On a superficial level, the right of repudiation is different; i.e., it is prospective in nature, relieving the representee of the *future* performance of obligations. However, this difference often has little meaning in practice as representees may, for example, possess certain restitutionary remedies by which they can (a) recover money transferred under the contract, or (b) claim payment on a *quantum meruit* basis for services rendered.

Damages

In misrepresentation damages will be assessed on a tortious basis, the general purpose being to place the victim in the position he occupied before the misrepresentation took place. This is often termed 'compensation for reliance losses' as it does not take account of the profit which the victim was expecting to derive from a proper performance of the contract. Conversely, damages for breach of contract often incorporate this wasted expectation loss under the heading of 'loss of bargain'. Here, the purpose of damages is to put the claimant, so far as possible, in the position he would have occupied had the contract been properly performed (see *Robinson* v *Harman* (1848) 1 Ex 850, 855), although a court, in appropriate circumstances, may protect a victim's reliance or restitution interests (see *Anglia Television Ltd* v *Reed* [1972] 1 QB 60).

A simple example illustrates the above distinction between contract and tort. X buys a car for £1,000 on the strength of the seller's statement that it is worth £1,200 but later finds out that the car is worth only £500. In contract, the starting point would be the loss of bargain, equivalent to £700, whereas in misrepresentation, the losses associated with X's reliance would suggest an initial figure of £500. Most textbooks consequently assert that damages in contract are normally higher than those in misrepresentation. There are, however, a variety of reasons why this may have changed recently.

As an introductory remark one might mention that prior to the passing of the Misrepresentation Act 1967 damages were only available for a fraudulent misrepresentation — an allegation of fraud being extremely difficult to substantiate. Damages were based on the tort of deceit, the representor being liable for *all* the losses flowing directly from his fraud even though such losses might not have been reasonably foreseeable (see *Doyle* v *Olby (Ironmongers) Ltd* [1969] 2 QB 158; *Smith New Court Securities Ltd* v *Scrimgeour Vickers (Asset Management) Ltd* [1996] 4 All ER 769). Moreover, apart from mere pecuniary loss the courts permitted the recovery of various types of non-pecuniary losses including damages for pain and suffering (see *Burrows* v *Rhodes* [1899] 1 QB 816), physical inconvenience and discomfort (see *Mafo* v *Adams* [1970] 1 QB 548) and mental disquiet (see *Archer* v *Brown* [1985] QB 401). Contrast this with the pre-1967 position for non-fraudulent misrepresentations where rescission was the primary remedy, if available, and damages took the very limited form of an 'indemnity' (see *Whittington* v *Seale-Hayne* (1900) 82 LT 49). Little wonder that an action for breach of contract contrasted favourably with that in misrepresentation. However, the passing of the Misrepresentation Act 1967 has changed this in at least four ways.

First, damages are now available for all non-innocent misrepresentations, innocence in this context proving difficult to establish (see *Howard Marine & Dredging Co. Ltd* v *A Ogden & Sons (Excavations) Ltd* [1978] QB 574). In particular, the burden of proof is reversed under s. 2(1) of the 1967 Act, requiring the representor to prove that he had reasonable grounds to believe and did believe up to the time the contract was made, that the facts represented were true.

Secondly, although there was some confusion as to basis upon which damages would be awarded under s. 2(1) it has now become clear that the measure of damages is based on the tort of deceit. This conclusion results from the peculiarity of the wording employed in the section. Specifically, if the representor would have been liable in damages had the misrepresentation been made fraudulently 'that person shall be so liable notwithstanding that the misrepresentation was not made fraudulently' provided objective innocence cannot be proven. The effect of this is that, unlike damages for breach of contract, which are limited by the reasonable contemplation of the parties (see *Hadley* v *Baxendale* (1854) 9 Exch 341), damages under s. 2(1) follow the test laid down in *Doyle* v *Olby (Ironmongers) Ltd* [1969] 2 QB 158. These damages are based on a direct consequence test in which reasonable foreseeability has no application. This indeed was the conclusion reached by the courts in such cases as *Naughton* v *O'Callaghan* [1990] 3 All ER 191, *Royscot Trust Ltd* v *Rogerson* [1991] 2 QB 297 and *Cemp* v *Dentsply R&D Corp. (No. 2)* [1991] 34 EG 62.

Thirdly, a further effect of the above is that many types of non-pecuniary loss which are not *normally* available for breach of contract can be recovered in the tort of deceit and also by using s. 2(1) of the 1967 Act (e.g. anxiety and stress).

Finally, two Court of Appeal decisions have even blurred the distinction between loss of bargain damages in contract and reliance losses in tort. In *East* v *Maurer* [1991] 2 QB 297 M owned two successful hairdressing salons. E bought one of them in 1979, being induced by M's representation that M had no intention of working in the other salon. In fact, M continued to work in the other salon, enticing many customers away from E's salon. After several abortive attempts, E sold out several years later at a considerable loss. The court held that a fraudulent misrepresentation had been made and, amongst other things, awarded E a sum of money equivalent to her lost opportunity cost. This sum reflected the profits which E would have derived from the purchase of a different salon if she had not been induced into buying M's salon. This measure seems very similar to awarding damages for loss of bargain (although see *McCullagh* v *Lane Fox & Partners* [1994] 1 EGLR 48) and reinforces the attraction of bringing an action under s. 2(1) of the Misrepresentation Act 1967, which employs the same measure of damages, as opposed to suing for breach of contract. More recently, in *Clef Aquitaine SARL* v *Laporte Materials (Barrow) Ltd* [2000] 3 All ER 493, it was stated that it will sometimes be possible for the claimant to prove that a different and more favourable transaction would have been entered into but for the fraud, and to measure and recover the claimant's loss on that basis.

In conclusion, where a pre-contractual statement constitutes *both* a breach of a contract and a misrepresentation, recent case law has suggested that the representee must think long and hard before choosing which action to pursue. The use of a deceit measure for all non-innocent misrepresentations, with its disregard of any foreseeability criterion, the potentially enhanced recovery of non-pecuniary losses, and even the award of quasi 'loss of bargain' damages, is clearly advantageous in many situations. Against this must be contrasted the problems of recovering any damages for purely innocent misrepresentations, the possible bars to the remedy of rescission, including the exercise of judicial discretion under s. 2(2) of the 1967 Act (see *William Sindall plc* v *Cambridgeshire County Council* [1994] 1 WLR 1016), and the general emphasis on reliance losses in tort.

Improper Pressure

Introduction

The formation of a contract requires the acceptance of an offer, the requisite degree of contractual intent and the presence of consideration. This 'indivisible trinity' is based on the notion of freedom of contract: parties give their consent to be legally bound. To a layman, freedom and consent would suggest a degree of choice and the exercise of free will. But this is not necessarily true. For example, a fundamental inequality of consideration might imply that improper pressure had been applied; nevertheless, it was only recently that courts were prepared to acknowledge this formal link (e.g. *Williams* v *Roffey Bros & Nicholls (Contractors) Ltd* [1991] 1 QB 1).

The tension in the law is clear. How does a court decide whether the parties intended that their bargained-for promises should create definite contractual relations? For example, if A signs away his property to B at a gross undervalue, should this suggest a lack of consent, the presence of some impropriety or merely crass stupidity? The basic answer requires one to focus on the relationship between the parties. Commonsense dictates that a court would be more fairly disposed to intervene where the relationship is of a more personal nature, based on confidence and trust, rather than where the parties are businessmen dealing at arm's length. This coincides with the current division in the law as represented by the twin doctrines of undue influence and economic duress.

The doctrine of undue influence covers a variety of personal relationships, fiduciary in nature, where trust is reposed and the possibility of its abuse by the dominant party necessitates adequate protection of the weaker party. Moreover, it is regularly invoked by sureties where their relationship with the creditor is manipulated when the debtor acts as intermediary; for example, a husband persuading his wife to guarantee his company's overdraft with a bank. Conversely, in the commercial field, although an emerging doctrine of economic duress has been employed to strike down some of the more morally reprehensible commercial activities, the doctrine is ring-fenced by a variety of restrictive conditions.

Undue Influence

There are two ways that a contract can be avoided for undue influence: (a) affirmative proof of undue influence, or (b) raising the presumption of undue influence which is not rebutted.

Affirmative Proof of Undue Influence

The courts have never attempted to define undue influence with any precision, but it has been described as:

> . . . some unfair and improper conduct, some coercion from outside, some overreaching, some form of cheating and generally, though not always, some personal advantage gained (*Allcard* v *Skinner* (1887) 36 Ch D 145 *per* Lindley LJ).

The following two factors, therefore, are normally required in order to establish affirmative undue influence:

(a) Evidence of victimisation and, inevitably, some personal gain by the dominant party (e.g. *Nottidge* v *Prince* (1860) 2 Giff 246; *Lyon* v *Home* (1868) LR 6 Eq 655; *Williams* v *Bayley* (1866) LR 1 HL 200).

(b) Lack of independent advice given to, or voluntary action by, the weaker party (see the comments of Bridge LJ in *Brocklehurst's Estate, Hall* v *Roberts* [1978] Ch 14).

In *CIBC Mortgages plc* v *Pitt* [1994] 1 AC 200, the House of Lords stated that there was no need for the weaker party to prove that the transaction had been manifestly disadvantageous.

Presumption of Undue Influence

The presumption arises where a 'special' relationship exists between the parties. Generally this relationship is fiduciary in nature: the weaker party reposes confidence and trust in the dominant party, giving the latter some authority over the decision-making powers of the weaker party and a consequential opportunity to enhance his position unfairly.

The categories of special relationships are not closed. As Sachs LJ indicated in *Lloyds Bank Ltd* v *Bundy* [1975] QB 326, 347, the presumption may arise in any situation where the dominant party has overstepped the boundaries of a normal confidential relationship. However, there are certain relationships where the existence of undue influence will be automatically presupposed, for example, solicitor and client, religious leader and disciple (e.g. *Allcard* v *Skinner*) and parent and child (e.g. *Lancashire Loans Ltd* v *Black* [1934] 1 KB 380).

In this area, the following questions should be posed:

(a) What is the relationship between the parties and is there a position of actual or potential dominance?

(b) Does the relationship between the parties fit one of the recognised categories where a presumption arises?

(c) If not, do the facts justify the existence of such a special relationship?

   (i) For example, has the dominant party taken on the role of advisor or has he encouraged the weaker party to place trust and confidence in the advice that is proffered?

(ii) Will the dominant party gain some form of personal advantage from the weaker party's reliance?

(iii) Is the transaction not readily explicable by the relationship of the parties?

An affirmative answer to the majority of these questions would imply that a presumption of undue influence has arisen. Note that the last question (c)(iii) must *always* be answered affirmatively, with the cogency of any explanation increasing in line with the seriousness of the disadvantage suffered by the weaker party (see *Royal Bank of Scotland* v *Etridge (No. 2)* [2001] UKHL 44, [2001] 4 All ER 449).

If the presumption has arisen the onus shifts to the dominant party. A successful rebuttal would *normally* require evidence that the weaker party, at the very least, was encouraged to seek independent advice. This advice must ensure that its recipient obtains a 'full, free and informed estimate' of the expediency of entering the transaction (see *Inche Noriah* v *Sheik Allie Bin Omar* [1929] AC 127).

Undue Influence and the Intermediary

A perennial problem facing banks and other money-lending institutions is the procedures that should be followed when dealing with married couples eager to use their marital homes as security for bank loans. In particular, how far should banks try to protect wives from the unreasonable pressures of their husbands? The potential for husbands to place unfair pressure on, or trick, their wives into signing away the matrimonial home for the purposes of securing business loans is all too clear. These issues have been the subject of continual litigation over the past last twenty years, requiring the courts to establish a clear set of guidelines that, if followed properly, would ensure that creditor institutions were not tainted by any undue pressure or deception employed by a husband over his wife.

When answering any question in this area, it is essential that you are fully conversant with the three pivotal House of Lords' decisions in *Barclays Bank plc* v *O'Brien* [1994] 1 AC 180, *CIBC Mortgages plc* v *Pitt* [1994] 1 AC 200, and *Royal Bank of Scotland* v *Etridge (No. 2)* [2001 UKHL 44, [2001] 4 All ER 449. For example, the legal framework created by the Law Lords flows from the important distinction that was drawn between wives acting as sureties for their husbands' entrepreneurial activities and those seeking to release the capital tied up within the matrimonial home for purely domestic reasons (e.g. buying a family car). The former type of transaction has an increased possibility that a husband, perhaps desperate to keep his business afloat, might have used 'emotional pressure tactics' in order to gain his wife's approval.

In answering a question in this area the following scheme should be considered (note that 'husband' and 'wife' are interchangeable terms for the purposes of this analysis):

(a) What type of transaction has the wife entered into? Was she (i) acting as surety for her husband's debts (see *O'Brien, Royal Bank of Scotland* v *Etridge (No. 2)*), or (ii) simply applying jointly with her husband for a straightforward loan (see *CIBC* v *Pitt*)?

(b)   In (a)(i) transactions the bank/creditor will automatically be 'put on enquiry', meaning that the bank/creditor will need to take certain steps to avoid being fixed with notice of any undue influence or misrepresentation employed by the husband against his wife (see *Etridge (No. 2)* [2001] UKHL 44). In (a)(ii) transactions a bank/creditor will not be tainted by a husband's improper behaviour unless it has clear evidence that such impropriety has occurred (e.g. the 'joint' loan will be used for the husband's sole purposes), or the nature of the transaction suggests that the potential for such conduct is too great to be ignored (draw an analogy with *Credit Lyonnais Bank Nederland NV* v *Burch* [1997] 1 All ER 144), or the risk/reward ratio is patently unreasonable from the wife's perspective (e.g. a joint loan to a jointly owned company where the wife's shareholding is grossly disproportionate to that of her husband—see *Goode Durrant Administration* v *Biddulph* (1994) 26 HLR 625).

(c)   If the bank/creditor is 'put on enquiry', what action did it take to ensure that the wife understood the consequences of her action? In particular, did she receive expert, independent advice? Note that the word 'independent' has been a restrictively interpreted, allowing a wife to be advised even by the husband's company solicitor as the latter could be trusted to decide whether any conflict of interest had arisen and act accordingly (see *Banco Externacional* v *Mann, Mann and Harris* [1995] 1 All ER 936).

(d)   As regards the independent advisor, did that person explain to the wife the nature of the documentation and her possible liability, and ask her whether she wished to proceed? If not, the wife may have an action founded upon negligence. However, the bank/creditor can assume that the advisor has acted properly provided it receives confirmation to that effect, though if it withholds material information or knows that the advisor has acted negligently then it proceeds as its own risk (see *Etridge (No. 2)* [2001] UKHL 44).

(e)   **What if the bank has failed to follow the proper procedures?** The House of Lords, in *Etridge (No. 2)*, stressed that this did not mean the wife would automatically avoid the transaction as against the bank/creditor. Proof was still required that the husband had used improper pressure, or some other form of deception, in order to gain the wife's agreement. Pre-*Etridge (No. 2)* this seemed a relatively easy burden for the wife to discharge. Post-*Etridge (No. 2)* the wife's ability to assert undue influence, or raise the presumption of undue influence, is no stronger than anybody else. Indeed, in *Etridge (No. 2)* Lord Nicholls stated that a wife's guaranteeing her husband's debts will not normally be considered a 'wrongful transaction' (i.e. one readily explicable only on the basis that it was procured by the exercise of undue influence); thus, the wife will often need to rely on her husband to confess to some form of overt, overbearing conduct or misrepresentation.

(f) What is the effect if the wife succeeds and is allowed to avoid the transaction (see *Midland Bank plc* v *Greene* [1994] 2 FLR 827, impliedly overruled by *TSB Bank plc* v *Camfield* [1995] 1 All ER 951 CA and *Dunbar Bank plc* v *Nadeem* [1998] 3 All ER 876)?

(g) Do the principles outlined above apply to any other relationships? In *Etridge (No. 2)* the House of Lords was content for the rules to be applied to all 'non-commercial' surety arrangements, (with regard to (a)(i) above) and, in general, to unmarried couples, whether in a heterosexual or homosexual relationship, whether cohabiting or not, provided the bank was aware of that relationship (see also *Massey* v *Midland Bank plc* [1995] 1 All ER 929). Moreover, cases such as *Avon Finance Co Ltd* v *Bridger* [1985] 2 All ER 281 and *Credit Lyonnais Bank Nederland NV* v *Burch* [1997] 1 All ER 144 demonstrate that the principles are potentially applicable to other family and employment relationships where the debtor stands in some form of dominant position *vis-à-vis* the potential surety.

Duress

There are two basic forms of duress: physical and economic. In its original form, the common law normally only recognised violence or its threat as sufficient to avoid a contract. This type of duress is rarely mentioned nowadays, as affirmative proof of undue influence would not be difficult to establish in such circumstances. Economic duress, on the other hand, is a very recent innovation, perhaps originating from Lord Denning's theory of inequality of bargaining power and from his judgments in cases such as *D&C Builders Ltd* v *Rees* [1966] 2 QB 617 and *Arrale* v *Costain Civil Engineering Ltd* [1976] 1 Lloyd's Rep 98.

Two cases are pivotal in the development of the new doctrine. First, in *The Siboen and The Sibotre* [1976] 1 Lloyd's Rep 293, Kerr J stated, *obiter*, that a court must 'in every case at least be satisfied that the consent of the other party was overborne by compulsion so as to deprive him of any *animus contrahendi*'. Secondly, in *Barton* v *Armstrong* [1976] AC 104, 121, Lords Wilberforce and Simon (dissenting) stated:

> In life many acts are done under pressure, sometimes overwhelming pressure, so that one can say that the actor had no choice but to act. Absence of choice in this sense does not negate consent in law; for this pressure must be one of a kind which the law does not regard as legitimate.

The link between these two statements was forged by Lord Scarman in *Universe Tankships Inc of Monrovia* v *International Transport Workers Federation* [1983] 1 AC 366: economic duress required evidence of illegitimate pressure by the dominant party *and* the resultant coercion of the weaker party. The problem is that illegitimate pressure does not necessarily negate consent and lack of consent does not necessarily establish wrongful pressure. For example, if X holds a gun to Y's head and tells him to sign a contract this might appear illegitimate but it hardly constitutes coercion if Y knows that the gun is not loaded. Moreover, as Lord Scarman recognised, pressure which appears legitimate might be illegitimate if applied for the wrong motives.

So what are the relevant factors in assessing the legitimacy of pressure? Recent case law indicates that the following questions should receive affirmative answers before a finding of economic duress can be supported:

(a) Was there a calculated threat of unlawful damage to the economic interests of the other party? A mere threat to break an existing contract is not enough (compare *Atlas Express Ltd* v *Kafco (Importers and Distributors) Ltd* [1989] QB 833 with *Williams* v *Roffey Bros and Nicholls (Contractors) Ltd* [1991] 1 QB 1).

(b) Was there a lawful excuse for the dominant party to pressure the weaker party, e.g. enforcing an existing contractual right (compare *CTN Cash and Carry Ltd* v *Gallaher Ltd* [1994] 4 All ER 715 and *Carillion Construction Ltd* v *Felix(UK) Ltd* [2001] BHR 1)?

(c) Were the effects of the pressure upon the weaker party recognised by the stronger party and was it exerted to bring about those effects (see *B&S Contracts and Design Ltd* v *Victor Green Publications Ltd* [1984] ICR 419)?

If the pressure is illegitimate, one must then ask whether the weaker party has been coerced. Lord Scarman, in *Pao On* v *Lau Yiu Long* [1980] AC 614, identified, *inter alia*, some of the relevant factors: did the party protest, did he possess an adequate alternative course of action, and did he take steps to avoid the contract after entering into it?

Subsequent case law has shown that the absence of effective choice is the cornerstone of this area, as noted in *Vantage Navigation Corporation* v *Suhail & Saud Bahwan Building Materials (The Alev)* [1989] 1 Lloyd's Rep 138. The other factors merely contribute to this finding; for example, lack of protest may simply demonstrate the futility of pursuing any other course of action.

Remedies for Undue Influence and Economic Duress

For the purposes of an examination, a student should know that the main remedy for a successful claimant is rescission of the contract. As with misrepresentation, certain bars operate to prevent rescission. In particular, relief will be refused if (a) the claimant has already affirmed the contract or waited too long before seeking to avoid the contract (note the tighter deadlines in economic duress — *North Ocean Shipping Co. Ltd* v *Hyundai Construction Co. Ltd* [1979] QB 705), (b) the parties cannot be restored substantially to their previous positions, or (c) third parties have acquired rights in the subject-matter of the contract prior to its avoidance. Note that in *TSB Bank plc* v *Camfield* [1995] 1 All ER 951, the Court of Appeal decided that it had no power to impose terms on the defendant when she sought to avoid the contract. Hence, where her husband had innocently represented that their liability would not exceed £15,000 (rather than unlimited liability as was the case) the court would not enforce the agreement against the wife to any extent. However, this 'all or nothing' approach is not absolute. In the recent decision of *Barclays Bank plc* v *Caplan* [1998] 1 FLR 532, the wife had originally been properly advised of her liability in 1986 when a new mortgage/guarantee had been agreed but that, subsequently, when her liability had been extended no further advice was proffered. The court held that these subsequent transactions could be severed, limiting the wife's liability to that which had been imposed under the 1986 mortgage.

Q Question 1

Marjorie, a firm believer in psychic phenomena, has recently been widowed. Her husband has left her a sizeable amount of money in his will as well as his business, Ghosthunters & Co.

She decides to communicate with the spirit of her husband through her medium, Spook. Spook tells Marjorie that her husband wishes her to donate £5,000 to the Spirit Appreciation Society Ltd (SAS), a company which publishes a journal entitled 'Supernatural Monthly'. Marjorie donates the money by gift under seal.

Meanwhile, Ghosthunters & Co. is facing financial collapse because its main creditor, Banshee, is threatening to call in an overdue loan of £50,000. In return for an extra six weeks to repay the loan, Marjorie agrees to transfer a 33% shareholding in Ghosthunters & Co. to Banshee.

Three months later, Marjorie finds out that Spook is a director of SAS. Moreover, she is becoming worried about the way in which Banshee is using his shareholding to redirect the policy of the business.

Advise Marjorie whether she can avoid either transaction on grounds of unfair pressure.

Commentary

In this problem, the victim of the pressure, Marjorie, is acting in two very different capacities. In her dealings with Spook she is just another private client seeking 'professional' advice. Spook is clearly the dominant party. If a special relationship between the parties is established, Spook will be expected to put Marjorie's interests first. In this context, the doctrine of undue influence is clearly the most relevant. A student should consider: Has Spook taken unfair advantage of Marjorie's recent bereavement? Has he acted in an unconscionable manner? Did she act in a spontaneous manner free from any improper pressure?

The relationship between Marjorie and Banshee is different. They are acting in their business capacities when arranging the shareholding transfer. The doctrine of economic duress is therefore more relevant. The type of questions which could be posed include: Is Banshee threatening to break an existing contract? Are his actions calculated to cause serious damage to Marjorie's company? Did Marjorie have an alternative course of action?

- **Is there any evidence of affirmative undue influence by Spook against Marjorie?**
- **If not, does the nature of their relationship suggest a presumption of undue influence and, if so, how can Spook effectively rebut it?**
- **What are the consequences of the contract between Spook and Marjorie being declared voidable?**
- **Has Banshee acted in an unconscionable manner, suggesting that he is applying some form of illegitimate pressure against Marjorie?**
- **Did Marjorie have any alternative course of action, as opposed to submitting to Banshee's demands?**

☼ Suggested answer

Marjorie v Spook

There are two possible ways in which Marjorie might argue that her donation to SAS is voidable for undue influence: affirmative proof of undue influence or a presumption of undue influence which is not rebutted. This distinction emphasises the shifting onus of proof resulting from the proximity of the parties' relationship.

In establishing affirmative proof the Court of Appeal in *Allcard* v *Skinner* (1887) 36 Ch D 145 defined undue influence as:

> some unfair and improper conduct, some coercion from outside, some overreaching, some form of cheating and generally, though not always, some personal advantage gained.

In so far as Spook has tricked Marjorie for the purposes of personal gain, it would seem that Spook's conduct is encompassed within the above definition. In particular, Majorie's recent bereavement and her belief in psychic phenomena is presumably known to Spook. These circumstances will clearly combine to cloud her judgment and make her extremely susceptible to Spook's suggestions. A parallel can be drawn with the cases of *Lyon* v *Home* (1868) LR 6 Eq 655 and *Nottidge* v *Prince* (1860) 2 Giff 246 to justify a finding of undue influence. The latter case is especially apposite as the plaintiff had visited the defendant, a spiritualist medium, in order to make contact with her late husband. The defendant's personal gain was more obvious as the plaintiff 's late husband apparently advised her to adopt the defendant as her son and ensure his future financial independence.

What is perhaps worth emphasising at this juncture is that it is the 'dominant' party's knowledge of the weaker party's desires and infirmities which is crucial to a finding of undue influence. Thus, if Spook was ignorant of Marjorie's psychic fixation then the difficulty of proof would be exacerbated.

If undue influence is established, the contract is *prima facie* voidable although the right to rescind is lost if the victim waits too long before seeking relief. As fraud is involved, it is generally thought that time runs from discovery of the fraud (e.g. *Leaf* v *International Galleries* [1950] 2 KB 86) although the alternative opinion is that time runs from when the pressure ceases to operate on the mind of the victim. On the present facts these tests are effectively contemporaneous as both would require Marjorie to unearth Spook's underhand dealing. However, if SAS has spent the donation in the meantime, any ensuing legal victory will be pyrrhic (see *Allcard* v *Skinner*) as damages are not available in this area. This might suggest that Marjorie should consider framing her action in misrepresentation (e.g. Misrepresentation Act 1967, s. 2(1), or the breach of a duty of care — *Cornish* v *Midland Bank plc* [1985] 3 All ER 513) but the likely attitude of a court dealing with the vagaries of psychic phenomena would probably be to discourage that sort of claim unless clear evidence of fraud existed.

Marjorie's alternative claim is that a presumption of undue influence has arisen. This requires proof that some form of quasi-fiduciary relationship exists between the parties, 'fiduciary' in this context requiring the dominant party to put the interests of the weaker party first. This expectation might result from a professional/client association such as solicitor/client or doctor/patient, but any relationship of trust and confidence has the *potential* to establish the necessary presumption. For example, in *Allcard* v *Skinner* it was found that these factors existed between a religious leader and his disciple. The considerations outlined above with regard to affirmative proof of undue influence would be equally applicable here (e.g. possible trickery, taking advantage of Marjorie's recent bereavement), as well as the fact that Spook gains some form of personal advantage from the transaction. Moreover, following *Royal Bank of Scotland* v *Etridge (No. 2)* [2001] UKHL 44, [2001] 4 All ER 449, Marjorie must adduce evidence to show that the transaction was in some way 'wrongful' (i.e. not readily explicable by the relationship of the parties). Does the amount of money transferred suggest this? If Marjorie is successful, Spook will be required to rebut the presumption that he exerted undue influence upon Marjorie when advising her to donate £5,000 to SAS.

In general, an effective rebuttal will require evidence that Marjorie's actions were 'voluntary'. This can take two forms: spontaneity of action or proper independent advice. The latter course seems difficult to substantiate as there is no evidence that any independent advice was given. Undoubtedly the concealment of Spook's true role in the transaction would intimate that Marjorie was unable to make a full, free and informed estimate of the expediency of the transaction (see *Inche Noriah* v *Sheik Allie Bin Omar* [1929] AC 127). The alternative is that for Spook to argue that Marjorie acted *spontaneously*, free of any undue pressures at that moment. The majority decision in *Re Brocklehurst's Estate, Hall* v *Roberts* [1978] Ch 14 supports the view that people should be free to do as they wish with their money and property, that friendship and eccentricity are human characteristics and that, as a result, courts should not interfere with such transactions in the absence of fraud or trickery.

As with the first area, if Marjorie were successful, she would need to show that she had not delayed unduly in seeking rescission. Moreover, the recovery of her donation would be subject to the decision in *Allcard* v *Skinner*, i.e. if the money has been spent then restitution becomes impossible (see, however, the more relaxed approach in *Cheese* v *Thomas* [1994] 1 All ER 35).

Marjorie v Banshee

Marjorie is attempting to avoid the contract in her capacity as proprietor of Ghost-hunters Ltd — thus the transaction is an arm's length commercial dealing. The doctrine of economic duress is therefore more appropriate.

Courts will not lightly infer economic duress. The *type* of pressure exerted is of paramount importance. Although one may act under overwhelming pressure the absence of choice will not negate consent in law unless it is of a kind that is regarded as illegitimate (see *Barton* v *Armstrong* [1976] AC 104, 121). Illegitimate pressure generally involves a threat by the dominant party calculated to cause unlawful damage to the economic interests of the other party; for example, a threat to break an *existing* contract which is vital to the economic well-being of the other party. In *Universe Tankships Inc. of Monrovia* v *ITWF* [1983] AC 366, Lord Scarman identified two aspects of illegitimate pressure: the nature of the pressure and the nature of the demand which the pressure was applied to support. This distinction demonstrates that pressure which appears lawful might still be considered illegitimate if exerted for unconscionable reasons.

On the present facts, one might pose the following questions. Is Banshee trying to hold Marjorie to ransom (e.g. *Atlas Express Ltd* v *Kafco (Importers and Distributors) Ltd* [1989] QB 833)? Is Banshee threatening to do something which may be construed as unconscionable, knowing the severe consequences which this will visit upon Marjorie's business (e.g. *Universe Tankships Inc. of Monrovia* v *ITWF* [1983] 1 AC 366)? Is Banshee threatening to break an existing contract (e.g. *North Ocean Shipping Co. Ltd* v *Hyundai Construction Co. Ltd* [1979] QB 705)? The last question deserves closer attention. There is nothing to suggest that Banshee does not have the right to call in the debt. If so, any advantage which Banshee gains from postponing repayment of the debt would normally be characterised as a simple forebearance. The doctrine of economic duress should not be employed to overturn such a contract *per se*. Conversely, if Banshee is wrongfully calling in the loan (e.g. prematurely) his action may be illegitimate assuming that he knows of Marjorie's plight and that the court is willing to stigmatise his acquisition of a 33% shareholding as being morally reprehensible. (Perhaps one could contrast *D&C Builders* v *Rees* [1966] 2 QB 617 with *CTN Cash and Carry Ltd* v *Gallaher Ltd* [1994] 4 All ER 715, those decisions being determined by the bona fide nature of the creditor's claim.)

Finally, although exercising an existing contractual right to call in an overdue loan seems perfectly reasonable, Lord Scarman in the *ITWF* case suggested that a lawful demand coupled with an 'illegitimate motive' might be illegitimate. Here, for instance, is Banshee's real motive the procurement of a 33% shareholding or the acquisition of a security to obviate any risks associated with non-payment of the debt at the later date?

If illegitimate pressure is identified, one must then ask whether Marjorie was coerced by this pressure. The first question must be whether she possessed any options other than to transfer the shareholding to Banshee. Could she have considered pursing an action for breach of contract? Would her business have survived in the meantime? Did she enter voluntarily into a compromise agreement, i.e. an extension on the time for repayment in return for a 33% shareholding? Could she have obtained appropriate refinancing of the debt from another source? If negative replies are forthcoming, it is arguable that the lack of any practicable available alternatives suggests coercion. For example, in *B&S Contracts and Design Ltd* v *Victor Green Publications Ltd* [1984] ICR 419 and *Carillion Construction Ltd* v *Felix (UK) Ltd* [2001] BLR 1 the timing of the threatened breach of contract left the plaintiff with no option other than to submit to the extra payment.

Another factor which has been considered relevant is the lack of any protest by the weaker party at the time the pressure was exerted. Marjorie seems to accept the new arrangement without a murmur. However, as Lord Scarman recognised in *ITWF*, protest is not always relevant if the pressure is so great as to make protest pointless.

Finally, Marjorie has already waited three months before seeking legal advice. The decision in *North Ocean Shipping Co. Ltd* v *Hyundai Construction Co. Ltd* [1979] QB 705 suggests that time runs quickly against a party seeking rescission. In that case the right to rescission was lost as the plaintiff had waited several months before instituting legal proceedings. In arm's length commercial dealings the defendant is entitled to know reasonably quickly whether his counterpart is considering any legal action. The only *caveat* is that time will probably run from release of the pressure, rather than its exertion. Thus, if Marjorie felt unable to question the shareholding transfer until the existing debt repayment had been resolved her right to rescind would remain intact.

Q Question 2

Ron is a retired lorry driver who has just set up his own distribution service. His first customer is Cottonvalue PLC, a company with a nationwide network of retail outlets. Cottonvalue wants to use Ron to deliver stationery to all its outlets in the North of England. A contract is signed whereby Ron will deliver a 'minimum 1,000 boxes of stationery' for Cottonvalue over the next twelve months, beginning on 1 January. No maximum figure for deliveries is specified. The stationery will be packed in specially selected boxes, of one size only, incurring a delivery charge of £0.50p per box irrespective of the distance travelled within the designated area. Both parties expect Ron to be called on to deliver far more than the 'minimum' specified in the contract.

Ron relies on the projected profits to take out a bank loan to upgrade his existing fleet of lorries. Unfortunately, midway through the contract, Cottonvalue expresses its wish to renegotiate the delivery charge, threatening immediate withdrawal unless the delivery charge is reduced to £0.40p. Ron agrees as the prospect of losing Cottonvalue's custom is unthinkable.

At the end of the year, Ron asks you for advice as to whether he can reclaim the lost 10p on every delivery he made on the ground that the contractual modification was voidable for improper pressure.

Commentary

This question concerns the limits which courts impose on the principle of freedom of contract as regards arm's length commercial dealings. Nineteenth century case law extolled the virtues of a *laissez-faire* philosophy refusing to interfere with business contracts unless clear evidence of fraud existed. However, more recently, courts have developed a doctrine of economic duress which limits the morally repugnant excesses of any unbridled freedom of contract principle. In particular, where a dominant party has exerted illegitimate pressure to coerce the other party's will, the ensuing contract may be voidable for economic duress. Thus for Ron to succeed he will need to establish that: (a) Cottonvalue exerted illegitimate pressure, and (b) as a consequence his will was coerced. In this context the good student might identify the factual similarities with *Atlas Express Ltd* v *Kafco (Importers & Distributors) Ltd* [1989] QB 833.

- Should Cottonvalue's demands be characterised as normal commercial pressure or illegitimate pressure?

- In particular, did Cottonvalue take advantage of its bargaining strength, knowing that Ron would submit because of his precarious financial situation?

- Was Ron coerced by Cottonvalue's request for re-negotiation of the contract?

- In particular, did Ron protest, possess an alternative course of action/legal remedy or demonstrate in some other way total submission to the wishes of Cottonvalue?

- What remedies would Ron possess if successful in his economic duress defence?

·Q· Suggested answer

Ron would be best advised to seek avoidance of the modified contract on the ground of economic duress. The doctrine of economic duress is still in its infancy but already it has become clear that a court will not set aside a contract merely because 'normal commercial pressure' has been exerted by the dominant party (*Barton* v *Armstrong* [1976] AC 104). What is needed is some evidence that the pressure which Cottonvalue exerted was of a type characterisable as 'illegitimate' and that Ron had no alternative but to agree to the new terms (i.e. his will was coerced).

Illegitimate Pressure

In *Universe Tankships Inc. of Monrovia* v *ITWF* [1983] AC 366, Lord Scarman identified two aspects of illegitimate pressure: the nature of the pressure and the nature of the demand which the pressure was applied to support. This distinction demonstrates that pressure which appears lawful might still be considered illegitimate if exerted for unconscionable reasons. Thus, even if Cottonvalue was contractually entitled to threaten withdrawal, this might not be considered legitimate *per se* (see however *CTN Cash and Carry Ltd* v *Gallaher Ltd* [1994] 4 All ER 715).

More often than not, illegitimate pressure involves a threat by the dominant party calculated to cause unlawful damage to the economic interests of the other party unless some demand is met. One example might be a threatened breach of an *existing* contract. However, additional evidence would be required as such threats are unlikely to be considered illegitimate *per se*. For instance, in *Atlas Express Ltd* v *Kafco (Importers & Distributors) Ltd* [1989] QB 833, it was the manner in which the plaintiff exerted the pressure which was crucial. In particular, compelling a re-negotiation of an existing contract purely for the plaintiff's benefit, leaving the communication of the threat to an innocent third party, timing its communication to correspond with his own absence, and judging the precise moment when the pressure would be heightened by the defendant's realisation that only the plaintiff was in the position to meet his needs (e.g. *Carillion Construction Ltd* v *Felix (UK) Ltd* [2001] BLR 1). In such situations, it is clear that the dominant party intends to apply the pressure and has sufficient knowledge of the weaker party's predicament to predict the impact of that pressure (e.g. *D&C Builders* v *Rees* [1966] 2 QB 617).

In the present situation, Cottonvalue has threatened to break an existing contract. Are there any facts which suggest that this threat is illegitimate? Does Cottonvalue recognise that Ron is relying upon the contract to service his existing indebtedness to his bank? Affirmative responses to these questions might suggest that the pressure is illegitimate.

However, one must recognise that hard bargaining is an everyday incident of normal business relationships (see *Barton* v *Armstrong* [1976] AC 104). For example, Ron was not obliged to upgrade his existing fleet of lorries, i.e. it was not a condition of the contract with Cottonvalue. A predicament of one's own making should not be used to label normal commercial pressure as something which is unconscionable. It is for this reason that Cottonvalue's knowledge of Ron's financial state and the serious economic consequences of withdrawing from the contract will be of paramount importance to a court. As was emphasised in *B&S Contracts & Design Ltd* v *Victor Green Publications Ltd* [1984] ICR 419, the pressure was illegitimate because it was an intentional threat of unlawful damage to the other party's economic interest. Remove this intent and duress becomes all the harder to establish.

Coercion

The next question is whether Ron has been coerced by the threat. The degree of pressure must be such as to vitiate consent. Various factors have been identified as being of importance: the protest of the weaker party, the unavailability of any other course of action (e.g. legal remedy), the lack of independent advice, and the attempted subsequent avoidance of the contract by the weaker party (see generally *Pao On* v *Lau Yiu Long* [1980] AC 614, 635). These factors are not of general application. Whereas protest demonstrates the weaker party's explicit reluctance to submit to the pressure, intentional submission (as in Ron's case) manifests an equally strong response, albeit implicitly, if it arises from the realisation that there is no practical alternative open to him. Moreover, subsequent steps to avoid the damaging effects of duress may indicate prior submission but such action cannot be expected if the illegitimate pressure has not yet ceased to operate.

The true hallmark of coercion is lack of effective choice: did Ron have an alternative course of action? It is the unavoidable and serious consequence of non-submission which lies at the heart of coercion. For example, in *Vantage Navigation Corporation* v *Suhail & Saud Bahwan Building Materials, The Alev* [1989] 1 Lloyd's Rep 138, the plaintiffs implicitly threatened non-delivery of the defendants' cargo, perhaps even to jettison or sell it, unless a contribution was made towards paying the increased port and discharge costs. The cargo was aboard ship thousands of miles away. The defendants needed the cargo to be delivered on time. A wait and see approach was not a realistic course of action, especially as other sources of purchase were out of the question. Coercion was thereby established.

What should Ron have done at the time of the threat? Perhaps he should have refused to re-negotiate? The answer, in turn, might depend upon whether Ron had already delivered the 'minimum' quantity of goods specified in the contract. If this had occurred then Cottonvalue would have a contractual right to employ other transport agencies to deliver their goods, leaving Ron with no remedy whatsoever. Conversely, if the 'minimum' had not yet been delivered it would be open to Ron to claim damages if Cottonvalue did not continue to employ his services until the minimum delivery had been fulfilled. But is this practical? The facts suggest that legal action is 'unthinkable'. Cottonvalue are threatening a complete withdrawal, with the clear implication that it might not employ Ron again. This must be preying on Ron's mind when he considers his existing indebtedness to his bank.

Moreover, how would damages have been assessed? Ron would be looking for loss of profits associated with his expected rate of delivery rather than his minimum specified delivery, but this presumably would be too remote in contract law. In truth, an available remedy in damages does not seem to have unduly influenced the courts in duress cases (e.g. *Atlas Express Ltd* v *Kafco (Importers & Distributors) Ltd*). Perhaps this is because litigation is a protracted affair often requiring considerable financial resources over a long period of time — Ron appears devoid of spare cash and needs to negotiate a solution immediately.

Finally, if Ron can successfully plead economic duress he should be advised to proceed quickly. Economic duress makes a contract voidable, allowing the victim the option of rescission. However, this right can be lost through effluxion of time. The question is whether a court would have expected him to have instituted legal proceedings against Cottonvalue at an earlier date. The basic principle as applied in *North Ocean Shipping Co. Ltd* v *Hyundai Construction Co. Ltd* [1979] QB 705 is that a victim of duress must seek rescission as soon as possible after the original pressure has ceased to operate.

In *North Ocean*, there was no evidence that, had the plaintiffs sought to reclaim their additional payment immediately, the defendants would have stopped the ship's construction. Equally, in Ron's situation is it reasonable for him to wait until the year has passed before seeking rescission of the modified payment schedule? He might argue that the pressure continued throughout the year as Cottonvalue had the right to redirect their delivery requirements to other firms once Ron had discharged his minimum delivery obligations. Perhaps there was a veiled threat that Cottonvalue might not negotiate with Ron over future delivery contracts. Without such evidence Ron's chances look bleak, as Cottonvalue will presumably contend that they were as interested as Ron in being informed of the legality of the contract modification and would have welcomed a clear ruling as quickly as possible. Whatever else, case law suggests that in business transactions *both* parties must be able to ascertain what their enforceable contractual rights are as quickly as possible so that they can take appropriate contingency measures in their subsequent dealings with each other. In Cottonvalue's situation, if the reduction in delivery charge had been unenforceable then alternative distributors might have been sought *after* Ron had fulfilled his minimum obligations but *before* the year had passed.

(Note: the very good student might also link, on the facts, the absence of consideration and the presence of duress. In particular, using the decision in *Williams* v *Roffey Bros and Nicholls (Contractors) Ltd* [1991] 1 QB 1, one might consider whether Ron had obtained a 'practical benefit' from the new arrangement or whether the reality of intent had been compromised by Cottonvalue's unconscionable behaviour.)

Q Question 3

Lincoln, who runs his own business, has decided to extend the family home in order to create an office for himself. He recognises that the best way of raising the necessary finance is to increase his existing mortgage, held with North Bank. He arranges to meet the bank manager, Peter, who is an old school friend.

Peter tells Lincoln that an increased mortgage is only possible if he takes advantage of the 'North Bank House Extension Policy'. This requires the bank, for a moderate fee, to arrange for the production of architect's plans and to apply for all planning consents. The bank also hires the building sub-contractors, with direct payment from the mortgage advance. Next day, Lincoln persuades his wife, Annabel, to sign the form on the pretext that it is needed as security for his company's existing overdraft. Annabel does not read the form which includes a statement to the effect that all signatories have received independent advice. The bank obtains the necessary planning consent and hires Slapjack & Co. to do the building work, a firm in which Peter is a sleeping partner. The building work commences while Lincoln and Annabel are away on holiday. However, on their return, Annabel is horrified to discover the truth and seeks to avoid the contract. Moreover, Lincoln discovers the connection between Peter and Slapjack & Co.

Advise the parties.

Commentary

This seems like a very straightforward question on undue influence in which the examinee should focus on the relationship between Lincoln and Peter. Recourse could be made to *National Westminster Bank plc* v *Morgan* [1985] AC 686 and *Lloyds Bank Ltd* v *Bundy* [1975] QB 326 in order to ascertain whether a presumption of undue influence arose or whether Lincoln would need to prove affirmatively the presence of undue influence.

But this is only half the question. Annabel's rights are equally important. The basic question is whether the bank is tainted by any undue influence exerted by Lincoln over his wife, Annabel. A spate of recent cases has shown the importance of banks dealing directly with wives and, if possible, either explaining the terms of any mooted agreement or encouraging the wife to obtain independent expert advice. You must consider whether the statement in the mortgage form, advising Annabel to seek independent advice, is sufficient for the bank to avoid liability.

- Can Lincoln establish affirmative proof of undue influence, or set up a presumption of undue influence?

- What type of transaction has Annabel entered into — a surety or joint loan arrangement? Why is this relevant to the application of the *O'Brien* and *Etridge (No. 2)* principles?

- Would the principles set out by the House of Lords in *Etridge (No. 2)* suggest that North Bank was 'put on enquiry'? If so, has North Bank followed the correct procedures?

- If Lincoln and Annabel are successful, what remedies will they possess as against North Bank?

:Q: Suggested answer

Lincoln

There are two possible ways in which Lincoln might argue that the mortgage arrangements with the bank are voidable for undue influence: affirmative proof of undue influence or a presumption of undue influence which is not rebutted. Although courts often do not make this distinction, it clearly emphasises the shifting onus of proof resulting from the closeness of the parties' relationship.

In establishing affirmative proof, the Court of Appeal in *Allcard* v *Skinner* (1887) 36 Ch D 145 defined undue influence as:

> some unfair and improper conduct, some coercion from outside, some overreaching, some form of cheating and generally, though not always, some personal advantage gained.

Has Peter tricked Lincoln for the purposes of personal gain? Peter is clearly in a dominant position as his bank is holding itself out as possessing some type of specialist skill, i.e. co-ordinating the planning and building of house extensions. But 'dominance' in itself is not sufficient (see *Goldsworthy* v *Brickell* [1987] Ch 378). Every professional/business relationship involves parties dealing with each other on some unequal footing. As *Allcard* v *Skinner* (1887) 36 Ch D 145 illustrates, there must be evidence of victimisation or improper conduct, generally leading to some personal advantage being gained.

On the one hand, Lincoln is not under pressure from the bank to extend his house. Nor has the bank any specific bargaining leverage, assuming Lincoln can obtain finance from an alternative source. On the other hand, there is a suggestion that Peter has gained from the transaction by using the services of a builder with whom he is financially associated and that by compelling Lincoln to use the bank's home extension service, the bank has also profited. Moreover, this must be viewed in the context of Peter's friendship with Lincoln over many years and Lincoln's desire to use the same bank with which he holds his current mortgage.

In summary, it must be said that the lack of any real pressure exerted by the bank should be contrasted with cases such as *Williams* v *Bayley* (1866) LR 1 HL 200, where success was in part attributable to the 'overbearing' nature of the dominant party and the lack of other choices open to the victim of that pressure. On this basis Lincoln's chances of success are slim.

An alternative course of action is for Lincoln to claim that a presumption of undue influence has arisen between him and Peter (i.e. the bank). This places the onus upon the bank to show that Lincoln acted voluntarily, after making a 'full, free and informed estimate' of the expediency of the transaction (see *Inche Noriah* v *Sheik Allie Bin Omar* [1929] AC 127). In *National Westminster Bank plc* v *Morgan* [1985] AC 686, the House of Lords considered the relationship that existed between a bank manager and client. Although recognising that the bank was in a dominant position, and possessed the confidence of its client, more was needed. Approving the words of Sachs LJ in *Lloyds Bank Ltd* v *Bundy* [1975] QB 326, the House stated that evidence was required that the bank had overstepped the boundaries of a normal confidential relationship before any presumption of undue influence could arise. Moreover, in the light of *Royal Bank of Scotland* v *Etridge (No. 2)*, Lincoln will need a show that the transaction was 'wrongful' in the sense that it was not readily explicable by the relationship of the parties.

On the present facts, the relationship is not altogether conventional. The bank has 'offered' a home extension service which takes the decisions out of the client's hands. In effect, Lincoln is putting the whole operation in the hands of the bank and is therefore demonstrating a considerable degree of trust. The bank is encouraging, rather than discouraging this reliance and all in the context of the bank manager, Peter, having formed a friendship with Lincoln over many years. The mixture of friendship, trust and expertise is a potent weapon, ripe for exploitation by the dominant party. It is arguable, in these circumstances, that the bank has overstepped the boundaries of an orthodox bank/customer relationship, especially in the light of its manager's secret connection with Slapjack & Co. However, in the light of *Etridge (No. 2)*, one might question whether the resultant transaction could be labelled as 'wrongful'. Lincoln has unloaded all the difficulties of organising a home extension on to the bank and stands to gain from owning an extended, more valuable house. Perhaps it will depend on how a court views Peter's apparent 'deception' and the secret profit he stands to gain. Clearly if a presumption of undue influence is successfully raised the bank will find it almost impossible to rebut in the light of Peter's deception.

Annabel

Current case law suggests that banks must take appropriate measures when dealing with wives who wish to act as sureties for their husbands and/or use the jointly-owned matrimonial home as additional security for their husbands' business dealings (see *Royal Bank of Scotland* v *Etridge (No. 2)* [2001] UKHL 44). Failure to do so may mean that North Bank is tainted by any undue influence of Lincoln, leaving it with little chance of enforcing the security against Annabel.

We must first ask whether North Bank was 'put on enquiry'. In considering the nature of the transaction it is apparent that we are not dealing with a 'non-commercial surety' arrangement so Annabel would normally face an uphill task (see generally *Royal Bank of Scotland* v *Etridge (No. 2)* [2001] UKHL 44). However, the facts suggest that Peter, as manager of North Bank, knew that the purpose of the loan was to benefit Lincoln's business activities. Perhaps one can draw an analogy with *Goode Durrant Administration* v *Biddulph* (1994) 26 HLR 625) and argue that Annabel's risk/benefit ratio is grossly disproportionate to that of Lincoln's. The Bank would attempt to refute these claims by simply arguing that the transaction appeared on its face to be a secured loan to a married couple for the purposes of extending the marital home. Relying on the earlier House of Lords decision in *CIBC Morttgages* v *Pitt* [1994] 1 AC 200, this would suggest that there was no reason for the Bank to enquire further as to whether the wife understood the transaction and her potential liability.

The above arguments are finely balanced but if Annabel successfully persuades the court that North Bank was 'put on enquiry' then the bank will need to demonstrate that it followed the procedures laid down in *Etridge (No. 2)*. What exactly were the actions of North Bank? According to *Etridge (No. 2)*, the bank should have persuaded Annabel to see an independent advisor who would explain the nature of the documentation and her possible liability, and ask her whether she wished to proceed? However, in our scenario, the bank simply relies upon Annabel's signature as evidence that she visited an independent advisor. It makes no attempt to discuss the matter with Annabel, nor does it attempt to discover whether Annabel read the forms, particularly the clause that encourages her to obtain independent advice. This seems to fall well below the standards expected in *Northern Rock Building Society* v *Archer* (1999) 78 P & CR 65 where the court berated the plaintiff for not informing the solicitor fully of the context in which the transaction was taking place (i.e. the underlying purpose for the loan). More importantly, the guidelines set out in *Etridge (No. 2)* clearly assume that it is the independent advisor who will confirm to the bank that proper advice has been given to the surety (i.e. Annabel), rather than relying upon the surety for such confirmation.

Finally, if it is found that North Bank has failed to comply with the spirit of *Etridge (No. 2)* Annabel will still need to establish that Lincoln had acted wrongfully towards her. Fortunately for Annabel the facts seem quite clear on this matter. Lincoln deceived her into signing the agreement on the pretext that the security was needed to secure his existing business overdraft, rather than to pay for a house extension. This is a clear misrepresentation, probably fraudulent in nature, which will enable Annabel to claim that the surety transaction was voidable.

Lincoln and Annabel: remedies

If Lincoln and Annabel are successful, their primary remedy will be one of rescission. The normal bars will apply such as lapse of time, affirmation and *restitutio in integrum*. Damages are not available for undue influence, although if the bank has broken a duty of care to Annabel damages may be available in negligence. The advice to both parties is to act sooner rather than later and notify the bank of their intention to avoid the contract. On the present facts complications might arise as the building work has already commenced. Regarding Lincoln, the Court of Appeal's decision in *Cheese* v *Thomas* [1994] 1 All ER 35 suggests some latitude on this point. Moreover, Annabel could invoke the authority of *TSB Bank plc* v *Camfield* [1995] 1 All ER 951 to argue hat no terms can be attached to the rescission of her contract with the bank. (Note: It is almost inconceivable that a student would be expected to consider this area in any further depth although a comment on the lack of privity between Slapjack & Co. and Lincoln/Annabel might be worth making.)

Q Question 4

The decisions of the House of Lords in *Barclays Bank plc* v *O'Brien* [1994] 1 AC 180 and *Royal Bank of Scotland* v *Etridge (No. 2)* [2001] UKHL 44 [2001] 4 All ER 449, have established a clearer, more coherent set of rules that strike an appropriate balance between the rights of creditors and those of wives who have been unduly influenced by their spouses.

To what extent do you agree with the above statement?

Commentary

Over the next few years, one should expect a question on this topic to appear on most Contract examination papers. The House of Lords' landmark decisions proffer important guidance to banks and other financial institutions on how to deal with wives who are acting as sureties for their husbands' debts, as well as those who secure joint advances with their husbands. It is important to note that the House of Lords' decision in *O'Brien* never intended to offer a definitive exposition of the law, applicable in every conceivable situation. Rather, it represented a framework of principle which lower courts would need to adapt and modify, interpret and re-interpret, in accordance with the facts presented to them. Unfortunately, the unpredictability of subsequent case-law suggested that greater clarity and specificity was required in this area, culminating in the *Etridge* decision. Interestingly, in both cases, the Law Lords did not merely direct their attention to wives but also to other types of relationship (e.g. unmarried cohabitees) whether heterosexual or homosexual, or any other relationship where the prospect of undue influence by the debtor was foreseeable (e.g. *Avon Finance Co.* v *Bridger* [1985] 2 All ER 281).

- **What was the state of the law prior to the House of Lords decision in *O'Brien*?**

- **What policy considerations influenced the House of Lords in *O'Brien*?**

- **To what extent did subsequent case-law depart from the spirit of *O'Brien*?**

- **To what extent did the House of Lords clarify any outstanding ambiguities in *Etridge*?**

⚙️ Suggested answer

When a bank entrusts certain duties to a debtor-husband who, as intermediary, is capable of exerting undue influence over his wife, the courts have always recognised the possibility that any ensuing transaction entered into between the wife and bank might be voidable for undue influence. Unfortunately, until 1994, there was considerable confusion regarding the specific conditions that were needed to justify judicial intervention on behalf of a wife. In particular, the courts appeared to adopt any one of three possible approaches, making it very difficult to predict the outcome.

Pre-O'Brien

First, there was the 'special equity theory', traceable to *Turnbull & Co* v *Duvall* [1902] AC 429, that seemed to reinforce the patronising nineteenth century attitude towards wives and their role and importance in marriage. Its modern reincarnation can be seen in *Yerkey* v *Jones* (1939) 63 CLR 649 where Dixon J. emphasised the importance of the creditor's actually proving that the wife understood the transaction she was entering into, thereby almost placing the bank in *loco parentis* to the wife. The implication was that a wife would be treated more like a child than an independent thinking adult. The second approach was termed the 'agency' theory: a creditor bank that 'left everything to the husband' might be tainted by any undue influence exerted by the husband over his wife (e.g. *Barclays Bank plc* v *Kennedy* [1989] 1 FLR 356). However, the use of agency principles is both illogical and artificial. It is rare for a bank to appoint a husband formally as its agent. Moreover, once an agency is established, notice by the creditor of an agent's improper conduct is irrelevant as the normal rule is that the principal (creditor) is *automatically* tainted by the actions of his agent. Finally, a line of Court of Appeal decisions from 1985 demonstrated a greater acceptance of notice as being pivotal to the determination of a creditor's liability (e.g. *Coldunell Ltd* v *Gallon* [1986] QB 1184, and *Midland Bank plc* v *Shephard* [1988] 3 All ER 17). Briefly, if the circumstances were such that creditor should have realised the possibility of the husband's using unfair means to procure his wife's signature, the creditor might be tainted by such impropriety. This latter approach was eventually adopted by the House of Lords in *O'Brien*, specifically focusing attention on the *nature* of the transaction between husband and wife, and the consequential probability of influence.

O'Brien and its aftermath

In *O'Brien* the House of Lords stated that where the creditor had notice, actual or constructive, of some possible impropriety occurring between husband and wife, reasonable steps had to be taken to ensure that the wife's consent had been properly obtained. To that end, the Law Lords distinguished two types of transactions. First, if the wife was acting as surety for her husband's business debts, the creditor would be put on notice if the transaction was financially disadvantageous and there was a substantial risk in such transactions that the wife's signature had been inequitably procured by her husband. Secondly, where the transaction simply involved a joint advance to a husband and wife (e.g. a joint loan to buy a family car) then, unless there were special circumstances known to the creditor, the latter would not be fixed with constructive notice of any impropriety between the married couple. For example, in *CIBC Mortgags PLC* v *Pitt* [1994] 1 AC 200 the creditor honestly believed that the husband and wife would use the joint advance for the purchase of a holiday home. Separate advice for the wife appeared unnecessary, as both appeared to benefit equally from the transaction.

The House of Lords also recommended that the husband and wife be interviewed separately, circumventing the problem faced by the interviewer in *Bank of Credit and Commerce International SA* v *Aboody* [1990] 1 QB 923 where the husband's hysterics at a joint meeting clearly affected the wife's will. In particular, it would be sufficient if the creditor insisted that the wife attend a private meeting (in the absence of her husband) with a representative of the creditor at which she was told of the extent of her liability, warned of the risk she was running and urged to take independent advice.

Subsequent case-law demonstrated a willingness to embrace the spirit of *O'Brien*, without in any way being restricted by specific rules of interpretation. Thus, in *Goode Durrant Administration* v *Biddulph* (1994) 26 HLR 625 the creditor was put on notice in a simple joint advance transaction (the loan financing a joint venture) because of the significant disparity between the wife's potential gain and the scale of her liability. As the creditor had done nothing to advise the wife, the transaction was tainted by the husband's undue influence. Unfortunately, this broad approach could be less than beneficial to the wronged wife. For example, in dealing with the actions of the bank, it seemed acceptable for the wife to be advised by the husband's solicitor (e.g. *Bank of Baroda* v *Rayarel* [1995] 27 HLR 387). To be specific, the bank was entitled to rely on the professional integrity of the solicitor and his/her ability to resolve conflicts of interest properly (e.g. *Banco Exterior Internacional* v *Mann, Mann and Harris* [1995] 1 All ER 936). Moreover, further cases reinforced the wider view that once advice had been given by a solicitor the bank was relieved of any further responsibilities, irrespective of whether the nature and type of advice that the wife received was appropriate to her needs and circumstances (see *Midland Bank plc* v *Massey* [1995] 1 All ER 929). It seemed that the best policy for banks to adopt was to leave everything to the solicitor, a state of affairs that was beneficial to the banks as it apparently exonerated them of any culpability in any circumstances.

Etridge No. 2

The House of Lords decision in *Etridge* attempted to address some of the deficiencies in the prevailing case-law ([2001] UKHL 44). It discarded notions of financially disadvantageous transactions, set out much clearer guidelines on the procedures that banks and independent advisers should adopt and, in particular, extended the principles so as to incorporate all 'non-commercial' debtor/surety relationships. Importantly, whilst accepting that the banks could rely upon the good sense and expertise of a solicitor, the Law Lords stressed that if the creditor withheld information from the solicitor or knew that no competent solicitor could ever advise the wife to enter such a transaction, then the availability of legal advice would be insufficient for the creditor to avoid being fixed by constructive notice of any legal impropriety perpetrated by the husband debtor upon his wife.

A fair balance?

The House of Lords has clearly stressed the need to retain a sense of balance in this area. In particular, excess sympathy for wives dealing with powerful banks can be counter-productive: courts need to ensure that the wealth currently tied up in matrimonial homes does not become economically sterile. If financial institutions are too hindered by the law then they will be unwilling to accept such security, thereby reducing the flow of capital to business enterprises.

Moreover, the law cannot operate in a social vacuum. For many years now society has promoted the equality of the sexes, attacking pre-conceptions that the wife is subservient to her husband in the management of the family's finances. What is important however is that a clear legal safety-net exists which can be used in circumstances where the husband possesses the business acumen and experience and the wife tends to follow her husband's advice in such matters. Courts still recognise that in many marriages the wife places confidence and trust in her husband in relation to their financial affairs, potentially raising the presumption of undue influence between the spouses. The House of Lords' decisions clearly offer a salutary warning to creditor institutions that unless they follow the correct procedures in good faith the ensuing financial transactions may become unenforceable as against wives.

Q Question 5

The doctrine of economic duress is a formal recognition of Lord Denning's theory of inequality of bargaining power. The latter provides the necessary juristic basis for courts to give relief to a weaker party who has entered into a contract upon terms which are very unfair or in return for a consideration which is grossly inadequate.
Discuss.

Commentary

In answering this question, a simple regurgitation of lecture notes on economic duress, adding a few of Lord Denning's famous judgments to spice-up the proceedings, would be unlikely to gain more than a simple pass mark. The central issue raised is the relationship between the very broad brushstroke approach taken by Lord Denning, in his emphasis upon inequality of bargaining power, and the rather more focused doctrine of economic duress. You must therefore set out the constituents of each theory and identify how they overlap.

The suggested answer below provides you with one of many possible approaches. The analysis is slightly unorthodox in that it argues that economic duress and inequality of bargaining power are not as dissimilar as many textbooks would suggest. Two alternative approaches would be: (a) to concentrate on the treatment that Lord Denning's judgments received by other courts, concluding that the development of a doctrine of economic duress rendered Lord Denning's general theory superfluous, or (b) to sidestep economic duress entirely and concentrate on non-commercial transactions where the doctrine of undue influence would be more apposite.

The following is one of many possible answer plans.

- Explain the basic constituents of economic duress.

- Giving examples, explain the meaning of 'inequality of bargaining power'.

- What is the difference between the above two approaches and to what extent can one identify Lord Denning's themes in the area of economic duress?

- Consider the impact of various judicial decisions in the post-*Bundy* era, such as *National Westminster Bank plc* v *Morgan*.

:Q: Suggested answer

In *Lloyds Bank Ltd* v *Bundy* [1975] QB 326, Lord Denning examined the various forms of improper pressure, attempting to identify a single thread which ran through the different categories of duress, undue influence and general unconscionability. His conclusion was that inequality of bargaining power represented the pervasive theme. The above quotation paraphrases Lord Denning's judgment but, in so doing, leaves out some important details. In particular, his Lordship stated that the law would give relief to a person who entered a contract:

> . . . on terms which are very unfair or transfers property for a consideration which is grossly inadequate, when his bargaining power is grievously impaired by reason of his own needs or desires, or by his own ignorance or infirmity, coupled with undue influence or pressures brought to bear on him by or for the benefit of the other.

In a series of subsequent decisions, Lord Denning continued to emphasise this aspect of improper pressure (see *Davis (Clifford) Management Ltd* v *WEA Records Ltd* [1975] 1 WLR 61; *Levison* v *Patent Steam Cleaning Co. Ltd* [1978] QB 69). It is important to recognise that 'inequality of bargaining power' was not the sole theoretical basis of Lord Denning's principle. Evidence was also required to show that (a) the terms of the contract were unfair, (b) the weaker party's bargaining power was affected by his own 'needs and infirmities', and (c) the stronger party exploited the position to his advantage. Note that this latter point does not require a formal finding of undue influence, duress, or similar wrongdoing — evidence of simple persuasion, explicit or implicit, in all its forms, would probably suffice.

Lord Denning's theory clearly emphasises the position of the weaker party. The unfairness of the contract is sufficient evidence of unconscionability — judicial intervention merely requires evidence of the weaker party's resultant coercion irrespective of whether the dominant party has acted unlawfully. It is little wonder that the theory was treated with considerable scepticism by subsequent courts. Seldom can one say that the bargaining power is equal in a transaction. Thus, as the resultant terms will reflect this disparity, judicial intervention would be possible in every transaction where the weaker party had been pressured in some way.

In *Pao On* v *Lau Yiu Long* [1980] AC 614, Lord Scarman preferred to concentrate on a doctrine of duress, opining that a broad theory of inequality of bargaining power would be an 'unhelpful development of law'. Subsequent courts followed this approach (e.g. *Burmah Oil Co. Ltd* v *Bank of England* [1979] 3 WLR 722). This reticence was best illustrated by Dillon LJ in *Lobb (Alec) (Garages) Ltd* v *Total Oil (GB) Ltd* [1985] 1 WLR 173 when stating that interference in arm's length commercial dealings was only acceptable where 'as a matter of common fairness it was not right that the strong should be allowed to push the weak to the wall'. Perhaps the death knell for Lord Denning's doctrine was sounded by Lord Scarman in *National Westminster Bank plc* v *Morgan* [1985] AC 686 when commenting that, in view of the increasing growth of statutory restrictions upon freedom of contract, it was questionable whether there was 'any need in the modern law to erect a general principle of relief against inequality of bargaining power'.

In each of the above cases reference was made to a new doctrine of economic duress. In what ways does this doctrine depart from Lord Denning's general theory of bargaining inequality? First, Lord Denning's judgments inevitably refer to consumer/ employment contracts whereas economic duress applies to businesses dealing at arm's length. Bargaining inequality is inevitable in the former situation as it results from lack of access to business/legal expertise and the general status of the parties. Conversely, in the latter circumstances, inequality results from the economic size of the businesses and, in general, the bargaining leverage which this gives the dominant party within an *existing* contractual or pseudo-contractual relationship.

Secondly, Lord Denning concentrated on the *existence* of bargaining inequality and its effect upon the weaker party. Economic duress, on the other hand, is at pains to point out that mere commercial pressure is insufficient to render a contract voidable. What is required is some evidence of illegitimate pressure which results in the coercion of the weaker party. It is the *use* that is made of the bargaining inequality which will determine whether the pressure is illegitimate.

For the above reasons, Lord Denning paid little attention to whether the dominant party had a lawful excuse for his actions whereas this becomes a central issue in economic duress. It was this vital omission which persuaded the Court of Appeal in *Lobb (Alec) (Garages) Ltd* v *Total Oil (GB) Ltd* to reject Lord Denning's theory. But to end here would cause considerable injustice to Lord Denning. In hindsight, many of his judgments could be regarded as laying down markers for a subsequent doctrine of economic duress. For example, in *D&C Builders* v *Rees* [1966] 2 QB 617 and *Arrale* v *Costain Civil Engineering Ltd* [1976] 1 Lloyd's Rep 98, Lord Denning set aside the contract on grounds that the weaker parties' consent was 'no true accord', that they had been 'held to ransom', and that no person 'can insist on a settlement procured by intimidation'.

The decision in *D&C Builders* is particularly worthy of consideration. There, the debtor *knew* that the builders were desperate for money and that they would accept part-payment of the existing debt. Refusal would have exacerbated their current liquidity problems and contributed to the firm's premature liquidation. If one were to apply the principles of economic duress to these facts the following remarks could be made. First, the debtor's action was not mere commercial pressure. The pressure was illegitimate because (a) it constituted a threatened breach of an existing contract; (b) the debtor knew that any refusal by the creditor to accept the settlement would have serious and damaging consequences for their business; and (c) the pressure was applied to bring about those effects. These points are ever-present in cases where economic duress has been established (see *Atlas Express Ltd* v *Kafco (Importers & Distributors) Ltd* [1989] QB 833; *Vantage Navigation Corporation* v *Suhail & Saud Bahwan Building Materials, The Alev* [1989] 1 Lloyd's Rep 138).

Secondly, the creditor could establish coercion because (a) there was very little alternative but to submit — seeking legal redress was unlikely in view of existing cash-flow problems and the time involved in litigating the issue, (b) it was clear that the creditor was reluctant to agree to the settlement, and (c) the creditor took immediate steps to avoid the transaction after the pressure ceased to exist. Yet again, this is a textbook scenario for coercion.

In conclusion, the basic approach adopted by Lord Denning often contains clear parallels with the newly developing doctrine of economic duress. The common denominator is that the type of action which encourages judicial intervention in both cases can be characterised as morally unconscionable. Although bargaining inequality and duress start from different positions, it is arguable that Lord Denning's theories provided the necessary stimulus for other courts to develop a more focused, rational and coherent doctrine of economic duress. These cases refined the use that could be made of bargaining inequality and placed it in its proper perspective as a useful contextual factor rather than as a *sine qua non* for judicial intervention.

Mistake

Introduction

The notion of mistake has a severely restricted ambit in the law of contract for several reasons. First, the parties commonly provide expressly for their rights and duties in the contract meaning that there will be a clear allocation of risks. Secondly, in the absence of contract terms, the notion of *caveat emptor* may apply placing the risk emphatically on one party. A buyer of goods may thus have made a bad bargain but, in the absence of contract terms describing the goods or some vitiating factor such as misrepresentation, the contract will be binding. If the law were otherwise, contracts could seldom be enforced against the unwilling and/or unscrupulous. Thirdly, the effect of an operative mistake at common law is to render the contract void *ab initio*. This means that the contract is a nullity and, for example, no title in goods can be transferred and none acquired by an innocent third party who may have to surrender the goods to the original owner or be liable in damages. In the interests of commercial certainty, the law is reluctant to widen the notion of mistake thereby invalidating contracts. Some of the older mistake cases are strongly influenced by notions of consensus imported from the civil law, but the modern view is that if the parties have ostensibly agreed in the same terms on the same subject matter the contract should be binding, even if *both* parties are mistaken. Equitable remedies might nevertheless be available to relieve one of the parties from the effects of mistake in three ways: (a) refusal of an order for specific performance, (b) rectification of a written agreement or, (c) rescission of the contract. The principles underlying equity's intervention have always been unclear and, in particular, *Solle* v *Butcher* [1950] 1 KB 671 was impossible to reconcile with *Bell* v *Lever Bros Ltd* [1932] AC 161. Most recently, in *Great Peace Shipping Ltd* v *Tsavliris Salvage (International) Ltd* (2002) *The Times*, 17 October, the Court of Appeal held that where a contract is valid and enforceable on ordinary principles of contract law, there is no jurisdiction to grant rescission of that contract on grounds of common mistake. After this decision, *Solle* v *Butcher* must be regarded as incorrecct.

Three broad classifications of mistake are widely recognised, *viz*, common, mutual and unilateral. In common mistake (confusingly referred to as mutual mistake in the older cases) both parties share the same mistake about a fundamental fact of the contract, e.g. A and B agree to buy and sell a painting by Picasso which, unknown to both, does not exist. With mutual mistake the parties are at cross-purposes but neither realises it, e.g. A and B agree to buy and sell a painting, A intending to sell a Picasso and B intending to buy a Constable. In unilateral mistake only one of the parties is mistaken and the other party either knows of the mistake or is deemed to know, e.g. B thinks he is buying a Picasso and thinks that A intends to sell one but A knows that it is a fake and that B is labouring under a misconception. If A does not know of B's mistake, the case would be one of mutual mistake for then A intends to sell a fake whilst B intends to buy a Picasso.

There are two distinct approaches in mistake cases. The first examines the formation and construction of the contract and attempts to decide what the parties have agreed. The contract may thus be valid and binding with one party bearing the risk of the mistake, e.g. the seller is liable if the painting is not a Picasso or the buyer runs the risk that it might be a fake. Using the same reasoning, the presence or absence of a fact might be an implied condition precedent to the operation of the entire contract, the contract then being rendered void for failure of that condition. This could happen where goods are non-existent, for example, when both parties might consider it an implied term that they should exist. It is difficult to imply such a term because it must be *necessary* and represent the parties' *common intention*.

The second broad approach is influenced by the civilian concept of *consensus* and postulates a separate doctrine of mistake based upon a fundamental error of substance which might destroy consent between the parties. The inherent difficulty here is determining the substance of the agreement in metaphysical terms and consequently divorcing substance from quality/attributes. In the above examples, is the substance of the contract 'a Picasso' or simply 'a painting' which has various attributes, one of which is that it is painted by Picasso? Both the constructionist and civilian theories are difficult to apply with any degree of certainty but English law favours an indecisive amalgam of both (see *Bell* v *Lever Bros Ltd* [1932] AC 161). The most recent decisions concerning common mistake confirm that the contract's construction must be examined first and that recourse can be had to mistake only if the contract is silent regarding material terms (see *Associated Japanese Bank (International) Ltd* v *Credit du Nord SA* [1989] 1 WLR 255; *William Sindall plc* v *Cambridgeshire County Council* [1994] 1 WLR 1016; *Great Peace Shipping Ltd* v *Tsavliris Salvage (International) Ltd* (2002) *The Times*, 17 October).

Common Mistake

The leading decision is *Bell* v *Lever Bros Ltd* (above) where it is possible to discern both approaches referred to above and consequently impossible to extract a definitive *ratio*. It appears that, in *Bell*, Lord Atkin sought to unite the constructionist/implied term theory with a doctrine of mistake in 'a common standard' of whether 'the state of the new facts destroy[s] the identity of the subject matter as it was in the original state of facts'. In other words, the contract will only be void if it is possible to imply a term that certain facts must either be present or absent, e.g. if A and B agree to buy and sell a painting which they both assume to be a Picasso when it is a fake, is it possible to imply a term that the painting should be by Picasso? If it is possible to make the implication it is also probable that the 'state of the new facts destroys the identity of the subject matter' for the mistake test. It is clear that it will be very difficult to satisfy these tests and often the contract will be binding, as it was in *Bell*. Certainly, most of the other leading decisions in this area have refused to conclude that the contract is void (see *Kennedy v Panama, New Zealand and Australian Royal Mail Co.* (1867) LR 2 QB 580; *Solle v Butcher* [1950] 1 KB 671; *Harrison & Jones Ltd v Bunten and Lancaster Ltd* [1953] 1 QB 646; *Frederick E Rose (London) Ltd v William H Pim Junior & Co. Ltd* [1953] 2 QB 450; *Cf Sheikh Bros Ltd v Ochsner* [1957] AC 136).

The cases of *res extincta* (where A and B enter into a contract regarding goods which do not exist) and those of *res sua* (where A attempts, for example, to buy something belonging to him) are often grouped within common mistake as examples of contracts void for common mistake. However, these are often cases of total failure of consideration and it does not matter whether the contract is valid or void as a purchaser cannot be made to pay for that which he has not received (see *Couturier v Hastie* (1856) 5 HL Cas 673) or may, alternatively, recover money so paid (see *Strickland v Turner* (1852) 7 Exch 208). Moreover, such cases may also be evaluated in the light of constructionist theory: i.e. it might be an implied condition precedent that the goods should exist, non-existence thus rendering the contract void (see *McRae v Commonwealth Disposals Commission* (1951) 84 CLR 377 — no such condition could be implied where a tanker was non-existent and the seller was liable in damages). In conclusion, the *Associated Japanese Bank* case should be read for Steyn J's delineation of the correct approach in this area.

In relation to equity's jurisdiction to grant relief in common mistake, the Court of Appeal has decided recently (*Great Peace Shipping Ltd v Tsavliris Salvage (International) Ltd* (2002), *The Times*, 17 October) that *Solle v Butcher* [1950] 1 KB 71 was wrongly decided.

Mutual and Unilateral Mistake

In common mistake, offer and acceptance coincide and the mistake relates to some underlying fact but in mutual and unilateral mistake there may be no genuine agreement. The general rule is that intention must be construed objectively and if the parties have reached an ostensible agreement the contract may be valid despite the parties' subjective, contrary intentions (see *Smith v Hughes* (1871) LR 6 QB 587; *Wood v Scarth* (1858) 1 F & F 293; *Scott v Littledale* (1858) 8 E & B 815). The approach of common mistake is therefore mirrored in mutual and unilateral errors in that agreement in the same terms on the same subject matter will normally constitute a binding contract and it is only a fundamental mistake as to substance which may engender an absence of agreement. Thus, in mutual mistake the parties may be so fundamentally at cross-purposes that offer and acceptance do not enmesh (see *Raffles v Wichelhaus* (1864) 2 H & C 906; *Falck v Williams* (1900) AC 176; *Scriven Bros & Co. v Hindley & Co.* (1913) 3 KB 564).

In unilateral mistake, the objective interpretation may be displaced in favour of subjective intention in some cases, but the dominant principle is still *caveat emptor* and the general rule is that one party is not under a duty to disclose information to the other or correct obvious errors of judgement. It follows that it is only the rarest of circumstances which will justify the finding of a void contract where one party knows the mistake of the other and is not allowed to take advantage of it. Again it must be a fundamental mistake and it is sometimes said that here it must be a mistake as to the terms of the contract or the promise itself, but this is singularly unhelpful in practice (see *Hartog* v *Colin and Shields* [1939] 3 All ER 566; *Smith* v *Hughes* (1871) LR 6 QB 597). It is unclear whether the mistake must be known to the other party or whether it is sufficient that it *ought* to be known using an objective test (see *Centrovincial Estates plc* v *Merchant Investors Assurance Co. Ltd* [1983] Com LR 158 where the latter view was apparently taken).

For cases where there has been equitable relief in mutual mistake, compare *Malins* v *Freeman* (1837) 2 Keen 25 with *Tamplin* v *James* (1880) 15 Ch D 215. For unilateral mistake see *Webster* v *Cecil* (1861) 30 Beav 62; *Garrard* v *Frankel* (1862) 30 Beav 445; *Torrance* v *Bolton* (1872) LR 8 Ch App 118.

Unilateral Mistake of Identity

The identity of the other contracting party is usually of no concern in commercial contracts and a unilateral mistake can only be operative in limited circumstances. As in the other areas of mistake, objective appearances are important and the contract may be binding despite the mistake. In this situation A accepts an offer of B thinking that B is C, intending therefore to contract with C. A must establish four requirements: (a) A intended to deal with some person other than B, (b) B knew of A's mistake, (c) identity is crucial to the contract, and (d) A took reasonable steps to verify B's identity.

The mistake of substance that is made here must relate to identity, not *attributes* such as honesty, social status or solvency (see *King's Norton Metal Co.* v *Edridge, Merrett & Co. Ltd* (1897) 14 TLR 98; *Cundy* v *Lindsay* (1978) 3 App Cas 459). Although criticisable in that a person's identity is the sum of his attributes, the distinction is tolerably clear and it is obviously helpful to A if there is another person in existence and identifiable, as in *Cundy*. It is probably not enough if A makes an offer to B simply thinking that B is not B unless it is possible for A's offer implicitly to exclude B, e.g. A's offer is made to the members of a club of which B is not a member (see the doubtful decision in *Said* v *Butt* [1920] 3 KB 497; *Sowler* v *Potter* [1940] 1 KB 271). Particular problems arise where the parties are *inter praesentes* in that it will be very difficult for A to prove that he wanted to contract with C when he is face-to-face with B (see *Phillips* v *Brooks* [1919] 2 KB 243; *Lake* v *Simmons* [1927] AC 487; *Ingram* v *Little* [1961] 1 QB 31; *Lewis* v *Averay* [1972] 1 QB 198). Often B is fraudulent and A's mistake is therefore induced by a misrepresentation. This means that decisions sometimes involve both mistake and misrepresentation and whilst the contract may not be void for mistake, it will be voidable for misrepresentation (see *Lewis* v *Averay*). B may transfer the goods to a *bona fide* third party and the question of rescission and acquisition of title then becomes important.

Q Question 1

Albert owns three Rolls Royce cars manufactured in 1950, 1960 and 1970 respectively. He wants to sell the 1970 model but ensure that the buyer should be a private car collector. Accordingly, he advertised it for sale in the local newspaper as 'For sale only to a private car collector.' Unfortunately, due to a printing error, the car advertised for sale was the 1960 model. Byron, a car dealer, wished to acquire the 1950 model and was informed incorrectly by a friend that Albert had the 1950 model advertised for sale in the newspaper.

Byron knew that, because he was a car dealer, Albert would not sell the car to him. He therefore telephoned Albert and said 'Hello, I am Mr Jones. I should like to buy the car that you have advertised in the newspaper and will give the full asking price of £80,000 for it.' Albert replied 'I am pleased to sell the car to you Mr Jones and I am glad it will have a good home.' When Albert delivered the 1970 model, he discovered the buyer's identity and refused to complete the sale but Byron wished to enforce the contract even though the car was not the 1950 model.

Discuss the legal position.

Commentary

This is a testing problem which, like the subject of mistake itself, appears easier than it is in reality. The problem involves mutual mistake and unilateral mistake which must be considered separately in the answer. As regards mutual mistake, it must be decided whether the parties are in agreement or sufficiently at cross-purposes to nullify any notion of contract. Does the fact that third parties (the newspaper and B's friend) induce the contracting parties' mistake make any difference? In unilateral mistake of identity, with whom must the mistaken party wish to contract? Must there be an identifiable, existing third party with whom A wants to deal or is it sufficient that he does not want to contract with B, as in the problem? Might the problem involve no operative mistake of identity but nevertheless an operative unilateral mistake? Is B guilty of misrepresentation and what effect might this have on the contract?

- What is the overall approach of the law when a mistake is made, on entering into a contract, by one or both of the parties? If a mistake is found to be an operative one, what effect does it have on the contract?

- In relation to the first part of the problem, there is a mutual mistake. How does the law evaluate this situation where the parties are at cross-purposes?

- In the second part of the problem, there is a unilateral mistake of identity. How does the law evaluate this situation where only one party is mistaken regarding the identity of the other party?

- If there is no operative mistake of identity in the second part of the problem, might there be an operative unilateral mistake as to the *terms* of the contract, in that A's offer excludes B and B knows that A would not contract with him?

- In the second part of the problem, is B guilty of misrepresentation? What effect would this have on the contract?

⋅Ọ⋅ Suggested answer

There are two different types of mistake to consider in this problem. First, the mistake between the parties regarding the year of manufacture of the car and, secondly, Albert's (A) mistake as to the identity of the other contracting party, Byron (B). It should be emphasised at the outset that although mistake permeates this transaction, it does not necessarily follow that the contract will be affected. The law adopts a particularly restricted view of mistake where only the most fundamental errors of substance will render a contract void *ab initio*. In the interests of commercial certainty the courts are thus loath to invalidate contracts without good reason. As a general rule, if the parties agree in the same terms on the same subject matter the contract will be binding even if both parties are mistaken. It remains to be seen which mistakes the law regards as sufficiently fundamental to render a contract void.

There is a mutual mistake in relation to which car is being sold, the parties therefore making different mistakes and being at cross-purposes but neither realising the other's mistake at the date of contract. Because of confusion caused by third parties, A intends to sell the 1970 model whereas B intends to buy the 1950 model. In order to be operative, a mutual mistake must entail an absence of genuine agreement, offer and acceptance thus failing to coincide. It is tempting to conclude that if the parties are at cross-purposes there can be no agreement but the test is an objective one and so real, subjective intentions may be dominated by ostensible objectivity, meaning that the contract is valid and binding. In *Wood* v *Scarth* (1858) 1 F & F 293, the defendant offered in writing to let a public house to the plaintiff for £63 per annum. The plaintiff had negotiations with the defendant's clerk and then accepted the offer by letter. The defendant intended that a premium of £500 be payable as well as the rent and assumed that his clerk had made that clear but the plaintiff thought that the only liability was the £63 rent. It was held that the contract was binding. Similarly, in *Scott* v *Littledale* (1858) 8 E & B 815 the defendants sold by sample to the plaintiff 100 chests of tea then lying in bond but later discovered that the sample was poorer in quality than the bulk. The defendants had made a bad bargain but the contract was held to be valid and the plaintiff's claim for non-delivery upheld. In both these cases the reasonable man would see a coincidence between offer and acceptance but it is equally possible to reach the opposite conclusion where the evidence is ambiguous and conflicting as in *Raffles* v *Wichelhaus* (1864) 2 H & C 906. There the defendant agreed to buy from the plaintiff a cargo of cotton to arrive '*ex Peerless* from Bombay'. There were two ships called *Peerless* both sailing from Bombay but the defendant meant a *Peerless* which sailed in October and the plaintiff a *Peerless* which sailed in December. The description of the goods pointed equally to either of the ships' cargoes. The court did not in fact decide whether there was a contract or not but upheld the defendant's refusal to accept the goods from the December shipment on the basis that he could show that the contract was ambiguous and that he intended the October ship. The buyer and seller were similarly at cross-purposes in *Scriven Bros & Co.* v *Hindley & Co.* (1913) 3 KB 564 where the plaintiff intended to sell a quantity of tow and the defendant to buy hemp, the court holding that there was such ambiguity that the subject matter of the contract could not be established with certainty. The same result was reached in *Falck* v *Williams* (1900) AC 176, and *Henkel* v *Pape* (1870) LR 6 Ex 7 illustrates that no contract will exist if the parties arrive at fundamental cross-purposes because of the act of a third party — there a telegram clerk who transmitted the wrong message.

It is arguable that these cases are not based upon an independent concept of mistake but, instead, are illustrations of lack of concurrence between offer and acceptance. In the problem, the parties are not *ad idem* and, moreover, there is nothing in the contract which could clarify the ambiguity. Indeed, the advertisement to which the parties refer advertises the 1960 model for sale and *neither* party wants to make that car the subject of a contract. That there is no contract on the facts of the problem may be tested by postulating facts which would point to an objective agreement. This would occur if A wished to sell the 1970 model but B wished to buy the 1950 model and the 1950 model was advertised for sale, the parties then referring to 'the car advertised in the paper.' It is suggested that the contract would be binding on those facts as A's mistake would not be apparent as in *Wood* v *Scarth*.

There are further difficulties if A attempts to prove that he did not intend to contract with B. If A apparently contracts with B yet alleges mistaken identity he must establish four factors, *viz*, A intended to contract with some person other than B, identity must be fundamental and material, B knew that fact and A took reasonable steps to verify B's identity. As elsewhere in mistake, the heart of these requirements is that the mistake must be a fundamental mistake of substance, meaning in this context a mistake of *identity* rather than one relating to the *attributes* or *qualities* of a person. Both *Cundy* v *Lindsay* (1878) 3 App Cas 459 and *King's Norton Metal Co. Ltd* v *Edridge, Merrett & Co. Ltd* (1897) 14 TLR 98 concerned swindlers who duped the plaintiffs into dealing with them. In *Cundy*, the swindler, Blenkarn, signed his name in a letter to resemble Blenkiron & Co., a prosperous business with whom the plaintiffs had dealt previously and the House of Lords held this to be a mistake of identity rendering the contract void. In contrast, the swindler in *King's Norton* invented an alias of 'Hallam & Co' in his letter, the Court of Appeal deciding that the plaintiffs intended to contract with the writer of the letter, i.e. the swindler. If there had been a separate entity of Hallam & Co, the plaintiffs might have been able to show that they intended to contract with that entity but, on the facts, the mistake was one of attributes/quality relating to solvency and respectability. The contract was thus not void for mistake but only voidable for misrepresentation. It is arguable from the decision in *Lake* v *Simmons* [1927] AC 487 that there need not be another entity in existence provided that A *believed* in the existence of someone else with whom he wanted to contract. In the instant problem, A intends to deal with the person to whom he speaks on the telephone, that is B, and it is not clear that there is anyone else with whom A wants to contract. If Byron's second name is Jones this adds to the presumption of A's choosing to deal with B. A's only argument would be a negative one that he did not want to deal with B rather than a positive one that he intended to deal with C. It would seem that this is insufficient for a mistake of identity and the contract will not be void by reason of such a mistake. This conclusion is fortified by A's negligence in not seeking to verify B's identity thus being content to contract with the person to whom he speaks as in *Phillips* v *Brooks* [1919] 2 KB 243. The court considered in *Ingram* v *Little* [1961] 1 QB 31 that the plaintiff's search of a telephone directory was sufficient to verify the address and telephone number provided by the swindler, but in the problem A does not even perform such a simple task.

However, B clearly knows that A does not want to deal with him as B is not in the relevant group of private car collectors with whom A wants to contract. In such cases, it is possible for A's offer to exclude B expressly or impliedly. One possible explanation of *Said* v *Butt* [1920] 3 KB 497 is that B knew from A's previous refusals that A would not contract with him and he could not avoid this and establish a binding contract by employing an agent to act on his behalf. It would appear in this situation that the mistake is a fundamental, unilateral one as to the terms of the contract or the promise itself as in *Hartog* v *Colin and Shields* [1939] 3 All ER 566. There the plaintiffs could not enforce the contract, the court holding that they must have known of the mistake of the defendants and could not therefore take advantage of the mistaken terms of the contract. This would appear to be the position in the problem because B *actually* knows of his *express* exclusion from the relevant class of car collectors and consequent inability to contract with A.

Finally, there is the possibility that B is guilty of misrepresentation which would render his contract with A voidable at A's option. However, if Byron is in fact Mr Jones, he has told the truth and his silence and non-disclosure regarding any other matters would not be actionable in misrepresentation.

In conclusion, there is probably a sufficient mutual mistake regarding the age of the car to render the contract void and if there is no operative unilateral mistake of identity there may well be such a mistake as to the terms of the contract and the promise itself. B may also be guilty of misrepresentation and it is most unlikely that he could establish any contract with A.

Q Question 2

The single thread of principle running through all types of mistake is that, no matter how serious, the courts will not relieve mistakes of quality.
  Discuss.

Commentary

This essay title demands a critical analysis of common, mutual and unilateral mistakes and an investigation of whether operative mistakes relate to substance or quality. Moreover, it should be asked if a meaningful distinction can be made between substance and quality in reality. A close knowledge of the cases is required coupled with an ability to compare and contrast the decisions and evaluate the rationale of the mistake doctrine.

- Explain why the law considers that the notion of mistake must be confined narrowly.

- Outline the principal theories underlying the decisions concerning mistake: (i) an analysis of the formation and construction of the contract, and (ii) an independent doctrine of mistake based upon the distinction between a mistake of substance and a mistake of quality.

- How can the distinction be made between substance and quality in the three recognised categories of mistake?

- Should a mistake as to quality be sufficient to render a contract void?

:Q: Suggested answer

At common law, the notion of mistake is confined within narrow limits but if it is operative its effect is to render a contract void *ab initio*. By placing mistake in a strait-jacket, both freedom of contract and certainty of contract are preserved. A man may make a very bad bargain due to his own error and thereby receive something of inferior quality in comparison with his expectations but the courts are not prepared to grant relief on that ground alone, for, otherwise, the very essence of bargain and *caveat emptor* would disappear. If the law were to grant relief for all complaints of inferior quality, bargains could never be enforced against the foolish, unwilling or unscrupulous. Accordingly, if the parties agree in the same terms on the same subject matter, the general rule is that they are bound and should look to the stipulations of the contract for 'protection from the effects of facts unknown to them' (*Bell* v *Lever Brothers Ltd* [1932] AC 161, *per* Lord Atkin).

  It is arguable that the so-called mistake cases really turn on questions of formation and construction of the contract rather than representing an independent theory of mistake. Thus, cases of common mistake, where the parties share a fundamental error, may be resolved by asking whether the contract terms put the risk on one or other of the parties or whether a term can be implied regarding the presence or absence of the fact at issue. For example, A sells a painting to B, both believe it to be a Picasso and worth several million pounds, but it is a fake. If the contract contains no express terms, is it an implied term that it should be a Picasso, lack of compliance with the term thereby rendering the contract void? In deciding the issue, it would be sensible to look at other facts such as the price paid for the painting and whether the seller was an expert, rather than dismissing the case as an inoperative mistake of quality and value. This was the approach taken in *McRae* v *Commonwealth Disposals Commission* (1951) 84 CLR 377. Similarly, the cases on mutual mistake where the parties are at cross-purposes and unilateral mistake where only one party is mistaken arguably involve nothing more than contract formation in terms of offer and acceptance. Although in *Bell*, Lord Atkin attempted to amalgamate the notion of the contract's formation/construction with ideas of mistake, the House of Lords appeared to acknowledge an independent doctrine of mistake based upon the distinction between substance on the one hand and quality/attributes on the other. Moreover, in the recent decision in *Associated Japanese Bank (International) Ltd* v *Credit du Nord SA* [1989] 1 WLR 255, it was held that the contract's construction should be considered first and separately from mistake, thereby acknowledging independent rules of mistake.

The substance/quality analysis is derived from Roman law and later civil law theories but the distinction has inherent difficulties of definition and there are almost insuperable problems in applying such a metaphysical abstraction to the facts of contractual disputes. In *Bell*, Lord Atkin considered that mistakes of quality would not affect assent unless there was a mistake made by both parties 'as to the existence of some quality which makes the thing without the quality essentially different from the thing as it was believed to be'. In *Bell*, the plaintiff was compensated for termination of his contract of service, both parties assuming the contract to be valid when, in fact, Bell could have been dismissed summarily without compensation because of breaches of duty. Lever Brothers sought recovery of the money. In terms of quality, both parties thought that Bell was worth £30,000 when he was in fact worth nothing. Although both the judge at first instance and the Court of Appeal held that the agreement was void, the House of Lords held the contract to be valid and binding. The ratio of *Bell* has never been ascertained but certainly mistake is cast in the narrowest terms, one interpretation being that this was only a mistake of quality which did not render the agreement 'essentially different' from that which the parties agreed upon. This would mean that the substance of the contract was a compensation agreement, that substance remaining unchanged. In terms of quality, the mistake could surely not be any worse, as it was equivalent to obtaining no value from the contract as opposed to reduced value. This has led some commentators to argue that a contract will only be void for common mistake when the contract has no subject-matter, that is cases of *res extincta* and *res sua*, and this would support the contention in the question that quality will never be a ground of relief. This would seem to be too narrow an interpretation: Lord Atkin's statement above allows relief in cases of essential difference, but when will the courts admit such a difference? Might a thing be so deficient in quality that it becomes a different thing?

In *Solle* v *Butcher* [1950] 1 KB 671, both parties entered into a lease of a flat thinking that structural alterations had altered its identity to make it a 'new' dwelling house, thus taking it outside the control of the Rent Restriction Acts, but the contract was not invalidated at common law. The same result was reached in *Leaf* v *International Galleries* [1950] 2 KB 86 where the parties entered into a contract to sell a painting which both erroneously believed to be painted by Constable. It is arguable that, for an operative mistake on the facts of *Leaf*, a sculpture would have to be tendered instead of a painting. It follows that quality defects in the thing itself, no matter how serious, are not a ground of relief and the threshold of operative common mistake is only reached in the most extreme cases thereby rendering it almost impotent as a remedy. Taken to its logical extreme, might a carthorse be validly tendered in place of a racehorse using the argument that both are horses, or might a cow be substituted on the basis that both horse and cow are animals with four legs? Greer LJ used the carthorse/racehorse example in *Bell* (Court of Appeal) as being a ground of relief but by most standards this would amount to a difference of substance, not quality.

The restrictive approach to mistake is also present in mutual mistake where the definition of an operative mistake means that the parties must be at fundamental cross-purposes such that it is impossible to construe an agreement between them. If the parties are crossed on the question of quality alone this will not render the contract void, one party thus profiting at the expense of the other. In *Scott* v *Littledale* (1858) 8 E & B 815, the defendants sold by sample to the plaintiff 100 chests of tea then lying in bond but later discovered that the sample was poorer in quality than the bulk. The defendants had made a bad bargain but the contract was held to be valid and the plaintiff's claim for non-delivery upheld. Similarly, in unilateral mistake where only one party is mistaken as to quality and the other party knows it, the contract is still binding on the basis of *caveat emptor*. If S sells a painting to B knowing that it is not a Constable yet knowing that B thinks it is a Constable, the contract is valid provided that S has not misled B. Here B's mistake simply relates to quality or his motive for entering the contract. It is only if B is mistaken as to the *promise itself* and S knows it, that S cannot take advantage of B, the contract then being void. Thus if S intends to sell a painting but B thinks S intends to sell a Constable and S knows of B's mistake, the contract is void for B is in error regarding the nature of S's promise. This is perhaps a fine distinction but it is supported by *Hartog* v *Colin and Shields* [1939] 3 All ER 566 and certainly points-up the substance/quality divide. In unilateral mistakes of identity, only identity is regarded as material and substantive. As in *Cundy* v *Lindsay* (1878) 3 App Cas 459, A must show that although he mistakenly contracted with B, he intended to contract with C and identity was material to the contract. It is insufficient if he contracted with B mistakenly believing him to be honest, respectable and solvent as these are mistakes as to attributes or qualities (*King's Norton Metal Co. Ltd* v *Edridge, Merrett & Co. Ltd* (1897) 14 TLR 98). Again this presupposes a metaphysical distinction between a person's identity on the one hand and his attributes on the other, a distinction which is hard to make with human beings where attributes and qualities usually define identity. Accordingly, in *Lewis* v *Averay* [1972] 1 QB 198, Lord Denning MR described this as a 'distinction without a difference'.

As a general rule, equity follows the law in not relieving a bad bargain simply on grounds of a mistake of quality. In *Tamplin* v *James* (1880) 15 Ch D 215, the defendant made a mistake of quality in buying a public house at auction thinking that a piece of land was included. As there was no ambiguity or misrepresentation in the sale particulars, specific performance of the contract was decreed. In contrast, the defendant in *Malins* v *Freeman* (1837) 2 Keen 25 successfully bid for one piece of land believing he was buying an entirely different lot and, although it was his own fault, specific performance was refused. The two decisions can be reconciled by arguing that *Malins* was a mistake as to substance, not quality.

It is arguable that a mistake as to quality should be sufficient to render a contract void if the quality is the dominant factor in the transaction. If A contracts with B because he mistakenly considers him reputable and solvent surely the contract can be avoided if it is discovered that he is disreputable and insolvent? Again, if the parties have contracted to buy and sell 'a Constable' it is this quality which is uppermost and it is hardly satisfactory to assert that the substance of the contract is a painting and the contract may thus be performed. At base, the mistake cases really involve separating acceptable from unacceptable business risks in unusual situations where the express terms of the contract do not solve the issue and the risk does not obviously fall on one of the parties by virtue of *caveat emptor*. It follows that the law cannot be a model of clarity and the substance/quality division provides a workable structure for decision making. Constructionist theory perhaps provides a clearer, more rational basis for decisions, with its assertion that the contract can only be void at law if a term can be implied in both offer and acceptance which prevents the contract from coming into operation, or if offer and acceptance do not coincide. It is thus arguable that this native test should be acknowledged as the rationale of the mistake cases thereby displacing the civil law theory of substance versus quality.

Q Question 3

Pike buys and sells paintings and antiques. He sees that Shark, an art dealer, has a Renoir for sale but he knows that Shark would never sell the painting to him as he (Pike) still owes a debt to Shark from a previous contract. Pike therefore telephones

Shark and says: 'This is Lord Chub speaking. I am staying at the Grand Hotel. I should like to acquire the Renoir that you have advertised for sale and will call at your galleries tomorrow to see if a price can be agreed.' Shark has to bribe the porter at the Grand Hotel in order to discover whether Lord Chub is staying there but when he discovers that Lord Chub is registered at the Hotel he is pleased to have attracted a prestigious customer. In fact, Pike is staying at the Grand Hotel in the name of Lord Chub having stolen the latter's cheque book.

The next day, Pike, heavily disguised, calls at Shark's premises. A price for the painting is agreed, Shark accepts a cheque from Pike and allows him to take the Renoir away with him. Pike displays the painting in his shop and sells it almost immediately to Rudd, a private collector, who pays in cash. Shark has now discovered that the cheque has been dishonoured and that Rudd is in possession of the Renoir.

Advise Shark.

Would your advice differ in any way if Shark had discovered that the cheque had been dishonoured before the sale to Rudd and had informed the Police?

Commentary

This problem concerns a unilateral mistake of identity. Students must be able to analyse the cases of mistake *inter absentes* and those *inter praesentes* and apply them to the problem. Does Shark make a mistake of identity or merely an error regarding the attributes/qualities of Pike? The contract is also voidable because of Pike's misrepresentation and it must be decided what effect this has on the third party, Rudd. The question also calls for a knowledge of rescission and the ways in which rescission can be communicated.

- Can Shark establish an operative, unilateral mistake of identity? If successful, what effect would this have on his contract with Pike?

- What are the conditions which Shark must fulfil if he is to be successful in establishing such a mistake regarding the identity of the other party to the contract?

- Is Pike guilty of fraudulent misrepresentation ? What effect does this have on the contract?

- Has Shark made any attempt to rescind the contract for fraudulent misrepresentation? What does rescission entail in this context?

- Is Pike a buyer in possession of the goods within the Sale of Goods Act 1979, s. 25(1) and the Factors Act 1889, s. 9 ? Does Rudd acquire title to the painting under the contract with Pike?

:Q̣: **Suggested answer**

Shark (S) has two possible remedies in this situation. First, he can try to establish a unilateral mistake of identity which, if operative, would render the contract with Pike (P) void. If successful, no title in the painting would transfer to P and, consequently, none to Rudd (R) who would be liable in conversion to S. Secondly, P is almost certainly guilty of fraudulent misrepresentation which would render his contract with S voidable at the latter's option. S could rescind the contract with P and, if communicated in time, the rescission would mean that no title could transfer to R. There are obvious difficulties here as to which of two innocent parties should suffer for the act of a swindler who probably cannot be traced. Consequently, there are conflicting policy decisions favouring either the owner or the *bona fide*, third party. This tends to distort the clarity of the law.

In order to establish an operative mistake of identity, S must show that he intended to deal with Lord Chub and that P knew this. Also, S must prove that identity was crucial in the circumstances and that, accordingly, he took reasonable steps to verify P's identity. It is clear that there is a real Lord Chub and that this is not simply an alias of P designed to impress S. This is in S's favour for if there had not been a separate entity apart from P, S could not prove a mistake of identity. In *King's Norton Metal Co. Ltd* v *Edridge, Merrett & Co. Ltd* (1897) 14 TLR 98, the swindler, Wallis, wrote to the plaintiffs using the alias of 'Hallam & Co' and was supplied with a quantity of wire which he sold to the *bona fide* defendants. It was held that the plaintiffs could not show that they intended to contract with 'Hallam & Co' as they did not exist and the contract was thus not void for mistake but only voidable for fraud. As the contract had not been avoided at the date of the sale to the defendants, they acquired a good title in the goods. The opposite conclusion was reached in *Cundy* v *Lindsay* (1878) 3 App Cas 459 where there was a separate, reputable company with whom the plaintiffs intended to deal, the contract with the swindler being void and the defendants therefore liable in conversion.

As P is fraudulent, it is self-evident that he is aware of S's mistake as he has induced it, and there should be no difficulty with this requirement. Moreover, as S bribes the porter at the Grand Hotel in order to discover whether Lord Chub is staying there, he has probably taken reasonable steps to verify Lord Chub's identity. In *Ingram* v *Little* [1961] 1 QB 31, the plaintiffs' cursory examination of the telephone directory was held to be a sufficiently onerous task in verification of the fact that the reputable third party lived at the address provided by the swindler. But can S prove that he intended to deal with Lord Chub, particularly as the contract is formed with P *inter praesentes*? What is there about Lord Chub's *identity* which would make S want to contract with him?

It is insufficient for S to prove that he does not want to contract with P — he must establish that he intends to contract positively with Lord Chub. Although subjective considerations are admitted in unilateral mistake, objective appearances are important here as with the other areas of mistake. In *Phillips* v *Brooks Ltd* [1919] 2 KB 243, a swindler named North entered the plaintiff's shop and selected some jewellery. He wrote a cheque for £3,000 saying that he was Sir George Bullough and giving an address in St James's Square which the plaintiff verified by consulting a directory. North was allowed to take a ring away with him which he pledged with the *bona fide* defendant. It was held that the contract was not void for mistake as the plaintiff intended to deal with the person in front of him and was simply impressed that he had secured a reputable customer. However, the contract was voidable for misrepresentation but had not been avoided, so the defendant acquired a good title. *Phillips* was distinguished by the House of Lords in *Lake* v *Simmons* [1927] AC 487. The appellant jeweller was insured against loss by theft with the exception of jewellery 'entrusted to a customer'. A woman entered the shop posing as the wife of a customer named Van der Borgh and was allowed to take away jewellery 'on approval' for her supposed husband. She absconded with the jewellery and the question was whether the loss was covered by the insurance policy or fell within its exclusion clause. It was held that the loss was covered by the insurance as the jeweller had not entrusted the goods to 'a customer' but thought, instead, that he 'was dealing with a different person, the wife of Van der Borgh'. It was pointed out that, in *Phillips*, the misrepresentation had not occurred until the sale was complete and it therefore only induced the delivery of the goods, not the contract itself. The contract was also void in *Ingram* v *Little*. Here the plaintiffs advertised their car for sale and were visited by a swindler posing as P. G.M. Hutchinson. The plaintiffs were reluctant to sell until they checked Hutchinson's address in the telephone directory but then they allowed the swindler to take the car, accepting a cheque which was subsequently dishonoured. The Court of Appeal held that the plaintiffs could recover their car from the defendant, a *bona fide* purchaser for value, on the basis that the contract with the swindler was void for mistaken identity. Finally, *Ingram* was criticised and not followed in *Lewis* v *Averay* [1972] 1 QB 198 where the facts were identical in all material respects to the former case except that, in *Lewis*, the swindler posed as the actor Richard Greene and showed an admission pass to Pinewood studios bearing a photograph of the swindler. The Court of Appeal emphasised that there is a strong presumption against a contract's being void where it is formed *inter praesentes* and, on the facts, the plaintiff intended to contract with the person in front of him, his only mistake being one of the attributes and credit-worthiness rather than identity. The defendant acquired a good title as the contract was voidable for fraud but had not been avoided by the plaintiff.

It seems that two lines of reasoning are evident in these cases. The first is that the contract cannot come into existence because there is a mistake regarding *the promise itself*, a term of the offer being that it is made only to the reputable third party, the swindler thus knowing that he is unable to accept the offer. This subjective test would accord with the reasoning in *Hartog* v *Colin and Shields* [1939] 3 All ER 566 regarding the promise itself, and *Boulton* v *Jones* (1857) 2 H & N 564 and *Hardman* v *Booth* (1863) 1 H & C 803 regarding mistaken identity. In *Boulton*, the defendant intended to contract only with the former owner of the business with whom he had a set-off and so the plaintiff, the new owner, could not accept the offer. This is, perhaps, too subjective a test as it would always allow the mistaken party to escape from the contract and it is more applicable to notions of *consensus* and small-scale transactions in the nineteenth century. Moreover, this approach has a catastrophic effect on the *bona fide*, third party buyer of goods who can virtually never acquire title. The second approach is objective and emphasises that it is difficult to rebut the presumption of a binding contract particularly when formed *inter praesentes* and, consequently, it is difficult to establish a *valid reason* for contracting with the third party other than that he has the attributes of good reputation and credit-worthiness. This line of reasoning is protective of *bona fide*, third party buyers but is, perhaps, too objective as it means that the mistaken party can rarely escape the contract. What, exactly, is the core of identity which the mistaken party must establish as the reason for wanting to contract only with the third party? This question is incapable of an accurate answer as it depends upon the ability to separate identity from attributes. In 1966, the Law Reform Committee recommended (Cmnd 2958) that in cases of mistaken identity the contract should be voidable in so far as the acquisition of title by third party buyers is concerned and much of the law would be clarified if statutory effect were given to this proposal.

Applying these conclusions to the problem would mean that in all probability the contract between S and P is not void for mistake. One difficulty remains unresolved in that P is said to be 'heavily disguised'. If this means disguised so that *his* identity is hidden, it adds nothing to the above conclusion but if it means disguised so as to resemble *Lord Chub* there is a much greater chance that S can prove that he wanted to deal only with the latter.

Finally, there is the question of S's rescinding the voidable contract made with P. It appears that R has acquired a valid title as S has made no attempt to rescind. If S had discovered the fraud before the sale to R the possibility of rescission must be considered. The general rule is that rescission must be communicated to the other party who has the voidable title but in *Car & Universal Finance Co. Ltd* v *Caldwell* [1965] 1 QB 525 it was recognised that a public act (there informing the police and Automobile Association) could suffice if the swindler is deliberately evading the plaintiff. Such would probably be the position in the problem. This rule is very protective of ownership and the Law Reform Committee recommended that it be abrogated but it is of limited application. P is clearly a buyer in possession of the goods by virtue of the Factors Act 1889, s. 9 and the Sale of Goods Act 1979, s. 25(1) and the decision in *Newtons of Wembley Ltd* v *Williams* [1965] 1 QB 560 establishes that the provisions of these statutes override an attempted rescission of the *Caldwell* variety meaning that the third party will normally acquire title. As P sells the painting to R in his (P's) shop and R appears to be *bona fide*, the other requirements of the above statutes would seem to be satisfied meaning that R should acquire a valid title in the painting.

Q Question 4

S and B were discussing the sale of works of art belonging to S. Discuss the legal position in the following separate situations:

(a) S offered to sell B 'that unsigned painting which you have always liked'. A price of £550 was agreed which included S's costs of having the painting cleaned and restored. The restorer discovered another painting beneath the one which was the subject of the sale which is believed to be by Goya and worth approximately £2 million. B claims the picture from S who refuses to deliver it to B.

(b) B was examining a painting at S's home which he (B) considered to be by Lowry and he offered S £150,000 for it. S agreed to the sale but neither S nor B said anything regarding the painting. Privately, S considered that it was only a good copy of a Lowry and worth £500. When B had the painting valued, he discovered that it was not a Lowry but that it was a good painting worth £10,000. B wishes to return the painting and have a refund of money but S refuses.

Commentary

Part (a) raises difficulties of common mistake. S and B make a common mistake but is it sufficient to render the contract void? Does part (b) involve a unilateral or a mutual mistake? It is arguable that the parties have agreed in the same terms on the same subject matter in both parts (a) and (b) and that the losses/gains should be regarded as part-and-parcel of the risks inherent in the bargains. The answer to the question must decide whether the law affords any grounds for relief from these ostensible contracts.

(a)

• What is meant by a 'common mistake' in the law of contract?

• Outline the two approaches to the notion of common mistake: (i) the existence of an express or implied term which provides who is to bear the risk of the mistake, and (ii) an independent doctrine of mistake based upon distinguishing a mistake of substance from a mistake of quality.

• Would either of the approaches, above, lead to this contract being declared void or, alternatively, is this a binding contract as both parties agree in the same terms on the same subject matter?

(b)

- What category of mistake is involved in this problem, mutual mistake or unilateral mistake?

- Define both these types of mistake and apply the definitions to the facts of the problem in order to establish whether there is an operative mistake of either sort.

ૐ Suggested answer

(a) S and B have clearly entered into a contract the *formation* of which is unimpeachable, but they have made a common mistake relating to the subject-matter. Both think that the painting is unattributed and worth £550 when, in fact, it is a Goya worth £2 million. The recent decision in *Associated Japanese Bank (International) Ltd* v *Credit du Nord SA* [1989] 1 WLR 255 confirms that the correct approach in such cases is to ascertain whether the contract itself, by express or implied terms, provides who bears the risk of the relevant mistake. The express terms of the contract only identify the painting and its price and thus the important question is whether it is possible to imply a term that, should the painting be found to be worth more than the contract price, the contract would be void. The initial reaction must be that such an implication is impossible in that it would negate the entire notion of a bargain and its attendant risks.

Many of the cases in this area have concerned non-existent subject matter or *res extincta*, where, contrary to the belief of both parties, the goods have perished at the date of contract or have never existed. One possibility in such cases is that there might be a total failure of consideration meaning that the contract is void; a buyer of goods, for example, does not have to pay for the goods if the seller cannot deliver as in *Couturier* v *Hastie* (1856) 5 HL Cas 673. Alternatively, it might be an implied condition precedent to the operation of the contract that the goods should exist, their non-existence rendering the contract void. If the seller has not impliedly warranted the existence of the goods (as he did in *McRae* v *Commonwealth Disposals Commission* (1951) 84 CLR 377) it might be possible to imply such a term as to existence as being both *necessary* to the contract and a manifestation of the *common* intention of the parties. In fact, such an implication was made successfully in the *Associated Japanese Bank* case regarding the non-existence of certain machines. But in the instant problem, it is the quality and value of the painting which is disputed and it is surely inconceivable that the tests for the implication of the above term could be satisfied.

The implied term is not *necessary* for the contract's performance nor could it represent the parties' *common* intention as B would certainly not assent to it. From the point of view of the contract's construction, it seems clear that S must bear the risk of this mistake. But might an independent doctrine of common mistake render this contract void?

In *Bell* v *Lever Brothers Ltd* [1932] AC 161, the House of Lords appeared to admit the existence of an extremely narrow concept of common mistake which would render the contract void. Lord Atkin proposed at least two tests, both being postulated upon the idea that only a fundamental mistake might invalidate a contract. The first was whether 'the state of the new facts destroy[s] the identity of the subject-matter as it was in the original state of facts'. Secondly, that 'the existence of some quality which makes the thing without the quality essentially different from the thing as it was believed to be' might render the contract void. Neither test was applied successfully in *Bell*; although both parties considered that Bell was worth £30,000, he was in fact worth nothing, yet this mistake of quality was insufficient to render the contract void. The later cases such as *Solle* v *Butcher* [1950] 1 KB 671 and *Leaf* v *International Galleries* [1950] 2 KB 86 took an equally restrictive approach to common mistake so that commentators began to think that perhaps only non-existent subject matter was sufficiently fundamental to render the contract void. This would mean that there was no meaningful doctrine of common mistake. In the *Associated Japanese Bank* case, Steyn J considered that common mistake existed as a doctrine but that the mistake 'must render the subject matter of the contract essentially and radically different'. These semantics are ultimately unhelpful in deciding the issues. In the problem, it is arguable that the subject matter of the contract is a painting which remains a painting in the light of the new facts. Indeed, the painting which is the subject of the contract is still present physically and its 'identity' is not therefore 'destroyed'. Alternatively, it may be asserted that a Goya worth £2 million is 'essentially different' from an unattributed painting worth £550. However, in *Bell*, Lord Atkin said that if A bought a picture from B which was believed by both to be the work of an old master, with a commensurately high purchase price, but which turned out to be a modern copy, A would have no remedy 'in the absence of representation or warranty'. This is most contentious and is at the heart of the debate relating to fundamental mistake. It is commonplace for a thing to be identified by a dominant quality which, if absent, makes the thing 'essentially different' and it is difficult to argue that 'a painting' and 'a Goya' are interchangeable. Nevertheless, the contract in the problem is probably valid and binding at common law.

As the contract would appear to be valid and enforceable under the ordinary principles of contract law, it is now clear that rescission cannot be granted in equity on the ground of common mistake (see *Great Peace Shipping Ltd* v *Tsavliris Salvage (Internatioinal) Ltd* (2002) *The Times*, 17 October).

(b) First, it must be decided what category of mistake is applicable to this problem and then ascertain whether it is an operative mistake rendering the contract void. This could be classified as a mutual mistake in that B thinks the painting is a Lowry whereas S thinks that it is a good copy, neither realising the other's error as nothing is said. On the facts, this mistake should not render the contract void as objectively there is an agreement in the same terms on the same subject matter: the parties are *ad idem*. Offer and acceptance might not have coincided if there had been two paintings, for example, S referring to one and B referring to the other, with nothing in the contract to identify which one was the subject of the sale. The facts would then approximate to *Raffles* v *Wichelhaus* (1864) 2 H & C 906 and *Scriven Bros & Co.* v *Hindley & Co.* [1913] 3 KB 564. In *Raffles*, there were two ships called *Peerless* both sailing from Bombay with cargoes of cotton, the buyer intending one ship and the seller the other. The buyer was not liable for his refusal to accept the cotton tendered. The facts of the problem resemble more closely those in *Wood* v *Scarth* (1858) 1 F & F 293 and *Scott* v *Littledale* (1858) 8 E & B 815. In the latter case, the defendants sold by sample 100 chests of tea but later discovered they had submitted a sample of poorer quality than the bulk. The contract was not void, the buyer thereby profiting from the transaction. It is clear that if the subject-matter of the sale is ascertained precisely, a mistake as to quality is immaterial, for otherwise, a buyer of goods who has made a bad bargain, as B has in the problem, would be able to re-open contracts at will.

Might it be argued that this is a unilateral mistake? If so B alone would have to be mistaken, S knowing of his mistake and attempting to take advantage of it. But again objective appearances count and if S has done nothing to mislead B the dominant principle is *caveat emptor*. Lord Atkin emphasised in *Bell* that this was still the position if S *knew* that B was labouring under a mistake. In these situations, B's mistake is one of quality and judgment which is not induced by S: if B has poor judgment he should make provision for it in the terms of the contract. However, this dominant principle does occasionally give way to evidence of subjective mistake. It is usually said that the contract will be void if one party is mistaken as to the *promise itself* and this is known to the other party. Here A makes or accepts an offer which he knows B understands in an entirely different sense. In *Hartog* v *Colin and Shields* [1939] 3 All ER 566, the defendants offered to sell 3,000 Argentine hare skins to the plaintiffs but, by mistake, offered them at so much per pound instead of so much per piece. Previous negotiations had been on the basis of price assessment per piece and this was trade practice but the plaintiffs, who would profit from the error, accepted the offer and sought damages for non-delivery. It was held that the plaintiffs must have realised that the offer did not express the defendants' real intent and the contract was therefore void. It is not clear whether the mistake must *actually* be known to the other party or whether it is sufficient that a reasonable man *ought* to be aware of it, but in *Centrovincial Estates plc v Merchant Investors Assurance Co. Ltd* [1983] Com LR 158, the Court of Appeal appeared to take the latter view. The *Hartog* analysis is said to relate only to mistakes regarding the terms of the contract and the promise itself rather than mistakes of quality, motive and judgement. This is a difficult distinction to make, although in *Bank of Credit and Commerce International v Ali* [1999] 4 All ER 83 the court again emphasised that the doctrine of mistake should not be used to extricate parties from 'bad bargains'. Does B's offer of £150,000 in the problem indicate that he is labouring under a mistake as to the terms of the contract, such that S ought to realise? It would seem not, as the terms of the contract relate to that particular picture and B's mistake relates only to the picture's quality.

It is doubtful whether any equitable relief would be forthcoming on the facts. B does acquire the picture that he bargained for rather than a different picture and so the court may think there is no hardship as in *Tamplin v James* (1880) 15 Ch D 215 where, on the facts, specific performance was ordered. Moreover, if the facts were that B's offer was an under-estimate for the painting such that he considered he would make a substantial profit on a re-sale, he could scarcely be heard to complain of hardship if the anticipated profits did not materialise. Indeed, it should be remembered that 'he who comes to equity must come with clean hands' and, depending upon the extent of any deception on B's part, he might be refused equitable remedies on this ground.

Illegality and Restraint of Trade

Introduction

The fundamental principle is that courts will not enforce an illegal contract. The most obvious example would be an agreement to commit a crime, e.g. A pays B £1,000 to shoot C. One can hardly imagine a court viewing with sympathy B's claim to payment after execution of the deed. Unfortunately, the simplicity of this example is rarely emulated in the field of illegality. For instance, few textbook writers agree on any appropriate classification. Should statutory and common law illegality be treated differently? What is the overlap between contracts which break the law and those which are contrary to public policy? Are uniform standards of unenforceability applied to all forms of illegal activity? Probably the best treatment of this area can be found in the current edition of *Cheshire, Fifoot & Furmston's Law of Contract*.

It is undoutedly true that illegality is the most confusing area within the law of contract, not least with regard to its lack of structure. For the sake of brevity the following comments classify the law into three parts: contracts contrary to law, contracts contrary to public policy and contracts in restraint of trade. The third category will be dealt with separately later in this chapter.

Contracts Contrary To Law

Obvious examples in this area include agreements to commit a crime (see *Bigos* v *Bousted* [1951] 1 All ER 92) or a civil wrong (see *Begbie* v *Phosphate Sewage Co. Ltd* (1875) LR 10 QB 491) or those which contravene an express statutory prohibition (*Harse* v *Pearl Life Assurance Co.* [1904] 1 KB 558). However, there are many other examples which fall into this category:

(a) A contract which has as its object something contrary to the law. Here, the state of the parties' minds can be crucial (see *Adamson* v *Jarvis* (1827) Bing 66); for example, a seller who knows that the buyer intends to put the goods to an unlawful use may not be allowed to recover the contract price (see *Pellecat* v *Angell* (1835) 2 Cr M & R 311).

(b) A contract which is performed in an illegal manner. Contracts can often be performed in several ways, some of which are perfectly lawful and others which are not (see *Cope* v *Rowlands* (1836) 2 M & W 149). If the method of performance is regulated by statute, the court will need to consider whether the statute penalises a particular method of performance or prohibits the contract *in toto* (see *St John Shipping Corp.* v *Joseph Rank Ltd* [1957] 1 QB 267).

(c) A contract contingent on the commission of an unlawful act. This would include an agreement to indemnify a party who commits a crime unless, in general terms, liability has been innocently or negligently incurred (see *Beresford* v *Royal Insurance Co. Ltd* [1938] AC 586 and *Osman* v *Ralph (J) Moss Ltd* [1970] 1 Lloyd's Rep 313).

(d) A contract contingent on the commission of a civil wrong. Thus, an agreement to indemnify a person against deceit would be illegal as deceit requires proof of *intent* (see *Brown Jenkinson & Co. Ltd* v *Percy Dalton (London) Ltd* [1972] 2 QB 621). However, an indemnity against civil liability which has been innocently or negligently incurred would be valid (see *Betts* v *Gibbins* (1834) 2 A & E 57).

Contracts Contrary to Public Policy

Contracts are said to be contrary to public policy when they have a clear tendency to bring about a state of affairs which the law regards as harmful or *contra bonos mores*. Obviously the courts will adapt to changes in social attitudes and economic conditions (compare *Cowan* v *Milbourn* (1867) LR 2 Ex 230 with *Bowman* v *Secular Society Ltd* [1917] AC 406). The main categories of such contracts are:

(a) Contracts which promote immoral conduct. For example, the hire of a carriage to a known prostitute so that she could ply her trade more effectively was considered illegal unless the hirer was ignorant of the intended use (see *Pearce* v *Brooks* (1866) LR 1 Ex 213). However, recent case law suggests that courts have adopted a more flexible approach to contracts promoting extra-marital sexual intercourse (see *Horrocks* v *Foray* [1976] 1 WLR 230) or, more recently, to contracts for the placing of advertisements in certain magazines advertising the defendant's pre-recorded sex messages and one-to-one conversations (see *Armhouse Lee Ltd* v *Chappell* (1996) *The Times*, 7 August).

(b) Contracts prejudicing the public service. This would include bribes for the acquisition of honours or contracts for the sale of public offices (see *Parkinson* v *Royal College of Ambulance* [1925] 2 KB 1).

(c) Contracts tending to pervert the course of justice. For example, criminal charges should not be compromised by private agreeement between criminal and victim, unless there is no strong public interest in prosecuting the offender (see *Fisher & Co.* v *Apolinaris Co.* (1875) LR 10 Ch App 297; *Elliot* v *Richardson* (1870) LR 5 CP 744). Other examples would include bribing a prosecution witness (see *R* v *Panayiotou* [1973] 3 All ER 112).

(d) Contracts prejudicial to public safety. This category covers agreements tending to benefit a country with which the UK is at war, or to disturb the good relations of the UK with a friendly country (see *Foster* v *Driscoll* [1929] 1 KB 470; *De Witz* v *Hendricks* (1824) Bing 314).

There are many other examples of contracts which would offend public policy such as unduly restricting personal liberty (see *King* v *Michael Faraday & Partners Ltd* [1939] 3 KB 753) and contracts to defraud the Inland Revenue (*Miller* v *Karlinski* (1945) 62 TLR 85). (Note: In applying public policy considerations the courts regard contracts that are in restraint of trade as being void rather than illegal — these contracts will thus be dealt with separately later in this chapter.)

Effects of Illegality

The most common effect of illegality, whether through being contrary to the law or as against public policy, is to prevent enforcement of the contract, either wholly or in part. It may even prevent a party who has transferred property or money from recovering it under the contract. In considering this area students are best advised to pose two questions:

(a) Was the contract (i) illegal at its inception, or (ii) only illegal in the manner of its performance? Category (i) includes contracts in which *both* parties intend, from the outset, to perform the contract in an illegal manner.

(b) If (ii) applies, is one of the parties innocent of any guilty intent? It will be seen that an innocent party often possesses the normal contractual remedies.

Illegal at Inception

In general the contract is void: there is no remedy of enforcement and no recovery of property transferred or money paid, although enforceable rights in the property may pass to a buyer *as against* a third party (see *Belvoir Finance Co. Ltd* v *Stapleton* [1971] 1 QB 210). Thus in an illegal sale of goods contract, the buyer who has paid the price cannot recover his money from the seller on grounds of non-delivery. Ignorance of the law is no excuse in this area (see *Nash* v *Stevenson Transport Ltd* [1936] 2 KB 128), although there is a suggestion that if performance of the illegal contract has some moral justification a court might adopt a more lenient attitude (see *Howard* v *Shirlstar Container Transport Ltd* [1990] 3 All ER 366).

However, there are some important exceptions to the general rule in which a court may permit the recovery of property or money. Thus, always consider the following questions:

(a) Is the disclosure of illegality essential to the claimant's cause of action? For example, in *Amar Singh* v *Kulubya* [1964] AC 142 the claimant recovered his property as he possessed an independent cause of action (see also *Bowmakers Ltd* v *Barnet Instruments Ltd* [1945] KB 65 and *Tinsley* v *Milligan* [1994] 1 AC 340).

(b) Are the parties *in pari delicto*? If parties have been pressured into contracts by misrepresentation, fraud, duress or oppression by others, they may recover property from, or money transferred to, those other persons (see *Hughes v Liverpool Victoria Legal Friendly Society* [1916] 2 KB 482). This principle has also been extended to cover parties who are protected by statute from the illegal activities of their contractual counterparts (see *Kiriri Cotton Co. Ltd v Dewani* [1960] AC 192).

(c) Did one of the parties 'repent' before performance of the illegal contract had begun (see generally *Kearley v Thomson* (1890) 24 QBD 742)? Note: (i) that the act of repentance must represent a *voluntary* abandonment of the contract (see *Bigos v Bousted* [1951] 1 All ER 92) or (ii) if the illegal transaction has not yet been performed, wholly or in part, then voluntary withdrawal will normally lead to the recovery of money or property already transferred (eg *Tribe v Tribe* [1995] 4 All ER 236).

Contracts Illegal as Performed

The general rule is that only parties to an agreement who possessed an unlawful intention are precluded from suing upon it. Thus, an innocent party possesses all the normal contractual remedies available, e.g. recovery of property and damages for breach (see *Marles v Philip Trant & Sons Ltd* [1954] 1 QB 29). Innocence in this context is objectively defined so the taint of illegality can be unwittingly transferred (see *Ashmore, Benson, Pease & Co. Ltd v AV Dawson Ltd* [1973] 1 WLR 828).

Statutory illegality generates its own problems. First, if the contract is absolutely prohibited then talk of rights and remedies is irrelevant (i.e. the contract is illegal at inception). Secondly, the statute might strike at the manner in which performance takes place, in which case any innocent party may possess the normal contractual remedies. Thirdly, the statute might provide certain classes of people with the normal contractual remedies even though they are aware of the illegal performance. Finally, the statute may contain its own regulatory sanctions (e.g. imposition of a fine) leaving the parties with their normal contractual remedies, irrespective of their state of knowledge (see *Hughes v Asset Managers plc* [1995] 3 All ER 669).

Thus, apart from innocence, there are two questions worthy of consideration:

(a) If illegality is imposed by statute, what is the purpose of the statute? For example, is it to protect a class of persons, regulate the manner in which a certain type of contract is performed, or simply to prohibit any such contract being formed? The answer will determine the remedies of the parties (see *Shaw v Groom* [1970] 2 QB 504).

(b) Is there a collateral warranty which stipulates that the defendant must perform the contract legally? Here, the claimant *might* be treated as if he were innocent (see *Strongman (1945) Ltd v Sincock* [1955] 2 QB 525).

Severance

An act of severance involves the court in removing the objectionable parts of a contract whilst enforcing the remainder (see *Storer* v *Gordon* (1814) 3 M & S 308). This power is seldom used by the courts as it is tantamount to condoning unlawful activities (see *Bennett* v *Bennett* [1952] 1 KB 249), although contracts in restraint of trade provide a marked exception to this policy (see below).

Q Question 1

Arnold, a professional burglar, plans a major robbery of the National Bank and enters into the following transactions in order to further his objective:

(a) Arnold agrees to use Buster's services as a 'safe-breaker' provided Buster pays him £500 immediately. Arnold promises to refund this payment after the robbery.

(b) Arnold purchases 50 kilos of dynamite from Crackit Ltd, the payment to be made in six one-monthly instalments of £500. The sales person fails to ask Arnold to produce a licence verifying his right to use dynamite.

(c) Arnold pressures Desmond into selling him a rifle. Desmond, the owner of a rifle-range, obtains the appropriate statutory licence and agrees to deliver to Arnold, within the month, certain personal documents establishing his ownership of the rifle. Payment is delayed for one week, by which time Arnold hopes he will be in possession of the proceeds of the planned robbery.

Buster never arrives at the bank to help Arnold but the robbery neverthless goes ahead as planned. However, there is much less in the safe than Arnold expected. He therefore refuses to pay the outstanding instalments on the dynamite and, in fact, sells some of it to Edward. Moreover, he refuses to pay Desmond for the rifle or return the £500 to Buster.

Discuss the legal position of all the parties.

Commentary

It is undoubtedly true that there is no easy problem question in the field of illegality. There are five parties involved and their rights will be determined by their state of knowledge, the purposes underlying existing statutory regulations and their comparative blameworthiness. However, as the facts are suitably ambiguous, you will need to consider how the addition of various hypothetical facts will affect your ultimate conclusions.

Clearly, the best approach is to look at each party individually, identifying the nature of the illegality, e.g. is the contract *ex facie* unlawful or unlawful as performed? This will ensure that you can identify more accurately the respective rights of the parties vis-à-vis the possible enforcement of the contract, the recovery of monies paid under the contract, and the recovery of property transferred.

- **Which of the contracts that Arnold entered into are potentially illegal at inception?**

- **Which of the contracts that Arnold entered into are potentially illegal only as performed?**

- **Does the licensing law regarding the use of dynamite completely forbid Arnold's contract, or merely render it illegal as performed?**

- **Has Buster repented in time and, if so, what are the consequences for Arnold?**

- **In what circumstances would a court allow Crackit Ltd or Desmond to recover their property?**

- **With regard to Desmond's contract, what is the effect if one of the parties is deemed 'innocent', or perhaps less blameworthy?**

⠶Ҩ⠶ Suggested answer

Arnold v Buster

In his contract with Arnold, Buster is clearly agreeing to aid the commission of a crime. As the contract is *ex facie* illegal, it will be declared void. This should mean that neither party will acquire any rights under the contract nor will a court permit the recovery of property or money transferred under the contract. If so, Arnold will be entitled to hide behind the illegality of the contract in order to retain the £500 payment (see *Re Mahmoud and Ispahani* [1921] 2 KB 716). But there is an alternative answer. The facts state that Buster did not arrive to help Arnold. Does this suggest that he 'repented'?

At present, the law on this point is in an extremely muddled state. However, two points seem reasonably clear. First, the act of repentance must represent a *voluntary* abandonment of the contract (see *Bigos* v *Bousted* [1951] 1 All ER 92). Thus, a plea of repentance would fail if Buster was prevented by external forces from helping Arnold (e.g. he crashed his car on the way to the bank, was incapacitated by illness, or was aiding the commission of a different crime). Secondly, repentance is impossible after the contract has been substantially performed (see *Kearley* v *Thomson* (1890) 24 QBD 742). However, provided Buster can argue that his failure to arrive before the robbery took place, constituted a genuine repentance, this should suffice. If Buster succeeds on both these points the court will allow him to recover his £500.

Crackit Ltd v Arnold

The facts are slightly more ambiguous on this point. For example, does Crackit know about Arnold's intended use of the dynamite? If this knowledge is established, the contract is unlawful from its inception (as with *Arnold v Buster*). Reference could be made to the case of *Pearce v Brooks* (1866) LR 1 Exch 213 in which the plaintiff's constructive knowledge of events was sufficient to defeat his claim of innocence. On the present facts, should Crackit Ltd be put on guard? Does the purchase of dynamite require some discussion with the customer regarding its intended use? This might be unnecessary if Arnold owned a quarrying business but would clearly be important if Arnold was a stranger purchasing the dynamite in a personal capacity.

This emphasises a more important point. The purchase of dynamite is clearly regulated by some form of statutory regulation. It is unlikely that a sale of dynamite over the counter is permissible without compliance with some further bureaucratic procedures. The vital issue for the court to resolve will be whether the relevant statute completely prohibits the type of contract under consideration (i.e. *ex facie* unlawful) or merely renders it illegal as performed.

If the statute expressly prohibited the sale of dynamite to unlicensed individuals under any circumstances, Crackit Ltd would have no right to sue Arnold for breach of contract or seek recovery of the unused dynamite (see generally *Cope v Rowlands* (1836) 2 M & W 149). Conversely, if the statute merely imposed conditions on the formation and execution of a dynamite sale, a different result might apply. For example, in *Shaw v Groom* [1970] 2 QB 504 the plaintiff landlord successfully sued the defendant tenant for rent arrears even though the former was liable to a fine for issuing the rent-book in contravention of the Landlord and Tenant Act 1962. The court held that the statute did not invalidate the tenancy agreement but merely regulated its circumvention through the imposition of fines. On our facts, this raises two possibilities. First, if Crackit Ltd is merely liable to a fine for selling to an unlicensed buyer, the company may still possess the normal contractual remedies, enabling it to recover the unused dynamite on learning of Arnold's repudiatory conduct and/or seek enforcement of outstanding contractual sums. Alternatively, if the statute prohibits the manner of performance, with no intention to substitute its own sanctions for those of the common law, Crackit Ltd's remedies will depend upon proof of innocence. This would be difficult to establish as the test is objective, preventing Crackit Ltd from arguing that it *honestly* thought that Arnold's intentions were lawful. The strictness of this objective test can be seen in *Ashmore, Benson, Pease & Co. Ltd v AV Dawson Ltd* [1973] 1 WLR 828.

Crackit Ltd v Edward

Even if the contract between Arnold and Crackit Ltd is illegal, the case of *Belvoir Finance Co. Ltd v Stapleton* [1971] 1 QB 210 may yet allow Crackit Ltd to recover the dynamite still in Edward's possession. In *Belvoir Finance* the plaintiffs bought various cars from dealers and sold them on hire purchase terms to X, all parties recognising that the transactions were illegal. In breach of contract, X's employee, the defendant, sold one of the cars to an innocent purchaser. It was held that the plaintiffs could successfully maintain an action in conversion against the defendant as they still enjoyed the 'general property' in the car. A similar finding was made in *Bowmakers Ltd v Barnet Instruments Ltd* [1945] KB 65, the Court of Appeal pointing out that as the illegal sub-sale constituted a fundamental breach of contract by the defendant, the plaintiffs could re-assert their original title to the goods. On our facts, Crackit Ltd would argue that in selling the dynamite to Edward, Arnold had committed a fundamental breach of contract, allowing Crackit Ltd to re-assert its title against Edward, irrespective of the latter's innocence.

Desmond v Arnold

Three questions could be posed here. What is Desmond's state of knowledge? What is the effect of Arnold's pressure tactics? What is the relevance of Desmond retaining the documents of title? Regarding the first point, if Desmond can establish his innocence he may be entitled to reclaim the contract price, subject to the comments below. Innocence in this context is objectively defined and is best illustrated by the case of *Pearce v Brooks* in which the plaintiff hired to the defendant an unusually designed carriage. It was held that the plaintiff's realisation that the defendant was a prostitute, who intended to use the carriage as a means of attracting customers, prevented him from recovering the outstanding hire fee. Note that an objective test of innocence entitled the jury to conclude that a reasonable person would make a connection between the defendant's calling and the peculiar design of the carriage. Does Desmond know the purpose for which Arnold intends to use the rifle? If he was aware of Arnold's criminal proclivities or Arnold had told him that the rifle would be useful in the planned robbery, the contract would be *ex facie* unlawful. On this basis, Desmond would have no right to enforce the contract (subject to the comments below). Alternatively, if Desmond is totally innocent he will possess all the normal contractual remedies available, e.g. recovery of property and/or damages for breach (see *Marles v Philip Trant & Sons Ltd* [1954] 1 QB 29).

However, there is evidence that Desmond was forced into the contract with Arnold. Even if Desmond knows of Arnold's intentions the question arises as to whether the parties were *in pari delicto*? If the court is convinced Arnold exerted sufficient pressure to break down the physical and emotional reserves of a reasonable person, Desmond may be allowed to recover his rifle. The principle being applied in this context is that the parties can never be considered equally blameworthy when 'one has the power to dictate, the other no alternative but to submit' (*Atkinson v Denby* (1862) 7 H & N 934, 936 *per* Cockburn CJ). Desmond's remedy would be the recovery of the rifle, not the right to enforce contractual payment.

Finally, even if the contract between Arnold and Desmond is *ex facie* unlawful,

Desmond may still be entitled to recover his rifle if he can frame his cause of action entirely independently of the contract (see *Tinsley* v *Milligan* [1994] 1 AC 340). For example, in *Amar Singh* v *Kulubya* [1964] AC 142, Ugandan law prohibited the lease of 'Mailo' land to a non-African without the permission of the Governor. The plaintiff leased his land to the defendant without obtaining the necessary consent. Several years later the plaintiff gave the defendant notice to quit under the lease agreement. It was held that although the lease was void for illegality, the plaintiff 's claim to possession would be upheld as it was not based upon the agreement but, rather, upon his independent and untainted ground of freehold ownership. On our facts, Arnold is now in possession of the rifle but Desmond has retained certain documents which would suggest that he is the rightful owner. It is submitted that Desmond has a stronger case as he can assert ownership on independent grounds which Arnold would be unable to rebut as their original agreement is void for illegality.

Q Question 2

In English Law only the innocent have rights under an illegal contract.

Discuss.

Commentary

This type of question does not simply require a summary of the law. Marks will be earned for a coherent structure, evaluation and analysis of existing precedent and, in particular, an ability to concentrate on those aspects of illegality relevant to the question.

In particular, your answer should focus on three issues. First, in dealing with a contract illegal at its inception, when will the innocence of either party be relevant to the determination of their rights under that contract? Secondly, is there a difference if the contract is only illegal as performed? Thirdly, are there any circumstances where a guilty party would possess rights under an illegal contract?

- **What is the difference between a contract *ex facie* unlawful and one that is only illegal as performed?**
- **When can a party reclaim property transferred under an illegal contract?**
- **In what circumstances will innocence entitle one party to enforce the contract?**
- **In what circumstances will a 'guilty' party retain the right to enforce the contract?**

Suggested answer

The general approach of the courts to illegal contracts is neatly summarised by the maxim *ex turpi causa non oritur actio* (no right of action arises from a base cause). On this basis, neither party would acquire enforceable rights under an illegal contract nor would they be entitled to sue on the contract for the return of any money or property transferred. But the *ex turpi* rule is subject to a variety of exceptions. In particular, a vital distinction must be drawn between contracts illegal at their inception and contracts which are only illegal because of the manner in which they have been performed. Judicial attitudes are far stricter when dealing with the first category, irrespective of the innocence of one or other party.

Contracts Illegal at Inception

In general, an agreement to do something which is expressly or impliedly prohibited by the law is unenforceable and property or money transferred under the contract cannot be recovered: *in pari delicto potior est conditio defendentis* (where both parties are equally at fault the position of the possessor is better). Neither party can assert that they had no intention of breaking the law, nor will any allowance be made for either party's ignorance of the law.

Notwithstanding the above, the courts will permit the recovery of property or money transferred under the contract where the *comparative innocence* of one party is established. Thus, if the parties are not *in pari delicto*, a court may allow the less blameworthy to recover money or property transferred under the contract. Available precedent suggests that there must be some evidence of oppression or misrepresentation by the defendant, or that the statute which prohibits the contract is aimed at protecting one of the parties. For example, in *Hughes* v *Liverpool Victoria Legal Friendly Society* [1916] 2 KB 482 the plaintiff was allowed to recover premiums paid under an illegal life insurance policy as he was induced to enter into the contract by the defendant's fraudulent misrepresentation that the policy was valid. However, a claimant's innocence is insufficient without evidence that the defendant acted in some unconscionable manner. Thus, in *Edler* v *Auerbach* [1950] 1 KB 359 the plaintiff lessee could not recover premiums, paid under an illegal lease, from the defendant lessor, as there was no evidence that the latter had been fraudulent. Regarding class-protecting statutes, in *Kiriri Cotton Co. Ltd* v *Dewani* [1960] AC 192, the landlord charged the tenant an illegal premium which the tenant then sought to recover. It was held that as the relevant statute placed the obligation firmly on the landlord, the tenant could recover the rent on the grounds that he was not *in pari delicto*.

One further example of 'comparative innocence' is provided by the principle of repentance. Specifically, the recovery of property and money will be permitted if the claimant repents by discontinuing his illegal activities before the contract has been substantially performed (see *Kearley* v *Thomson* (1890) 24 QBD 742). Moreover, repentance must be voluntary, the defendant thereby demonstrating that he has seen 'the error of his ways'. For example, in *Bigos* v *Bousted* [1951] 1 All ER 92 the plaintiff agreed to purchase Italian lire from the defendant. Payment was to be made in sterling, which contravened existing exchange control regulations. When the defendant failed to deliver the lire, the plaintiff claimed back his money, arguing that he had repented. The claim failed as there was no evidence that the claimant would have withdrawn from the contract if the defendant had supplied the lire.

Contracts Illegal as Performed

In this area an innocent party possesses all the normal contractual remedies available, e.g. recovery of property and/or damages for breach of contract (see *Marles v Philip Trant & Sons Ltd* [1954] 1 QB 29). Here again the test of innocence is objectively applied. Thus, in *Ashmore, Benson, Pease & Co. Ltd v AV Dawson Ltd* [1973] 1 WLR 828 the contract involved the transportation of a load in excess of the legal limit for the lorries used. The claim by the plaintiff's transport manager, who supervised the loading of the lorries, that he had not noticed the error, was rejected by the court.

The same principles apply to contracts which are performed in ways prohibited by statute: the innocent party will possess all the normal remedies whilst the guilty party will have none (see *Anderson Ltd v Daniel* [1924] 1 KB 138). Naturally, if the claimant's 'innocence' is compromised then he may forfeit his rights, e.g. perhaps the innocent party ought to have recognised that the contract could only be performed in an illegal manner, though this seems less important if the statute is there to protect him in the first place (see *Shaw v Groom* [1970] 2 QB 504). This general objective test has been applied, in a different context, to a collateral contract which stipulated that the defendant would obtain the required statutory licence before commencing work. The defendant failed to do so. Nevertheless, the 'innocence' of the plaintiff persuaded the court to afford him an independent cause of action based on the collateral contract (see *Strongman (1945) Ltd v Sincock* [1955] 2 QB 525).

So far we have seen that an innocent party posseses better remedies in comparison with his guilty counterpart. But the latter is not completely denuded of rights.

Rights of a Guilty Party

The general rule that no rights emerge from a contract illegal at inception can often be successfully utilised by the defendant as an effective defence against a claimant who seeks enforcement, damages or recovery of property (see *Re Mahmoud and Ispahani, Re* [1921] 2 KB 716). For example, in *Pearce v Brooks* (1866) LR 1 Ex 213, although the prostitute used the carriage, she could successfully rely on the illegality of the contract when the plaintiff sued for the hire-charge. Moreover, there is a suggestion that although a claimant cannot generally rely upon the contract to recover goods transferred to the defendant, the defendant can use the contract as a means of protecting himself against third parties who claim to have acquired rights in the subject-matter (see *Belvoir Finance Co. Ltd v Stapleton* [1971] 1 QB 210).

Other than this, a guilty party can seek recovery of property under an illegal contract provided disclosure of the illegality is not essential to his cause of action. For example, in *Amar Singh v Kulubya* [1964] AC 142 the plaintiff was the owner of land leased unlawfully to the defendant. It was held that he could recover his land on the basis of his untainted, independent title of freehold ownership. Equally, in *Edler* v *Auerbach* [1950] 1 KB 359, although the landlord was unable to sue on the illegal lease he was entitled to assert his untainted title to other property on the premises, thereby obtaining damages for the tenant's unlawful removal of a bath. Naturally, if the illegality is apparent from the evidence brought before the court, it is questionable that the guilty party will be entitled to recover his property (see *Snell* v *Unity Finance Co. Ltd* [1964] 2 QB 203). However, in *Tinsley* v *Milligan*, the House of Lords allowed the defendant's counterclaim on the ground that evidence of illegality only emerged in cross-examination rather than in her original pleadings.

Finally, there has been a recent suggestion that if the guilt of one party does not amount to an affront to public conscience, the courts may be more lenient. For example, in *Howard* v *Shirlstar Container Transport Ltd* [1990] 3 All ER 366, the plaintiff, who was a pilot, agreed to recover a plane that was being held by the Nigerian authorities. Although clearly illegal, the Court of Appeal upheld his claim to the agreed payment. If this approach is followed, the effects of illegality may reflect more accurately the relative fault and guilty intentions of the parties. Admittedly, the House of Lords, in *Tinsley* v *Milligan* refused to accept a test based on public conscience. Although recognising the deficiences in the present law, Lord Goff considered that Parliamentary intervention was required if two hundred years of precedent was to be swept aside. Nevertheless, more recent case law has again highlighted the importance of the parties' respective blameworthiness (e.g. *Mohamed* v *Alaga & Co.* [2000] 1 WLR 1815).

Contracts in Restraint of Trade

Many employment contracts possess the customary restraint clause directed towards restricting employees' activities during the course of employment and after its termination. Restraint clauses are traditionally drafted in terms of restricting activities within a certain geographical area and for a certain time; for example, the employer might wish to prevent departing employees from working for any competing firm within a two mile radius and for six months thereafter. Restraint clauses can also appear in commercial dealings between businesses such as where the purchaser of a business wishes to protect its goodwill.

The common starting point is that all restraints of trade are presumed void unless shown to be reasonable as between the parties and to be in the public interest, the latter point rarely proving critical as a distinct point. The test for reasonableness is seen at its most stringent when dealing with employment contracts because restricting employees' freedom of operations may deny them the opportunity to earn a living.

Employees

The enforceability of restraint clauses in employment contracts is dependent upon the employer establishing two things: that a legitimate proprietary interest is being protected, and that the restraint is not unreasonably wide in terms of protecting those interests.

The following questions should therefore be considered in answering any question on this topic:

(a) Is the employer protecting a legitimate proprietary interest? The most common example involves the protection of confidential information (e.g. trade secrets) or trade connections (see generally *Thomas Marshall (Exports) Ltd* v *Guinle* [1979] 1 WLR 251).

(b) Is the clause unreasonably wide in terms of the *type* of activities which it restricts? A general non-competition clause may be too wide (see *GW Plowman and Son Ltd* v *Ash* [1964] 1 WLR 568) whereas a clause which only prevents soliciting of former customers will be viewed more favourably.

(c) Is the clause unreasonably wide in terms of the employer's activities and what the employee was employed to do? For example, there must be a functional correspondence between the area circumscribed by the clause (e.g. not to work within 5 miles) and the area particularly associated with the employee's place of work (see *Spencer* v *Marchington* [1988] IRLR 392).

(d) Is the clause unreasonably wide in terms of the *type* of employee involved and the influence that he could exert over the employer's customers? For example, non-solicitation clause for employees who have little personal contact with their employers' customers may be unreasonable (see *SW Strange Ltd* v *Mann* [1965] 1 WLR 629).

(e) Is the clause unreasonably wide in terms of the time and area restraints that it imposes? For instance, a time constraint should not last longer than the projected useful life of the information it is attempting to protect (see *Littlewoods Organisation* v *Harris* [1977] 1 WLR 1472).

As mentioned above, the whole doctrine of restraint of trade is based on the concept of public interest; the balancing of an individual's liberty with principles of freedom of contract. Courts can therefore 'fall back' on pronouncements of public interest or public policy in order to strike out clauses which, though reasonable perhaps as between the parties, offend some vague judgment as to what is acceptable. For example, in *Panayiotou* v *Sony Music Entertainment (UK) Ltd* [1994] EMLR 229 the court held it would be against public policy to allow the plaintiff singer/songwriter to question the enforceability of a previous bona fide compromise settlement which he had later affirmed voluntarily.

This brings us to one final point: the doctrine of restraint of trade has developed rapidly in the post-war years and has been used successfully in quasi-employment situations. For example, in the music industry, although the plaintiff failed in *Panayiotou*, others have met with greater success (e.g. *ZTT* v *Holly Johnson* [1993] EMLR 61, *Silverstone Records Ltd* v *Mountfield* [1993] EMLR 152, *Schroeder Music Publishing Co Ltd* v *Macaulay* [1974] 1 WLR 1308).

Moreover, current litigation demonstrates the link between this area, undue influence and the wider notions of inequality of bargaining power (e.g. *O'Sullivan* v *M.A.M. Ltd* [1984] 3 WLR 448, *John* v *James* [1991] FSR 397). Students would therefore be well-advised to recognise that cases of this nature can be of use in answering questions on improper pressure (e.g. **Chapter 8**, Question 5).

Sale of a Business

Clearly the purchaser of a business does not wish to see its assets diminished by the vendor's post-completion activities. If the vendor was able to entice all his old clients away from the purchaser then the latter would be left with a worthless asset. A purchaser will therefore consider the insertion of restraint clauses which consolidate the business's commercial assets. Are such clauses enforceable? As with employment contracts, the basic test is whether the clause is reasonably protecting the legitimate proprietary interests of the purchaser, the courts striking a balance between the public policy implications of anti-competitive behaviour and the contractual freedom of commercial parties who are often of equal bargaining strengths. For example, in *Nordenfelt* v *Maxim Nordenfelt Guns and Ammunition Co.* [1894] AC 535, the plaintiff sold his armaments business to the defendant and undertook not to carry on such a business for 25 years, except on behalf of the company, anywhere in the world. It was held that this condition was valid and enforceable given the plaintiff's reputation and the global nature of the armaments trade.

In dealing with this area the following questions seem the most appropriate to ask:

(a) Is the purchaser protecting a legitimate proprietary interest? The customer-base and goodwill of the business are invariably the most important protectable interests.

(b) Is the clause unreasonably wide in terms of the *type* of activities which it restricts? A clause should not restrict competition *per se* as this would be unduly wide in terms of the protectable interest (see *British Reinforced Concrete Engineering Co. Ltd* v *Schelff* [1921] 2 Ch 563 where the restraint was more subtly framed).

(c) Is the clause unreasonably wide in terms of the time and area restraints that it imposes? The *Nordenfelt* decision clearly demonstrates that the clause must reflect the extent of the vendor's sphere of influence, his geographically located client base, and the period of time over which both would evaporate.

(d) Can the restraint doctrine apply to contracts other than sales of businesses? The doctrine has been used to control the growth of solus agreements, i.e. those which restrict a retailer's distribution network, pricing policies or chain of supply (see *Esso Petroleum Co. Ltd* v *Harper's Garage (Stourport) Ltd* [1967] 1 All ER 699, *Alec Lobb (Garages) Ltd* v *Total Oil Great Britain Ltd* [1983] 1 WLR 87). In this area, the public interest assumes greater importance as a restraint clause might affect the public in terms of prices charged or the choice of goods available for purchase (see generally *Schroeder (A) Music Publishing Co. Ltd* v *Macaulay* [1974] 1 WLR 1308).

Severance

Generally, a contract will not be nullified simply because it is found that one of its clauses constitutes an unreasonable restraint of trade. Rather, the objectionable clause will, if possible, be severed completely or reduced in its effect.

The complete elimination of a clause will only be allowed if it forms a subsidiary rather than a substantial part of the consideration, otherwise the contract becomes totally unenforceable (see *Goodinson* v *Goodinson* [1954] 2 QB 118). Alternatively, it may be possible to sever specific parts of a clause by employing the 'blue pencil' test. This test provides that the objectionable part of a clause will only be severed if it leaves the remainder in a grammatically correct and understandable form (see *Goldsoll* v *Goldman* [1915] 1 Ch 292). The only pre-condition is that the clause itself is divisible in nature; that is, that the clause is not a single covenant but is in effect a combination of several distinct covenants (see *Attwood* v *Lamont* [1920] 3 KB 571).

Q Question 3

(a) Sam is employed as Deputy Accountant by Albright Ltd, a firm of financial analysts located in Cardiff, Wales. Most of Sam's work involves sitting in front of a computer predicting the future profit expectations of Albright's clients located in Wales. His work has always greatly impressed these clients. Recently, Sam resigned from his job and joined a similar firm located in Swansea. A number of Albright's clients heard about this move and transferred their allegiance to the Swansea firm. Albright Ltd has now written to Sam pointing out that there was a clause in his original contract which stated that on termination of employment he must not 'for a period of two years solicit custom from any Albright client with whom the employee has had contact in the year prior to termination of the contract, or join any firm of financial analysts located in Wales'.

Discuss. (66%)

(b) John owns a very profitable business, Wacko Enterprises Leeds, a firm specialising in the provision of professional entertainment for birthday parties,
e.g. magicians and musician bands. He decides to sell this firm to Mary with
an undertaking that he will not 'start up any new firm within five miles of
Leeds which specialises in any form of adult entertainment'. John now
wants to start up a travel agency in Leeds, specialising in adult adventure
holidays.

Discuss. (34%)

Commentary

The question clearly weights the different parts unequally. Your answer must reflect this
disparity in the length of treatment accorded to each part. The basic issue in part **(a)** will be
resolved by posing the following questions: What is Albright's protectable proprietary interest? Is the clause unduly wide in protecting this interest? Can the offending portions be
severed whilst allowing the remainder to remain enforceable?

Similar considerations apply in part **(b)**. Mary has the right to prevent John from unfairly
competing with her after the purchase has been completed; otherwise John could entice his
old customers away. The issue is whether the clause effects this in a reasonable manner. In
particular, if the clause restricts John's subsequent commercial aspirations in areas that have
no connection with Wacko Enterprises then, unless severance is possible, the clause would
fail in its entirety.

- What proprietary interests is Albright attempting to protect?

- Is the clause used by Albright unreasonably wide, in terms of Sam's existing
  duties and his degree of influence over Albright's clients?

- Is the clause used by Albright unreasonably wide, in terms of Albright's
  geographical area of influence and the commercial duration of any trade
  secrets?

- Has Mary drawn her net too widely in terms of protecting her existing client
  base?

- Are Sam's legitimate career aspirations being unreasonably constrained?

- In either contract, what scope is there to sever the offending parts of the
  clauses?

⠟ **Suggested answer**

(a) The simple issue is whether the restraint clause is enforceable by Albright Ltd. The presumption with all restraint clauses is that they are void unless shown to be reasonable. 'Reasonableness' depends upon whether Albright Ltd can establish that it has a legitimate proprietary interest to protect and that the clause is not drafted in unreasonably wide terms for the protection of those interests.

Does Albright Ltd possess such legitimate interests? This is debatable as regards the protection of business connections because Sam seems to have little personal contact with Albright's clients. If he does have the opportunity to exert personal influence over the clients, or possibly if his reputation is such that clients might move their accounts when he leaves Albright, such an interest will exist. After all, Albright is attempting to prevent departing employees from poaching their existing clients: an important asset within any firm (see *Plowman (GW) and Son Ltd v Ash* [1964] 1 WLR 568). Moreover, Sam has access to a considerable amount of confidential information which could be used unfairly in this context and will, therefore, constitute a proprietary interest (see *Roger Bullivant Ltd v Ellis* [1987] ICR 464).

Assuming a protectable interest, is the clause unreasonably wide in terms of the *type* of activities which it restricts? Insofar as the clause prevents the solicitation of clients this is likely to be reasonable if the two-year period accurately reflects how long it would take the employer to reinstate *influence* over the clients; and should receive a more sympathetic hearing from a court because it is limited in the scope and range of clients affected (see *Plowman (GW) and Son Ltd v Ash, supra*). However, the clause also prevents Sam from joining a competing firm. This is much more difficult to defend. Reasonableness here will depend upon: (a) Sam's duties and his degree of influence over Albright's clients and, (b) the area and time-limits imposed within the clause.

First, as noted above, Sam was employed as a back-room expert with little personal contact with clients. This would suggest that the clause is unreasonable (see *Strange (SW) Ltd v Mann* [1965] 1 WLR 629) because the clause does not reflect the employee's job. However, Sam did occupy a senior position within the firm and his work impressed the clients for whom he worked. This may represent an effective substitute for personal contact as clients are often more interested in ability and results, rather than general personality traits. As these positive factors induce reliance and some degree of attachment, a properly-drawn restraint might be considered reasonable (see *Marley Tile Co. Ltd v Johnson* [1982] IRLR 75). The actual wording of the clause imposes a blanket prohibition on working for another firm of 'financial analysts'. There is no mention in what capacity Sam would seek employment, e.g. as a clerk, an auditor or an accountant. As such, the clause may appear too widely drawn insofar as it prevents Sam from diversifying into other types of employment. The question notes that the clients have moved their business. It is irrelevant here whether they would or would not wish to continue dealing with Albright in any event.

On the second point, there must be a functional correspondence between the area circumscribed by the clause (i.e. not to work in Wales) and the area particularly associated with the employee's place of work (see *Spencer v Marchington* [1988] IRLR 392). The guiding principle is that the wider the geographical area of restraint, the more likely that it is unreasonable, although density of population should be taken into account (see *Mason v Provident Clothing and Supply Co. Ltd* [1913] AC 724). In Sam's position we do not know whether his clients are located throughout Wales or are limited to a narrower area. If the clients are widely dispersed, the clause seems more reasonable, whereas if they are all situated within a few miles of Cardiff, a court might reach a different conclusion.

Regarding the time constraint, this period must not be longer than the projected useful life of any trade secrets which Albright Ltd is attempting to protect (see *Faccenda Chicken v Fowler* [1986] ICR 297). Nor must any restraint regarding trade connections be longer than it would take Albright to recruit a replacement and for that employee to gain the same status and contacts as Sam possessed. Both these points are questions of fact, although current precedent suggests that one year is often a generally accepted norm for protecting trade connections.

Finally, can any reasonable portions of the clause be enforced? The principle of severance does not countenance the rewriting of contracts by the courts. The 'blue pencil test' ensures that an objectionable part of a clause can only be severed if it leaves the remainder in a grammatically correct and understandable form and does not radically alter the original agreement (see *Goldsoll v Goldman* [1915] 1 Ch 292). On our facts, it would be possible to delete the words 'or join any firm of financial analysts located in Wales', leaving the non-solicitation clause intact. However, it would not be possible to substitute a different length of time for the restraint, so if the existing period was unreasonable the clause would fail in its entirety. Equally, if the court decided that the clause was not a combination of two undertakings but, rather, an indivisible covenant, the clause would again fail completely (see *Attwood v Lamont* [1920] 3 KB 571).

(b) The starting point is that the clause will be presumed void unless reasonable as between the parties and in the public interest. The clause is clearly attempting to protect Mary's legitimate proprietary interests by conserving the existing client base of Wacko Enterprises. However, is it framed too widely in terms of the *type* of activities which it restricts? For example, in *British Reinforced Concrete Engineering Co. Ltd v Schelff* [1921] 2 Ch 563, it was held unreasonable for the defendant to be precluded from engaging in the manufacture or sale of road-reinforcements generally, as the business that he sold was concerned with the manufacture of a specialised road improvement product.

On our facts Wacko deals with a very limited type of entertainment, providing services for birthday parties. However, the clause restricts John's activities far beyond such provision, employing the words 'any form of adult entertainment'. On the one hand the parties were presumably of equal bargaining strength when they entered into the contract — the freedom of contract principle is influential in this area. On the other hand, John's subsequent entrepreneurial flair is being subdued thereby depriving the public of his talents in his newly discovered 'vocation' of adult adventure holidays. It is submitted that the latter argument is stronger as (a) Mary has no legitimate interest in preventing John from taking up his new business activity as there appears to be very little overlap with Wacko, and (b) even if a substantial overlap existed, a non-solicitation clause would seem more appropriate in the circumstances. This analysis is reinforced by the fact that the clause includes no time restraint, thereby restricting John's business aspirations for the whole of his life. Is this not unduly onerous? Existing precedent would certainly agree (see *Pellow* v *Ivey* (1933) 49 TLR 422) except in very exceptional circumstances (e.g. the enforceable 25 year restraint in *Nordenfelt* v *Maxim Nordenfelt Guns and Ammunition Co.* [1894] AC 535).

Finally, severance of the objectionable part seems inappropriate. As the court cannot re-write the clause (e.g. add a reasonable time constraint) and use of the blue pencil test would produce grammatical nonsense, the restraint would appear completely unenforceable. If this happens Mary may argue that the remainder of the contract has suffered from a substantial failure of consideration and is *completely* unenforceable (see *Goodinson* v *Goodinson* [1954] 2 QB 118 and *Stenhouse Australia Ltd* v *Phillips* [1974] AC 391). This is difficult to assess as the purchaser of a small business may rightly argue that goodwill and existing trade connections are the only important assets for which the contract price is paid. Naturally, if Mary succeeds, the contract will be void and she will be entitled to the return of her purchase monies.

Frustration

Introduction

The doctrine of frustration evolved during the mid-nineteenth century to moderate the common law's uncompromising insistence on the literal performance of absolute contractual obligations (e.g. *Paradine* v *Jane* (1647) Aleyn 26). The hallmark of frustration is that it refers to a supervening event not reasonably contemplated by the parties at the time of contracting which radically alters the foundation of the contract or renders it physically or legally impossible to perform. For example, in *Taylor* v *Caldwell* (1863) 3 B & S 826 the hiring of a music hall was held to be frustrated when the hall burnt down. The event, however, must have a fundamental impact on performance of the contract; thus, disappointed expectations, hardship or mere inconvenience, do not in themselves give rise to frustrated contracts (e.g. *Davis Contractors Ltd* v *Fareham Urban District Council* [1956] AC 696). Note that frustration refers to events that take place *after* the contract was made, whereas if the change of circumstances was *pre-contractual* recourse would be made to the law of mistake and the presumed allocation of risks between the parties.

In answering a problem question on frustration three questions will always need to be posed, as outlined below.

Is there a Radical Change in Circumstances?

Perhaps the event has made the contract physically incapable to perform, or a change in the law has had the same effect? Alternatively, performance remains possible but would bear no relation to what was intended. In these circumstances it is often said that the contract has been struck by commercial sterility. Relevant questions include:

(a) Is the contract physically incapable of performance in the business sense (compare *Condor* v *Barron Knights Ltd* [1966] 1 WLR 87 with *Marshall* v *Harland and Wolff Ltd* [1972] 1 WLR 899)?

(b) Did an unexpected interruption in performance delay, to an unacceptable degree, the eventual completion of the contract (see generally *Metropolitan Water Board* v *Dick, Kerr & Co.* [1918] AC 119 and *Chakki* v *United Yeast Co. Ltd* [1982] 2 All ER 446 on the specific problem of employees being temporarily unavailable for work)?

(c) Was the non-occurrence of a specified event central to the contract? (e.g. *Krell* v *Henry* [1903] 2 KB 740).

(d) Did the supervening event *fundamentally* alter the obligations of the parties or merely increase the costs of performance, rendering it unprofitable in the short-term, or causing some other additional inconvenience (see *Davis Contractors Ltd* v *Fareham UDC* [1956] AC 696)?

In answering these points it may be necessary to identify the 'object' of the contract. This requires a separation of the parties' motives in entering into the contract from the object of the contract itself. For example, X purchases a train ticket (Crewe to St Andrews, weekend return) in order to take him to the venue of the British Open Golf Championship in Scotland. The Open is cancelled owing to appalling weather conditions. In these circumstances, although the train journey is now pointless as the *motive* for going no longer exists, the object of the contract is still performable, i.e. to take X to St Andrews and back. Thus, the contract would not be frustrated. However, X's motive and the contract's object could become inseparable if, for example, the railway company had advertised in the following way: 'Travel in style to the British Open. First class seats at second class prices.' This might suggest that fare payers were travelling for the express purpose of seeing the Open, i.e. the object of the contract was to facilitate the viewing of the Golf Open rather than to transport a passenger from A to B (see *Krell* v *Henry* [1903] 2 KB 740).

Finally, some understanding of the juristic basis of frustration may be important. Two tests have been adopted over the years with varying degrees of success: implied terms and construction. The implied terms theory was pre-eminent at the turn of the century, necessitating an *objective* assessment of the hypothetical reactions of a party to an unforeseen event (e.g. *Tamplin (FA) Steamship Co. Ltd* v *Anglo-Mexican Petroleum Products Co. Ltd* [1916] 2 AC 397, 404). The question, put simply, was whether a term covering the frustrating event could be implied into the contract on the basis that it was so obvious and necessary that it went without saying that both parties would have assumed its inclusion when the contract was made. The weakness of the test is that as the supervening event is supposedly unforeseen, the idea that either party would have considered the automatic inclusion of a term to cover the event at the time of the contract is patently contradictory. Nowadays, the 'construction' test has supplanted the implied term theory. This test requires a court to examine the terms of the contract in order to construe the intentions of the parties at the time the contract was made and, in that context, impose upon the parties a just and reasonable solution which the new circumstances demand.

> The event is something which happens in the world of fact, and has to be found as a fact by the judge. Its effect on the contract depends on the meaning of the contract, which is a matter of law. Whether there is frustration or not in any case depends on the view taken of the event and of its relation to the express contract by 'informed and experienced minds' (*Denny, Mott and Dickson Ltd* v *James Fraser & Co. Ltd* [1944] AC 265, at 276 *per* Lord Wright).

Does any Rule of Law Render Frustration Inoperative?

The central question here is whether the supervening event was foreseen by either party and, in particular, whether either could be assumed to take the risk that such an event might occur. For example, if parties accept the risk of a particular event occurring then it ill-behoves them to claim frustration when that event materialises. In these circumstances a court would only reluctantly discharge the parties. Why? Because it is reasonable to assume that they would have sought adequate insurance cover against such contingencies or, if that was not possible, that the terms of the contract would have counterbalanced the risk in some other way (see *Bank Line Ltd* v *Arthur Capel & Co.* [1919] AC 435). Equally, if, for example, an agreement trades certainty for the risks of the uncertain, or achieves finality where rights are subject to protracted negotiations, courts will be extremely unwilling to embrace the doctrine of frustration (e.g. *Amey* v *Amey* [1992] 2 FLR 89).

The element of risk, in many ways, lies at the heart of frustration. The following examples illustrate this point: (a) neither party is assumed to take the risk of subsequent illegality unless there is an express clause to the contrary; (b) destruction of the subject-matter will frustrate the contract unless, for example, one party is expected to take out appropriate insurance against such an event, insurance in this context intimating an acceptance of risk; (c) if the event is foreseen but the contract makes no provision for it then it is unlikely that a plea of frustration will succeed, the *normal* assumption being that the parties have accepted the risk of that event. These points clearly show that any discussion of frustration must consider if and how risks have been apportioned between the parties.

Other than foreseeability and risk it may be necessary to consider the potential applicability of the following rules: neither party can take advantage of self-induced frustration (see *Maritime National Fish Ltd* v *Ocean Trawlers Ltd* [1935] AC 524), clauses which purport to cover frustrating events must do so unequivocally and unambiguously (see *Metropolitan Water Board* v *Dick, Kerr & Co.* [1918] AC 119), and a contract of lease can hardly ever be frustrated (*National Carriers Ltd* v *Panalpina (Northern) Ltd* [1981] 1 All ER 161).

What are the Effects of Frustration?

Generally the parties are discharged from the performance of any future obligations. However, the Law Reform (Frustrated Contracts) Act 1943 adds to this in three ways. Under the 1943 Act the general rule is that any money paid or payable before the frustrating event ceases to be payable or is recoverable by the payee. This rule is subject to two exceptions: (a) any advance payment (paid or payable) may be retained in full or in part by the payee (subject to the discretion of the court) in order to reimburse the payee for specific expenses incurred in performing the contract (see the interesting exercise of discretion in *Gamerco SA* v *ICM Fair Warning Ltd* [1995] 1 WLR 1226); and (b) if either party obtains a valuable benefit a court may require the recipient to pay for it (see *BP Exploration Co. (Libya) Ltd* v *Hunt (No. 2)* [1979] 1 WLR 783).

In conclusion, as with previous areas, there are no definite answers in a problem question on frustration. Try to consider both sides of the argument. For example, if there are strong arguments for saying that the supervening event will not radically affect the performance of the contract, do not stop there. Consider whether a court might decide otherwise. If there are *any* reasons then proceed to questions two and three (i.e. consider rules of law and effects).

Q Question 1

IMC own a piece of land in Dorset, 80 square miles in area, with planning permission to mine for tungsten ore. IMC agree to lease this land to Dig Deeper Ltd (DD Ltd) who will extract the ore. The contract provides that DD Ltd will supply all relevant plant, machinery and technology for the extraction of the tungsten ore and that the lease rental will become payable when the first tonne of tungsten has been extracted from the land.

A year later, when the site has been developed and mining operations are due to commence, local pressure groups force a public enquiry. As a result of the enquiry, planning permission for mining operations is restricted to an area of 20 square miles. DD Ltd claims that the contract has been frustrated.

Advise the parties.

Commentary

The above problem covers all the main areas of frustration. You should consider: whether the mining of 20 square miles is radically different from the mining of 80 square miles or does it merely cause additional hardship and a consequential reduction in profitability, whether the object of the contract is to lease land or extract ore, whether either party foresaw the possibility of the public enquiry and, if the contract is frustrated, has a valuable benefit been conferred on either party? The following answer adopts the structure outlined in the introduction to this chapter.

- Does the reduction in planning permission represent a sufficiently radical change in circumstances to frustrate the contract?

- What is the common objective of the contract and how has this been affected?

- Was it reasonably foreseeable/foreseen that a subsequent planning enquiry might be set up that would lead to the current planning permission being scaled down?

- Is a specialist mining lease capable of being frustrated?

- As there is no pre-payment, can DD Ltd claim any wasted expenditure?

- Has either side received a valuable benefit and, if so, how will this be valued?

Suggested answer

Is the Event Capable of Frustrating the Contract?

The doctrine of frustration applies when a change of circumstances renders a contract physically or legally impossible to perform or the changed circumstances transform the expected contract performance into something which is radically different from that which the parties intended when they entered into the contract. On the present facts the mining of tungsten ore is still physically possible, albeit restricted to only 20 square miles. The same considerations apply to legal possibility. Two questions arise in this context: first, what is the object of the contract and, secondly, in the light of this object, has the contract become commercially sterile?

How clear is the object of the contract? For example, it might be: (a) to lease land; or (b) to lease land for the purpose of mining tungsten ore; or (c) to mine the land for tungsten ore. This is particularly important, for if object (a) was correct, frustration would be difficult to argue as the actual lease would remain unaffected by the changed circumstances. Although the problems of leases will be considered later, it would seem appropriate to state that claim (a) is the least likely to succeed. First, IMC are not just leasing land and washing their hands of it; rather, IMC's future profits are linked inextricably with DD Ltd's effective use of the land. Secondly, the pre-contractual negotiations between IMC and DD Ltd must have focused on DD Ltd's intended use of the land. One can hardly imagine IMC advertising the availability of a lease without a clear and specific reference to the presence of tungsten deposits. Clear parallels could be drawn with *Krell v Henry* [1903] 2 KB 740 where the initial advertisement stated the intended use to which the room and balcony would be put, that use eventually constituting the object of the contract. If claim (b) or (c) is correct the next question is whether the planning limitations constitute a sufficiently radical change in circumstances to warrant a finding of frustration.

On a purely mathematical basis, the 75% restriction in the mining area appears fundamental. But what if the ore is primarily located in the specified area? If so, the public enquiry has made little difference to the expectations of the parties. Note that a reduction in profitability, increased logistical hardship and inconvenience are not, in themselves, sufficient to frustrate the contract as demonstrated in *Tsakiroglou & Co. Ltd v Noblee Thorl GmbH* [1962] AC 93 where the increased costs of carriage attributable to the closure of the Suez Canal found no sympathy with the court. Conversely, if the ore is distributed evenly across the whole 80 square miles and the initial site development costs remain the same, it is more arguable that there has been a radical change in circumstances. Reference to a case such as *Herne Bay Steamboat Co. v Hutton* [1903] 2 KB 683 might be appropriate. There, as the defendant could attain one of the two primary objectives from performance of the contract, his plea of frustration failed. However, on the present facts, a 75% reduction appears rather more drastic.

Will any Rule of Law Render Frustration Inoperative?

There are two important questions here: (a) was the decision of the public enquiry foreseen by either party and/or did either party take the risk of such an event's occurring and, (b) can the mining lease be frustrated?

Generally, where land is intended to be redeveloped it is the buyer who is assumed to take the risk that planning permission will be refused unless the contract states otherwise. For example, in *Amalgamated Investment and Property Co. Ltd v John Walker & Sons Ltd* [1956] 3 All ER 509, the buyer purchased a warehouse for business redevelopment purposes. The building was worth over £1.7 million with planning permission, without which it was worth only £200,000. Subsequent to the sale the warehouse was legally designated as a building of historic importance, making the intended re-development all but impossible. The court concluded that in such circumstances the buyer was taken to have accepted the risk of such an event. But the present facts are slightly different. When IMC and DD Ltd entered into the contract, planning permission had already been successfully obtained. In these circumstances it might be difficult to place the risk on DD Ltd unless, for example, it was clear at the time of contracting that local pressure was mounting for a public enquiry. Equally, in a more environmentally friendly society it might indeed be reasonably foreseeable that large scale projects might attract unfavourable media comment but unless the contract specifically allocates this risk to one or other of the parties, there is nothing to prevent a court from discharging them. For example, in *Ocean Tramp Tankers Corporation v VO Sovfracht, The Eugenia* [1964] 2 QB 226, involving carriage of goods via the Suez Canal, Lord Denning MR recognised that *both* parties had foreseen the possible closure of the canal. However, as they had been unable to reach agreement on any provision to meet this contingency, Lord Denning was quite prepared to make a finding of frustration when the relevant vessel became trapped in the canal. In the present case, there is nothing to suggest that the parties turned their minds to the possibility of a planning limitation so frustration seems possible.

The second point concerns leases of land. Traditionally it has been argued that a lease cannot be frustrated as it not only creates a contract but also an estate in land. If land is requisitioned by the government, for instance, the lessee would still be expected to pay the rent as the act of requisition has not affected the ownership of the estate (e.g. *Whitehall Court Ltd v Ettlinger* [1920] 1 KB 680). But there are two cases of more recent origin which have doubted that, *as a matter of law*, leases are incapable of being frustrated. First, in *Cricklewood Property and Investment Trust Ltd v Leighton's Investment Trust Ltd* [1945] AC 221, the Law Lords were divided equally on the matter (Lord Porter expressing no view). Lords Simon and Wright argued persuasively that a special purpose lease (e.g. a building lease), in which that purpose could not be performed, might be capable of being frustrated. Secondly, in *National Carriers Ltd v Panalpina (Northern) Ltd* [1981] 1 All ER 161, the House of Lords expressed the opinion that frustration should 'hardly ever' apply to leases rather than discounting the possibility entirely. For our purposes, as DD Ltd have taken a lease exclusively for the mining of ore (i.e. a special purpose lease), which may now be commercially redundant, it is arguable that the lease has been frustrated (see also *BP Exploration Co. (Libya) Ltd v Hunt (No. 2)* [1979] 1 WLR 783, affirmed [1983] 2 AC 352, where an oil concession, similar in many ways to a mining lease, was held capable of being frustrated).

Effects

If a contract is frustrated it is discharged from the date of the frustrating event and thereafter both parties are excused further performance. However, the position at common law has been qualified, to some extent, by the Law Reform (Frustrated Contracts) Act 1943.

Under the 1943 Act, the general rule is that any money paid or payable before the frustrating event ceases to be payable or is recoverable by the payee. There is no evidence of such a payment so the general rule is inapplicable. Moreover, as the lease rental was only payable when mining had actually commenced, this liability is extinguished under the normal common law rules (e.g. *Fibrosa Spolka Akcyjna v Fairburn Lawson Combe Barbour Ltd* [1943] AC 32). Finally, insofar as s. 1(2) offers the possibility of wasted expenses being recovered, this again has no application in the absence of any obligation to make payments *before* the frustrating event.

However, under s. 1(3) of the 1943 Act, the court may award a 'just sum' where one party has obtained a 'valuable benefit' before discharge of the contract. Can DD Ltd claim that IMC has retained the benefit of land which has been suitably adapted to mineral extraction? Recourse should be made to the judgment of Goff J in *BP Exploration Co. (Libya) Ltd v Hunt (No. 2)* on this point. The learned judge stressed that the value of any benefit must be equated with the end-product of services not their cost of provision. This causes DD Ltd some difficulty as much of the site development may be worthless *to IMC* in the light of planning restrictions. In particular, Goff J commented that the effect of the frustrating event might be to reduce, or even extinguish, the value of the benefit received. If DD Ltd has built roads on IMC land which are now unusable, there appears to be little benefit to IMC.

Q Question 2

Victor, as Secretary of a local tennis club, hires a bus from the Rambler Bus Company (RBC) to take 45 members of the club to see the Final of the Mens' Singles Championships, held at Wimbledon. A term of the contract provides: 'This contract may be cancelled provided that notice of 3 working days is given to the company, otherwise the full hire charge is payable.'

RBC charges £1,500 for fares and Victor pays a deposit of £250 in advance. As RBC guarantees the roadworthiness of all of its buses, the designated bus is

properly serviced the day before its intended use. However, on the morning of the trip it is announced that none of the tennis matches will be played as political demonstrators have dug holes in the tennis courts. Victor immediately claims that the contract has been frustrated and demands the return of the £250 deposit.
Advise the parties.

Commentary

Here again it is useful to begin by identifying the 'object of the contract'. Is it to hire a bus or to facilitate the viewing of the sporting event? If the former, a plea of frustration will almost certainly fail. Beyond this the following questions may be considered: is there a radical change in circumstances, what is the effect of the cancellation clause, was the event foreseen or foreseeable, can RBC recover its servicing costs and has any valuable benefit been conferred on either party?

What is important, especially in frustration, is that you try to look at the potential arguments of *both* sides. Thus, a student who recognises all the points but whose analysis is superficial will often do worse than a student who concentrates in-depth on a few selected issues.

- What is the common object of the contract and has it been radically changed by the subsequent events?

- Was the cancellation of the tennis tournament a reasonably foreseeable event?

- Can the cancellation clause be used by RBC to prevent Victor from claiming frustration?

- As Victor paid a deposit of £250, can this money be claimed by RBC to cover for any expenses incurred in performing the contract?

- Has either party received a valuable benefit?

Suggested answer

Is the Event Capable of Frustrating the Contract?

A contract will be discharged by frustration where unforeseen events render performance of the contract radically different from that which was originally intended by the parties: *Non haec in foedera veni*. 'It was not this that I promised to do' (*Davis Contractors Ltd* v *Fareham UDC* [1956] AC 696 at 729 *per* Lord Radcliffe).

On the present facts, the contract to hire the bus can still be performed, as RBC would readily argue. However, from Victor's viewpoint, performance would be pointless as the *motive* for hiring the bus has disappeared. How would a court decide this issue? Clearly one must identify the *object* of the contract. Have the changed circumstances made performance of this object radically different from the original intentions of the parties? The starting point is *Krell* v *Henry* [1903] 2 KB 740 which considered the hypothetical example of a contract for the hire of a cab to go to Epsom on Derby day. The races were subsequently cancelled. The court felt that the contract would not be frustrated as it would be viewed as one in which the passenger was transported to Epsom, his motive of seeing the Derby being irrelevant to the cabby. This argument would be used by RBC, contending that the contract was merely to transport Victor and his passengers rather than to facilitate the viewing of Wimbledon tennis matches.

Conversely, Victor would rely on the actual decision in *Krell* v *Henry* where the contract was frustrated as the court considered that the basis of the contract was to afford a private view of the coronation procession rather than the simple hire of a room.

Which argument is stronger? Although both are possible, it is submitted that the court's decision will be determined by the manner in which RBC advertised its services and the general intentions of the parties. In *Krell*, for example, the plaintiff advertised the room specifically for the purpose of viewing the coronation — the room hire and its intended use became inseparable. If the facts show that RBC advertised their services in this way (e.g. 'hire our bus and see Wimbledon tennis') Victor may be successful on this point. If not, RBC will be entitled to claim that the contract remains in force and that, consequently, the cancellation fee is payable.

If Victor's arguments prevail it is clear that the cancellation of Wimbledon will be of sufficient magnitude to frustrate the contract. Whether it will be on the grounds of physical impossibility (e.g. *Taylor* v *Caldwell* (1863) 3 B & S 826) or that non-occurrence of the event would render performance of the contract pointless (e.g. *Krell* v *Henry*) is not especially relevant in this context. It is proposed to proceed on the basis that Victor succeeds on this first point.

Will any Rule of Law Render Frustration Inoperative?

A party is rarely able to rely on an event which he has foreseen in order to claim frustration (e.g. *Walton Harvey Ltd* v *Walker & Homfrays Ltd* [1931] 1 Ch 274). The rationale is that if an event has been foreseen, then in the absence of an express provision covering that event, one or other of the parties must be taken to have accepted the risk of its occurring. In short, the element of foreseeability often determines the allocation of risk.

In considering this issue courts have, on occasion, distinguished between events that were foreseen by the parties (or one of them) and events which were foreseeable at the time of the contract. In the first situation if the event and its magnitude have been foreseen then a plea of frustration will fail except, perhaps, where there is evidence that the parties intended 'to leave the lawyers to sort it out' (see *The Eugenia* [1964] 2 QB 226, *per* Lord Denning MR). On the present facts, there is nothing to intimate that the parties foresaw that a policitical demonstration would lead to the event's cancellation. (Note: in this context, see below for the possible effect of the cancellation clause.)

If the event was foreseeable at the time of the contract it becomes a question of construction as to whether the contract allocates the risk of the event to one or other of the parties (e.g. *Larraga & Co.* v *Societe Franco-Americaine des Phosphates de Medulla* (1923) 92 LJKB 455). On the present facts, it is arguable that in the modern age of violent political demonstration, the possibility that people will resort to such activity to enhance the publicity of a particular campaign cannot be discounted. If so, the disruption of a major event is foreseeable. The question then becomes: have the parties made provision for this eventuality by incorporating a clause which restricts the effects of the potentially frustrating event? In particular, what is the effect of the cancellation clause?

Victor appears to have accepted responsibility for any cancellation which takes place *within* three days of the anticipated performance. However, in this area, courts apply a very strict test: as the frustrating event, by very definition, is unforeseen (though not unforeseeable) clear evidence is required that the parties intended the clause to cover the said event (e.g. *Metropolitan Water Board* v *Dick, Kerr & Co.* [1918] AC 119).

On the present facts, it is arguable that the parties merely intended the clause to cover a situation where, for example, Victor was unable to find enough passengers to make the trip cost-effective. Moreover, if the object of the contract is to arrange transport to a sporting event, it is arguable that Victor does not so much 'cancel' the contract as that the political demonstrators 'frustrate' it; i.e. Victor does not notify a desire to cancel as the events have already brought the contract to an end. On this basis it might be justifiably concluded that as the cancellation clause does not cover political demonstration, there is no other evidence from which one could deduce that the parties had allocated that particular risk in a certain way. Hence, although the event might be foreseeable, the contract is still capable of being frustrated.

Effects

Under the Law Reform (Frustrated Contracts) Act 1943 the general rule is that any money paid or payable before the frustrating event ceases to be payable or is recoverable by the payer. However, if the payee incurred expenses in performance of the contract, a court has a discretion to allow that party to retain some or all of the specified pre-payment. On the present facts, Victor will be claiming a refund on his £250 deposit whereas RBC will argue that it should retain some part of the deposit as compensation for its servicing costs. It is submitted that RBC's claim is unlikely to attract judicial sympathy as RBC presumably services its buses at periodic intervals anyway, making it unfair to saddle Victor with the ensuing costs. Support for this can be found in *Gamerco SA* v *ICMFair Warning Ltd* [1995] 1 WLR 1226 where the court refused to deduct an amount from the pre-paid sum to cover the defendants' expenses as the plaintiff's loss had been so much greater. However, an alternative argument might be that servicing only takes place because the buses are actually hired for future use, i.e. without use, the need to service disappears.

Has any valuable benefit been conferred on either party? Technically speaking RBC is now in possession of a 'recently serviced' bus but there are two reasons why the court would probably ignore this: under s. 1(3) the valuable benefit must be conferred by the other party, whereas here RBC does its own servicing; as this benefit is paid for by RBC, s. 1(3)(a) would expect the court to take account of the servicing costs when determining the real benefit received.

Q Question 3

When comparing the common law with the Law Reform (Frustrated Contracts) Act 1943, it becomes clear that the latter is more clearly directed towards equitably apportioning the loss between the parties.
  Discuss.

Commentary

There are few hidden depths to this question. The answer divides itself broadly into two parts. First, a brief description of the common law and an assessment of its advantages and disadvantages, setting this in the context of the House of Lords decision in *Fibrosa Spolka Akcyjna v Fairburn Lawson Combe Barbour Ltd* [1943] AC 32. Secondly, the changes brought about by the 1943 Act and whether they improved the situation, focusing especially upon the analysis adopted in *BP Exploration Co. (Libya) Ltd v Hunt (No 2)* [1979] 1 WLR 783. The better students will try to answer the question by including their own evaluation of whether the 1943 Act ensures a more equitable apportionment of loss.

- What was the approach of the common law prior to the passing of the Law Reform (Frustrated Contracts) Act 1943?

- What inadequacies remained after the House of Lords' decision in *Fibrosa*?

- How did the 1943 Act change the law?

- What discretion does a court have under the 1943 Act to compensate either party for wasted expenditure, or even to apportion losses?

- How have the courts interpreted and applied the 'valuable benefit' rule?

- What weaknesses remain under the present system?

:Q: Suggested answer

When a contract is frustrated the parties are excused from the performance of any future obligations. This is because at the date of discharge further performance has become impossible in circumstances which involve no liability in damages for the failure of either party (see *Fibrosa Spolka Akcyjna* v *Fairburn Lawson Combe Barbour Ltd* [1943] AC 32 *per* Lord Wright).

At common law the logical corollary was that any obligation that had accrued before the frustrating event still had to be performed. This could cause considerable injustice as illustrated in *Chandler* v *Webster* [1904] 1 KB 493 where the plaintiff hired a room for the purpose of overlooking the coronation procession but the coronation was subsequently cancelled. The price exceeded £140 and was payable in advance. Although the plaintiff actually paid £100 he was still held liable for the balance. The Court of Appeal rejected counsel's submission that there had been a total failure of consideration. As the doctrine of frustration only released the parties from *future* performance, as opposed to past and future obligations, the absence of consideration was irrelevant.

In *Fibrosa*, the House of Lords mitigated the harshness of the common law by ruling that a total failure of consideration, in terms of non-performance, released the parties from the performance of existing obligations and allowed either to recover payments already made. The actual facts bear repetition. The respondents agreed to make and deliver machinery according to the appellant's specifications. The contract price was £4,800, £1,600 payable in advance of which only £1,000 had been paid at the time of the frustrating event. As no machinery had been delivered, the House of Lords held that the appellants need not pay the outstanding £600 and were entitled to recover their £1,000.

At first glance the *Fibrosa* decision appears perfectly logical: the appellants did not receive any benefit so they were not expected to pay any money. However, closer examination reveals certain flaws. First, the respondents were merely performing their contractual obligations by manufacturing machinery in accordance with the appellant's specifications. Why should the respondents bear the whole loss when their performance was stipulated by the appellants? Secondly, the machinery was almost complete when the contract was frustrated; on the facts, it seems that it could have been sold without loss. But what if the machinery had been 'custom-built' and was only saleable at a loss? Would it be just and equitable for the respondents to receive no recompense for work done? On these hypothetical facts, the respondents' prudence in stipulating for a pre-payment would be accentuated, especially in view of their blameless conduct. Yet the common law would still place the whole loss on their shoulders. Thirdly, consider a variation on the above facts in which the appellants received a very small part of the anticipated delivery of machinery. Insofar as this represented only a partial failure of consideration, the appellants would have forfeited their £1,000 and be liable for the balance of £600, even if the delivery had been unusable without the remainder of the consignment.

The above points demonstrate the inadequacies of the common law even after *Fibrosa*. Moreover, that decision was limited to the recovery of money payments and did not offer any general restitutionary relief for the conferment of non-monetary benefits.

The Law Reform (Frustrated Contracts) Act 1943 implicitly addressed some of these issues. It introduced a general principle that all money paid or payable before the frustrating event was recoverable or ceased to be payable, irrespective of whether there had been a total failure of consideration. However, this rule was subject to two exceptions.

First, under s. 1(2) a court could disregard this general rule by allowing the payee to retain the whole or part of any advance payment (paid or payable before the frustrating event) in order to compensate for expenses incurred in performance of the contract. Applied to the facts of *Fibrosa*, this might have allowed the respondents, subject to the court's discretion, to retain and/or claim a part of the £1,600 advance payment as recompense for their manufacturing expenses. However, this exception only applies if the contract provides for an advance payment prior to the frustrating event (or an actual payment *is* made), otherwise compensation for expenses is unavailable. Equally, if expenses exceed the advance payment, a court is powerless to award the excess under this provision, emphasising another deficiency in the 1943 Act. The moral is to negotiate for payment of the entire contract price in advance. These two points, taken together, suggest that the 1943 Act was never intended to apportion losses equitably as, otherwise, the expenses rule would operate without the need for an advance payment.

Secondly, under s. 1(3) of the 1943 Act the court may award a 'just sum' where one party has obtained a 'valuable benefit' before discharge of the contract. Recourse should be had to the judgment of Goff J in *BP Exploration Co. (Libya) Ltd* v *Hunt (No. 2)* [1979] 1 WLR 783 (affirmed [1983] 2 AC 352) in which a number of useful observations were made.

Most importantly, the value of any benefit was to be equated with the end-product of services, not the cost of their provision. Perhaps for this reason Goff J emphasised that the 1943 Act was more concerned with preventing unjust enrichment rather than providing for an equitable apportionment of loss. For example, if the benefit conferred was destroyed by the frustrating event no sum would be payable except, possibly, where one party had benefited from insurance cover. This confirms that a valuable benefit must be conferred, rather than payment made for *work done*. Thus, if the facts of *Fibrosa* were to be repeated, there would be no valuable benefit as no machinery had been delivered.

Goff J's interpretation has been criticised by many commentators. It is true that under s. 1(3)(b) the court must take account of the effect of the frustrating event upon the said benefit, thereby suggesting that destruction of the benefit will render it value-less. However, s. 1(3) expects a court to value the benefit *before* the time of discharge and then have 'regard to all the circumstances', including the effect of the frustrating event. This implies that a court could value a benefit before discharge and only *partially* reduce its value in the event of its subsequent destruction. The decision in *BP* v *Hunt* ignores this potential flexibility, thereby emphasising the role of undue enrichment at the expense of an equitable apportionment of loss. As the law stands, the effect of Goff J's judgment would be that if the facts of *Appleby* v *Myers* (1867) LR 2 CP 651 were to be repeated, the claimants would still bear the whole loss as the frustrating event destroyed the machinery.

Goff J's judgment also considered that, although the Act was silent on the matter, the best guide to valuing a benefit was the contract price. Thus if a party's expenditure exceeded the contract price, conferring a benefit which also exceeded the contract price, the party would be unlikely to recover all his expenses under s. 1(3).

The above points, taken together, establish clear limits on a court's flexibility to apportion losses fairly. Nevertheless, there are exceptions.

First, s. 1(3) requires a court to take into account any advance payment made which the court has allowed the payee to retain under s. 1(2), thereby preventing a double payment for the same benefit. In the same context, any expenses incurred by the benefited party have to be deducted from the benefit received rather than the 'just sum' which is eventually awarded by the court. Secondly, the Act can apportion benefits, i.e. if both parties confer benefits on each other a court would be entitled to award the balance to the less favoured party. Thirdly, s. 1(3) can include 'benefits' of a more intangible nature, such as the knowledge and experience gained from pre-frustration contractual performance (e.g. *BP* v *Hunt*). This might allow the provider of specialist advice to be paid a reasonable sum of money for its potential post-frustration use by the recipient.

In summary, the 1943 Act offers considerable advantages over the common law by allowing courts greater flexibility in the awards that can be made. However, the scheme is not perfect. Expenses cannot be recovered in the absence of a provision for pre-payment or actual payment and compensation for benefits conferred is dependent upon those benefits surviving the frustrating event. This clearly falls short of any scheme aimed at apportioning losses equitably between the parties.

Q Question 4

The Marine Biology Unit (MBU) at Poppleton University has received a six-month government grant to study the effects of oil pollution off the coast of England. MBU approach Cumbrian Trawlers & Co. (CTC) to negotiate a six month charter of an appropriate vessel to perform daily off-shore pollution checks. CTC, which owns a fleet of five 'B51' trawlers, allocates one of these trawlers to the MBU charter-party. The final contract states that: (a) MBU will take possession of the designated trawler from 1 June, (b) one-half of the charter rates (£5,000) is payable in advance, and (c) the trawler will be returned for servicing at the end of each month.

At the end of the first month's charter MBU sends back the trawler for its routine servicing. However, a fire in CTC's dry dock badly damages the trawler. CTC refuses to allocate another B51 trawler to MBU, claiming that all other trawlers are fully utilised. CTC adds that if specialist parts are available the trawler will be ready 'in the not too distant future'. As pollution testing is at a critical stage, MBU has entered into negotiations with another company to hire a substitute trawler.

Advise the parties.

Commentary

The main questions raised by the facts are: what is the effect of the interruption upon the contract, who takes the risk of the fire, what is the effect of CTC refusing to allocate one of its remaining trawlers to the contract with MBU, what if CTC was responsible for the fire, what are the effects if the contract has been frustrated, what if MBU was found to have acted prematurely in breaking the link with CTC?

Permeating your answer must be a consideration of what happens if the contract is not frustrated. For example, would MBU's hire of an alternative trawler constitute repudiatory conduct entitling CTC to sue for breach of contract? Can MBU sue CTC for failure to provide a trawler?

• Did the interruption to the performance of the contract radically change the nature of that contract?

• Did the contract allocate the risk of the fire to either party?

• In the light of the *Super Servant Two*, is there any evidence that CTC might have induced the frustrating event (Note: this could be dealt with earlier as it raises the question of whether it is the fire or the refusal by CTC to allocate another trawler that 'potentially frustrated' the contract)?

• In the light of the stipulated pre-payment, can CTC claim for all its expenses?

• Has a valuable benefit been conferred on either party?

⃝ Suggested answer

Radical Change in Circumstances

Frustration occurs whenever a court recognises that, without default of either party, the contract has become incapable of further performance because a supervening event has rendered it radically different from that which was originally undertaken by the parties (see *Davis Contractors Ltd v Fareham UDC* [1956] AC 696). The present facts require the court to consider whether the anticipated delay in repair of the trawler was of sufficient duration to render further performance commercially impracticable. This question must be considered in the light of the circumstances existing at the moment when the fire occurred. What view would a reasonable person have formed at that moment, without regard to the fuller information available to the court at the time of the trial? One month of the contract has already been performed so five months remain. At what point will the *predicted* delay make complete nonsense of the contract?

Part of the answer lies in identifying the object of the contract. MBU had very specific reasons for chartering a trawler. Conversely, provided the trawler's use was not illegal or dangerous, CTC would not be particularly concerned with the purpose for which MBU chartered it. In short, as MBU's *motive* for using the trawler would not represent the object of the contract the court would probably ignore the reasons for MBU's requiring immediate access to another trawler. If so, there is a need to establish whether the predicted delay, on a purely mathematical basis (e.g. 2, 3 or 4 months use out of 6), was of a sufficient extent to frustrate the contract. In *Tamplin (FA) SS Co. Ltd v Anglo-Mexican Petroleum Products Ltd* [1916] 2 AC 397, a five-year charter agreement, of which just over two years had elapsed, was held not to be frustrated by requisitioning of the vessel by the Government. However, this decision was influenced by the fact that the vessel might still be usable by the charterer for certain periods during the remainder of the charterparty. (Note: recourse might also be had to the decisions in *Morgan v Manser* [1948] 1 KB 184 and *Metropolitan Water Board v Dick, Kerr & Co.* [1918] AC 119.)

In the end it becomes a matter of fact for the judge to decide. What is important is that neither party has acted precipitately. It may be that the fire does not automatically frustrate the contract but, rather, the subsequently predicted length of delay in relation to the intended duration of the contract. Perhaps the reasonable person would have postponed any decision until the duration of the repairs had been more accurately gauged (see *Finelvet AG v Vinaya Shipping Co. Ltd, The Chrysalis* [1983] 2 All ER 658; *Pioneer Shipping Ltd v Btp Tioxide Ltd, The Nema* [1981] 2 All ER 1030, 1047). If a 'wait and see' policy was expected, any premature withdrawal would constitute repudiatory conduct entitling the other side to damages for breach of contract. In summary, the longer the predicted delay the more likely that there has been a radical change in circumstances — the shorter the delay the more likely this will be a case of mere hardship and inconvenience insufficient to frustrate the contract.

Will any Rule of Law Render Frustration Inoperative?

Two issues might be considered in this context: (a) who took the risk of the fire's occurring and was CTC in any way responsible? and (b) was CTC's decision to refuse the allocation of another trawler tantamount to inducing the frustrating event?

The first question concerns the cause of the frustrating event. Must the party seeking discharge of the contract be free of any blame or fault? This issue has generated considerable debate. In *Bank Line Ltd v Arthur Capel & Co.* [1919] AC 435, 452, Lord Sumner asserted that frustration 'arises without blame or fault on either side'. This definition was confined by an *obiter dictum* of Lord Wright in *Joseph Constantine Steamship Ltd v Imperial Smelting Corporation Ltd* [1942] AC 154 to positive acts against the faith of the contract which amounted to a repudiation and would justify rescission. Furthermore, doubt was expressed over whether 'mere negligence' would render an event 'self-induced'.

However, more recently, in *Lauritzen (J) A/S v Wijsmuller BV, The Super Servant Two* [1990] 1 Lloyd's Rep 1, Bingham LJ regarded responsibility for and control over the event as the key issues (see also *The Hannah Blumenthal* [1983] 1 AC 854, 882 *per* Griffiths LJ). CTC clearly possessed the requisite degree of control over their servicing operations. Thus, if CTC claimed frustration it would need to show that the fire precautions were adequate, that the fire was not caused by the negligence of any of its employees or that in some other way it was responsible. Failure to achieve these standards might allow MBU to claim that the resultant non-availability of a trawler constituted a breach of contract by CTC.

An additional argument would be that the risk of fire in a boatyard is always foreseeable and that one normally expects the owner (CTC) to insure against any ensuing losses. Thus, unless MBU had agreed to take out appropriate insurance cover for the six-month period, the risk seems to lie squarely with CTC, i.e. CTC cannot claim frustration. If so, the remaining arguments on self-induced frustration are academic insofar as they relate to CTC claiming frustration.

In refusing to allocate another trawler to MBU, has CTC induced the frustrating event? Two cases are clearly relevant in this context. First, in *Maritime National Fish Ltd v Ocean Trawlers Ltd* [1935] AC 524 the defendants allocated government licences to their fleet of trawlers in such a way that their contract with the plaintiffs became illegal to perform. The Privy Council concluded that the defendants had *elected* not to supply the necessary licence and, therefore, could not rely upon frustration. Speculation as to why the defendants preferred to allocate the licences to other trawlers was considered irrelevant. Equally, in *The Super Servant Two*, Bingham LJ stated that the doctrine of frustration could not depend on 'any decision, however reasonable and commercial, of the party seeking to rely on it'. The court did not accept the argument that conscious election was irrelevant when the only choice was which contract to frustrate.

Both cases emphasise the 'election' of the defendants as corroborative proof of self-induced frustration. Investigation as to what constraints operated on the minds of the defendants in cancelling the contracts appears superfluous. This leaves CTC in a particularly unenviable position. Whatever decision CTC made they would open themselves to a breach of contract action from a disgruntled client. The only defence on the present facts is for CTC to argue that from the start only one trawler was designated for performance of the contract and that there was no suggestion that a substitute would be found if the designated trawler became unusable. This would distinguish the facts from those of the above two cases. Put simply, in *Maritime National Fish* no trawlers had been designated with an appropriate licence at the time of the contract whilst in *The Super Servant Two* the defendants did not nominate a specific vessel for the towing contract. Thus, in both those cases election took place *after* the supposed frustrating event.

Effects

Under the Law Reform (Frustrated Contracts) Act 1943 the general rule is that any money paid or payable before the frustrating event ceases to be payable or is recoverable by the payee. However, if the payee incurred expenses in performance of the contract, a court has a discretion to allow that party to retain some or all of the specified pre-payment. On the present facts, if the contract is discharged by frustration, MBU will claim a refund of its initial £5,000 payment whereas CTC will argue for its partial retention as compensation for its costs.

Presumably CTC may have spent money in preparing the trawler for use from 1 June. However, such a claim is unlikely to attract judicial sympathy for two reasons. First, CTC have guaranteed the trawler's seaworthiness. If a court allowed CTC to recover expenses for its servicing costs it would be tantamount to making MBU pay for this guarantee. Secondly, although MBU cannot be classified as a 'payee' it would not weigh heavily on the scales of justice if CTC recovered expenses for the type of activity which MBU had also performed; that is, MBU must also have incurred expenses in preparing for the charter of the trawler but would be unable to use s. 1(2) for its benefit — a point which clearly influenced the decision in *Gamerco SA v ICM/Fair Warning Ltd* [1995] 1 WLR 1226.

Finally, has any valuable benefit been conferred on either party? MBU have certainly obtained one month's use of the trawler. The question must be whether this has benefitted MBU. For instance, will an interruption at this stage put paid to the experiments already carried out? Is six months use of the trawler a minimum requirement for the pollution survey? Negative responses might suggest that no benefit has been conferred. Moreover, s. 1(3)(a) would require a court to take account of any expenses recoverable by CTC under s. 1(2) before awarding a 'just sum' for the benefit conferred on MBU.

Damages

Introduction

The victim of a breach of contract may claim specific relief, damages or restitution. Specific relief normally involves an order for specific performance or an injunction, requiring the addressee to perform, or desist from performing, a specified act. Conversely, in an action for damages the victim of a breach is seeking compensation for the fact that he has not received the bargained-for performance. Finally, in the context of breach of contract, a restitutionary remedy is most appropriate where a party has performed his side of the contract but has not received the agreed counter-performance. It should be added that although specific relief will be considered in the next chapter, the law of restitution has not been examined as most institutions offer this area as a separate option within their LLB courses.

A brief perusal of any contract law textbook demonstrates the clear emphasis that is placed on damages as the primary remedy for breach of contract. This is reinforced by the fact that although a victim of a breach may seek specific performance or an injunction, such orders are equitable in nature and therefore discretionary. Thus, unlike our European neighbours, contractual rights are perceived more in terms of their breach than in terms of their performance.

Damages: Basis for Award

Damages for breach of contract are available as of right even if no loss has been suffered. In such cases damages are said to be nominal. The purpose of awarding damages is to *compensate* the victim for the loss caused by the defendant's breach of contract, rather than to punish the wrongdoer (see *Surrey County Council* v *Bredero Homes* [1993] 3 All ER 705). For example, what happens if A, in breach of contract, fails to deliver goods to B? In such cases, damages will primarily reflect the difference between the original contract price and the price which B has to pay for identical goods from an alternative supplier. A court will not penalise the contract-breaker by arbitrarily increasing the damages payable to the victim, nor will the court be swayed by evidence that A had no legitimate excuse for non-delivery. Moreover, as compensation is the overriding principle, if B is able to purchase the goods at a lower price elsewhere no damages will be payable, subject to such matters as the additional expense of arranging alternative supplies.

The award of damages itself is intended to place the victim in the position that he would have occupied if the contract had been properly performed, i.e. loss of bargain is the main yardstick for awarding damages. However, this principle should be treated with a certain degree of caution.

First, a court may adopt a different basis for awarding damages where appropriate. This might occur if the injured party seeks the return of wasted expenditure (see *Anglia Television Ltd* v *Reed* [1972] 1 QB 60) or where a claim to lost bargain damages would appear too speculative (*McRae* v *Commonwealth Disposals Commission* [1951] 84 CLR 377). Secondly, a direct causal link between a breach and the victim's loss does not automatically entail recovery of all the resultant loss. In particular, the victim of a breach must fulfil three main conditions:

(a) that the damages are not too remote (REMOTENESS);

(b) are of a type recoverable in law (TYPES);

(c) could not have been mitigated (MITIGATION);

In answering any question on damages, you must always consider these issues, citing case law where appropriate. For example, under point (a), the victim of a breach may need to establish that his counterpart possessed specific knowledge which would allow the latter to predict accurately the loss caused to the victim by a particular breach. Under point (b), the fact that the victim suffers considerable distress may be irrelevant if the contract is not of a kind which guarantees peace of mind. Finally, under point (c), the victim whose tender of performance has been rejected is not expected to sit back and claim the full contract price — where reasonable he must consider making alternative arrangements with potential customers in order to lessen his current losses.

Once these issues have been discussed, you must then consider whether any difficulties emerge in quantifying the recoverable loss.

Remoteness

The claimant must first establish a sufficiently strong causal connection between the breach of contract and the loss claimed. See, for example, the recent decisions in *Galoo Ltd* v *Bright Grahame Murray* [1995] 1 All ER 16 and *Beco Ltd* v *Alfa Laval Co. Ltd* [1994] 4 All ER 464 that clearly state that the breach must be the dominant or effective cause of the loss. Once causation has been established then the claimant must address the general issue of remoteness. Adopting the principle first enunciated by Alderson B in *Hadley* v *Baxendale* (1854) 9 Exch 341, damages are only recoverable if:

(a) they were fairly and reasonably considered to arise naturally from the breach, OR

(b) they were in the reasonable contemplation of the parties as liable to result from the breach.

This offers a single test for awarding damages for breach of contract based on the 'reasonable contemplation' of the parties, the level of liability depending upon the degree of knowledge possessed by the contract-breaker. Put another way, the greater knowledge that the contract breaker possesses, the greater his horizon of contemplation when predicting the consequences of his breach.

In considering the issue of remoteness within an examination context you will be expected to consider the following types of question:

(a) What is the actual knowledge of the parties? (This was critical in *Hadley* v *Baxendale* as the carrier was not told that the mill possessed no spare shaft);

(b) What type of loss might the relevant breach be expected to produce in the ordinary course of events? (Consider *Victoria Laundry (Windsor) Ltd* v *Newman Industries Ltd* [1949] 2 KB 428 where the boiler manufacturer could foresee loss of normal profits but not the exceptional profits associated with the dyeing contract);

(c) Does the contract-breaker possess any special knowledge, skill or calling which would allow him to contemplate additional loss? (In *Koufos* v *Czarnikow (C) Ltd, The Heron II* [1969] 1 AC 350 the background knowledge of the shipowners was crucial.)

Types of Damages

In the normal course of events the victim of a breach will be seeking to recover loss of bargain damages. For example, the non-delivery of goods will cause the buyer two types of loss: loss of expected profits (difference between market value and contract price) and the lost opportunity of using them, whether in an existing manufacturing process or by their profitable sub-sale.

However, as mentioned earlier, an award of damages may cover other types of loss. For example, if a claim to damages based on lost profits appears too speculative, the claimant might consider the recovery of post-contractual reliance losses (see *McRae* v *Commonwealth Disposals Commission, supra*). Alternatively, pre-contractual expenses may be recoverable in certain situations, such as a solicitor's fees in an abortive conveyancing transaction (see the limits imposed by *Lloyd* v *Stanbury* [1971] 1 WLR 535). The claimant will need to formulate his claim with precision although both reliance and expectation losses are recoverable provided the claimant does not recover more than once for the same loss (see *Cullinane* v *British 'Rema' Manufacturing Co.* [1954] 1 QB 292).

Injured Feelings and Disappointment

This is a particularly controversial area. In *Addis* v *Gramophone Co. Ltd* [1909] AC 488 it was stated in general terms that damages in a contractual action would not include injured feelings. Thus, when the defendant company dismissed the plaintiff employee in a most humiliating manner, his claim, insofar as it related to injured feelings, failed. However, there are a number of exceptions.

It is important to identify the type of contract which has been broken. In particular, is *one of the main objects* of the contract to guarantee peace of mind, freedom from distress or the provision of pleasure and enjoyment (see *Farley* v *Skinner* [2001] UKHL 49, [2001] 3 WLR 899)? If so, a claim to damages for disappointment, injured feelings and/or inconvenience may be successful. Within this category the following have been included: a holiday that falls short of the standard promised (see *Jarvis* v *Swan Tours Ltd* [1973] 2 QB 233, a breach of contract regarding the taking of wedding photographs (see *Diesen* v *Samson* 1971 SLT (Sh Ct) 49), physical inconvenience associated with a solicitor's negligent handling of a conveyancing transaction (see *Bailey* v *Bullock* (1950) 66 TLR (Pt 2) 791), distress caused to a client because a solicitor negligently fails to take necessary steps in non-molestation proceedings (see *Heywood* v *Wellers* [1976] 1 QB 446), loss of a pleasurable amenity (see *Ruxley Electronics and Construction Ltd* v *Forsyth* [1995] 3 All ER 268), and sensory inconvenience caused by unexpectedly high levels of aircraft noise (see *Farley* v *Skinner* [2001] UKHL 49).

However, if the avowed aims of a contract do not correspond with the above situations, damages for such non-pecuniary losses will not be awarded (see *Bliss* v *SE Thames Regional Health Authority* [1987] ICR 700). Arguably, the underlying reason for this is that in most arm's length commercial contracts neither party would reasonably contemplate specific psychological suffering or disappointment resulting from a breach.

Injured Reputation

Here again, damages for injured reputation are difficult to recover, especially as the law of tort offers remedies in defamation and malicious falsehood. But there are exceptions such as injury to business reputation from the wrongful dishonour of a cheque (see *Gibbons* v *Westminster Bank Ltd* [1939] 2 KB 882), loss of customer goodwill (see *Anglo-Continental Holidays Ltd* v *Typaldos Lines (London) Ltd* [1967] 2 Lloyd's Rep 61), wrongful expulsion from a trade union (see *Edwards* v *SOGAT* [1971] Ch 354, 378–9) and wrongful conviction owing to a solicitor's negligence (see *McLeish* v *Amoo-Gottfried* (1993) *The Times*, 13 October). Ironically, one of the most recent decisions in this area appears to have limited the general application of the original *Addis* approach. In *Malik* v *Bank of Credit and Commerce International SA* [1998] AC 20 the House of Lords accepted the theoretical recovery of damages for injured reputation where the employer had carried on its business in such a way as to besmirch the professional reputations of all its employees (but see the practical limits of this approach in *Johnson* v *Unisys Ltd* [2001] UKHL 13; [2001] 2 WLR 1076).

Speculative Damages

In all of the above cases it is clear that the quantification of loss is at best speculative. This will not deter a court from awarding damages. For example, in *Chaplin* v *Hicks* [1911] 2 KB 786 the claimant was awarded damages for the loss of a right to belong to a limited class of competitors.

Mitigation

The victim of the breach has a duty to mitigate any loss. This means that the victim must minimise the loss, not act unreasonably to increase the loss, and account for any benefits received. It is important to realise that a court does not expect the claimant to take the *most* reasonable course of action or explore *every* avenue in order to minimise his losses. Sometimes the issue is easily decided. For example, if a buyer refuses to take delivery of goods then one would reasonably expect the seller to find an alternative buyer. Equally, if the seller refuses to deliver, the buyer should find an alternative supplier. As to whether the buyer would be expected to find the *best* price, this would require a court to balance the inconvenience of attempting to find the most competitive source against the unfairness to the seller if the buyer takes the first offer that comes along, however high the price.

In dealing with the issue of mitigation, consider the following questions:

(a) In an effort to mitigate losses, what courses of action would it be reasonable for the victim to take? If an employee is wrongfully dismissed it may be reasonable to accept an offer of re-engagement from his previous employer, or refuse the offer and seek employment elsewhere, but it would not be reasonable to sit at home and watch the television (see generally *Yetton v Eastwood Froy Ltd* [1967] 1 WLR 104).

(b) Is there any particular course of mitigation which it would be unreasonable for the victim to take? Consider *Pilkington v Wood* [1953] Ch 770 in which the plaintiff was not expected to take steps that would involve him in complicated litigation against a third party.

(c) In an effort to mitigate losses, when can a victim recover additional losses *caused* by this process of mitigation? See *Banco de Portugal v Waterlow & Sons* [1932] AC 452 and *Hoffberger v Ascot Bloodstock Bureau Ltd* (1976) 120 SJ 130 which illustrate the leniency of the courts in this respect.

(d) Has the victim obtained any additional benefits in the course of mitigation? A court will normally expect the victim to account for this benefit (see *British Westinghouse v Underground Electric Railways Co. of London* [1912] AC 673) although this is not necessarily the case if the claimant, as a result, is unfairly penalised (see *Bacon v Cooper (Metals) Ltd* [1982] 1 All ER 397).

Note that the duty to mitigate may not compel the claimant to accept an anticipatory breach even if, by continuing with the contract, he increases the defendant's loss (see *White & Carter (Councils) Ltd v McGregor* [1962] AC 413). However, in *Clea Shipping Corporation v Bulk Oil International Ltd* [1984] 1 All ER 129, the court stipulated that the plaintiff must possess a 'legitimate interest' before refusing the defendant's repudiatory conduct and continuing with the contract.

Finally, recent case law has questioned whether the Law Reform (Contributory Negligence) Act 1945 applies to breach of contract actions. The 1945 Act affords courts discretionary powers to apportion liability on the basis of the respective parties' fault. This generally refers to an assessment of who contributed to the initial loss, rather than how the parties reacted thereafter. Although normally applicable to actions in tort it has been held that the 1945 Act is relevant where the contractual duty (which has been broken) is co-extensive with such a duty in tort (see generally *Barclays Bank plc* v *Fairclough Building Ltd* [1995] 1 All ER 289).

Measure of Damages

This is an extremely wide-ranging area. Your knowledge will be determined by the particular emphasis which your lecturer places on selected aspects of quantification. For example, a clear distinction might be made between reliance losses and loss of bargain/expectation. Alternatively, a comparison might be made between restitutionary relief and breach of contract damages. However, there are several general rules which will be covered within most contract law syllabi. These normally relate to the non-delivery or non-acceptance of goods and can be summarised generally in the following ways:

(a) If a seller fails to deliver goods the buyer is entitled *prima facie* to claim the loss which he sustains in buying identical goods at a higher price from an alternative source (see Sale of Goods Act 1979, s. 51(3)). A subsale by the buyer is generally disregarded unless contemplated by the seller at the time of the original contract (compare *William Bros* v *ET Agius Ltd* [1914] AC 510 with *Williams* v *Reynolds* (1865) 6 B & S 495).

(b) If a buyer refuses to accept delivery, the seller's recoverable loss will consist *prima facie* of the difference between the contract price and the market value (see *Kwei Tek Chao* v *British Traders Ltd* [1954] 2 QB 459). This is subject to a variety of exceptions discussed in Question 3 of this chapter.

(c) If a seller delivers defective goods the normal measure of damages will be the difference between the value of the goods as warranted and the value of the goods actually delivered (see also Sale of Goods Act 1979, s. 53(3)). However, this presumption can be displaced, for example, if the seller knows that the buyer intends to sell the goods onwards to another person. In such circumstances, damages may be based on the loss that the buyer sustains from an abortive or defective sub-sale (see *Bence Graphics International Ltd* v *Fasson UK Ltd* [1998] QB 87).

(d) In general terms, if the claimant is claiming reliance losses, as opposed to loss of bargain/expectation losses, damages must return him to the position he occupied before he entered into the contract.

Note that the issue of the appropriate measure of damages has been recently considered by the House of Lords in *Ruxley Electronics and Construction Ltd* v *Forsyth* [1995] 3 All ER 268. The case involved a completely different area of contract law: defective performance of building contracts. The question arose as to whether a court should award damages based on diminution in value or cost of cure. On the facts, the former was preferred but with a separate sum being awarded for loss of amenity. More importantly, the speeches contain important guidance on the purpose of awarding damages and choosing the appropriate *measure*.

Agreed Damages Clauses

It is the inherent difficulties in estimating the likely recoverable damages flowing from a breach which encourage so many businesses to consider the insertion of a 'damages' clause. This clause is supposedly designed as an alternative to litigation, offering a sum of money by way of compensation to the victim of a specified breach of contract.

However, the potential for abuse is clear. An agreed damages clause can be used as a threat, compelling performance of a contract as the consequences of any breach are too disastrous to contemplate; for example, specifying the payment of £100,000 in damages if a builder is one day late in completing the construction of a £20,000 house. For this reason courts attempt to distinguish between legitimate clauses aimed at avoiding the vagaries of litigation and those clauses which are merely inserted by a dominant party to compel performance. If the agreed sum is a *genuine pre-estimate of likely loss* then it will be classified as a liquidated damages clause. This clause is enforceable irrespective of the loss actually suffered — the normal rules of remoteness, mitigation and so forth do not apply. Conversely, if the agreed sum is merely inserted in order *to exert pressure on one party to perform*, it will be considered a penalty clause and therefore invalid. Here, a court will disregard the clause in its entirety and, instead, have recourse to the normal common law principles regarding the recovery of damages (e.g. remoteness). The rules for distinguishing such clauses are contained in *Dunlop Pneumatic Tyre Co. Ltd v New Garage and Motor Co. Ltd* [1915] AC 79 and will be the subject of further explanation below.

Q Question 1

Jack is a manufacturer and seller of frozen food. Botchit & Co. agree to lay the floor in Jack's newly constructed factory, the work to be completed on 1 April, at a cost of £25,000. Clause 12 of the contract provides: 'If Botchit & Co. fail to complete the contract within the stipulated time, we undertake to pay, by way of penalty, a sum of £10,000 in full satisfaction of our liability.'

Marko & Co. have a contract with Jack to instal machinery in the factory between 5 and 10 April at a cost of £750,000.

Jack intends to commence production of frozen food on 15 April, and, in consequence, he has a contract with Fatts Ltd for fresh food to the value of £200,000 to be delivered to the factory on 14 April.

Botchit & Co. only complete the floor on 15 April. As a result, Jack has to pay

Marko & Co. an extra £50,000 to allow for overtime payments to its employees in order that the machinery can be installed as quickly as possible. Jack finally commences frozen food production on 18 April. The fresh food which had been delivered on 14 April was sold by Jack for £10,000 as pig food.

Advise the parties.

Commentary

This represents the archetypal damages question. It contains the main ingredients of the law relating to damages: remoteness, mitigation and agreed damages clauses. Note that if clause 12 is a liquidated damages clause then Jack would receive £10,000 in full and final settlement of his claim, no more and no less.

- Is the agreed damages clause a penalty clause or an enforceable liquidated damages clause; e.g. was it a genuine pre-estimate of likely loss or simply inserted in order to exert pressure on one party to perform the contract?
- Is the additional overtime payments to Marko & Co a 'natural loss' resulting from Botchit's delay?
- What 'special knowledge' did Botchit & Co possess regarding Jack's business plans (e.g. the intended date for manufacturing operations to begin)?
- Can Jack claim damages for loss of reputation?
- Did Jack take reasonable steps to minimise his losses and avoid taking any unreasonable steps that might result in his losses being increased?

☼ Suggested answer

The difficulty in predicting the damages recoverable for a breach of contract often encourages the parties to insert an agreed damages clause, thereby obviating the need to seek legal redress. However, a court will intervene if it believes that the clause is not truly an expression of the freedom of contract principle but rather an attempt by a dominant party to exert unfair pressure on the weaker party. Does this happen here?

Agreed Damages Clause

The general principle is that any damages clause which makes a genuine attempt at pre-estimating likely loss will be enforceable, whatever the actual loss suffered. As the common law rules (e.g. remoteness) are disregarded by the courts, the parties can rely on specific sums being paid in the event of specified breaches and order their affairs accordingly. Conversely, if the underlying purpose of a damages clause is to exert pressure on one party to perform his contractual obligations then it will be labelled as a penalty clause. In effect, the clause shows that the parties have not made a genuine attempt to pre-estimate the likely loss resulting from a particular breach. Such a clause is void, allowing the court to award damages in accordance with the normal rules of contract. Into which category does this clause fit?

In *Dunlop Pneumatic Tyre Co.* v *New Garage and Motor Co. Ltd* [1915] AC 79 the following guidelines were formulated by the House of Lords. First, the clause will be considered penal if the sum stipulated is extravagant or unconscionable in comparison with the greatest conceivable loss which could arise. On the facts, Botchit is expected to pay Jack £10,000 for the delay. It is arguable that this is not an exorbitant sum bearing in mind the expected loss of production and the dislocation of other arrangements caused by a two-week delay.

Secondly, the clause is one of liquidated damages if the consequences of the breach are such as to make precise pre-estimate impossible and the actual amount specified bears a reasonable relation to the probable consequences of the breach (see the facts of *Dunlop* v *New Garage*). Superficially, it would appear difficult to estimate the real loss resulting from delay but this argument would be found lacking. The specified sum is not graduated in accordance with the severity of the breach. For example, the loss sustained by Jack might be minimal if Botchit delayed by only one day, but it might be considerable if the delay exceeded two months. Thus, it is difficult to argue that the sum bears a reasonable relation to the probable consequences of the breach. Put another way, the clause is not making a genuine attempt to pre-estimate the likely loss and so should be considered a penalty clause.

(Note: for the sake of completeness, one might mention the third rule, although this would seem unnecessary in an examination: there is a presumption of a penalty clause where the sum is payable on one or more of several breaches which must cause different amounts of loss (see *Ford Motor Co. (England) Ltd* v *Armstrong* (1915) 31 TLR 267). Here the clause covers only one type of breach, namely delay, so it would seem irrelevant.)

On the basis that the damages clause is penal, the court will have to assess Jack's actual losses under the normal common law rules of recovery. Particular emphasis will be placed on remoteness and mitigation.

Remoteness

There are three potential losses which Jack suffers: the delay in commencing production, the additional payment of £50,000 to Marko & Co. and the sale of the fresh food consignment as pig food. (Note: the very good student *might* also consider the loss to Jack's reputation, resulting from the delay in commencing production and meeting customer's requirements (see below).) Are any of these losses too remote?

The basic principle is contained in *Hadley* v *Baxendale* (1854) 9 Exch 341 which can be distilled in the following way. Losses are too remote if, at the time of the contract, they were not in the reasonable contemplation of the parties as liable to result from the particular breach. This requires the court to consider the actual knowledge of the parties, eliciting responses to the following types of question: in the ordinary course of events would one expect a customer such as Jack to adopt such a tight schedule for the completion of all the desired works? Was Botchit & Co. expected to know, or were they informed, of the consequences of a delay in completion? Is the trade experience of Botchit & Co. a relevant consideration?

The answers to the above questions will form the basis of the court's decision. For example, if Botchit & Co. knew about the anticipated installation of machinery from 5 April, and expressly or by implication accepted liability for any delay, then damages may be awarded to recompense Jack for the increased payments to Marko (see generally *Koufos* v *Czarnikow (C) Ltd, The Heron II* [1969] 1 AC 350). The reverse would equally hold true: if Botchit is not informed of the tight schedule, would the urgency of completion by 5 April be considered a reasonably contemplatable event? In this context, the decision in *Hadley* v *Baxendale* provides useful support for this analysis: the carrier was not expected to foresee the consequences of his delay as the mill owner failed to inform him of the absence of any spare shaft.

Alternatively, the knowledge of the defendant may arise from his special calling or the capacity in which he contracted. For example, in *Heron II* the shipowners were expected to know of the fluctuating prices on the commodity markets. It was therefore within their reasonable contemplation that a delay might cause loss to their clients if the market price moved against them. Equally, as Botchit & Co. are assumed to be experienced builders they might be expected to predict more accurately the consequences of their actions. As a factory floor is often laid as a precursor to the installation of machinery, any delay in completion may cause a consequent delay to that installation.

As all these issues raise questions of fact, it is difficult to come to a specific conclusion. However, in practice, it is likely that of the three potential losses outlined above, the first (delay in commencing production) seems the most foreseeable as Botchit must realise that Jack is a frozen food manufacturer who wishes to utilise his assets (factory) as quickly as possible. Conversely, the third item (sale of the fresh food) seems the most remote as it requires Botchit to contemplate the tight works schedule, the preparedness of Jack to organize a consignment of food before the works have definitely been completed and the lack of available storage food facilities if delay occurs.

Special Types of Damage

At first glance, this seems irrelevant. There is no evidence of any non-pecuniary loss suffered by Jack. However, one might consider the possible impact of delay on Jack's reputation. Generally, damages for injured reputation are difficult to recover, especially as the law of tort offers remedies in defamation and malicious falsehood. But there are exceptions. In particular, it may be possible to claim damages for injury to commercial reputation. In *Anglo-Continental Holidays Ltd* v *Typaldos Lines (London) Ltd*

[1967] 2 Lloyd's Rep 61, for example, a travel agent recovered such damages from the defendant shipowner who was in breach of contract in failing to provide passengers with accommodation on a pleasure cruise. Jack's reputation might also suffer if he has entered into contracts to supply frozen food to certain customers by a particular date. However, it is submitted that Jack would fail in such a claim as these losses would be considered too remote by a court.

Mitigation

Jack has a duty to mitigate any loss. A court will not expect him to take the *most* reasonable course of action or explore every avenue in order to minimise his losses. Rather, he must adopt a reasonable course of action. What options were available to Jack? Was the course that he pursued reasonable? Presumably, Jack must have known by 2 April that Botchit would not be completing on time. Should he have contacted Fatts Ltd and delayed delivery until he was confident that his processing plant would be operational by a specific date? Ought he to have considered the temporary storage of the fresh food, assuming that such facilities were available? Could he have obtained a better price for the food? If an affirmative answer to *any* of these questions is forthcoming, it will raise serious doubts as to whether Jack's course of action could be regarded as 'reasonable'. Alternatively, if the court decided that delayed delivery, possible storage or more profitable re-sale, involved too much inconvenience for Jack, then such courses of action might be ignored (see generally *Pilkington* v *Wood* [1953] Ch 770).

Q Question 2

Deco Ltd purchased an eighteenth century property to be used as its new business premises from 19 April. The property needed to be completely repainted and a central heating system to be installed. Deco Ltd hired Jerry for the sum of £1,000 to do the painting, all work to be completed by 18 April, otherwise a deduction of 5% in the contract price would be made for each day that completion was delayed. Deco Ltd also purchased a new heating system from Warmwall & Sons. The contract stipulated that the system needed to be installed by 18 April, with Warmwall being required 'to pay £100 by way of penalty to Deco Ltd for any late completion of the work'.

Jerry did not complete the work until 28 April (ten days late). This meant that Deco Ltd was unable to operate normally from its new premises until 29 April, causing an approximate loss of profits in the region of £500 per day (from 18 April).

Coincidentally, the heating system was not fully installed until 28 April, so Deco Ltd was required to hire six portable electric heaters as the house was cold and damp — total hire charge and electricity was approximately £150 per day, for ten days. Moreover, two days later, owing to a gas leak, the heating system exploded causing severe structural damage to the property and ruining an antique tapestry which had recently been acquired by Deco Ltd for hanging within its client reception area.

Advise Deco Ltd.

Commentary

As mentioned in the introduction to this chapter, consider adopting a simple structure to your answer: remoteness, special types of damages, mitigation and agreed damages clauses. Clearly one cannot predict the decision of the court on any issues involving a question of fact. What is important is that you state the law accurately, identify any specific problems and make several remarks on how the law might sensibly be applied to the facts.

- Did Deco Ltd sustain its losses in the normal course of events?

- What special knowledge did Jerry and/or Warmwall possess that might suggest either could have reasonably contemplated some or all of Deco Ltd's losses?

- Can a court award damages for any non-pecuniary losses that Deco Ltd might have suffered, such as inconvenience or loss of reputation?

- Did Deco Ltd act reasonably in order to mitigate its losses?

- Are the agreed damages clauses penal in nature or genuine attempts to pre-estimate likely losses?

:Q: Suggested answer

Deco must first establish that the damages it has suffered are not too remote from Jerry or Warmwall's breaches of contract; i.e. that there is a sufficiently strong causal connection between the breach of contract and the claimed loss. Adopting the principle first stated by Alderson B in *Hadley* v *Baxendale* (1854) 9 Exch 341, damages are only recoverable if: (a) they were fairly and reasonably considered to arise naturally from the breach, or (b) they were in the reasonable contemplation of the parties as liable to result from the breach. This offers a single test for awarding damages for breach of contract based on the 'reasonable contemplation' of the parties, the level of liability depending upon the degree of knowledge possessed by the contract breaker. If the remoteness test is successfully negotiated, Deco will need to show that the losses were of a type that are recoverable for breach of contract and that it was not expected to mitigate those losses in any reasonable manner.

Remoteness

Clearly Jerry and Warmwall have been asked to complete their respective contractual duties by the 18 April. As traders they must encounter many situations where time limits are imposed and, consequently, late completions will inevitably cause their customers some inconvenience. However, Deco's losses generally result from the need to occupy and operate from their premises from April 19. Was this fact known to Jerry and Warmwall, and that delays in completion might prevent Deco opening for business? Unless this knowledge is established, it would seem that Deco's only argument is that under the first rule in *Hadley* v *Baxendale* (1854) 9 Exch 341, the losses that were incurred were fairly and reasonably considered to arise naturally from the breach. This seems unlikely, especially when one considers the facts in *Hadley* where failure to tell the carrier that no spare shaft could be used in the meantime prevented the mill owner from claiming loss of profits resulting from delay in the carrier's returning the repaired shaft. If, however, Jerry and/or Warmwall are aware of the reasons for the work being completed by April 18 then the second rule in *Hadley* comes into play. Relying on *The Heron II*, and the experience of the parties, it is certainly arguable that any delay might prevent Deco operating effectively from its new premises.

The damage caused by the gas leak offers interesting possibilities. Assuming that Warmwall was considered to have been the cause of the leak, and that Deco was not expected to have been checking for such problems (compare this with *Beco Ltd* v *Alfa Laval Co. Ltd* [1994] 4 All ER 464), it would seem that the two rules in *Hadley* would cover the situation. The only issue would be whether the purchase of the antique tapestry, *after* the contract with Warmwall had been entered into, was a relevant consideration. Is it likely that gas leaks will cause damage to any artefacts stored on premises and that Deco, as a company, might well have expensive ornaments in order to impress its clients. Arguing that Warmwall should have been told the value of the precise items on the premises as a pre-condition of liability would appear needlessly burdensome for Deco.

Types of Damage

Apart from the normal pecuniary loss, it seems unlikely that Deco could recover any other special damages. The main objects of the contract are all business related. It may well be that the owners of Deco will be 'disappointed' by the delays but that is insufficient. In *Bliss* v *SE Thames Regional Health Authority* [1987] ICR 700 it was clearly stated that such damages were irrecoverable in an arm's length commercial contract, although certain *obiter* comments in *Farley* v *Skinner* [2001] UKHL 49 would suggest that the distinction between 'business' and 'non-business' contracts should not be the critical determinant in such circumstances. Similar reasoning could be used as regards any physical inconvenience suffered by Deco employees. Presumably, the purpose of the contract is primarily to enhance the earnings potential of Deco, not to improve the working environment of its employees.

Mitigation

To what extent would Deco be expected to mitigate its losses? It will only be expected to act reasonably, rather than taking the *most* reasonable course of action. Could Deco have stayed at its old premises for another few days, or was the move irreversible? Was alternative accommodation available or would the inconvenience and disruption caused to Deco make that option unreasonable? Finally, the hire of portable heaters at that cost seems extravagant. What other options did Deco consider and with which other suppliers did it communicate? (Note that the purpose of posing such questions, although unanswerable on the paucity of facts given, demonstrates to the examiner an understanding of how the rules of mitigation would be theoretically applied by a court. On this basis, reference to cases such as *Banco de Portugal* v *Waterlow & Sons Ltd* [1932] AC 452 and *Hoffberger* v *Ascot Bloodstock Bureau* (1976) 120 SJ 130 might be helpful as it demonstrates the latitude that the courts afford to innocent parties when responding to a breach of contract).

Agreed Damages Clauses

A fuller discussion of this topic can be seen in Question 1. The overall purpose of the rules expressed in *Dunlop* v *New Garage and Motor Co. Ltd* [1915] AC 79 is to distinguish clauses which legitimately attempt to pre-estimate likely loss resulting from a breach and those which penalise one of the parties for a breach of the contract. At first glance the sums of money mentioned in either clause do not appear to be unduly extravagant. However, Jerry might be deprived of any payment if he is more than 20 days late. Is this a genuine pre-estimate of likely loss? If not, then it is a penalty clause and void — requiring the court to apply the normal common law rules regarding the recovery of damages.

Secondly, although both sums of money are payable for one particular type of breach, the clause in Warmwall's contract does not appear to graduate its liability. Whether Warmwall completes one hour late or one year late seems to make no difference: the same amount of money is payable. Thus, under the second rule in *Dunlop*, it might be difficult to argue that the sum of £100 bears a reasonable relation to the probable consequences of the breach. As above, this would make the clause penal in nature, again requiring the court to resort to the normal common law rules on recovery.

Q Question 3

(a) Estelle Restaurant contracts with Janice to provide a buffet lunch for her wedding celebrations. Estelle is paid on the basis that sufficient food will be supplied for 50 guests and the resident photographer will be engaged to take appropriate photographs of wedding guests and the happy couple. On the day of the wedding, Janice is informed that, owing to a clerical over-sight, the buffet room has been double-booked. As a result, a smaller room has been allocated for the buffet. Janice has the embarrassing task of turning away half of the wedding guests. Moreover, the photographer fails to arrive and no other substitute can be found in the time available.

Advise Janice.

(b) John owns a garage which specialises in the sale of Bentley cars. James agrees to purchase one of the Bentleys for £40,000. At this price, John would expect to make a profit of £5,000. Unfortunately, James later decides that the price is too high and refuses to take delivery of the Bentley.

Advise John.

Commentary

This is a popular type of question in certain institutions, especially where damages are concerned. The question comprises two completely separate short problems. Unless otherwise stated, both parts are equally weighted so it is important that your treatment is similarly apportioned. In particular, the fact that the length of the questions varies does not mean that the length of each of your answers should be similarly different. Rather, it suggests that the shorter of the two questions is more general in nature, encouraging you to speculate on other possible factual variations which might lead to different responses.

- What exactly are Janice's losses and are they too remote?
- Is this the type of contract where courts will award damages for non-pecuniary losses (e.g. disappointment and inconvenience)?
- Has Janice acted reasonably in attempting to mitigate her losses?
- What is the normal measure for awarding damages in breach of contract actions?
- Identify the precise losses that John has sustained?
- What reasonable steps should John take to mitigate his losses?

☀ Suggested answer

(a)   The main thrust of Janice's claim to damages for breach of contract will be that she has suffered two forms of non-pecuniary loss: (i) she has been deprived of photographs of her wedding buffet and, (ii) she has suffered personal humiliation in having to turn away half of the wedding guests. Presumably she will also be successful in reclaiming part of the contract price on grounds of the reduced value of the services supplied, i.e. a smaller room and a buffet for only 25 guests. Will her two-part claim also succeed?

The question of remoteness and mitigation hardly arises. It must clearly have been in the reasonable contemplation of the parties that a smaller room would take fewer guests, necessitating some form of rationing of places (see, generally, the test laid down in *Hadley* v *Baxendale*). Equally, as the acquisition of a substitute professional photographer at such short notice would be unlikely (i.e. mitigation impossible), Janice would be permanently deprived of a photographic souvenir of her wedding day. We should therefore concentrate on the issue of the recovery of non-pecuniary loss.

In general, courts limit the recovery of damages for disappointment and injured feelings to those contracts where one of the main objects is to provide for pleasure and/or peace of mind (e.g., *Jarvis* v *Swan Tours Ltd* [1973] 1 QB 233). This must be contrasted with the normal commercial contract where courts have restricted the recovery of such damages (see *Bliss* v *SE Thames Regional Health Authority* [1987] ICR 700; *Hayes* v *James and Charles Dodd* [1990] 2 All ER 815).

One must therefore identify the main objects of the contract. Presumably they must be to provide peace of mind (stress-free organisation of buffet) and some sentimental benefit (photographs). As such, it seems reasonable to award damages for injured feelings and inconvenience against a party who defeats that object. In *Diesen* v *Samson* 1971 SLT (Sh Ct) 49, a father arranged for a photographer to attend his daughter's wedding. The photographer failed to arrive. The father was awarded substantial damages for being permanently deprived of the pleasure that he would obtain 'in years ahead' from 'the recollection of a happy occasion'. Equally, in *Hotson & Hotson* v *Payne* 1988 CLY 1047, a father was awarded damages when buffet arrangements went awry. There, as the father had to organise a buffet at another location, using a smaller room, he was left with the humiliating task of deflecting a large proportion of the invited guests.

The above analysis clearly supports Janice's claim to the recovery of non-pecuniary losses. But there *may* be one particular limitation. In awarding Janice damages for the inconvenience of re-arranging the buffet guest list one must be careful that any award of damages is not seen as compensation for loss of reputation. This head *may* apply only to loss of commercial reputation, as evidenced in *Rae* v *Yorkshire Bank* [1988] FLR 1. However, in *Kpoharor* v *Woolwich Building Society* [1996] 4 All ER 119, the court refused to award damages for loss of reputation to a private individual whose cheque had been wrongfully dishonoured by his bank (compare this with the rights of a commercial customer — *Rolin* v *Steward* (1854) 14 CB 595). Whether the decisions in *McLeish* v *Amoo-Gottfried*, (1993) *The Times*, 13 October and *Farley* v *Skinner* [2001] UKHL 49, will affect these issues may depend upon how broadly one can define the words 'reputation' and 'inconvenience'.

(b) The general principle of awarding damages in a breach of contract action is that the victim of the breach must be placed in the position he would have occupied had the contract been properly performed. In assessing John's recoverable loss one must first consider the principle of remoteness as outlined in *Hadley* v *Baxendale*. Briefly, damages are recoverable provided (i) they were fairly and reasonably considered to arise naturally from the breach, or (ii) they were in the reasonable contemplation of the parties as liable to result from the breach.

On this basis, it is clear that John has been deprived of a sale and will be claiming the resultant loss of profit. But the issue is not that clearcut. In circumstances where a seller has been deprived of a sale, the law distinguishes between sellers who are private individuals and those who are dealers. In the former case, for example, s. 50 of the Sale of Goods Act 1979 provides that where there is an 'available market' for the goods in question the measure of damages will be the difference between the contract price and the market price. However, John is a dealer, so separate considerations apply.

As a dealer, John is entitled *prima facie* to recover his lost profit. The case of *WL Thompson Ltd* v *Robinson (Gunmakers) Ltd* [1955] Ch 177 suggests that James will be unable to claim that John could have sold the Bentley to another customer as, in these circumstances, if he successfully arranges a substitute sale he will only have profited from one, not two sales. In particular, Upjohn J, commenting on s. 50 of the Sale of Goods Act 1979, stated that the phrase 'available market' referred to conditions in a particular trade in which goods could be readily and freely resold in the event of the buyer's default. On the facts in *WL Thompson*, as the supply of particular cars exceeded demand, the dealer's loss was clearly a loss of profit on the sale of the car.

Hence, if excess demand for Bentley cars applies in John's situation, it would appear that a claim to lost profits will succeed. But what if demand exceeds supply? In this case John's claim will fail as the number of car sales that he can successfully negotiate will depend upon the supply of cars rather than the supply of buyers (see *Charter* v *Sullivan* [1957] 2 QB 117). In short, in refusing to accept delivery, James has not reduced the number of sales that John could conclude, assuming an excess demand.

Finally, the above analysis is based on the assumption that James is buying a new Bentley car. What if the car is second-hand? If so, different considerations apply. In *Lazenby Garages Ltd* v *Wright* [1976] 1 WLR 459 it was held that a second-hand car was a 'unique' object, presumably because each such car is different in terms of its mileage, condition of its bodywork and so forth. As such, if the car was resold for a higher price to another customer then the original customer would not be liable for loss of profit. Moreover, the possibility that the dealer might have sold a different, second-hand car to the second customer was dismissed as being too remote. On our facts, there is no evidence that John has found another customer although a court would expect him to mitigate his losses by attempting to do so. But even if this occurs, James will still be liable for any expenses incurred by John in negotiating a second sale of the Bentley and, in addition, any loss of profits sustained from selling the car at a lower price (i.e. below £40,000).

Q Question 4

The overriding principle in the award of damages for breach of contract is that the victim should be fully compensated for all the losses which flow from that breach. Discuss.

Commentary

In many ways, the rules regarding the recovery of damages for breach of contract represent a process of elimination. A court will identify the actual damage caused by the breach and then scale down these damages, where appropriate, on grounds that they are (a) too remote, or (b) not of a type that are recoverable, or (c) should have been mitigated by the claimant. The net result is that a claimant may not recover *all* the losses directly caused by the breach of contract.

Good students will not merely regurgitate their lecture notes but will try to identify particular situations where the claimant's actual losses are not fully recoverable. The answer below adopts one of many possible structures. As an alternative, one might consider other aspects such as the basis upon which damages are awarded (e.g. compare reliance and expectation losses), or the quantification of loss (e.g. non-delivery of goods which thwarts a profitable sub-sale by the buyer), or the enforceability of agreed damages clauses which often do not fully compensate the victim of a breach.

- What is the meaning of causation?

- How will the contract-breaker's knowledge at the time of contracting affect the application of the remoteness test?

- Contrast direct consequence and reasonably contemplated losses

- What limitations are imposed on the recovery of non-pecuniary losses?

- What steps should the victim take in order to minimise his losses?

- Give examples throughout your answer that illustrate how the victim's damages do not fully compensate him for all the losses resulting from the breach.

☼ Suggested answer

Few people would question that the purpose of awarding damages for breach of contract is to compensate the claimant rather than punish the defendant. Thus, although damages can be claimed as of right by the victim of a breach, such damages will only be nominal, substantial damages requiring proof that actual losses were sustained as a result of the breach. Equally, exemplary damages, often termed punitive, cannot be awarded in a pure contract action. The claimant will fail even if there is proof that the defendant's breach was committed deliberately and with a view to profit, unless the court is prepared to disguise such an award under the general heading of injury to the claimant's feelings (e.g. *Cox* v *Phillips Industries Ltd* [1976] 1 WLR 638).

However, three questions emerge from the quotation. How does one assess whether the loss suffered is actually *caused* by the breach? Is the recovery of damages based upon an assessment of the direct consequences of the breach or is it limited by a test of foreseeability? Finally, will the victim be fully compensated for *all* the losses suffered?

Causation

It is often said that there must be a sufficiently strong causal connection between the loss suffered and the actual breach. In this context, causation is not exclusively subsumed within the remoteness principle. For example, if the breach of contract is one of two causes for the loss suffered, both causes acting concurrently, then a court will still award normal damages (see *Heskell* v *Continental Express Ltd* [1950] 1 All ER 1033). Thus, in *Smith, Hogg & Co.* v *Black Sea Insurance Co. Ltd* [1940] AC 997, the cargo was lost because of bad weather and also because, in breach of contract, the ship did not fulfil the seaworthiness criterion. It was held that the breach was sufficient to support a claim for damages. However, if the bad weather had been so extreme that no ship would have survived, then damages might not have been recoverable (see generally *Monarch SS Co.* v *Karlshamns Oljefabriker (A/B)* [1949] AC 196). In this way, the principle of causation ensures that the claimant does not recover for losses under the notional pretext that a breach has occurred.

One further point on causation is that the contract breaker will be liable for loss aggravated by a third party if the intervening act was foreseeable. For example, in *Stansbie* v *Troman* [1948] 2 KB 48 a painter who left his client's house unlocked was held liable for the value of the goods taken by thieves. In short, the breach had caused the claimant specific losses and it was no excuse to transfer responsibility to a third party (the burglar) who profited from that breach.

Remoteness

The principle of remoteness clearly limits the recovery of losses directly caused by the breach. The courts have adopted a test which limits recoverable loss to that which was in the reasonable contemplation of the parties as liable to result from the particular breach (see *The Heron II*).

The knowledge of the parties is the determining factor and can be illustrated by a comparison of the following two cases. In *Diamond* v *Campbell-Jones* [1961] Ch 22 the defendant, in breach of contract, refused to sell a house to the plaintiff. The defendant knew that the plaintiff was a dealer in real property but not that he intended to redevelop the premises, converting them into offices and flats. It was held that, as the defendant did not possess any knowledge of the plaintiff's specific intentions, he was not liable for the loss of redevelopment profits. Conversely, in *Cottrill v Steyning & Littlehampton Building Society* [1966] 1 WLR 753, the vendor of a hotel knew that the purchaser intended to convert the premises into flats, as well as erecting a further six houses on the land. It was held that in refusing to sell the hotel, in breach of contract, the vendor was liable to pay damages assessed upon the lost redevelopment potential. It can be seen that in both cases the defendant *caused* the plaintiff's losses, but the defendants' state of knowledge prevented their full recovery (see also *Seven Seas Properties Ltd v Al-Essa (No 2)* [1993] 3 All ER 577). (Note: a comparison of any two cases would have sufficed in this context, e.g. *Horne v Midland Railway* (1873) LR 8 CP 131 versus *Simpson v L & NW Railway* (1876) 1 BD 274.)

Recovery of Losses

There are two general issues which arise under this heading: the recovery of non-pecuniary loss and the general duty imposed on the claimant to mitigate his losses.

With regard to the first aspect, there are clear limitations on the recovery of such losses. In the seminal case of *Addis v Gramophone Co. Ltd* [1909] AC 488, the House of Lords stated in general terms that damages for injured feelings were not recoverable in a pure contract action. Subsequent decisions appeared to disregard this decision, allowing the recovery of losses for disappointment, inconvenience and distress (see *Cox v Phillips Industries Ltd* [1976] 1 WLR 638). However, in modern times, the courts have somewhat retreated from this expansive approach, limiting recovery to those contracts which have, as one of their main objects, the provision of enjoyment, peace of mind and freedom from distress. Examples would include holidays and house purchases. But in the general arena of commercial/employment contracts even the clearest indications that the claimant will suffer psychological trauma as a result of the breach will be insufficient (see *Bliss v SE Thames Regional Health Authority* [1987] ICR 700; *Hayes v James and Charles Dodd* [1990] 2 All ER 815). The *Bliss* decision demonstrates that the current limitations that are being imposed are not explicable by recourse to the principle of remoteness (i.e. the defendant could not have been expected to contemplate such losses) but are referable to wider policy considerations. However, the recovery of damages for mental distress in *McLeish v Amoo-Gottfried* (1993) *The Times*, 13 October and the more relaxed approach of the House of Lords in *Farley v Skinner* [2001] UKHL 49 may presage some changes in this area.

(Note: the good student might also consider the difficulties of recovering damages for injured reputation, that being the basis for an action in tort. A summary of the general principle linked to a couple of exceptions might demonstrate to the examiner a useful breadth of knowledge, e.g. the dishonour of cheques and *Gibbons v Westminster*

Bank Ltd [1939] 2 KB 882; *Kpoharor v Woolwich Building Society* [1996] 4 All ER 119; damage to reputation and *Anglo-Continental Holidays Ltd v Typaldos Lines (London) Ltd* [1967] 2 Lloyd's Rep 61; or even damage to *personal* reputation and *McLeish v Amoo-Gottfried*, above.)

Finally, even if the loss which the claimant has suffered is recoverable in principle, damages will be reduced on evidence that the victim failed to mitigate his loss properly. This duty requires the claimant to act reasonably in trying to minimise his loss and not to act unreasonably in increasing his loss. Available precedent suggests that the claimant need only adopt a reasonable course of action rather than the *most* reasonable course of action. Thus, an employee who is wrongfully dismissed must take reasonable steps to find another, hopefully comparable, position. But he would not be expected to accept an offer of re-engagement from his original employer where his original dismissal occurred in particularly humiliating circumstances (compare *Payzu v Saunders* [1919] 2 KB 581 with *Brace v Calder* [1895] 2 KB 253). One can justify this rule of mitigation on the following grounds: either that a claimant's inaction causes the loss to occur rather than the defendant's being in breach, or that the defendant reasonably contemplated that the claimant would wish to minimise his loss rather than seek redress through the courts (but see *White & Carter (Councils) Ltd v McGregor* [1962] AC 413). Either way, the effect is seemingly that the defendant should not be liable for losses which are not of his own making.

Conclusion

The foregoing analysis demonstrates the limits on the recovery of loss caused by the defendant's breach. In a commercial sense it seems fair that the defendant should not be liable for losses which he could never have contemplated. Both parties take risks when entering into a contract and part of the allocation of those risks is that non-recoverable loss might be suffered by the victim of a breach. (Note: the very good student might at this point highlight the discrepancy that exists between actions brought for breach of contract and those under the Misrepresentation Act 1967, s. 2(1). The latter can appear more attractive in that it offers a direct consequence test, as opposed to the 'reasonable contemplation' test adopted in contract, and may well ignore any duty to mitigate loss — see *Gran Gelato Ltd v Richcliff* [1992] Ch 560. It also imposes fewer limitations on the recovery of damages for non-pecuniary loss — see *Mafo v Adams* [1970] 1 QB 548; *Archer v Brown* [1985] QB 401.)

Equitable Remedies

Introduction

There are times when the remedy of damages will prove inadequate to the victim of a breach of contract. This might occur where the claimant wishes to purchase a unique artefact which cannot be acquired elsewhere (see *Falcke* v *Gray* (1859) 4 Drew 651 — the sale of two china jars). Equity therefore developed a number of remedies, discretionary in nature, directed towards ensuring that a claimant was not unjustly treated by his being confined to a remedy in damages. In this part two such remedies will be considered: specific performance and injunctions.

Specific Performance

An order for specific performance will compel the addressee to fulfil the terms of a contract. These terms must be positive in nature (e.g. to deliver goods), whereas negative stipulations are normally enforced by an injunction (e.g. a restraint of trade clause).

Any question concerning specific performance inevitably requires a consideration of three issues. First, are damages an adequate remedy? An order for specific performance will rarely be granted if damages would be adequate. This would occur, for example, if the claimant was able to acquire an equivalent performance from a third party (e.g. substitute goods). Conversely, if the quantum of damages is difficult to assess or, as occurred in *Beswick* v *Beswick* [1968] AC 58, the award of damages would be unfair to the claimant, then specific relief will be granted.

Secondly, is there any reason why the court would refuse an order in the exercise of its equitable discretion? There are a variety of existing precedents which circumscribe this discretion. In particular, an order may well be refused if there is a lack of mutuality (see *Sutton* v *Sutton* [1984] 1 All ER 168) or the claimant has acted unfairly (see *Walters* v *Morgan* (1861) 3 DF & J 718).

Finally, is the contract of a type where an order would normally be refused? The two traditional examples where this is the case are personal service contracts and building contracts. The former situation is generally justifiable on the grounds that the mutual trust and confidence that exists between the parties has irretrievably broken down (especially in employment contracts). In the latter example, justification results from the difficulty of continually supervising the building work (i.e. enforcing the order) and often because damages provide an adequate remedy.

Injunctions

An injunction seeks to restrain the defendant from committing a breach of contract. If the injunction is prohibitive in nature (restraining a *future* breach) a court, in the exercise of its discretion, will not be influenced by the fact that the defendant's compliance with the injunction would be unduly onerous or that the breach would cause the claimant little prejudice (see *Marco Productions Ltd* v *Pagola* [1945] KB 111). However, if the injunction is mandatory in nature, requiring the defendant to reverse the effects of an *existing* breach, a court will apply the 'balance of convenience test', refusing relief if the hardship caused to the defendant by compliance with the order outweighs the consequential advantages to the claimant.

The basic rule is that an injunction will not be awarded if it would compel the defendant to perform acts which in themselves cannot form the basis of an order for specific performance. The most obvious example would be a contract of employment in which an employer seeks to enforce a restraint clause in such a way that the employee's only option is to work for the employer (see *Ehrman* v *Bartholomew* [1898] 1 Ch 671). However, there are exceptions to this basic rule as will be outlined in the question below.

Damages in Equity

Under s. 2 of the Chancery Amendment Act 1858 (Lord Cairns Act), a Court of Chancery has a discretion to award damages in lieu of, or in addition to specific performance provided the contract is of a type that is specifically enforceable (see now the Supreme Court Act 1981). It is possible that the assessment of damages under the Act may be more favourable to the claimant than at common law (see *Wroth* v *Tyler* [1974] Ch 30) but this was doubted by Lord Wilberforce in *Johnson* v *Agnew* [1979] 2 WLR 487).

Q Question

In the light of existing precedent, in what circumstances will a court grant an order for specific performance? Do the same considerations apply to the award of an injunction?

Commentary

Thankfully most institutions have discarded this type of question. It is somewhat unfair to the examinee as there is little indication as to what weight should be attached to the parts. Some help might be gained from the amount of time spent on each area in lectures. If not, the best advice would be to concentrate more on specific performance as the case law is more settled and expansive. Note also, that it is very unlikely that a question would be set exclusively on equitable remedies. Rather, some aspect may arise in a damages question. For an example, see **Chapter 15** in which equitable remedies form *part* of a mixed question.

- **What is the general attitude of courts to making orders for specific performance of contracts?**

- **In what circumstances would damages for breach of contract be considered an adequate remedy? (Give at least two examples)**

- **What factors affect the use of a court's discretion in this area?**

- **Are there any specific types of contracts where specific performance would rarely be granted?**

- **Why is injunctive relief more likely where the breach refers to a negative stipulation within the contract?**

⚡ **Suggested answer**

Specific Performance

An order of specific performance is perceived by courts as a drastic remedy. For example, in many instances it will involve some form of personal constraint over the defendant. The courts are therefore cautious in granting such an order: 'The court gives specific performance instead of damages, only when it can by that means do more perfect and complete justice' (*Wilson v Northampton and Banbury Junction Ry Co.* (1874) 9 Ch App 279 at 284 *per* Lord Selborne). In particular, a court will pose the following questions: Are damages an adequate remedy? How should the court use its discretion? Is the contract of a type that is specifically enforceable?

Damages are an Adequate Remedy

Specific performance is rarely ordered of contracts for the sale of commodities which are readily available in the market. For example, in the face of non-delivery, a purchaser would be expected to purchase the required goods elsewhere. If the alternative source charged a higher price, or the purchaser was put to costly inconvenience, the court would award damages to cover these items. In short, damages would be an adequate remedy. Conversely, if the purchaser finds that he cannot obtain a satisfactory substitute elsewhere, damages would be inadequate (see *Phillips v Lamdin* [1949] 2 KB 33, at 41 involving the wrongful removal of an Adam door).

Inadequacy may also be asserted successfully, subject to the court's discretion, where:

(a) the claimant has contracted for services of a personal nature from the defendant;

(b) damages are too speculative;

(c) damages would be difficult to prove;

(d) the loss is not legally recoverable (see generally *Decro-Wall International SA* v *Practitioners in Marketing Ltd SA* [1971] 1 WLR 361);

(e) damages would be purely nominal (*Beswick* v *Beswick* [1968] AC 58); or

(f) under s. 52 of the Sale of Goods Act 1979, the seller refuses to deliver 'specific or ascertained' goods.

Judicial Discretion

'Equity will only grant specific performance if, under all the circumstances, it is just and equitable to do so' (see *Stickney* v *Keeble* [1915] AC 386, at 419). However, the exercise of this discretion is circumscribed by a number of well-known rules:

(a) the claimant will only succeed if the contract could also be enforced by the defendant, at the time of the hearing (see *Sutton* v *Sutton* [1984] 1 All ER 168);

(b) the claimant will fail if it is impossible for the defendant to comply with the order (see *Watts* v *Spence* [1976] Ch 165 — sale of land not owned by the vendor; *The Sea Hawk* [1986] 1 WLR 657 — defendant owned no assets within the court's jurisdiction);

(c) specific relief will be refused if the claimant has taken unfair advantage of the defendant or has acted dishonestly (e.g. negotiating with a drunkard) — this will also be the case where the claimant's conduct offends the conscience of the court (compare *Watkin* v *Watson-Smith* (1986) *The Times*, 3 July with *Shell UK Ltd* v *Lostock Garages Ltd* [1976] 1 WLR 1187); and

(d) an order for specific relief will be refused if it would cause *severe* hardship to the defendant (see *Patel* v *Ali* [1984] Ch 283), or the costs of performance would be wholly out of proportion to the benefit conferred on the claimant (see *Tito* v *Waddell (No. 2)* [1977] Ch 106, 326). On a general note the claimant who seeks specific relief must not delay too long as the doctrine of *laches* may operate to bar his claim.

Specific Types of Contracts

First, equity will rarely enforce a contract of personal service. Thus employees cannot be forced to work for their employer and an employer who is found to have unfairly dismissed an employee cannot be compelled to re-instate or re-engage him (notwithstanding ss. 69–71 of the Employment Protection (Consolidation) Act 1978, as amended by the Employment Act 1980, s. 5 & sch. 1). Moreover, this exception encompasses other types of personal service contracts such as partnerships.

Secondly, building contracts will rarely be enforced on grounds that damages would normally be an adequate remedy, the court cannot supervise the work, and the building specifications are often too imprecise. However, if the first and last reasons are inapplicable then the second ground can be disregarded (see *Carpenters Estates Ltd v Davies* [1940] Ch 160). The particular difficulty of a court's supervising continuous contractual duties *may* also prevent specific relief in a variety of other situations; for example, an agreement to provide a porter for flats (see *Ryan* v *Mutual Tontine Association* [1893] 1 Ch 116, cf *Posner* v *Scott-Lewis* [1987] 3 All ER 513).

Thirdly, if the contract is entire and cannot be severed, specific relief will be refused for the performance of particular obligations within that contract (see *Ryan* v *Mutual Tontine Association*, above).

Injunctions

The general rule is that an injunction will be refused if it would force the defendant to perform acts which could not form the basis of a decree of specific performance. Thus an injunction will not normally be granted in the case of contracts of personal service (see *Chappell* v *Times Newspapers Ltd* [1975] 1 WLR 482). There are, however, some important exceptions to the general rule.

First, if the contract contains a negative stipulation it may be possible for the injunction to be framed in such a way as to enforce this negative aspect without compelling positive performance of the whole contract. For example, consider an employee who has resigned and taken up employment with another firm. The ex-employer now wishes to enforce an existing restraint clause which prevents ex-employees working for competing firms within a specified area. A properly framed injunction could enforce this negative obligation without forcing the employee to work for his old employer; for example, he could find work outside the specified area or join a non-competing firm (see *Fitch* v *Dewes* [1921] 2 AC 158; *Littlewoods Organisation Ltd* v *Harris* [1977] 1 WLR 1472). However, the employee must possess a reasonable, alternative way of earning his living otherwise an injunction serves as a disguised form of specific performance (see generally *Page One Records* v *Britton* [1968] 1 WLR 157).

Secondly, except in contracts of personal service, courts have been prepared to *imply* negative stipulations even though the contract as a whole may not be specifically enforceable. Thus in *Associated Portland Cement Manufacturers Ltd* v *Teigland Shipping A/S* [1975] 1 Lloyd's Rep 581, an injunction was granted to prevent a shipowner from employing a ship under charter in ways that were inconsistent with the charterparty.

Finally, a negative stipulation which is too wide can be severed and enforced in part. For example, in *Warner Bros Pictures Inc* v *Nelson* [1937] 1 KB 209, the defendant undertook not to act for third parties without the plaintiff's consent nor to 'engage in any other occupation' without requisite permission. The latter undertaking was considered unenforceable as it would force the defendant, an actress, to work for her existing employer, but an injunction was awarded to enforce the former obligation.

Privity of Contract

Introduction

The doctrine of privity of contract, which only became entrenched in the latter half of the nineteenth century, is the mechanism by which contractual rights and liabilities are limited to the parties to the contract. The theory is simple: contract is based upon agreement and therefore only the parties to that agreement have consented to contractual responsibility. The common law reasoned that, first, only a promisee may enforce the promise, meaning that if the third party is not a promisee he is not privy to the contract. Thus if A promises B that, in return for a consideration provided by B, A will do something for C, C is not a promisee and is unable to enforce the promise. Secondly, there is the principle that consideration must move from the promisee. Thus A may make a promise to both B and C, with a consideration provided by B, that he will do something for C's benefit. Here C is clearly a promisee but no consideration has moved from him, meaning that he is unable to enforce the promise. The two principles of privity and consideration have become entwined, but the Law Commission has recently suggested (Privity of Contract: Contracts for the Benefit of Third Parties, Consultation Paper No. 121, 1991) that two separate policy issues can be identified, *viz* privity relates to those *who* can enforce a contract whilst consideration concerns the *types* of promise that can be enforced. The leading decisions which should be read are *Tweddle* v *Atkinson* (1861) 1 B & S 393; *Dunlop Pneumatic Tyre Co. Ltd* v *Selfridge & Co. Ltd* [1915] AC 847; *Midland Silicones Ltd* v *Scruttons Ltd* [1962] AC 446.

The Law Commission's provisional suggestions (Consultation Paper No. 121, 1991) were, for the most part, subsequently enacted in the Contracts (Rights of Third Parties) Act 1999.

Effects of the Doctrine of Privity

Although the third party, C, cannot enforce the contract, it is obviously a valid undertaking between the contracting parties, A and B. It follows that the promisee, B, can enforce the contract, there being three possibilities:

(a) B may obtain a decree of specific performance against A thereby compelling him to confer the benefit on C (see *Beswick* v *Beswick* [1968] AC 58).

(b) B might sue A for damages for breach of contract for refusing to confer the benefit on C. The problem here is to ascertain the measure of damages, one view being that

B may only obtain nominal damages as he has suffered no loss (see *West* v *Houghton* (1879) 4 CPD 197; *Beswick* v *Beswick*, above). In *Jackson* v *Horizon Holidays Ltd* [1975] 1 WLR 1468, the Court of Appeal took the view that the promisee should be able to recover damages for the loss suffered by the third party but this seems unlikely in view of what was said in the House of Lords decision in *Woodar Investment Development Ltd* v *Wimpey Construction UK Ltd* [1980] 1 WLR 277. This question remains unresolved.

(c) If A takes action against C in breach of his contract with B, B may obtain an injunction to restrain A (see *Gore* v *Van Der Lann* [1967] 2 QB 31; *Snelling* v *John G Snelling Ltd* [1973] 1 QB 87).

Common Law Attempts to Evade Privity

Trusts

Privity applies only to contracts whereas a trust can attach to property of any kind including choses in action, e.g. rights under contracts. It follows that where A makes a promise to B for the benefit of C, C can enforce the promise if B has constituted himself trustee of A's promise for C. Early in the twentieth century it seemed that the trust device might be the method by which privity could be avoided (see *Affréteurs (Les) Réunis SA* v *Leopold Walford (London) Ltd* [1919] AC 801). However, it fell by the wayside because of the strict requirements of constituting a trust and most particularly that there should be a specific intention on the part of the person declaring the trust that it should be a trust, the courts being unwilling to imply such an intention (see *Vandepitte* v *Preferred Accident Insurance Corp.* [1933] AC 70; *Re Schebsman* [1944] Ch 83).

Restrictive Covenants

The concept derived from land law that a vendor of property may impose restrictive covenants which 'run with the land' and restrict its future use was carried over into the law of contract by the Privy Council in *Lord Strathcona SS Co.* v *Dominion Coal Co.* [1926] AC 108. Again, the notion has little scope for extension after Diplock J's refusal to follow the decision in *Port Line Ltd* v *Ben Line Steamers Ltd* [1958] 2 QB 146. Most recently, in *Law Debenture Trust Corp. plc* v *Ural Caspian Oil Corp. Ltd* [1993] 2 All ER 355, Hoffmann J held that this concept did not provide 'a panacea for outflanking the doctrine of privity of contract'. Moreover, it was emphasised that the principle permitted no more than the grant of a negative injunction to restrain the person acquiring the property from doing acts which would be inconsistent with the performance of the contract by his predecessor and had never been used to impose upon a purchaser a positive duty to perform the covenants of his predecessor.

Collateral Contracts

A contract between A and B may be accompanied by a collateral contract between B and C relating to the same subject-matter and is a very effective means by which to avoid privity (see *Shanklin Pier* v *Detel Products Ltd* [1951] 2 KB 854; *Charnock* v *Liverpool Corporation* [1968] 1 WLR 1498).

Liability in Tort to Third Parties

Where A and B have a contract it may impose upon A a duty of care which is owed to C, and C may be able to sue A in the tort of negligence if the duty is breached. The most controversial extension of tortious liability was made in *Junior Books Ltd* v *Veitchi Co. Ltd* [1983] 1 AC 520 where B and C had a contract whereby B agreed to build a factory for C, C having the right to nominate sub-contractors. C nominated A and a contract was formed between A and B, but there was no contract between A and C. It was held that A was liable in tort to C for the financial loss caused by a defective floor which had to be re-laid. Later cases have virtually interpreted *Junior Books* out of existence and, whilst it is clear that a manufacturer may be liable in tort for injury to persons or damage to property caused by a defective chattel, he will not be liable in tort to persons who suffer economic loss simply because the chattel is defective in quality. Such claims are properly the province of the law of contract. (See *D & F Estates Ltd* v *Church Commissioners for England* [1989] AC 177; *Simaan General Contracting Co.* v *Pilkington Glass Ltd (No. 2)* [1988] QB 758; *Murphy* v *Brentwood District Council* [1991] 1 AC 398).

Agency

The concept of agency is an exception to the doctrine of privity in that an agent may contract on behalf of his principal with a third party and form a binding contract between principal and third party. Agency has also provided a fertile ground for evading privity in relation to exclusion clauses. A third party may be able to take the benefit of an exclusion clause by proving that the party imposing the clause was acting as the agent of the third party, thereby bringing the third party into a direct contractual relationship with the claimant (see *Elder, Dempster & Co. Ltd* v *Paterson, Zochonis & Co. Ltd* [1924] AC 446; *New Zealand Shipping Co. Ltd* v *AM Satterthwaite & Co. Ltd (The Eurymedon)* [1975] AC 154).

Statutory Developments

Contracts (Rights of Third Parties) Act 1999

The Contracts (Rights of Third Parties) Act 1999 fundamentally modifies the doctrine of privity. Section 1 provides third parties with the right to enforce a term contained within a contract if the contract expressly so provides or the term purports to confer a benefit on the third party. The latter possibility depends on whether, in construing the contract, the contracting parties intended the particular term to be enforceable by the third party. In exercising this right the third party will possess any remedy that would have been available to him in an action for breach of contract if he had been a party to the contract (e.g., damages, injunctive relief). Moreover, s. 1(6) makes it clear that a third party should have the benefit of any exclusion clause, provided that the third party is referred to in the clause, thereby circumventing the rather artificial analysis employed by the common law to secure this result (e.g. *New Zealand Shipping Co. Ltd* v *AM Satterthwaite & Co. Ltd (The Eurymedon)* [1975] AC 154).

Section 2 limits the power of the contracting parties to vary the terms of the contract unless such power has been expressly included in the contract. Any alteration of a term covered by s. 1 requires the consent of the third party if that person has already communicated his assent to the term, or it is known that the third party has relied upon the term, or it is reasonably foreseeable that such reliance would, and in fact did, take place. Further sections address the availability of defences (s. 3), double liability (s. 4), exempted contracts (s. 6), and the compatibility of other legislation (s. 7).

Overall, the 1999 Act will have important consequences for common law precedent. Under the Act cases such as *Beswick* v *Beswick* [1966] Ch 538 will no longer be good law — clearly the parties intended Mrs Beswick to have a legally enforceable right to claim payment from her nephew. However, the Act gives freedom to the contracting parties to exclude expressly the provisions of the Act or to set out procedures for post-contractual variation of arrangements that avoid the need to obtain the third party's consent. On this basis, any suggestion that common law precedent is rendered redundant by the 1999 Act is indeed premature.

Q Question 1

It is clearly desirable to amend the rule that a third party may not sue on a contract which is made for his benefit.
Discuss.

Commentary

This essay title requires an understanding and evaluation of the traditional rules of privity regarding contracts which are made for the benefit of third parties. A critical examination should also be made of whether the law was ripe for reform in 1999 and, consequently, students should be acquainted with the Law Commission's provisional recommendations regarding contracts made for the benefit of third parties (Consultation Paper No. 121, 1991) and the Contracts (Rights of Third Parties) Act 1999.

- What purpose did the courts originally intend the doctrine of privity to serve?

- How does this rule inter-relate with the modern doctrine of Consideration?

- Why did so many exceptions develop to the privity rule?

- What are the guiding principles of the Contracts (Rights of Third Parties) Act 1999?

- What limits are imposed on those contracting parties who wish to amend their existing contractual arrangements?

:Q: Suggested answer

Before the passing of the Contracts (Rights of Third Parties) Act 1999 it was clear that a third party could not sue on a contract to which he was not privy, even if the sole purpose of the contract was to benefit the third party. This rule is relatively modern and only became entrenched in the nineteenth century. In *Price* v *Easton* (1833) 4 B & Ad 433, the defendant promised B that if B did certain work for him he would pay money to the plaintiff. B did the requisite work but the defendant refused to pay the money. It was held that the plaintiff could not sue, the court advancing two reasons for the decision. First, that the plaintiff could not show any consideration for the promise moving from him to the defendant and, secondly, that the plaintiff was not privy to the contract made between the defendant and B. The decision in *Tweddle* v *Atkinson* (1861) 1 B & S 393 firmly established the privity rule in its modern form. There the fathers of a husband and wife agreed in writing that both should pay money to the husband, adding that the husband should have the power to sue them for the respective sums. The husband's claim against his wife's father was dismissed, the court justifying the decision largely because no consideration moved from the promisee i.e., the husband. Important decisions of the House of Lords have strongly supported the privity rule (*Dunlop Pneumatic Tyre Co. Ltd* v *Selfridge & Co. Ltd* [1915] AC 847; *Midland Silicones Ltd* v *Scruttons Ltd* [1962] AC 446) but in *Beswick* v *Beswick* [1968] AC 58 and *Woodar Investment Development Ltd* v *Wimpey Construction UK Ltd* [1980] 1 WLR 277, the House of Lords continued to comply with the rule whilst strongly criticising it.

The injustice of the doctrine of privity was further reinforced by the rules relating to damages. In *Jackson* v *Horizon Holidays Ltd* [1975] 1 WLR 1468, the defendants contracted with the plaintiff to provide holiday accommodation for the plaintiff, his wife and their two children. The accommodation was totally inadequate and the plaintiff recovered damages including £500 for 'mental distress'. Lord Denning MR considered that £500 would have been an excessive amount for the plaintiff's own distress but regarded the award as adequate on the basis that the plaintiff had made a contract for the benefit of himself and his family and that he could recover in respect of their loss. This approach to damages was strongly disapproved by the House of Lords in *Woodar* but the promisee's inability to recover damages in respect of loss suffered by the third party was described as 'most unsatisfactory' and in need of re-evaluation by the legislature or by the House itself. Moreover, in *Forster* v *Silvermere Golf and Equestrian Centre* (1981) 125 SJ 397, Dillon J described the position as 'a blot on our law and most unjust'. There the plaintiff transferred land to the defendant who agreed to build a house on it and to allow the plaintiff and her children to live in it rent-free for life. It was held that the plaintiff could recover damages in respect of her own loss but not in relation to any rights of occupation which the children might have enjoyed after her death. It is scarcely surprising that this arbitrary rule engendered attempts at its circumvention in the guise of trusts (*Affréteurs (Les) Réunis SA v Leopold Walford (London) Ltd* [1919] AC 801) and restrictive covenants (*Lord Strathcona SS Co. v Dominion Coal Co.* [1926] AC 108), but no single attack by the common law courts successfully abrogated it. Moreover, the inroads upon the rule were created on an *ad hoc* basis and were both artificial and over-complicated (e.g. *New Zealand Shipping Co. Ltd v AM Satterthwaite & Co. Ltd (The Eurymedon)* [1975] AC 154). One might therefore question whether the doctrine of privity was ever justifiable and, if not, whether its fundamental modification by the Contracts (Rights of Third Parties) Act 1999 was the most appropriate way forward.

Several justifications have been advanced in denial of rights to third parties under the privity rule. First, it is argued that rights and duties remain the personal domain of those who create them and, as the third party has played no part in the technical formation of the contract, he should obtain no contractual rights. In particular, the Law Commission (Consultation Paper No. 121, 1991) emphasised that the purpose of requiring consent in contracts is to protect personal autonomy but that allowing third parties to obtain *benefits* under a contract would not undermine such autonomy. Indeed, where both parties have agreed to benefit the third party, his right of enforcement gives effect to their intention and promotes the essence of agreement. Secondly, the third party's failure to furnish any consideration is often thought to be fatal to his having any rights under the contract, a point which is reinforced by asserting that the third party beneficiary should not be better off than a gratuitous promisee who has provided no consideration. Again, the Law Commission pointed to the fact that consideration was provided by the promisee meaning that the promisor's promise had been paid for, albeit not by the third party; the gratuitous third party thus has rights under a valid contract whereas in the case of a gratuitous promisee there is no valid contract to enforce. Thirdly, it is suggested that it is unjust that a person should be treated as a party to a contract for the purpose of suing on it when he could not be sued. It is clear, however, that the promisor's interests are protected by his having a claim against the promisee whereas the third party has no such security under the existing rule of privity. Fourthly, there is the argument that the promisor could be liable to two actions from both the promisee and the third party but, as the Law Commission suggested, one answer is to say that there is only one promise giving rise to one cause of action and, once the promise is enforced it is extinguished, the promisor then ceasing to be liable. Fifthly, there is the assertion that, whilst privity does not permit the creation of contractual rights in third parties, it does not prohibit the achievement of the same result in practice provided that the appropriate drafting is used, e.g. collateral contracts. But the Law Commission emphasised that laymen will often fail to draft around the rule and that problems are still engendered where the parties have taken legal advice (e.g. *Beswick* v *Beswick*, above). Finally, it is argued that the ability of third parties to sue on the contract made for their benefit would detract from the rights of the contracting parties to rescind or vary their contract and would expose the promisor to a potentially wide range of possible third party claimants. The Law Commission acknowledged that reform would need to safeguard the rights of the parties and that provision should be made for a circumscribed definition of third parties in order to prevent a flood of litigation.

The Law Commission's proposals for reform were that nothing short of a 'detailed legislative scheme' would suffice to guarantee the rights of third parties. In this regard the 1999 Act appears to have fulfilled the Law Commission's plea. On the central issue of the test of an enforceable benefit, s. 1 provides that a third party will be entitled to enforce a contractual term in his own right if either the contract 'expressly' so provides (s. 1(1)(a)), or the term 'purports to confer a benefit' on the third party (s. 1(1)(b)). As regards the latter possibility, the Act, in effect, sets up a rebuttable presumption that if the parties confer a benefit on a third party, they intend that the third party is empowered to enforce the term that creates the benefit (see s. 1(2)). Inevitably, we must await judicial clarification of such words as 'purports to confer a benefit', but clearly there is room for litigious dispute. For example, if the primary contractors simply *wished* to benefit a third party, or their agreement *appeared* to benefit a third party, would such situations fall within the meaning of 'purport to confer'? One can only assume that such intentions will not easily be inferred and that, before any rebuttable presumption has been established, the necessary objective legal intent has been ascertained. Certainly the vagaries of such factual analysis have been partially avoided by s. 1(3), which requires any third party to be expressly identified in the contract. On this basis, if the facts of *Jackson* v *Horizon Holidays* were to be repeated one would assume that as the family members had all been referred to in the contract (i.e. satisfying s. 1(3)), all members were travelling together, all arrangements concerned a 'family trip', and the cost clearly encompassed all the family, that a court would conclude that the contract had purported to confer the benefit of the contract terms on all the claimant's family.

Section 2 concerns the difficult issue of variation and rescission. In general it recognises that where a third party has a right under s. 1 to enforce a term of the contract, the parties to the contract cannot, by agreement, rescind the contract, or vary it in such a way as to alter that right without prior permission from the third party. This restriction pre-supposes that the third party has communicated to the promisor his assent to the term, or the promisor is aware that the third party has relied upon the term, or the promisor could reasonably foresee reliance by the third party on the term and such reliance has in fact occurred. In so doing, the Act seems to uphold the right to vary subject only to express intervention by the third party. In practice, the power to vary will be much weaker. As it will often be reasonably foreseeable that the third party might rely on the term in question, the parties will be best advised to contact the third party before any agreed variation has occurred in order to check whether such reliance had indeed taken place.

Finally, the 1999 Act makes no mention of consideration. Are we to infer that the decision in *Tweddle* v *Atkinson* is preserved, thereby representing a major loophole to the Act? It would appear not, because the Law Commission seemingly re-interpreted *Tweddle* by distinguishing promises that are supported by consideration (albeit enforced by a third party) and promises that are wholly gratuitous. The resultant interpretation of the 1999 Act will therefore focus on the right to enforce a promise supported by consideration, even though the third party himself conferred no benefit.

In conclusion, many of the artificial and often questionable exemptions that the common law created to circumvent the unfairness of the privity rule can now be laid to rest. Attention has moved away from the direct contractual relationship embodied in the bargained-for exchange of promises. Instead, the 1999 Act gives effect to the intentions of the contracting parties and the legitimate expectations of named third parties, raising a different set of complex legal issues. Indeed, the skeletal nature of the statutory provisions will require future explanation and elaboration by the courts regarding some fundamental points. First, it will sometimes be difficult to ascertain the intention of the contracting parties as to when the third party is to benefit from the contract. Secondly, a degree of uncertainty remains regarding the freedom of the parties to vary their contract where the third party's views are unknown. Nevertheless, legislation openly acknowledging the third party's rights is long overdue and removes the need for the common law to construct artificial and elaborate mechanisms in order to confer benefits upon third parties.

Mixed Questions

This final chapter introduces students to those examination questions which contain overlapping topics. For example, a contract question might include aspects of mistake, undue influence and misrepresentation. Clearly, if students identify all the relevant areas then they will have established a firm base from which a good answer can be developed.

As the main purpose of reading this chapter is to test your ability to identify different topics contained within one question, the suggested answers offer a *broad outline* of the issues raised rather than a more detailed analysis of relevant points which would be required by an examiner.

Q Question 1

The NSC is a government body which arranges for the salvaging of shipwrecks lying within the coastal waters of the UK. Recently, the *Hesperus* was reported as having been damaged in heavy seas and that its captain had run the ship aground on a remote Scottish island. The NSC invites salvage operators to bid for the salvage rights of the *Hesperus* in the following terms: 'We imagine great interest in the ship as its cargo includes a quantity of Roman coins. Bidding is by sealed competitive tender. Only one bid will be accepted from any one company. All bids will remain confidential. We bind ourselves to accept the highest bid.'

Scrappit Ltd and Junkit Ltd both bid for the salvage rights. Scrappit Ltd bids £100,000 whilst Junkit Ltd bids '£90,000 or £10,000 more than the next highest bid, whichever is the greater'. NSC assumes that Junkit Ltd's bid is the highest (i.e. £110,000) and therefore accepts it. Scrappit Ltd now claims that its bid is the highest and that NSC is in breach of contract in accepting Junkit Ltd's bid.

Discuss the legal position of the parties.

Would your answer differ in each of the following separate situations:

(a) *Hesperus* is found to have survived the heavy storms and is sailing off the coast of South America.

(b) The 'Rare Coins and Antiquities Act 1964' prevents the sale of Roman coins without the prior permission of the Department of the Environment, with an unlimited maximum fine being payable for any transgression.

 **Suggested answer**

This question deals with offer and acceptance, terms, mistake and illegality.

Regarding the formation of a contract four questions arise: was the invitation to bid an offer; if so, did it form a unilateral contract; if so, was it the intention that referential bids would be excluded; if so, does Scrappit Ltd have an enforceable contract with NSC? The starting point would be to define an offer as opposed to an invitation to treat: it must be specific, certain and display sufficient legal intent to be bound. Although the facts appear similar to an auction, in which it is the bidder who makes the offer, there are some important differences. NSC's invitation clearly demonstrates an intention to be bound as NSC is willing to 'bind itself' to accept the highest bid. The words are very clear and unambiguous. Moreover, although the invitation is directed to the world at large this might not detract from its being an offer (see *Carlill* v *Carbolic Smoke Ball Co.* [1893] 1 QB 256). Parallels could also be drawn with the *obiter* statements in *Warlow* v *Harrison* (1859) 1 E & E 309 in which it was stated that advertising an auction without reserve constituted an offer to sell to the highest bidder (see also *Barry* v *Heathcote Ball & Co (Commercial Auctions) Ltd* [2000] 1 WLR 1962). Is not NSC offering to do exactly that? Finally, the House of Lords decision in *Harvela Investments Ltd* v *Royal Trust Co. of Canada (CI) Ltd* [1986] AC 207 should be mentioned in which, on similar facts, the invitation was treated as an offer to accept the highest bid. Lord Diplock went so far as to say that the offer constituted a unilateral contract which would be followed by a bilateral contract with the person who made the highest valid bid.

So far this would suggest that Junkit Ltd should succeed. However, the *Harvela* decision also dealt with the problems of referential bids. The House held that on the facts referential bids were invalid, thereby leaving the only other remaining valid bid as representing the highest bid submitted. This conclusion was reached because referential bids would undermine the purpose of sealed confidential bids which was to obtain the maximum bid that any bidder was prepared to make. On our facts, if the same result followed, Scrappit Ltd would have submitted the only valid bid and would thus have a legally binding contract with NSC.

(Note: the very good student who has read the *Harvela* decision might recognise that Lord Diplock, in particular, placed emphasis on the defendant's inviting bids from two specified individuals. There was an implication that an invitation to a random number of individuals would have been treated differently.)

(a) The altered facts are reminiscent of those in *McRae* v *Commonwealth Disposals Commission* (1951) 84 CLR 377, except that unlike *McRae*, the tanker does exist albeit, in an unsalvable form! If a contract has been formed between the parties it becomes a question of construction whether: (i) NSC should accept the risk of the vessel not being shipwrecked off Scotland — following the *McRae* decision, or (ii) that there is an implied condition precedent that the specified vessel exists and is subject to salvage rights — if this fails the contract would be void (see *Couturier* v *Hastie* (1856) 5 HL Cas 673). Under point (ii) you would probably mention the doctrine of common mistake, drawing appropriate support for your arguments from *Bell* v *Lever Bros* [1932] AC 161 and *Associated Japanese Bank (International) Ltd* v *Credit du Nord SA* [1989] 1 WLR 255.

(b) This deals with illegality. Is the contract illegal as formed or as performed? Although ignorance of the law is no excuse it would seem that the relevant statute does not prohibit the sale of Roman coins but merely imposes a condition upon NSC to obtain prior government approval, on pain of an unlimited fine. Thus two questions arise: how does one interpret the underlying purpose of the statute, and what is the effect of the illegality? Cases such as *Hughes* v *Asset Managers plc* [1995] 3 All ER 669 and *Shaw* v *Groom* [1970] 2 QB 504 could be used in the analysis of the first point, one possible conclusion being that the statute merely represents a bureaucratic procedure by which sales of Roman coins are monitored. Consider also the importance of whether the statute places the burden on NSC's shoulders to obtain approval. If, in these circumstances, the buyer is considered innocent then all the normal remedies for breach of contract will be available. Alternatively, if the contract is completely prohibited, there may have been an implied collateral warranty that NSC would obtain a licence (see *Strongman (1945) Ltd* v *Sincock* [1955] 2 QB 525) or that for public policy reasons the innocent party should be allowed some form of restitutionary relief anyway (see *Phoenix General Insurance Co. of Greece SA* v *Administratia Asigurairilor de Stat* [1988] QB 216).

Q Question 2

For the past five years Fastbuild Ltd, a company that specialises in the building of housing estates, has entered into one-yearly contracts with Bricklast Ltd for the supply of house bricks. Each of these contracts has been preceded by protracted negotiations in which new terms and conditions have been agreed between the parties. In the most recent set of negotiations, for a proposed contract in 1993, the parties had agreed the type and quantity of bricks to be supplied, the specified quantity easily exceeding Bricklast Ltd's expectations bearing in mind previous contracts. Fastbuild Ltd thereupon sends Bricklast Ltd a letter of intent which includes the following statement: 'As per negotiations we intend to contract with you, purchasing 2.5 million bricks (type agreed) for the year 1993 at a price to be confirmed.' Bricklast Ltd purchases additional machinery in order to manufacture the increased quantity of bricks and goes into immediate production.

Consider the legal position of the parties if negotiations between them break down and Fastbuild Ltd refuse to purchase any bricks from Bricklast Ltd.

:Q: Suggested answer

This question deals with formation of contracts and involves a consideration of offer and acceptance, certainty, intent and consideration.

First, does the letter of intent constitute an offer? An offer has to be certain, specific and demonstrate an intention to be bound. Leaving aside the particular problems associated with letters of intent, Fastbuild Ltd's communication does contain specific terms (quantity and period of delivery) but two problems remain: use of the word 'intend' and omission of an agreed price. The word 'intend' imports some degree of reticence and might be referring merely to *future* intentions. For example, in *Clifton* v *Palumbo* [1944] 2 All ER 497 the claimant's statement that he was 'prepared to offer' was held to constitute a mere invitation to treat (see also *Gibson* v *Manchester City Council* [1979] 1 WLR 294). Equally, omission of an agreed price should detract from the letter's certainty although use of the word 'confirmed' might suggest that the parties have already reached a definite agreement elsewhere. Contrast the cases of *Hillas & Co. Ltd* v *Arcos Ltd* (1932) 147 LT 503 and *Scammell (G) and Nephew Ltd* v *Ouston* [1941] AC 251, the first case showing that the omission of a price might not affect contractual validity if viewed in the light of the parties' previous course of dealing. Note the general policy that courts will always seek to implement rather than defeat the reasonable expectations of the parties. It might also be relevant to consider the impact of *Blackpool & Fylde Aero Club Ltd* v *Blackpool Borough Council* [1990] 1 WLR 1195 in that the clear intentions of the parties might override the technical requirements of offer and acceptance. Finally, lack of certainty might be argued with reference to *Walford* v *Miles* [1992] 2 AC 128 — even if the letter implies an undertaking not to contract with anyone else this does not establish an enforceable, positive contract to negotiate in good faith as it is too uncertain. (Note: many of the issues raised on the certainty of an offer would be equally applicable, if an offer and acceptance has occurred, to the certainty of the final contract, e.g. *Foley* v *Classique Coaches Ltd* [1934] 2 KB 1.)

Regarding the issue of letters of intent, the decision in *Kleinwort Benson Ltd* v *Malaysia Mining Corporation Bhd* [1989] 1 WLR 379 shows that the courts have no preconceived notion as to the enforceability of letters of comfort. Rather, the enforceability of such letters will depend upon the precise wording used. In *Kleinwort*, the words 'it is our policy' were not considered to be promissory in nature. On the present facts the word 'intend' might be considered to import an unacceptable degree of uncertainty, although contrast this with the decision in *Wilson Smithett & Cape (Sugar) Ltd* v *Bangladesh Sugar and Food Industries Corporation* [1986] 1 Lloyd's Rep 378.

Secondly, if an offer has been made, has there been an acceptance? Acceptance can take many forms: written, spoken or conduct. Although there is no suggestion that Bricklast has responded formally to Fastbuild's letter, there is clear evidence of reliance. At first glance, *Brogden* v *Metropolitan Railway Co.* (1877) 2 App Cas 666 seems applicable but in that case *both* parties acted on the strength of the new agreement (see also *Wettern Electric Ltd* v *Welsh Development Agency* [1983] QB 796). This is important as, in general, acceptance is ineffective until it has been communicated (see *Powell* v *Lee* (1908) 99 LT 284). Thus, no contract will have come into existence unless Bricklast Ltd can argue that starting work is sufficient in itself to create a contract. Consider the effect of *Trollope & Colls Ltd* v *Atomic Power Constructions Ltd* [1963] 1 WLR 333 and, in particular, *British Steel Corporation* v *Cleveland Bridge and Engineering Co. Ltd* [1984] 1 All ER 504 which concerned the twin impact of an existing letter of intent and reliance by the recipient that a contract would be finalised. An alternative approach would be to consider cases where courts have been prepared to adapt, if not modify, the orthodox rules of offer and acceptance (e.g. *Blackpool; Kleinwort, supra*, [1988] 1 WLR 799 (High Court); *Evans (J) & Son (Portsmouth) Ltd* v *Andrea Merzario* [1976] 1 WLR 1078). Naturally it would help if the parties, during their negotiations, had set up independent machinery (e.g. arbitration) for determining the meaning of uncertain terms (see *Sudbrook Trading Estate Ltd* v *Eggleton* [1983] 1 AC 444).

Finally, even if a court is prepared to find an offer that has been accepted, is there consideration for this agreement? Briefly, as there has been no exchange of promises a court would find great difficulty in identifying valid consideration (see *Combe* v *Combe* [1951] 2 KB 215). Traditionally, reliance would be considered too uncertain in English law to constitute consideration. But we are dealing here with a specific promise rather than one which is random. Perhaps one could circumvent this problem by arguing that the original letter sent by Fastbuild Ltd constituted an offer leading to a unilateral contract and that Bricklast Ltd's reliance demonstrated that they had embarked upon a course of performance leading to acceptance, thereby making the offer irrevocable (see *Daulia Ltd* v *Four Millbank Nominees Ltd* [1978] Ch 231).

Q Question 3

John, who is the son of James, is engaged to be married to Janet. He owes Grabbit, a moneylender, £5,000. James discovers his son's debt and writes to Grabbit: 'I enclose a cheque for £4,000 plus two free tickets for this year's FA Cup Final match. This is all you will get from either of us. Now get lost.' Grabbit cashes the cheque without reply.

In an attempt to make his son settle down, James agrees to buy him a house and pay the mortgage instalments provided he marries Janet within one year. John agrees so James purchases the house. However, John also agrees to lease a flat from George, payment to be made by 12 monthly payments of £180.

John and Janet move into the house but separate after six months. James, on hearing this, stops paying the mortgage. John offsets this problem by forcing George to accept a 50% reduction in the remaining six monthly payments on the flat, thereby allowing John to maintain both properties.

Another four months pass and John now wishes to enforce the mortgage agreement with his father, James, especially as Janet has moved back and accepted an engagement ring. Furthermore, John is being sued by Grabbit and George for the *full* amounts owing to them.

Discuss the legal position of all the parties concerned.

⋮Ọ⋮ Suggested answer

This answer deals with consideration, promissory estoppel, economic duress and intent to create legal relations. The good student might also see two further issues; namely, privity and unilateral contracts.

John v Grabbit

The general rule is that part-payment of a debt is insufficient to release the debtor (see *Foakes* v *Beer* (1884) 9 App Cas 605). However, part-payment from a third party which has been accepted by the creditor constitutes one of the exceptions to this rule as otherwise a fraud would have been perpetrated on the former (see *Welby* v *Drake* (1825) 1 C & P 557). The first question is whether cashing a cheque constitutes a voluntary acceptance of the new arrangement. There is a suggestion that James is holding Grabbit to ransom (see *D & C Builders Ltd* v *Rees* [1966] 2 QB 617). Does it matter whether Grabbit is in financial difficulties and James knows of this? Probably yes. A fleeting reference to economic duress might be worthwhile.

The second question concerns the use to which Grabbit puts the two match tickets. As four months has elapsed, it may well be that he has attended the football match. If so, this will signify an irrevocable, voluntary acceptance of James's offer. See *Pinnel's Case* (1602) 5 Co Rep 117a in which it was stated that a court would always assume that the creditor's acceptance of a chattel (e.g. match tickets), with or without additional payment, discharged the debt.

John v James

Is there an intention to create legal relations? There is a general presumption against such intent in family arrangements, although the parties are dealing with property and the agreement affects legal relations between James and a building society (see *Merritt* v *Merritt* [1970] 1 WLR 1121; *Pettitt* v *Pettitt* [1970] AC 777). Is there consideration? Perhaps John is suffering a potential financial detriment or James will feel happier when his son settles down (contrast *White* v *Bluett* (1853) 23 LJ Ex 36 with *Ward* v *Byham* [1956] 1 WLR 496 and *Williams* v *Williams* [1957] 1 WLR 148). Consider also the relevance of executory consideration — a promise in return for a promise is enforceable although John might sue for breach of an existing contract when the couple separate.

Two further points could be touched upon: (a) Janet is not privy to the contract and provides no consideration (see *Tweddle* v *Atkinson* (1861) 1 B & S 393) unless Janet can argue that she is a joint promisee (see *Coulls* v *Bagot's Executors and Trustee Co. Ltd* [1967] ALR 385), and (b) there are factual similarities with *Errington* v *Errington & Woods* [1952] 1 KB 290 — is there a unilateral contract and can James stop paying when John and Janet split up?

John v George

Two main issues are raised: (a) On the facts, is there a promissory estoppel which circumvents the part-payment rule? If so, what are the effects? (b) Is there any evidence of economic duress? On the first point, there is a promise to modify an existing contract which is acted upon by John (see *Central London Property Trust Ltd* v *High Trees House Ltd* [1947] KB 130). But has the promise been inequitably extracted (see *D & C Builders* v *Rees*)? If not, the *High Trees* decision would suggest that George cannot recover the lost rent (notice of reversion to the original agreement for the future is probably irrelevant). Has George derived a practical benefit from the arrangement in not having to find another tenant (see *Williams* v *Roffey & Nicholls (Contractors) Ltd* [1991] 1 QB 1). On the second point, one might link comments on *D & C Builders* v *Rees* with economic duress. Has John exerted illegitimate pressure (e.g. blackmail)? Did George have an alternative course of action (e.g. finding another tenant)?

Q Question 4

S & M Ltd agree to purchase 100,000 towels, of specified dimensions, over the next year from TT Ltd. The contract is signed on 1 January.

Six months later S & M Ltd tell TT Ltd that they are so impressed by the quality of the towels supplied that, as a goodwill gesture, an extra payment of £1 would be made at the end of the year for the delivery of every towel outstanding under the existing agreement. S & M Ltd add that they 'hope to negotiate a new contract for further supplies on similar terms for the next year'. With this in mind, TT Ltd purchase additional factory machinery.

On 1 December, S & M Ltd tell TT Ltd that they have no intention of paying the additional £1 per towel. Moreover, although TT Ltd is expecting to deliver the remainder of the towels in December (approximately 10,000 towels) S & M Ltd refuse to accept any more unless TT Ltd deliver the remainder at a 50% discount. S & M Ltd's manager adds: 'I hope that you adopt a constructive attitude or this will jeopardise our future relations.' TT Ltd agree to deliver the remaining 10,000 towels at the required discount as the loss of future contracts with S & M Ltd would probably lead to the company's going into liquidation.

Subsequently, negotiations between S & M Ltd and TT Ltd regarding a new contract, are terminated. TT Ltd now seeks your advice as to the possibility of recovering the 50% discount as well as enforcing the July promise to pay an extra £1 per towel.

☼ Suggested answer

This question primarily involves an analysis of economic duress and promissory estoppel, perhaps brought together within the wider context of consideration.

The additional payment is linked to promissory estoppel. TT Ltd provide no consideration for the additional payment. The promise is gratuitous, modifies an existing contract, and is equitably created. The only two question marks concern (a) S & M Ltd's intent, and (b) TT Ltd's reliance. On point (a) the promise appears specific and certain. But was it made in circumstances which would suggest an intention to be bound? The evidence suggests that it is a gesture of goodwill which might militate against an affirmative answer (but see the useful comments in *Scandinavian Trading Tanker Co.* v *Flota Petrolera Ecuatoriana, The Scaptrade* [1983] QB 529). On point (b) has TT Ltd acted upon the promise or, as some judges have stated, altered their position on the faith of the promise? Probably no. The towels had to be delivered anyway — although it might be arguable that TT Ltd purchased additional machinery not just because of future potential contracts with S & M Ltd but also because of the additional payment for 1992. If an estoppel is established one would probably follow *Central London Property Trust Ltd* v *High Trees House Ltd* [1947] KB 130, arguing that it would be inequitable to revert to the original position as TT Ltd has relied upon the extra payment. Moreover, as the year has already passed, there is no scope for S & M Ltd to give reasonable notice to return to its original position.

On the face of it, the December re-negotiation should fail for lack of consideration, i.e. TT Ltd do not derive any benefit from the change. However, reference should be made to *Williams* v *Roffey & Nicholls (Contractors) Ltd* [1991] 1 QB 1 in which the Court of Appeal appears to have extended the definition of consideration so as to include 'practical benefits'. Does TT Ltd receive any benefit? Possibly, in that there is an enhanced possibility of forging future, profitable links with S & M Ltd. Whether a practical benefit can include a future potential benefit is as yet a moot point. One might also mention Russell LJ's famous *dictum* in *Williams* v *Roffey* in which courts were encouraged to identify consideration if the parties clearly intended to be bound by new contractual arrangements. However, this approach emphasises the importance of the doctrine of economic duress as a means of policing the possible abuse arising from a marked inequality in bargaining powers between the parties.

The facts incorporate all the hallmarks of economic duress: a threatened breach of an existing contract (*North Ocean Shipping Co. Ltd* v *Hyundai Construction Co. Ltd* [1979] QB 705), disastrous consequences of non-compliance with this threat (*B & S Contracts and Design Ltd* v *Victor Green Publications Ltd* [1984] ICR 419), and perfect timing of the threat (*Atlas Express Ltd* v *Kafco (Importers and Distributors) Ltd* [1989] QB

833). But this is not enough. TT Ltd must establish that the pressure exerted by S & M Ltd was illegitimate and that TT Ltd's will was resultingly coerced. The above points would be helpful in demonstrating the first point, especially if linked with the comments of Lord Scarman in *Universe Tankships Inc. of Monrovia v International Transport Workers Federation* [1983] 1 AC 366. Regarding the issue of coercion, the litmus test appears to be whether the victim had an alternative course of action. This is assessed objectively, irrespective of the pressure which the victim *feels* is being exerted. Could TT Ltd have found other customers? All this should be seen in the context of TT Ltd's reliance on future links with S & M Ltd which, even if encouraged, should not be taken too seriously in a commercial world. Support for this might be gained from *Lobb (Alec) (Garages) Ltd v Total Oil (GB) Ltd* [1985] 1 All ER 303 where the court was not impressed by the plaintiff's argument that the defendant offered the only source of financial backing.

Q Question 5

The principle of freedom of contract has allowed courts to elevate the needs of certainty and predictability above those of reasonableness and fairness.

In the light of modern case law, to what extent do you agree with this statement?

ⵒ Suggested answer

There are innumerable ways in which you can answer this question. This is because you can draw upon most topics within a law of contract syllabus to support your arguments. Thus, the suggested outline merely gives you three possible structures for your answer. Option 1 offers the most restrictive treatment of the question, concentrating on the more obviously relevant features of a contract law syllabus. Option 2 builds on this base by adding aspects of statutory regulation. Option 3 provides the most expansive treatment, drawing together the effect of case law across the whole range of contract law.

Whichever option is selected, a student would be expected to provide a brief introduction to the principle of freedom of contract: nineteenth century principles of *laissez-faire*, the need to ensure predictability and certainty when dealing with arm's length commercial dealings, and the growing preparedness of courts in the twentieth century to intervene in consumer/ business transactions. Following from this:

Option 1

This would restrict attention to the more obvious areas, dealing with developments in undue influence and economic duress as well as the decline in Lord Denning's theory of bargaining inequality. Undue influence could be considered in the context of judicial intervention where trust which has been reposed by a weaker party is abused by the dominant party. The increased tendency for courts to intervene was perhaps illustrated, at its extreme, in *Lloyds Bank Ltd* v *Bundy* [1975] QB 326, with clear limits being subsequently imposed by the House of Lords in *National Westminster Bank* v *Morgan* [1985] AC 686. The most recent developments in this area centre upon the rights of wives who act as sureties for their husbands' debts, or elderly parents who finance their offspring's entrepreneurial activities (see for example *Barclays Bank plc* v *O'Brien* [1994] 1 AC 180; *Barclays Bank* v *Kennedy* [1989] FLR 356; *Avon Finance Co. Ltd* v *Bridger* [1985] 2 All ER 281). Compare this with the more restricted approach shown in commercial transactions where the doctrine of economic duress has been used sparingly (see *Lobb (Alec) (Garages) Ltd* v *Total Oil (GB) Ltd* [1985] 1 WLR 173). The clear conclusion is that courts prefer to encourage predictability and certainty in commercial transactions but place concepts such as fairness and reasonableness on a higher plane when dealing with personal, and especially fiduciary, relationships.

Option 2

This would draw on the above comments whilst emphasising the limits of judicial intervention. For example, in dealing with unconscionable exclusion clauses the common law has imposed restrictions upon the incorporation of such clauses, requiring reasonable notice to be given of these clauses (see *Parker* v *South Eastern Railway* (1877) 2 CPD 416) and the special highlighting of onerous clauses (see *Interfoto Picture Library Ltd* v *Stiletto Visual Programmes Ltd* [1989] QB 433). A more concerted and successful effort to curb the excesses of exclusion clauses materialised with the rule that the consequences of a fundamental breach could not be excluded (see *Karsales (Harrow) Ltd* v *Wallis* [1956] 1 WLR 936). However, the courts recognised that the common law had almost abrogated freedom of contract/intent and consequently restored these notions in such cases as *Photo Production Ltd* v *Securicor Transport Ltd* [1980] AC 827. You might therefore focus on statutory intervention as represented by the Unfair Contract Terms Act 1977 and the Sale of Goods Act 1979. UCTA 1977 applies a reasonableness test to certain types of exclusion clauses, with a complete prohibition of clauses which seek to exclude liability for negligence causing death or personal injury. The Act polices specific types of clauses such as those excluding liability for breach of the implied terms contained in ss. 13–15 of the SOGA 1979. In such cases, these clauses are prohibited in consumer sales but are subjected to a reasonableness test in commercial transactions. Yet again there is a clear link between the hands-off, non-interventionist approach to commercial parties (subject to economic duress and so forth) and the interventionist stance adopted with regard to consumers (see also the protection of consumers in the Unsolicited Goods and Services Act 1971).

Option 3

This would draw upon a number of disparate points within a contract syllabus ranging from economic duress/undue influence, as well as statutory intervention, through to offer and acceptance, intent, frustration, damages and illegality. Options 1 and 2 cover a number of these points but the following additional aspects could be considered:

(a) the possible modification of offer and acceptance rules in the interests of fair dealing and the reliance of the parties (see *Blackpool & Fylde Aero Club Ltd* v *Blackpool Borough Council* [1990] 1 WLR 1195; *British Steel Corporation* v *Cleveland Bridge and Engineering Co. Ltd* [1984] 1 All ER 504);

(b) the growing emphasis upon the role of intent in contract formation in order to support the legitimate expectations of commercial parties and, in particular, their post-contractual re-allocation of risk (see *Williams* v *Roffey & Nicholls (Contractors) Ltd* [1991] 1 QB 1);

(c) the greater flexibility that the Law Reform (Frustrated Contracts) Act 1943 offers courts in terms of the equitable apportionment of loss where a contract has been discharged on gounds of frustration;

(d) the distinction which courts make between liquidated damages and penalty clauses, thereby preventing the abuse of a dominant position (see *Dunlop Pneumatic Tyre Co. Ltd* v *New Garage and Motor Co. Ltd* [1915] AC 79); and

(e) the compromises which courts have reached in assessing the rights of innocent parties under illegal contracts, or the rights of employees under contracts in restraint of trade (see *Strongman (1945) Ltd* v *Sincock* [1955] 2 QB 525; *Phoenix General Insurance Co. of Greece SA* v *Administratia Asigurairilor de Stat* [1988] QB 216; *Plowman (GW) and Son Ltd* v *Ash* [1964] 1 WLR 568).

Q Question 6

Dick has inherited a substantial amount of money and seeks advice regarding its investment. He approaches Stirling, a 'financial consultant' who, for a fixed fee, advises him on the investment potential of paintings and antiques. Stirling suggests that Dick should visit Cheetham & Co., fine art dealers of Bond Street, as 'they have always given sound advice to my clients in the past'.

Dick studies the soaring prices fetched at auction by the French Impressionists and, desirous of buying a painting from this school, he visits Cheetham & Co. He is introduced to Fortescue, who has recently bought the gallery from Cheetham but carries on the business in the former trade name for the purposes of business goodwill. After two hours perusing the paintings, Dick is particularly taken with a painting described in the gallery's catalogue as painted by Renoir. Fortescue informs Dick that 'the French Impressionists continue to rocket in price and these type of lake scenes by artists such as Renoir are particularly in vogue'. Accordingly, Dick buys the Renoir for £850,000.

Six months later, Dick has the painting valued for insurance purposes and is told that it is definitely not by Renoir but that it is nevertheless an important picture and thus worth £200,000. Dick has discovered that Stirling and Fortescue are both directors of a separate company which specialises in the renovation of dilapidated Georgian mansions. Moreover, in their dealings with Dick they both disclaimed liability in writing in the following terms: 'No liability can be accepted for loss arising from advice given or statements made to clients who should verify the accuracy of statements for themselves.'

Advise Dick.

:ℚ: Suggested answer

Dick v Stirling

Breach of Contract:

(a) Implied term by statute — Dick (D) has contracted for the supply of advice on the 'investment potential of paintings and antiques' which is a contract for the supply of a service. In these circumstances it is an implied term that the service will be provided with reasonable care and skill (s. 13 Supply of Goods and Services Act 1982). Liability is based on fault; can D prove that Stirling (S) was negligent?

(b) Express term — was the statement by S intended to be a contractual promise (*Heilbut, Symons & Co.* v *Buckleton* [1913] AC 30)? What about the parol evidence rule?

Negligent misstatement: can D show a special relationship (*Hedley Byrne & Co. Ltd* v *Heller & Partners Ltd* [1964] AC 465)? If so, can D prove a breach of duty and that loss was foreseeable (note s. 2(1) of the Misrepresentation Act 1967 is not applicable as D is induced to enter into a contract with Fortescue (F) not S).

Disclaimer: subject to the clause being validly incorporated, ss. 2(2) and 3 of the Unfair Contract Terms Act 1977 subjects the disclaimer to the reasonableness test (s. 11 and sch 2). As the clause potentially excludes liability for fraud it is probably unreasonable (see *Stewart Gill Ltd* v *Horatio Myer & Co. Ltd* [1992] 1 QB 600; *Thomas Witter Ltd* v *TBP Industries* [1996] 2 All ER 573).

Dick v Cheetham

Misrepresentation:

(a) '. . . described in the gallery's catalogue as painted by Renoir'. This is clearly a statement of fact (e.g., *Atlantic Estates plc* v *Ezekiel* [1991] 2 EGLR 202).

(b) '. . . the French Impressionists continue to rocket in price and these type of lake scenes by artists such as Renoir are particularly in vogue'. This might be an opinion (*Bisset* v *Wilkinson* [1927] AC 177), but what of F's purported expertise (*Smith* v *Land & House Property Corp* (1884) 28 Ch D 7)?

Inducement and reliance: has D relied upon any representation in entering the contract, rather than his own judgment (*Attwood* v *Small* (1838) 6 CL & F 232)? Type of misrepresentation? Any evidence of fraud (*Derry* v *Peek* (1889) 9 App Cas 187)? Is there a special relationship between C and D (see, for example, *Hedley Byrne; ESSO Petroleum Co. Ltd* v *Mardon* [1976] QB 801). Section 2(1) of the Misrepresentation Act 1967 — can C discharge the burden of proof (see *Howard* v *Marine & Dredging Co Ltd* v *A Ogden & Sons (Excavations) Ltd* [1978] QB 574)?

Remedies for Misrepresentation:

Has any right to rescind been lost through time (*Leaf* v *International Galleries* [1950] 2 KB 86)?

Damages: available for fraudulent, s. 2(1) and negligent misrepresentations. Under s. 2(1) (Misrepresentation Act 1967), D can recover damages which are assessed as if the misrepresentation had been made fraudulently. What about lost opportunity costs in not having a Renoir which may have '. . . rocketed in price . . .' (*East* v *Maurer* [1991] 2 All ER 733)?

Breach of contract: is there an express term that the painting is a Renoir? Difficulties in proving objective contractual intent (*Heilbut*). Apply general guidelines: has C suggested that D should verify the statements (*Ecay* v *Godfrey* [1974] 80 Ll LR 286) or is it normal practice in this area not to rely on such statements of attribution (*Harlingdon & Leinster Enterprises Ltd* v *Christopher Hull Fine Art Ltd* [1991] 1 QB 564)? Implied term? Consider the relevance of the SGA 1979 to this transaction. Is there a *sale by description*, i.e. has the buyer relied on the description (e.g. *Harlingdon*)? Is there a breach of the implied term relating to *satisfactory quality* (s. 14 of the SGA) although in the light of *Harlingdon* this is unlikely as s. 14 probably does not apply to non-physical defects.

Disclaimer: has the clause been incorporated at common law? Does s. 3 of the Unfair Contract Terms Act 1977 apply or is the clause merely defining liability rather than excluding it? (Note also that as regards any breach of contract exclusion, if there has been a breach of an implied term — e.g. s. 13 of the SGA 1979 — then the disclaimer will be subject to s. 6 of the UCTA 1977 and consequently void.)

Other Issues

Undue Influence (*Dick* v *Stirling*): this is not an obvious category of a special relationship in which a presumption of undue influence would automatically arise (*Lloyds Bank Ltd* v *Bundy* [1975] QB 326). But is it arguable that a fiduciary type relationship exists between D and S: S is a paid professional adviser, D is relying upon the advice, S is cheating by not disclosing his alliance with F? If the presumption is made then S will need to show that D exercised his own independent will (*Inche Noriah* v *Sheik Allie Bin Omar* [1929] AC 127). Would this be possible without S at least recommending D to see another professional arts' adviser? Finally, is there a manifest disadvantage to D at the time he entered the contract?

Breach of a collateral contract (D v S): this would be relevant only if it is objectively established that the statement was intended to be a contractual term of a collateral contract (e.g. *Heilbut*) *and* the statement is supported by separate consideration. In these circumstances it would be difficult to prove that the statement was intended to *guarantee (promise)* the soundness of Cheetham's advice (see *ESSO Petroleum Co. Ltd* v *Mardon* and *Kleinwort Benson Ltd* v *Malaysia Mining Corp Bhd* [1989] 1 All ER 785 — statement of present intention) and to find separate consideration. Further, this situation differs from other collateral contract cases in that the statement concerns the advice of a third party and not the properties of a product (e.g. *Andrews* v *Hopkinson* [1956] 3 All ER 422) or the terms of another contract between the parties (e.g. *City & Westminster Properties* v *Mudd* [1959] Ch 129).

Mistake (*D* v *C*): common mistake — it would be difficult to establish a fundamental mistake here since it is likely to be treated as a mistake of quality (*Bell* v *Lever Brothers*; *Leaf* v *International Galleries*).

Unilateral mistake: unlikely, as it is not clear that F is aware of D's mistake (*Hardman* v *Booth* (1863) 1 H & C 803); moreover, how important was it to D to contract only with the previous proprietor (*Phillips* v *Brooks* [1919] 2 KB 243)?

Third party undue influence: this would be relevant only if it could be established that S had made a misrepresentation which induced D to enter the contract with F, who had actual or constructive knowledge of S's wrongdoing; if this was established, D may be able to avoid the contract with F (*Barclays Bank* v *O'Brien* [1994] 1 AC 180).

Q Question 7

Rex entered a jeweller's shop and asked Barker, the proprietor, 'How much is that gold necklace in the window?' Barker replied, '£1,250 to you, Sir.' Rex said: 'Good, I'll take it then.'

Consider the contractual position in EACH of the following circumstances:

(a) Rex thinks that the necklace is pure gold, and so worth £1,250, whereas in reality it is only gold-plated.

(b) There are two necklaces in the window, one worth £500 and the other worth £1,250. Rex intends to buy the valuable necklace whilst Barker intends to sell the cheaper one.

(c) Rex purports to be Rover, an accounts' customer of Barker's, signing the proffered credit slip and showing identification stolen from Rover's wallet. Rex sells the necklace to Setter.

(d) Having concluded the sale, Barker's shopwindow is smashed by a gang of robbers who steal all the items on display, including the necklace. Rex demands another, identical necklace. Rex replies that it was unique and, therefore, an irreplaceable piece of jewellery.

∶Q∶ Suggested answer

This question deals with misrepresentation, all forms of mistake, breach of contract and frustration. A small point on specific performance might also be considered.

(a) *Misrepresentation:* Does Barker make a false statement of fact? For example, Barker's initial response implies a confirmation that the necklace is gold — is this a half-truth? Inducement and reliance present no problems, assuming Rex did not attempt to verify that the necklace was pure gold before purchase. In considering the type of misrepresentation, it is unlikely that Barker could establish innocence — fraud and s. 2(1) of the Misrepresentation Act 1967 seem more relevant. Rescission seems possible in which case damages would appear unlikely. Alternatively, Rex may wish to keep the necklace provided he is awarded appropriate damages.

Mistake: The principle of *caveat emptor* suggests that Rex bears the risk that the necklace might not be solid gold. Alternatively, does Rex's initial enquiry imply that it is an implied condition precedent that the necklace is solid gold? If the parties' intentions cannot be gauged the doctrine of mistake might be applied (*Associated Japanese Bank (International) Ltd* v *Credit du Nord SA* [1989] 1 WLR 255). The goods are still in existence but does the common law recognise mistake as to quality (see *Leaf* v *International Galleries* [1950] 2 KB 86)? One might use Lord Atkin's test in *Bell* v *Lever Bros* [1932] AC 161 (does the state of the new facts destroy the original identity of the subject-matter); or, consider whether there has been a total failure of consideration. However, equity may declare the contract *voidable* on grounds of mistake as to quality, imposing additional terms by which Rex is given the right to buy the necklace for its true value (see *Grist* v *Bailey* [1967] Ch 532). Rex will lose his right of rescission if he waits too long.

(Note: *common* mistake may be difficult to establish as there is no evidence that Barker believed the necklace to be solid gold. Unilateral mistake would require proof of Barker's fraud and the fundamental nature of the mistake.)

(b) This is a simple case of mutual mistake. Generally, the reasonable person will favour one side's interpretation of events. If a figure of £1,250 is mentioned then, objectively speaking, it may more obviously relate to one of the two necklaces. If the reasonable person is truly confused then the contract will become void for mutual mistake (i.e. no correspondence of offer and acceptance — *Raffles* v *Wichelhaus* (1864) 2 H & C 906).

(c) Fraudulent misrepresentation will not avail Barker as third party rights have already accrued (Setter has bought the necklace). Barker must show that the contract is void for unilateral mistake. Apply the relevant conditions: (i) there are presumably two distinct entities; (ii) the transaction is not a simple cash sale — it is a credit agreement with an accounts' customer so Barker can argue that anyone who does not possess the features of an accounts' customer is 'crucially different' (use *Lake* v *Simmons* [1927] AC 487 to reinforce this point). Alternatively, it could be argued that Barker is merely mistaken as to credit-worthiness, especially in the light of the face to face dealings, i.e. contract not void for mistake (see *Phillips* v *Brooks Ltd* [1919] 2 KB 243; (iii) did Barker take reasonable steps to verify identity? — if cheque guarantee cards are acceptable then surely the relevant stolen identification card will suffice?

(d) As the robbery is post-contractual the doctrine of frustration would be relevant. In a commercial sense, as the subject-matter is irreplaceable, it no longer exists. However, is Barker insured against theft? Was this a foreseeable event? Was Barker at fault in not protecting his shop-window more effectively? Affirmative answers would suggest that frustration is inappropriate, in which case Barker is in breach of contract. If so, Rex would claim his money back as well as damages for loss of bargain, provided such damages were not too conjectural. Specific performance would be refused provided it is not in Barker's power to locate an identical necklace.

Q Question 8

Hiss & Co. agree with Harvey to supply Harvey with a new boiler for Harvey's factory for the sum of £8,500, delivery to take place on or before 1 June. The agreement incorporates Hiss & Co.'s standard form terms by which their liability to Harvey for any breach of contract will not exceed £300. Consider the legal position of Harvey in each of the following sets of circumstances:

(a) Instead of supplying a boiler of the agreed size, Hiss & Co. supply a boiler half that size invoicing Harvey for £5,000; in consequence, Harvey makes up the lack of productive capacity by obtaining another boiler elsewhere costing £6,000 but which is more efficient.

(b) Instead of delivering the boiler on 1 June, Hiss & Co. deliver it on 1 August. In consequence of the delay, Harvey suffers a loss of £5,000 in production.

(c) While delivering the boiler to Harvey by road, Hiss & Co.'s lorry is involved in a serious accident with the result that the boiler is damaged beyond repair. Hiss & Co. cannot deliver another boiler for at least six weeks.

☼ Suggested answer

This question covers damages, frustration and exclusion clauses.

The first point must be to consider the enforceability of the limitation clause. Note that the subject of liquidated damages/penalty clauses should not arise as the sum of money contained in the clause is not a *set* figure but, rather, specifies an *upper limit* for which Hiss & Co. might be liable for any breach. Recourse should be had to the various provisions of the Unfair Contract Terms Act 1977 by which the reasonableness of such clauses will be judged. On the facts, the following sections may be relevant: ss. 3, 11, 13 and sch. 2. Section 3 applies as the parties are businesses dealing on standard terms. The question will be whether Hiss & Co. is rendering a substantially different performance from that which is reasonably expected (this should be yes in parts **(a)** and **(b)** but possibly not in part **(c)**). If yes, the question of reasonableness will be resolved by applying s. 11 and sch. 2 of UCTA. The good student will spot the importance of s. 11(4) in this context and the guidelines contained in sch. 2 such as the equality of bargaining power. Section 13 might also be relevant as the clause is applying a 'restrictive or onerous condition'. If the clause is held to be unreasonable then it will be void.

Parts **(a)** and **(b)** concern the application of the common law regarding the recovery of damages. In particular, one would concentrate on remoteness and mitigation drawing on cases such as *Hadley* v *Baxendale* (1854) 9 Exch 341, *Koufos* v *Czarnikow (C) Ltd, The Heron II* [1969] 1 AC 350 and *Victoria Laundry (Windsor) Ltd* v *Newman Industries Ltd* [1949] 2 KB 528. For example, what knowledge does Hiss & Co. possess of Harvey's planned manufacturing operations? Is it reasonable to expect Hiss & Co. to recognise the potential loss caused to Harvey by a delay in delivery? Is Harvey claiming the loss of normal or exceptional profit? Furthermore, in part **(a)** Harvey has attempted to mitigate his losses by purchasing another boiler but this action has benefited him — compare *British Westinghouse Electric & Manufacturing Co. Ltd* v *Underground Electric Railways Co. of London Ltd* [1912] AC 673 with *Bacon* v *Cooper (Metals) Ltd* [1982] 1 All ER 397, the latter suggesting that Harvey might not have to account for this benefit if all other suppliers would have provided a more efficient boiler at the price stated.

Part **(c)** involves a possible frustration of the contract. The boiler has been destroyed but a replacement can be delivered in approximately six weeks. Is there a radical change of circumstances? Is the delay causing Harvey mere inconvenience and hardship or can Harvey establish the necessity for prompt delivery? If the road accident was a result of the driver's negligence, has Hiss & Co. induced the frustrating event (see *Lauritzen (J) A/S* v *Wijsmuller BV, The Super Servant Two* [1990] 1 Lloyd's Rep 1)? Was the event foreseeable, did either party insure against the accident's occurring and does the contract allocate the risk to one or other party? What is the effect of the limitation clause? The clause seems to be insufficiently explicit to cover the dramatic effect of the accident. If the contract is frustrated, what are the effects? If Harvey was required to make a pre-payment can Hiss & Co. retain all or part of that sum on grounds of expenses incurred in performance of the contract (see s. 1 of the Law Reform (Frustrated Contracts) Act 1943). Note that if the contract is not frustrated Hiss & Co. is in breach of contract — allowing Harvey to recover all losses that are not too remote after the issue of mitigation has been resolved.

Index